Palestinian Society
and Politics

Written under the auspices of
the Center for International Affairs,
Harvard University

A list of other Center publications of related
interest appears at the back of this book

Palestinian Society and Politics

Joel S. Migdal

WITH CONTRIBUTIONS BY

Gabriel Baer   *Donna Robinson Divine*

Mark Heller   *Ylana N. Miller*   *Shaul Mishal*

Shimon Shamir   *Kenneth W. Stein*

Rachelle Taqqu

Princeton University Press

Princeton, New Jersey

Dedicated to my second parents,
Reba and Asher Alexander

Contents

Maps, Figures, and Tables

Preface

Palestine has become such a sensitive, emotion-laden issue that comparatively little sound historical research has been carried out on it. The Arabs of Palestine, as much as any component of the issue, have been subjects of emotional defenses and attacks and of chauvinistic jingoism. Only the first tentative steps have been taken by historians to unravel the events of the past from partisan slogans. Social science literature has been even more scant. After J. C. Hurewitz's pioneering study, *The Struggle for Palestine*, which has recently been reissued in paperback, this kind of scholarship has been limited to a few scattered researchers.

Originally, I had two goals for this volume. The first was to present serious, scholarly research that would aid in fostering a meaningful understanding of the complex relations between society and politics among the Palestinian Arabs. The second aim was to assemble in the volume the writings of Israeli and Palestinian scholars, as well as those of other academics working on the subject.

Much to my regret, the second goal was not achieved. In the spring and summer of 1976, I wrote to a large number of academics (including Americans, Arabs, Britons, and Israelis) inviting them to submit articles or suggest others who have undertaken research on the Palestinians. A rigid schedule was dictated (contributions were to be submitted by early spring of 1977), and a broad framework for the articles was suggested. That framework emphasized the effects of different regimes (or environments) on the interaction between society and political community among the Palestinians. The articles in Book II are by authors who, for several years, had already been collecting and analyzing material within that broad framework. The essays were written independently of each other and of my own contribution in Book I.

Despite my hopes for assembling the writings of scholars from a variety of backgrounds, only one Arab scholar responded that he was completing research on a subject that fell within the scope of the framework. Unfortunately, later, even he found himself overcommitted and unable to complete his article in time to be included in this volume. It was with much regret, then, that I finally decided to put it together without the contributions of any Palestinian scholars. My regrets were even greater since some important social science research has been undertaken by them, both under the auspices of the Institute for Palestine Studies in Beirut and in a number of American uni-

versities, but, to date, relatively little of their published research has
been on the historical sociology of the Palestinians. My hope is that
the volume will achieve the primary aim of giving as scholarly and informed a picture of Palestinian society as possible even while it fails to
achieve the elusive "balance" of contributors I had sought.

The picture of Palestinian society and politics that is presented here
is far from complete, and the interpretations from author to author
are far from unitary. The authors have relied on two principal types
of sources, archival materials and interviews. Many additional standard sources remain to be tapped, such as Arabic newspapers during
the Mandate. And Divine's use of obituaries demonstrates that many
interesting patterns can be uncovered through new types of research
sources. Also, after 1948 and the creation of hundreds of thousands
of refugees, Palestinian society has included both those within and
those outside Palestine. The book does not attempt to analyze all
Palestinian society after 1948, but focuses principally on the West
Bank. The nine authors, including five historians and four political
scientists, frequently differ greatly from one another in both methodology and analytic perspective. In short, the book is not and could not
be a comprehensive statement on Palestinian society.

The aim of this work is, through varied methods and perspectives,
to shed light on certain crucial aspects of Palestinian Arab life: the
changing nature of the population in Palestine and of the leadership
to which that population looks. To help understand these changes,
the volume focuses on the Palestinian village and its inhabitants, who
have constituted the overwhelming majority of the Arab population;
on the elites, principally urban, that have vied for national leadership;
and on the nodes of interaction between these villagers and leaders.

The main argument in Book I is that many critical changes at the
base of the society—the village—as well as those at the level of social
and political leadership can be understood in the context of major
changes in regime policies. Major policy changes have resulted most
dramatically from three catastrophic episodes in Palestinian history:
World War I, the War of 1948, and the War of 1967. Each catastrophic event brought a new regime (or regimes) to rule Palestine.
Book I is a comparative study, viewing the changes and structure of
Palestinian society under the impact of four regimes, within the
framework of specific, classifiable regime policies. These policies, it is
suggested, are of prime importance in explaining the changing nature of the population and of the leadership to which the population
looks, as well as in understanding the great impact of Zionism and of
the spread of capitalism to the area. This approach, in brief, dis-
aggregates the concept of imperialism into two sets of interrelated
forces, economic ones (especially spreading capitalism) and political-

administrative ones (seen through regime policies). Only very partial
and distorted explanations of changes in Palestinian society, I believe,
result from approaches that focus entirely on only one set of forces,
e.g., spreading capitalism.

In Book II, eight studies of continuity and change in Palestinian society are presented. Book II is divided into three parts: the first focuses on the village, the second on the urban elites, and the third on
the nodes of interaction between followers and leaders. The essays
span the changes of the last century. Villagers have gone from subsistence agriculture to working in Israel's complex, industrial economy. Leadership has shifted from locally based, rural leaders to the
professionals and intellectuals of the Palestine Liberation Organization, who are part of Palestinian society but are located outside Palestine itself. These changes in Palestinian social structure—and the continuities that have withstood these changes—are discussed in detailed
case studies in Book II.

It would be a distortion of the articles in Book II to read them as
mere extensions of Book I. All the articles were originally written
without seeing the material included in the first book, and a number
of the authors would argue with the framework and the analytic perspectives presented there. Each article stands on its own, and each of-
fers a distinct approach to and interpretation of Palestinian social and
political history. There are, nonetheless, important similarities among
the essays, as the reader will see. Most importantly, all are concerned
with the delicate interplay among three factors: the Palestinian population, its leadership, and key outside forces (particularly political and
administrative forces). Together, they give us important new insights
into the historical sociology of the Palestinian Arabs.

A word should be said about terminology. Political and military
conflicts generate rhetorical conflicts as well. Almost no descriptive
term having to do with the Arab-Israeli conflict is shared by both
sides. What the Arabs call the "Arab Revolt," the Israelis call "disturbances"; what Yasir Arafat calls an "occupied territory," Menachem
Begin calls a "liberated territory"; what the PLO refers to as Palestinians, the Israeli government calls the "Arabs of Eretz Israel," and so it
goes on and on. There is no way to escape this dilemma other than to
assure readers that the descriptive terms used are not intended to
carry ideological connotations and then to make some arbitrary
choices.

In this volume, Palestine refers to the territory Britain included in
its Mandate after it had separated Trans-Jordan from the territory to
the West, or in more familiar terms, it refers to pre-1967 Israel plus
the West Bank and Gaza Strip. The term Palestinians refers to the
Arabs living in Palestine as well as those living in Palestine until

1947-1948 and their descendants who have continued to think of themselves as Palestinians. The West Bank refers to the territory annexed to Jordan after the 1948 War.

Finally, many people helped in my study of the Palestinians since the conception of this project in 1972. At the early stages, numerous colleagues from Tel-Aviv University gave invaluable, encouraging criticism. I would also like to cite my debt to the Tel-Aviv University Social Science Research Fund for a grant early in the project. Later, Harvard University's Center for International Affairs and a small grant from the Harvard Graduate Society gave me time and assistance to complete it. I would like to thank friends and colleagues who read and criticized earlier drafts, including Benjamin Brown, Theda Skocpol, Penina M. Glazer, Myron Glazer, and R. Marcia Migdal. Nancy Hausman did a fine job of editing all of Book I. Two first-rate research assistants worked with me for two years in collecting and making sense of materials. They are Zipporah Kleinbaum and Ariela Sturm. Mary Hilderbrand helped get the entire manuscript ready. A special word of thanks goes to Nicholas Saba, who served as both a research assistant and an interviewer. I also want to thank Jeffrey Rosen who prepared the censual material and accompanied me on a number of interviews. A note of appreciation is in order to the Harvard Semitic Museum for the cover photograph. The Museum has undertaken an international search to identify whatever nineteenth-century photographic material depicting the Near East has survived, and to assemble a comprehensive photo archive of the nineteenth-century Near East. Lastly, I want to express my gratitude to all my respondents in West Bank villages, who gave much of themselves with no personal reward in sight in a very trying period of their lives.

Contributors

Gabriel Baer is Professor of Middle East History at the Hebrew University of Jerusalem. He has written extensively on the social history of the Middle East. Among his books are *A History of Landownership in Modern Egypt* (1962), *Egyptian Guilds in Modern Times* (1964), and *Studies in the Social History of Modern Egypt* (1969).

Donna Robinson Divine is Associate Professor of Government at Smith College. She has contributed articles on the Middle East to the *International Journal of Middle East Studies* and to other journals.

Mark Heller is Assistant Professor of Political Science at Boston College. He has written on the Middle East in *Armed Forces and Society* and *Leviathan* and has contributed articles and book reviews in other professional and popular journals.

Joel S. Migdal is Associate Professor of Government at Harvard University and a Research Fellow of Harvard's Center for International Affairs. He is the author of *Peasants, Politics, and Revolution* (1974) and co-editor of *Patterns of Policy* (1979).

Ylana N. Miller is Assistant Professor of History at Rutgers University. She received her Ph.D. from the University of California at Berkeley. Currently, she is working on a manuscript on government and society in rural Palestine.

Shaul Mishal is a Lecturer in the Department of Political Science at Tel-Aviv University. His book *West Bank/East Bank, The Palestinians in Jordan* appeared in 1978.

Shimon Shamir is Associate Professor of Middle Eastern History at Tel-Aviv University. He was instrumental in the establishment of its Department of Middle Eastern and African History and the Shiloah Center for Middle Eastern and African Affairs. His books include *A Modern History of the Arabs in the Middle East* and *Egypt under Sadat* (both in Hebrew).

Kenneth W. Stein is Assistant Professor of Near Eastern History at Emory University and a Resource Associate at the Southern Center for International Studies in Atlanta. His doctoral dissertation, "The Land Question in Mandatory Palestine, 1929-1936" (University of Michigan, 1976), is currently being revised for publication.

Rachelle Taqqu has taught at Cornell University and currently teaches at Hobart and William Smith Colleges. She received her Ph.D. in history from Columbia University, where she was a Faculty Fellow and a Woodrow Wilson Dissertation Fellow.

The Effects of Regime Policies
on Social Cohesion and Fragmentation

Introduction

In the wake of the third Arab-Israeli war in 1967, the Palestinian Arabs catapulted into public view and consciousness throughout the world and have remained highly visible ever since. The period since those fateful six days in June has also generated a wealth of new literature on the Palestinians. Despite the outpouring of new books and articles, however, there has tended to be a reiteration of the same two themes that have dominated literature on the Palestinians since the 1930s.

A first theme has been the confrontation of Palestinian Arabs with Jewish settlers in Palestine since the beginning of the century. Writers sympathetic to Zionism have often emphasized the minimal detrimental impact of Jewish activity on the Arabs during the British Mandate or even during the post-1967 period, and have stressed the social and economic benefits of close Jewish-Arab interaction.[1] Their explanations for the clear pathology of Jewish-Arab relations have centered on what they consider the irresponsibility and extremism of Palestinian leadership from Haj Amin al-Husayni during the British Mandate to Yasir Arafat and George Habash in the post-1967 era. A minority of pro-Zionist writers blamed the poisonous relations on the policies of the British imperialists during the Mandate.

Authors sympathetic to the Arab cause, on the other hand, have focused on the repeated displacement of Arabs by Jews from both homes and homeland. And their explanations for the unmitigated hostility that has characterized communal interaction in historic Palestine focus on what they consider to be the extremism of Zionist leadership.[2]

A second common theme among those writing about Palestinian Arabs has dealt with the nature of the organizations at the pinnacle of Palestinian politics. Here the emphasis has been on the organizational structure and ideology of the Palestine Liberation Organization

[1] See, for example, F. H. Kisch, *Palestine Diary* (London: Victor Gallancz, 1938); and Arie Bregman, *Economic Growth in the Administered Areas, 1968-1973* (Jerusalem: Bank of Israel Research Department, 1975), p. 4.

[2] See, for example, Ann Lesch's essay describing Arab perceptions of the Jewish-Arab confrontation in William B. Quandt, Fuad Jabber, and Ann Mosley Lesch, *The Politics of Palestinian Nationalism* (Berkeley: University of California, 1973).

(PLO) and its components, much as it was on the characteristics of the Arab Higher Committee thirty and forty years ago.[3] Questions of cliques and cleavages and policy issues (will the PLO recognize Israel? will it accept a West Bank-Gaza Strip state?, etc.) have been consuming for some writers. But questions of day-to-day politics have been too frequently analyzed as if they were divorced from the society that those politics are supposed to steer.

Unfortunately, the literature has not only been all too polemical in its treatment of these two major themes, but the themes themselves offer a very abbreviated view of Palestinian politics and society. A richer, more complex view of Palestinian life is needed. First, it is important to understand the society upon which Palestinian politics rests. What have been the major institutions and patterns of social dynamics? Second, this society and the smaller communities that are parts of the society have changed dramatically over time. What has been the effect, not only of Jewish settlers, but also of the four different regimes that have ruled Palestine during this century—the Ottoman Empire, the British Mandate, Jordan, and Israel—in precipitating social change among the Palestinians?

In beginning to explore such questions, it is important to consider that conditions faced by Palestinians have often resembled those confronted by other peoples. In many parts of the Third World, the explosive changes that have undermined old inward-oriented peasant communities have not necessarily led to strong, centralized national societies instead. The changes associated with rapid social mobility—urbanization, higher literacy, nonagricultural occupations, rising incomes—have not always had the expected reinforcing effect on the growth of a "modern" society and strong state. Rather than gaining new social cohesion and coherent stratification patterns, many societies have experienced new kinds of social fragmentation and continuing political weakness.[4]

[3] Examples of this genre include Quandt's essay in ibid; Ehud Yaari, *Strike Terror* (New York: Sabra Books, 1970); Y. Harkabi, "Fedayeen Action and Arab Strategy," *Adelphi Papers*, No. 53 (London, Institute for Strategic Studies, December 1968); Gerard Chaliand, "The Palestinian Resistance Movement (in early 1969)" (Beirut: Fifth of June Society, n.d.); Hisham Sharabi, "Palestine Guerrillas: Their Credibility and Effectiveness," *Middle East Forum*, 46 (1970), 19-53; and Mehmood Hussain, *The Palestine Liberation Organization* (Delhi: University Publications, 1975). For an excellent annotated bibliography on the Palestinians and their interaction with the Jews, see Walid Khalidi and Jill Khadduri, *Palestine and the Arab-Israeli Conflict* (Beirut: Institute for Palestine Studies and University of Kuwait, 1974).

[4] By a coherent (or comprehensive) pattern of stratification, I refer to a highly interactive society (one with high levels of social communication) in which the interdependent parts respond to or assign power or status in very similar ways. Social cohesion is the cohering of the diverse elements of the society through a common understanding

Although in many ways unique in their tumultuous twentieth-century history, the Arabs of Palestine have been faced with frustration in devising and achieving their goals of national independence and integration, in large part, because of just such fragmentation and weakness. Book I of this volume presents an overview of the major changes in Palestinian society and politics during the last century. One aim is to offer a systematic analysis of Palestinian society and politics under the four regimes that have ruled Palestine in the modern era. A second purpose is a more general one: to ferret out some of the main causes and conditions that deny societies the expected social cohesion and coherent patterns of stratification.

During this last century and even somewhat earlier, the Palestinians found themselves subjected to many of the same forces that were radically changing other societies in Asia, Africa, and Latin America—and, at first glance, with many of the same effects. The spread of capitalism and Western institutions, as early as the eighteenth century, brought new educational opportunities, new measures of public health, new modes of behavior, and, most importantly, new economic relationships. Results included a substantial increase in population, a more centralized and interactive society, new patterns of population movement, and new types of leaders and leadership resources. How radically such changes can affect even small, remote communities can be seen, in part, by the following population growth figures for the village of Bitunia, located near the West Bank town of Ramallah:

Table 1
Population of Village of Bitunia

Year	Population
1838	90
1922	948
1931	1213
1967	1984

And these figures do not include the considerably more than 1,000 people who now live abroad but maintain close ties with relatives and consider Bitunia their home.

In a comparative context, the changes in numbers, movement, critical resources, and social interaction among Palestinians are not so startling. What is more important in sound comparative historical sociology is discovering patterns beyond such broad outlines, beyond longtime secular trends induced by the nebulous "West" or "capitalism."

---

of the ordering or layering of society. Fragmentation is the absence of such cohesion when separate elements in the society recognize different orderings or layerings, each with its own criteria for what constitutes power or status.

Once we begin to understand the *content* of those patterns of change in specific contexts, we start to gain insight into the different routes along which the interaction of society and politics has taken place in various countries around the globe. In Book I, change in social cohesion / fragmentation will be analyzed by an examination of (a) stratification patterns (who are the elites? what is the basis of their social control and influence? how do people make their living and which resources are crucial to those ends?) and (b) population patterns (including both growth and movement). The underlying argument is that the most crucial changes in a society, including stratification and population patterns, cannot be understood by analyzing only the spread of capitalism and the diffuse effects of the expansion of the world-system centered in Europe.[5] The specific results of the enormous impact of capitalism must be seen within the context of the states that ruled the society and the different policies those states adopted.[6]

One problem in any comparative study is that there has been little progress by scholars in developing frameworks that would make the numerous and diverse policies of different states comparable. To look at the interaction of state and society among Palestinians, I have developed a model that groups regime policies into three clusters: *investment policies*, including investments (or lack of them) by the regime itself and those the regime encouraged or permitted by others; *policies establishing political alliances*, focusing on those elements among the Palestinians with whom the regime chose to deal; and *security policies*, including measures taken by the regime to insure both physical safety and a social climate that encourages some to risk new types of social behavior. The analysis in each chapter of Book I is based upon the impact of the three clusters of policies on Palestinian stratification and population.

Change in societies is not simply depicted by a smooth curve. Critical events give rise to new attitudes and opinions, as well as to new situations. The spread of capitalism and particular regime policies work most dramatically in an environment that has been "shaken-up," an environment in which specific crises have rapidly and profoundly weakened important social bonds. Effects of capitalism and of new regime policies were most dramatic in the Palestinian context, as we shall see, in the aftermath of three "catastrophic" events:

[5] See Immanuel Wallerstein, *The Modern World-System* (New York: Academic Press, 1974).

[6] Of course, there is also a feedback loop that indicates the effect of the society and changes in the society on the ruling regime and its policies. The hypothesis developed in this essay, however, can be stated in rather bold terms without an initial elaboration of the feedback effect.

the establishment of British rule during World War I and the wars of
1948 and 1967.

Chapter 1 examines the effects of Ottoman policies prior to World
War I. In Chapter 2, change in Palestinian society is analyzed under
the tremendous impact of Western rule and intensive Zionist settlement. Chapter 3 covers the Jordanian period after the most traumatic
event in modern Palestinian history, the creation of Israel and, simultaneously, of the refugees and the diaspora Palestinians. All of these
chapters view the changes in Palestinian stratification and population
resulting from the three clusters of policies—investment, alliance, and
security.

The changes of the contemporary period, the years of Israeli occupation after the Arabs' devastating 1967 defeat, are looked at within
the same framework but in more detail. Chapter 4 is an analysis of the
impact of the three Israeli policy clusters on patterns of stratification
and population at the macro-level of Palestinian society. Chapter 5
looks beyond the seeming stability of such patterns since 1967 and
analyzes the great changes in stratification at the micro-level. These
changes have been unintended results of Israeli investment policies,
specifically the policy of employing Arabs from the occupied territories in Israel proper. Interestingly, these micro-level changes have
differed from area to area in the West Bank.

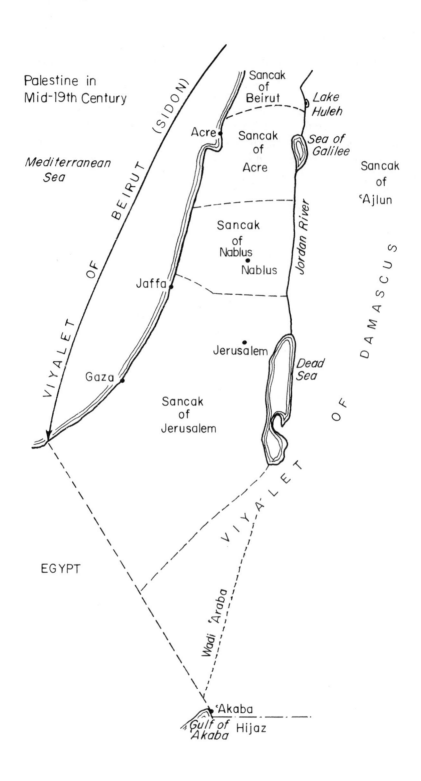

Palestine in
Mid-19th Century

Mediterranean
Sea

VIYALET OF BEIRUT (SIDON)

Sancak
of
Beirut

Lake
Huleh

Acre

Sancak
of
Acre

Sea of
Galilee

Sancak
of
ʿAjlun

Sancak
of
Nablus

Nablus

Jordan River

Jaffa

Gaza

Jerusalem

Dead
Sea

DAMASCUS

VIYALET OF

Sancak
of
Jerusalem

EGYPT

VIYALET OF

Wadi ʿAraba

ʿAkaba

Gulf of
Akaba

Hijaz

The Two Faces of Ottoman Rule: Palestinian Society before World War I

The First Face of Ottoman Rule

By the early decades of the nineteenth century, conditions in the provinces of the Ottoman Empire that constituted historic Palestine had deteriorated badly. The effects of all three governmental policies—security, investment, and alliances—were to make life precarious and to drive communities to be inward oriented. The security policy of the Empire, resulting from its low level of capabilities, was to provide as few police and military forces as possible while still maintaining Ottoman suzerainty. The small number of billeted soldiers did not (and probably could not) control the wanton violence that permeated the area.[1]

One old Arab proverb states, "Four are the ravages of the land: mice, locusts, Kurds and Bedouins."[2] The Kurds may no longer have been a problem, but the Bedouins certainly continued to make the life of the *fellahin* (peasants) extremely difficult through raids and plunder. A vicious cycle of desertion of the land by the peasants and infiltration by Bedouins from the desert existed. The result was the depopulation of the central plains and valleys by the peasantry. Some relief from the physical insecurity came after the Egyptian-based conquest of the provinces by the forces of Muhammad 'Ali (1832-1840), but conditions again worsened after the Ottomans reestablished their rule. Settled agriculture in the most fertile parts of the country be-

---

[1] One source estimated that in 1852, there were only 976 Ottoman soldiers in what today constitutes the West Bank and only 160 of them stood ready for immediate use by the Ottoman ruler (pasha). A. N. Poliak, *The History of Land Relations in Egypt, Syria and Palestine at the End of the Middle Ages and in Modern Times* (Jerusalem: Avar, 1940), p. 85 (Hebrew). The small number of soldiers also gave the villagers the opportunity to avoid them when they were used for extractive purposes. At times, the soldiers sought shaykhs who had not delivered the collected taxes, and instead found whole villages deserted. See R. A. Stewart Macalister and E.W.G. Masterman, "A History of the Doings of the Fellahin during the First Half of the Nineteenth Century, From Native Sources, Part I," *Palestine Exploration Fund Quarterly* (October, 1905), 344.

[2] Quoted in *Palestine, A Study of Jewish, Arab, and British Policies*, Vol. I, published for the Esco Foundation for Palestine (New Haven: Yale University Press, 1947), p. 510.

came almost an impossibility given the Ottoman policy of providing insufficient local security forces.

There was a lack of integration of Arabs due to the administrative divisions of the Empire. In fact, there was no administrative unit known as Palestine. This lack of integration was compounded by the effects of Ottoman security policy. Inhabitants of Palestine tended to cluster in inward-oriented villages located in the mountains and hills of what is today called the West Bank. There they gained some measure of refuge not available in the low-lying areas and planted a variety of crops that would not be subjected to repeated plunder.[3] Others sought security behind the walls of the towns, trekking long distances each day to reach their fields. Caprice entered their lives not only through the raids of the Bedouins but through the rapaciousness of tax-farmers and through largely uncontrolled, intermittent village feuding.[4] Shifting cleavages and coalitions among the Arabs formed and re-formed in response to the ongoing feuds and internecine warfare.[5] There was almost no governmental intervention to stem the ravages of outside raids by Bedouins, strong-arm tactics by the private armies of tax-farmers, and the pathology of intervillage warfare.

Just as the security furnished by government forces was minimal, so too was any investment in an economic or political infrastructure in the area. On the contrary, port facilities, for example, deteriorated badly in the latter centuries of Ottoman rule. Also, to offset the weak outside economic infrastructure, small communities utilized a number of cooperative economic and social measures. Lands, for example, were not registered to individuals but to communities that were considered the basic administrative units. Within these communities, modes of mutual aid and communal interaction developed to offer some limited means of protection to the individual.[6]

---

[3] E. Robinson and E. Smith, *Biblical Researches in Palestine, Mount Sinai and Arabia Petraea*, Vol. II (London: John Murray, 1841), p. 387. Also, for an interesting (if prejudiced) view of peasant life, see Rev. F. A. Klein, "Life, Habits and Customs of the Fellahin of Palestine," *Palestine Exploration Fund Quarterly* (April and October, 1881, and January, 1883), 110-18, 297-304, and 41-48.

[4] Philip J. Baldensperger, *The Immovable East* (London: Sir Issac Pitman, 1913), pp. 115-16. Also on intervillage warfare and banditry, see James Finn, *Stirring Times*, Vol. II (London: Kegan Paul, 1878), pp. 193-210 and 286ff. The violence involved in village justice is described in P. J. Baldensperger, "Morals of the Fellahîn," *Palestine Exploration Fund Quarterly* (1897), 123-34.

[5] The major cleavage was between the factions called Qays and Yaman, which seemed to have no ideological or interest basis. See R. A. Stewart Macalister and E.W.G. Masterman, "A History of the Doings of the Fellahin during the First Half of the Nineteenth Century, From Native Sources, Part III," *Palestine Exploration Fund Quarterly* (January, 1906), 33-50.

[6] For a discussion of types of land ownership in Ottoman law, which often promoted communal interdependence, see Z. Abramovitz and Y. Gelfat, *The Arab Holding in Pales-*

Ottoman neglect forced the fellahin to use their own communal devices in order to survive. By no means did this type of insulation make village life idyllic. The Ottoman policy of alliances in the province was a major factor leading to internally harsh conditions on a local basis. Rural *shaykhs* (chieftains who usually inherited their positions) formed alliances with the Ottoman rulers in order to gain authorization to collect taxes within the village. Such an authorization enabled resourceful shaykhs to wield considerable power in the Palestinian countryside, often with private armies.

The Second Face of Ottoman Rule

By the latter half of the nineteenth century, significant changes began to occur. Now outside forces exposed peasants to new risks and troubles. The protection of shaykhs and village institutions was insufficient. Ottoman rulers began shifting their alliances, leaving the village shaykhs and joining with more powerful city dwellers. Tax-farming, with collection rights now going to the highest bidders instead of automatically to the shaykh, was increasingly in the hands of urban forces, and war powers and judicial powers were also passing from the hands of the shaykhs. The new position of *mukhtar* (village leader) was mandated, creating weaker and more accountable village chiefs.

New patterns of political alliance by Ottoman rulers with town notables (*a'yan*) and local mukhtars resulted in subtle but critical changes in stratification patterns in Palestine. These changes included the predominance of a single, more cohesive leadership group (urban notables displacing rural shaykhs); more interdependence among different elements of the society; and greater social gaps between the layers of society. Most obvious was the accrual of broad, autonomous powers throughout the countryside by the rising, tax-farming townsmen.[7]

Slowly, there was a drift away from a pattern characterized by wanton intervillage warfare, by nonclass and nonideological cleavages (such as the split between the camps of Qays and Yaman), and by the

---

tine and in the Countries of the Middle East (Palestine: Hakibutz Hameuchad, 1944) (Hebrew). Also, see Raphael Patai, "Musha'a Tenure and Co-operation in Palestine," *American Anthropologist*, 51 (1949), 436-45; Samuel Bergheim, "Land Tenure in Palestine," *Palestine Exploration Fund Quarterly* (1894), 191-99; and A. Granott, *The Land System in Palestine* (London: Eyre and Spottiswoode, 1952). Granott also discusses the intervillage warfare still common in the first half of the nineteenth century.

[7] Also, within the villages, fellahin continued to avoid Turkish law courts to settle their disputes and to rely on village elders. Mrs. Finn, *Palestine Peasantry* (London: Marshall Brothers, 1923), p. 89. Though the political (and, often, economic) power of the shaykhs was broken, they remained strong socially. Y. Porath, *The Emergence of the Palestinian-Arab National Movement 1918-1929* (London: Frank Cass, 1974), p. 10.

autonomous power of rural strongmen who had few ties to one another. The new tendency was marked by less fragmentation and a more comprehensive pattern of stratification. The new town notables were developing into a self-conscious social class. Villagers came to be dependent, not on leaders whose power extended over only one or several villages, but on these urban leaders, whose power reached out from the cities to whole networks of villages.

These changes in Arab society were accelerated in the last four decades of the nineteenth century. Ottoman authorities renewed their attempts to strengthen the Empire internally by adopting the successful techniques of the West.[8] There were efforts at political centralization that could lead to increased production and extraction of surplus from the provinces. The aim was to develop strong, centralized political institutions capable of fostering capitalist economic growth, and, in turn, drawing further political and military strength from that economic growth. Reform was not an isolated ploy by the Ottomans, but was almost identical in nature to reform programs undertaken in numerous other countries at the time, such as Mexico, Bolivia, Colombia, and in the colonies of India and Indonesia.

The goal was to increase production without direct investments by the regime. The authorities hoped to use to their advantage new and renewed alliances with those thought to be able to help increase central administrative control of rural areas and able to effect greater economies of scale. In different places these people were called *effendi*s, *hacendado*s, or *zamindar*s. In almost all cases, one of the most critical components in dealing with the perceived threat of the West's capitalism was a change to more so-called "liberal" land tenure laws— laws that greatly aided the regime's new political allies in establishing their predominance.

The Change in Land Tenure

Whether called the *ley de desamortización*, as in Mexico, or the *Tapu* Law, as in the Ottoman Empire, the statute had the ultimate effect of undermining the peasants' ability to maintain relatively autarchic, inward-oriented communities. In Palestine, peasants were given the option to demand a permanent division of the village-held land that had previously been redivided every few years (*musha'a*). Also, the law forbade the periodic redivision of state land (*miri*), which instead would be held in permanent tenure by the individual. The central aspect of the law was the call for all lands to be officially registered.

[8] On the attempts at internal reform (the Tanzimat) from the period after Muhammed 'Ali's rule, see Moshe Ma'oz, *Ottoman Reform in Syria and Palestine 1840-1861* (Oxford: the Clarendon Press, 1968).

What is so interesting about this law is what it reveals about the changing relationship between peasants and government and the ability of new elites to establish themselves between the two. Peasants traditionally had received very little in services from the government and nevertheless had been made to pay a significant share of their incomes as a tithe to the tax-farmers appointed by the Ottoman authorities. Even the minimal service of defense came only intermittently, as we have seen. When the peasants heard of the new Tapu Law, they had two reactions. The first was fear—fear that it was a means to erase their anonymity within the village. They saw the law as an attempt by the government to extract higher taxes from individual households and to draft them into the imperial army.

Their second reaction was that it was possible to maneuver around the law given the usually limited administrative capabilities of the central institutions. In some cases, they continued to work the land jointly but registered it under one or several names such as that of a village elder or a head of a clan (hamula). Frequently, peasants sought the protection of a powerful figure and sold their land or handed it free to a tax-farmer, some other strongman, or a religious foundation (waqf) in return for the right to continue working it. In other cases, they simply neglected to register the lands they were working.

The maneuverings of the fellahin turned out disastrously for them. Unregistered lands were reclaimed by Ottoman authorities, who auctioned them off at incredibly low prices to the urban notables.[9] Where peasants had jointly registered their lands under the name of a single elder, they often found that the elder's heirs later claimed full ownership, thus changing the peasants into mere tenants. Powerful notables also turned peasants into tenants, and religious foundations absorbed lands into their other holdings.

Other techniques were also adopted by the Ottomans in an effort to copy the West's successful formula. Attempts were made, for example, to increase tax rates, to reform tax collection, and to expand the base upon which taxes were levied.[10] It was not overlooked that the British and French used their colonial presence in other parts of the world to increase greatly the amount of collected taxes. One goal was to shift from collection of taxes in kind to collection of money taxes. According to Granott, the tax was fixed on the basis of the aver-

[9] Abromovitz and Gelfat, *The Arab Holding*, p. 16. Huge tracts, such as the Jezreel Valley which included 20 villages and 4,000 people, were sold in single transactions. Two-thirds of the purchase price went to the Turkish intermediary who arranged the sale and one-third to Ottoman coffers. Poliak, *The History of Land Relations*, p. 86.

[10] The tithe was traditionally 10 percent. In 1886, it was raised to 11.5 percent and, in 1897, to 12.5 percent. See Chaim Halperin, *The Agricultural Legislation in Palestine* (Tel-Aviv: Sifriat HaSadeh, 1944), p. 119 (Hebrew).

age yield for the five previous years. Yearly fluctuations in prices for crops, however, put tremendous economic pressure on the peasants in particular years.[11]

The Changing Structure of Palestinian Society

Ironically, it was not the Ottoman authorities who benefited most from the reforms. Unlike the Western regimes they were trying to imitate, the Empire lacked the capability to achieve significant centralization and administrative penetration. It was characterized by an endemic weakness in administrative control. What it did succeed in doing, however, was changing the social structure in the provinces. Peasants increasingly found the basis of their self-subsistence and autarchic communities slipping from under them.[12] Power was not accruing to officials in Constantinople but increasingly was in the hands of Constantinople's local political allies, the provincial urban leaders.

Demands for taxes in cash, for example, forced peasants to put their produce on the market and often to deal with powerful moneylenders (none other than urban notables, often Christians). There were perfunctory efforts to control the effects of such moneylending through an 1887 law that fixed the maximum rate of interest at 9 percent and that prohibited the amount of interest from exceeding the amount of principal. The Ottoman Agricultural Bank also lent money at an interest rate of 6 percent. In practice, however, interest rates were much higher, and the Ottoman Agricultural Bank could sell the farmer's land to the top bidder if a payment was missed.

In short, through the middle and latter parts of the nineteenth century, the Ottoman authorities shifted the emphasis of their policies in Palestine. Political alliances were forged with a less localistic, urban-based Palestinian elite. Local councils established as part of the reforms came to be dominated by these urban notables. Preeminent families consolidated their influence, controlling critical municipal offices in the towns and gaining control of huge tracts of land in the countryside.[13]

Although the Ottoman policy was not to promote government investment, there was a new emphasis on generating local investment by creating the conditions for greater economies of scale. In some in-

[11] Granott, *The Land System in Palestine*, p. 60. Also, see the Johnson-Crosbie Report: Government of Palestine, *Report of a Committee on the Economic Conditions of Agriculturists in Palestine* (Jerusalem, 1930).

[12] Hubert Auhagen, *Beiträge zur Kenntnis der Landesnatur und der Landwirtschaft Syriens* (Berlin: Deutsche Landwirtschaft, 1907), gives figures indicating the degree to which holdings had slipped out of the hands of the peasants.

[13] Some major families owned from 7,000 to 15,000 acres each.

stances, local investment began to be achieved with growing export-oriented agricultural ventures such as large citrus groves.[14] In other cases, the new policies resulted only in the dispossession of the peasants and their change to tenancy status. By the end of Ottoman rule, about one-half the landowning population was short of land and about one-third of all lands were leased to tenants.

Another investment policy was to permit and/or encourage investment by limited numbers of German and Jewish settlers. Some economic growth did result from these investments, and the economic expansion probably did begin to affect the Arab population.[15]

Also important to the structure of Palestinian society was a change in Ottoman security policy in the course of the nineteenth century. Slowly, violence began to be curbed. Efforts were made to prevent Bedouin raids against the settled population. A number of campaigns were launched against private, local armies. Intervillage warfare subsided.

The results of improved security were manifested most explicitly in population issues. First, there was resettlement of the plains and valleys in the center of the country. In fact, a long-term trend of westward shift of population began around 1860. New settlements, *khirbes*, were established in areas that had previously been used only as village security outposts. Dyadic ties were established between original villages and their khirbes in the western, low-lying areas. An increase in missionaries, active foreign consuls, and tourists and travelers also lent security to the country.

Second, the number of Arabs in Palestine began to grow, inaugurating a lasting trend of relatively rapid natural increase. From a low point of about 200,000 Arabs west of the Jordan River in 1800, the numbers grew to about a half million at the turn of the twentieth century.[16] One major outcome of this population growth was a change from labor shortages to land shortages. Especially in the ref-

[14] Abromovitz and Gelfat, *The Arab Holding*, p. 53. There was a big increase in Arab cultivation of bananas and citrus fruit for export. Whereas the average Jewish grove was 7.5 acres, the average Arab grove was 12.5 acres. Groves demanded bigger investments than other crops and were thus planted by large landholders.

[15] Michael Assaf, *History of the Arabs in Palestine, Vol. III: The Arab Awakening and Flight, Part 2: Arab-Jewish Relations in Palestine (1860-1948)* (Tel-Aviv: Tarbuth Vehinuch, 1970) (Hebrew). Assaf indicates that the economic expansion could be seen in the increase in trade at Jaffa port. Later, World War I's high agricultural prices helped peasants eliminate their debt, but the period was also one of negative investment. Settlers emigrated. The Ottomans engaged in such practices as destruction of forests. These conditions probably led to more subsistence-oriented production by Arab farmers.

[16] Assaf, *History of the Arabs*, III, p. 160, bases his estimates on travelers such as Robinson and Bazili. Also, see Abromovitz and Gelfat, *The Arab Holding*, p. 3.

uges of the rocky hill country, village agriculture was increasingly becoming insufficient to meet the population's needs.

Population growth undermined villages as corporate units. Villages
found it more and more difficult to maintain their institutions as there
were many more peasants living on much less peasant-owned land.
The crucial point is the terrible bind in which poor peasants found
themselves. They had viewed the world outside as basically exploitative, extracting much and giving little. The community, located on
rocky Palestinian soil, had shielded and protected them from facing
that world alone. They had lived under the umbrella of the village
organization with the tacit consent of weak governments and powerful notables. The changes emanating from Europe, however, now
made the village an inadequate framework. Self-sufficiency was no
longer a viable strategy. Their choice was between a now inadequate
inward-oriented village or greater ties with the perceived exploitative
world outside.

The demographic character of the country was changing significantly, as the population grew, as people migrated from country to
city,[17] and as the center of population gravity shifted from east to
west. Ottoman reforms did not create political centralization. Instead
these policies led to an increase in power of local notables living in the
cities. By World War I, they owned great tracts of land in the plains
and valleys of Palestine.

The dynamic relationships between politics and society—between
the Empire's policies and patterns of stratification and population—
are summarized in Table 2.

[17] In 1875, there were four cities with more than 10,000 people: Jerusalem (40,000),
Gaza (18,000), Hebron (17,600), and Nablus (15,000). By 1895, the number had grown
to seven: Jerusalem (45,400), Nablus (21,000), Jaffa (17,700), Gaza (17,700), Hebron
(14,200), Safed (12,900), and Acre (10,500).

Table 2
Effects of Ottoman Policy on Patterns of Stratification and Population

Type of Policy		Stratification Patterns	Population Patterns
Investment	Early 19th century	Villages left to own devices; development of autonomous village institutions and village-oriented stratification	Lack of a central infrastructure led to population that was village-bound
	Late 19th century	Laws leading to greater economies of scale increased gap between notables and peasants—increasing tenancy and debt	Investment by notables causing a movement westward to larger agricultural enterprises
Alliance	Early 19th century	Support of rural shaykhs led to village-oriented stratification and non-interest based cleavages	Reliance on shaykhs encouraged population to remain rural and village-bound
	Late 19th century	Support of urban notables led to a more comprehensive stratification and a growing gap between notables and peasants	Renewed prominence of the towns; growing urbanization
Security	Early 19th century	Lack of central security led to reliance on powerful shaykhs and their private armies	Insecurity resulted in de-population and concentration in mountainous villages
	Late 19th century	Campaign by government to end private armies started undermining shaykhs	Increased security led to population growth, beginning of westward movement and resettlement of coastal plain

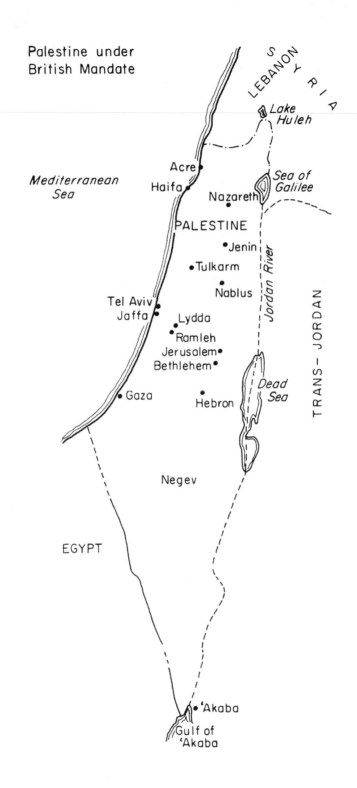

Palestine under
British Mandate

S Y R I A

LEBANON

Lake
Huleh

Mediterranean
Sea

Acre

Haifa

Sea of
Galilee

Nazareth

PALESTINE

Jenin

Tulkarm

Nablus

Jordan River

TRANS - JORDAN

Tel Aviv
Jaffa

Lydda

Ramleh

Jerusalem

Bethlehem

Dead
Sea

Gaza

Hebron

Negev

EGYPT

'Akaba

Gulf of
'Akaba

CHAPTER 2

Direct Contact with the West:
The British Mandate

Establishing British Rule

A major effect of British rule in the period between the world wars was to intensify and institutionalize many of the patterns begun in the Ottoman period. The Arab population swelled, movement to cities and the western portion of the country grew, and more comprehensive, coherent stratification patterns predominated as people became more and more interdependent. At the same time, new policy orientations by the British, particularly in the realm of investment policies (including regulations relating to Zionist land-buying and settlement), brought new Arab elites into existence by the 1940s. New bases for social institutions *and* cleavages among Palestinian Arabs were being laid.

The period between the last two years of World War I and the formal beginning of the Palestine Mandate on September 29, 1923 was unprecedented in the turbulence of its politics for the Arabs. After four hundred years, Ottoman rule ended and the British assumed control.[1] Palestine was now a separate entity. After a brief flirtation with the possibility of Palestine's inclusion in a Greater Syria under Faysal (who was awarded the kingdom of Iraq by the British after the failure of his Syrian adventure), Palestinian notables began to come to terms with that separateness. Their eyes turned from Constantinople and Damascus towards Jerusalem, which gained preeminence in the new political arrangements. In Jerusalem the Arabs warily viewed the execution of British rule, and it was there that they haltingly began to build their own political apparatus.

British rule was anomalous in the Arab experience. The new rulers

[1] British rule began as a military administration of the area east and west of the Jordan River in the last year of World War I. On July 1, 1920, a civil administration was instituted under High Commissioner Herbert Samuel. By 1921, the High Commissioner was responsible to the Colonial Office. The beginning of the civil administration followed the San Remo Conference in April 1920, which divided the Arab Middle East into French and British mandates. The Council of the League of Nations approved the Mandate in August 1922. The area east of the Jordan River was then separated from the Palestine Mandate and established as Trans-Jordan under Amir 'Abdallah.

had come with military and civilian institutions much more capable
and efficient than those of the Ottomans; yet, they came as outsiders,
perceived as imperialists and carriers (at least, for the Muslim majority) of an alien, Christian culture. Moreover, the threat the British
presented was greatly magnified by the specific terms of the Mandate,
which incorporated the Balfour Declaration and its legitimation of a
Jewish national home in Palestine.

The first major hurdle the British had to overcome in order to establish some kind of working order was to institute an effective policy
of political alliances with the Arab population. Their targets for these
alliances were precisely those who had gained so handsomely from
Ottoman policies in the previous century, the leading urban families.
In particular, Kamil al-Husayni, mufti of Jerusalem and a member of
one of the most powerful families, was rewarded for his early cooperation by being elevated to an unprecedented combination of powerful
religious posts, head of the Central Waqf Committee and president of
the Shari'a Court of Appeal in Jerusalem. In addition, the British
secured him the title of grand mufti, a title new to Palestine, which
gave the Husaynis and the city of Jerusalem an even more central role
among the Palestinian Muslim population. Another member of the
clan, Mussa Kazim al-Husayni, headed the Arab Executive Committee, which was established by the leading clans to press their claims to
the British.[2]

Political Alliances with the Notables

After Kamil's death in 1921, the British continued their policy of political alliances along the same lines. Within a short time, a young
member of the Husayni clan, Haj Amin, was maneuvered by the British to win the combined election and appointment process as the new
grand mufti. And, what is more important, Haj Amin was made president of a newly constituted Supreme Muslim Council (1922) having
wide powers and great discretion over disbursement of considerable
sums of money (waqf funds). British policy on political alliances, then,
was one of personal rewards coupled with institutional changes that
made the positions of their allies within the indigenous community
seemingly inviolable.

Even stronger institutional resources were offered to this Arab
landowning elite. The Mandate's incorporation of the Balfour Declaration led the Arab leaders to a policy of noncooperation with the
British in realms other than religion. As such, Arab political institutions lacked the explicit recognition, cooperation, and autonomy that

---

[2] The Arab Executive Committee dissolved in 1934 upon the death of Mussa Kazim
al-Husayni.

Jewish Palestinian institutions came to enjoy. Nevertheless, the religious offices under British control loomed very large in the exercise of power within Arab society. The British granted the Supreme Muslim Council wide-ranging powers that one official called ". . . to some extent almost an abdication by the Administration of Palestine of responsibilities normally incumbent upon a Government."[3]

It was within this context of political-religious alliances that Haj Amin, the Mufti, as he came to be known, moved to consolidate power within Palestinian Arab society. Links between the Husayni clan and a pyramidal structure beneath it tied even the smallest Palestinian villages into political life. Leaders in small villages attached their clans to those in larger villages, and the latter were tied directly to major city families. Haj Amin utilized the considerable yearly budget of the Supreme Muslim Council to bind the links.[4] These ties were quite selective, so that funds intended for restoration of mosques or construction of schools, for example, went to the Mufti's loyal followers, who were located predominantly in the districts of Jerusalem, Jaffa, and Nablus. Those outside his pyramid, including many in Hebron and Haifa-Acre, were relatively neglected.[5]

Opposition to the power of the Husaynis grew among certain other urban clans, particularly centered around the Jerusalem family of Nashashibi.[6] Raghib Bey al-Nashashibi followed Mussa Kazim al-Husayni as mayor of Jerusalem and used that base to establish his own links down to the villages of Hebron and Haifa-Acre. In the Arab Executive Committee, the Nashashibis and their allies constituted the opposition.

Cleavages and conflict among the prominent clans were probably less important from our point of view than what they had in common. All were using the resources afforded by their political alliances with the British (legitimacy, institutions and their posts, and revenues), and all were using (in varying degrees) their symbolic opposition to the British. And, of course, they still maintained their major basis of power and social control—ownership of land.

British political alliance policy, then, reinforced the elite that was already entrenched on the strength of its social and economic characteristics. In the 1920s, the power derived from landholding was considerable, even though there were clear signs of the radical changes

---

[3] Quoted in Y. Porath, *The Emergence of the Palestinian-Arab National Movement 1918-1929* (London: Frank Cass, 1974), p. 198.

[4] The waqf funds were 12.75 percent of the total tithe revenues for the country.

[5] See Yehoshua Porath, "Al-Hajj Amin Al-Husayni, Mufti of Jerusalem—His Rise to Power and the Consolidation of his Position," *Asian and African Studies*, 7 (1971), 148-49.

[6] See Yuval Arnon-Ohanna, "The Internal Political Struggle within the Arab Palestinian Community, 1929-1939," unpublished Ph.D. dissertation, Tel-Aviv University, April, 1978 (Hebrew).

that were to overtake Palestinian agriculture shortly.[7] Farming was
still the main occupation in the country and was still carried on primarily for subsistence needs.[8] Increasingly, from 1919 on, taxes and rent
had to be paid by the fellah in cash. Given his low income and periph-
eral relationship to the market, he was forced to turn to the landowner for loans. Dependency remained strong as families averaged
an expenditure of 20 percent of their incomes on interest payments.[9]
Interest rates hovered around 30 percent per annum but soared in
some cases to 50 percent for three months. Rents further increased
dependency, averaging about 30 percent of a peasant's gross income.
With families such as ʿAbd al-Hadi in Nablus owning 15,000 acres of
land, and Husayni 12,500 acres of land, the notable families were able
to exercise tremendous influence over the daily decisions of the population. Disbursement of patronage through waqf funds by the
Husaynis and their allies only increased their leverage.

British Security and Investment Policies

British security policy had a less clear-cut result in comparison with their
policy of political alliances. On the one hand, stabilization measures
were instituted to decrease the dependency of the fellah. An order
guarded tenants' rights. A land court was established. Bedouin raids
from across the Jordan River were eliminated. Roads were built at an
unprecedented rate, greatly increasing mobility in this small country.
Orders, on the other hand, did not always guarantee execution. "No
occupancy right exists in favour of the Arab tenant in Palestine,"
wrote Sir John Hope Simpson in 1930. "As a rule he holds his land on
a yearly tenancy, terminable by his landlord at will."[10]
    British attempts to offer tenant security were negligible through the
1920s. As more security from physical harm (except during the Arab
Revolt of 1936-1939) and more security of life through new public
health measures contributed to the beginnings of a real Arab popula-

[7] For example, from 1923 to 1930, the percentage of lands that continued to be redivided under the mushaʿa system declined from 56 to 46. John H. Simpson, *Report on
Immigration, Land Settlement and Development* (Palestine: October, 1930), pp. 31-34.

[8] The Johnson-Crosbie survey of 1930 estimated that 80-90 percent of a peasant's net
staples were consumed in the home. According to the 1931 census over 60 percent of
the Arab work force was engaged in strictly agricultural occupations. Note the Muslim
(about 65 percent)-Christian (about 15 percent) split in agricultural activity. Also, see
Simpson, *Report on Immigration*.

[9] Over 30 percent of the peasants were tenant farmers. Many others (probably
around another 20 percent) had small, fragmented holdings that did not supply subsistence needs. See the Johnson-Crosbie Report; and Simpson, *Report on Immigration*,
p. 26.

[10] Simpson, *Report on Immigration*, p. 34.

tion explosion (mostly through natural increase), tenant *insecurity* became magnified with increasing pressure on the land. The Arab population of Palestine grew 120 percent between 1922 and 1947.[11] This growth rate was one of the highest in the world at the time, but took place within the context of an even more rapid and threatening Jewish growth. British security policy, leading to decreased violence as well as increased public health measures, was partly responsbile for the Arab population explosion. Muslim infant mortality, for example, dropped from 187 to 128 per 1,000 between 1931 and 1946.

Jewish land-buying contributed to land pressure as well.[12] Rents, Simpson reported, were rising rapidly. One way of dealing with the problems arising from those pressures was for Arabs to continue seeking some sense of security in their families and clans.[13]

Despite the dependency and social control that were magnified by British policies of political alliance and security, the third area of British policy, investment, had a contradictory effect. The effect was to undermine the monopolistic control of the Arab notable families and thus very much attenuate the strength of the pyramidal structure they had used to create peasant dependency upon them. Although the Mandate itself had been envisioned as temporary and as entailing in-

[11] Although we came upon our statistics independently, both the following citation and this work relied upon many of the same, far from totally accurate sources: Edward Hagopian and A. B. Zahlan, "Palestine's Arab Population: The Demography of the Palestinians," *Journal of Palestine Studies*, 3 (Summer, 1974), 32-73. The British conducted two full censuses—in 1922 and 1931—as well as a population survey in 1946. Many have argued over the veracity of the results of all these enumerations. In 1946, there were approximately 1.1 million Muslims and 145,000 Christians. There were also almost 600,000 Jews in Palestine. According to another source, in 1947 there were 1.125 million Muslims (58 percent); 175,000 Christians (9 percent); and 625,000 Jews (32 percent). Georges Montaron, "Le Fait National Palestinian," *La Palestine* (*Notre Combat*) (Janvier-Fevrier, 1970), 5. Probably somewhere around three-quarters of the Arab growth was through natural increase, which would have meant a phenomenally high rate of natural increase of between 3.5 and 4.0 percent. See *Supplement to Survey of Palestine* (Jerusalem: Government Printer, June, 1947). Also, see Fred M. Gottheil, "Arab Immigration into Pre-State Israel: 1922-1931," *Middle East Information Series*, 24 (Fall, 1973), 13-22; and Aharon Cohen, *Israel and the Arab World* (New York: Funk and Wagnalls, 1970), p. 224.

[12] See John Ruedy, "Dynamics of Land Alienation" in *The Transformation of Palestine*, ed. by Ibrahim Abu-Lughod (Evanston, Ill.: Northwestern University Press, 1971), pp. 119-38.

[13] As late as 1944, a survey of five villages showed that almost 60 percent of all marriages were intra-clan, and there was even a tendency to have intra-subclan marriages. There was a wide variation (from 37.5 percent to 76.0 percent) among villages. Government of Palestine, Department of Statistics, *Survey of Social and Economic Conditions in Arab Villages*, Special Bulletin no. 21 (1944), pp. 18-19.

direct British rule, British investment policies from the beginning had a very direct impact on daily life in Palestine. Legitimation of a Jewish national home opened the door for unprecedented Jewish investments.[14] A good share of the huge sums spent on Jewish land acquisition went to absentee landowners but "probably much more than half constituted a direct transfer of capital to the Palestine Arabs. In addition, the payments by Jews to Arabs for agricultural produce, building materials, wages, rents, and services expanded until they reached an estimated peak of $13,750,000 in 1935."[15] Although Jewish-Arab interaction is not the main focus here, it should be noted that Jewish influence on numerous aspects of Arab life was momentous. Whether they were land sellers, tenants leaving the newly sold land, or workers in the burgeoning towns, Palestinians were finding great changes in their lives and the resources critical to those lives in the wake of growing Jewish settlement and investment.

The British themselves added significant sums in the 1920s and 1930s, mainly in public works (especially roads) and salaries for workers in the Palestine administration. In the 1940s, British investment increased substantially as army camps were built *and* serviced, industrial activity on a cost plus basis was encouraged, and agricultural produce became important to the war effort.[16] The British became the largest employer, with estimates running up to one-quarter of the Arab work force British-employed. In addition the climate established by the British rulers was encouraging the investment of some other foreign capital as well.

The Impact of British Policy

All the unprecedented, vast influx of capital into Palestinian Arab society had significant effects on the distribution of resources among Arabs and on the relative importance of the resource that had been the key to social and political power, land. These effects were on the numbers and location of the Arab population and on the stratification patterns of the society.

It is important to note here that the most intense effects of the British investment policy were occurring at the same time that there was a distinct change in its political alliance policy. By 1936, Arab political frustration over Zionist gains broke out in overt acts: a general strike

[14] J. C. Hurewitz reports that Jews invested over $400 million between 1919 and 1936. J. C. Hurewitz, *The Struggle for Palestine* (New York: Greenwood Press, 1968), p. 30.

[15] Ibid., p. 31.

[16] Ibid., p. 191, reports that from 1943-1945 British military expenditures alone averaged $100 million a year.

in 1936 was followed by a period of unrest through 1939 that came to be known as the Arab Revolt. The Arab Higher Committee, formed in April 1936 to coordinate the strike and the battle against Jewish settlement and ultimately against the British presence, was led by the notable families and, more particularly, by Haj Amin and his Husayni clan.[17]

Under the pressure of escalating violence, the British withdrew their support of Haj Amin. On October 1, 1937, they stripped the Mufti of his posts as president of the Supreme Council and as chairman of the General Waqf Committee with its abundant patronage funds. In addition, they dissolved the Arab Higher Committee and deported six of the leaders, while the Mufti fled the country under the threat of arrest. The notables (the Husaynis and their allies, in particular) suddenly found themselves without the three key resources supplied by the tacit alliance with the British: legitimacy, institutions and posts, and revenues. It was within this context that the landowning families had to face the added challenge created by British investment policies.

With the push of severe drought in the early 1930s and the pull created by British investment policies, two interrelated processes increasingly characterized the *movement* of Arab population: urbanization, and a growing flow from east to west. Peasants were seeking relief and opportunities outside the village and the domain of the large landowner. The fellahin began to move physically—to urban areas and westward—and to move figuratively out of the networks controlled by the old elites.

The Christian Arab population had always been more urban oriented than its Muslim counterpart. By the 1940s, almost 80 percent of the Christian Arabs were living in cities, while about 30 percent of the Muslims were urban dwellers. Even for the Muslims, however, the Mandate brought a significant increase in their connection to the city and to outside institutions. The smallness of the country allowed for considerable commuting from village home to city or public works job, and thus probably kept down the numbers of those who left the village permanently.[18] Also, many Arabs resettled in vil-

[17] In the early 1930s, the tight grip of the notable families on the course of Palestinian politics was institutionalized through the establishment of six narrowly based parties: Istiqlal, Youth Congress, National Defense Party (Nashashibis), the Palestine Arab Party (Husaynis), Reform Party, and National Bloc. The Arab Higher Committee brought the rival families together for a short period, but the old cleavages reappeared and the Nashashibis withdrew into renewed opposition on July 21, 1937.

[18] The overall non-Jewish urban population (including nomads) grew from 29 percent in 1922 to 34 percent in 1944. *A Survey of Palestine*, Vol. II, Prepared in December 1945 and January 1946 for the information of the Anglo-American Committee of Inquiry (Palestine: Government Printer).

lages surrounding major cities.[19] The cities themselves were growing rapidly as well. Haifa's Arab population grew by 87 percent between 1922 and 1931 and Jaffa's by 63 percent, and they continued to grow in the early 1930s and then again in the 1940s. And these cities began to display the characteristic signs of a rapidly urbanizing society. One source reports that in the mid-1930s in Haifa, for example, 11,160 Arab workers lived in nearly 2,500 gasoline can huts.[20]

Urbanization in itself along with jobs in public works would not have spelled a decrease in the social control of the powerful families if they could have gained control over access to new opportunities—and to a considerable degree they did enter into the new economic activities. The notables had the advantage of already being urban-based. Nevertheless, the nature of the movement of the Arab population—from the eastern portions of Palestine to the Western coast—spelled the end of the old monopoly over crucial resources in the life of the Arab worker or peasant. The continuing shift from east to west grew in intensity throughout the Mandate. Eastern areas, such as the surroundings of Bethlehem, Nablus, Hebron, and Jenin, grew moderately, near or below the rate of overall increase, while areas around Jaffa and Haifa were mushrooming. (See Table 3.) It was within these western coastal areas, particularly around Haifa, that the notable families had the weakest ties and links.

Probably no counter-elite could have emerged in Jerusalem, where the old ties and networks of the notables were so firmly entrenched. To establish a new infrastructure, new elites needed the sheer space between themselves and Jerusalem with its symbolic importance as a center and with its vigilant old landowning elites. The growth of an infrastructure—an institutional nexus—on the coast, and the movement of the population westward, were part of a self-reinforcing process. As the center of gravity of the Arab population moved from around the middle of the country (Jerusalem) to the west, there were more and more people seeking roles in the host of new institutions there.

The following statistics give some indication of the decline in the dominance of Jerusalem. In 1922, Jerusalem was the city with the largest Arab population, containing 38 percent of the total Arab population of the three largest cities (Jaffa and Haifa were the others). By 1944, Jerusalem had the *third* largest Arab population, with 32 percent of these cities' Arab population. Also, significantly, Jerusa-

[19] Between 1922 and 1931, the overall Arab population grew by approximately 28 percent while the villages around Jaffa grew by considerably more than 100 percent. In the same period, the Jewish population grew by well over 100 percent, also principally concentrated in the Tel-Aviv area.

[20] G. Mansur, *The Arab Worker under the Palestine Mandate* (Jerusalem, 1936), p. 14.

Table 3
Growth of Arab Population in Districts with More than 25,000 Arabs in 1922

	1922	1931	Percent increase 1922-1931	1944***	Percent increase 1931-1944***
Eastern districts*	362,231	414,935	15	540,700	30
Western (coastal) districts**	235,456	340,581	45	518,750	52

* Includes subdistricts of Beersheba, Hebron, Bethlehem, Jerusalem, Ramallah, Tulkarm, Nablus, Jenin.
** Includes subdistricts of Gaza, Jaffa, Ramle, Haifa, Acre.
*** Estimates. Also the figures are not strictly comparable, since the 1944 estimates excluded the nomadic population and collapse several subdistricts, and I had to adjust them accordingly.

lem's percentage of Muslims in the three cities fell to only 26 percent. Haifa, the city with least control by notables, grew from having one-quarter of the Arab population of the three cities to having one-third.

No direct political challenge to the preeminence of the notables was mounted on any serious level.[21] For the most part, the new institutions in the western portion of the country were economic (and, to a lesser degree, social) in character rather than political. Although Arab industry never grew to significant proportions, it did expand dramatically from its previously very small base. It moved from almost sole production of handicrafts[22] to production that included some large-scale enterprises. The number of Arab industries more than quadrupled from 1939 to 1942 (although many of those were still small handicraft establishments), doubling the number of Arab workers employed.[23] One source states that from 1920-1940, the number of workers in Arab industry and crafts tripled, the output more than tripled, and the invested capital quadrupled—and all this even before the great expansion of the war years.[24]

[21] For the nature of the struggle between the new forces and the old, see Arnon-Ohanna, "The Internal Political Struggle."
[22] See Sa'id B. Himadeh, "Industry" in *Economic Organization of Palestine*, ed. by Himadeh (Beirut: American University, 1938), pp. 216-21.
[23] The figures come from the censuses of industry by the Department of Statistics in 1940 and 1943. The average number of employees in Arab industries was 5.6 in 1942 (while for Jewish industries the figure was 19.8). See *A Survey of Palestine*, Vol. I, p. 508; and Government of Palestine, Department of Statistics, *Statistical Abstract of Palestine 1944-5* (Jerusalem, 1945).
[24] Z. Abromovitz and Y. Gelfat, *The Arab Holding in Palestine and in the Countries of the Middle East* (Palestine: Hakibutz Hameuchad, 1944), pp. 61 and 78 (Hebrew). From 1941-1944, several textile factories were established that were mechanized and

In addition to Arab industries, the growing Arab labor organizations were another vital part of the new infrastructure. By the end of World War II, the labor movement represented about 20,000 Arab workers.[25] Other institutions, such as Arab banks, were also growing quickly.

It was not only the distance from Jerusalem that encouraged the development of new Arab economic and social organizations along the coast. Movement westward was also fostered by the rapid growth of non-Arab institutions in these areas, which in themselves were shattering the monopoly of social control the notables had exercised. (See Table 4.) In the earlier part of the Mandate, Jewish economic activity

Table 4
Growth of Arab Population by Concentration of Jewish Population

	1922	1931	Percent increase 1922-1931	1944**	Percent increase 1931-1944**
Districts with high Jewish population*	219,487	338,693	54	505,000	49
Districts with low Jewish population	444,427	512,417	15	695,000	36

* Subdistricts with more than 3,000 Jews in 1922 (there was a gap between Safed with 3,844 and the next highest subdistrict with only 700).
** Estimates.

had generated employment in settlements and in industry, but the turbulence of 1936-1939 reduced the interdependence of the two communal groups.[26] Foreign concerns employed several thousand workers as well. But the major alternative sources of employment were due to the British. In 1939, government agencies employed 15,000 daily workers, not counting government clerks; by 1942, the

employed from 50-100 workers. Capital invested in industry also tripled from 1939 to 1942.

[25] Hurewitz, *The Struggle for Palestine*, p. 123 and p. 189. The Palestine Arab Workers Society was on the right-wing of the labor movement, growing out of the Federation of Arab Trade Unions and Labor Societies, on the left. The Congress of Arab Workers was another union that grew out of the break-up of the Federation. The very small Palestine Labor League was the Arab subsidiary of the Jewish Histadrut.

[26] Assaf estimates that 1,000-2,000 Arab workers were employed by Jewish industry until the late 1930s. Michael Assaf, *History of the Arabs in Palestine, Vol. III: The Arab Awakening and Flight, Part 2: Arab-Jewish Relations in Palestine (1860-1948)* (Tel-Aviv: Tarbuth Vehinuch, 1970), p. 195. In the 1920s Jewish building stimulated lime and coal extraction by Arabs. See Henry Rosenfeld, "The Arab Village Proletariat" in *Revadim B'Yisrael*, ed. by S. N. Eisenstadt et al. (Jerusalem: Akadamon, 1968), pp. 478-79.

number was 80,000 (probably 60,000 or more of whom were Arabs).[27] They worked building army camps, airfields, and roads. Others were policemen or gave personal service to British officials and army officers. The standard of living increased significantly, the old indebtedness lessened considerably, and Arab financial assets multiplied. Even agriculture changed in nature due to labor shortages and capital intensification.[28]

All the new prosperity and new activity of the mandatory period—stimulated by British investment policies that allowed for an influx of outside capital and new uses of Arab capital—meant that formerly self-sufficient Arab peasants or landless agricultural workers were now tied into much more complex economic frameworks. Stratification patterns were altered significantly. As new groups generated new sources of employment, those at the bottom of the social scale were able to free themselves from complete dependence on landowners.

Although Arab political leadership for the most part remained the bailiwick of the notable families until the end of the Mandate, the nature of the leadership they exercised was greatly affected by changes in British actions and changes in Palestinian society itself. The British used suppression, exile, and arrest, and all took their toll on Palestinian politics beginning in the latter part of the period of the Arab Revolt. The years of World War II were marked by Arab political quiescence in Palestine (except, as throughout the Mandate, at the municipal level). The major political figures were in exile. Status was increasingly expressed through economic means or professional standing.

Only the pan-Arab Istiqlal Party made appreciable headway during

[27] *The Settlement Economy Book for 1947* (Tel-Aviv: Ha'vaad Ha'leumi, 1947), p. 513 (Hebrew). The total number of nonseasonal employees was 42,000 and about two-thirds were Arabs. Military expenditures in Palestine grew by almost a factor of five between 1940 and 1942. Hurewitz, *The Struggle for Palestine*, p. 121.

[28] The standard of living rose dramatically during the war years. In industry, wages went up from between 124 percent to 277 percent from 1939 to 1945, with all but one industry's wage rises far exceeding the cost of living. In agriculture, the labor shortage generated wages that were, at times, 300-400 percent above prewar levels. *A Survey of Palestine*, Vol. III, pp. 1337-38. Indebtedness had fluctuated widely during the Mandate. Numerous village credit societies were established and, finally, the high prices and inflation of the war period eliminated the debt for most peasants. See Abromovitz and Gelfat, *The Arab Holding in Palestine*, pp. 38-44; and *Palestine, A Study of Jewish, Arab, and British Policies*, Vol. II, published for the Esco Foundation for Palestine (New Haven: Yale University Press, 1947), p. 723. Agriculture was increasing in acreage, undergoing capital intensification, and increasing output of cash (export) crops. See *The Settlement Economy Book*, pp. 509-13. Hurewitz, *The Struggle for Palestine*, pp. 191-92, reports on the Arabs' increase in foreign assets (also see p. 32 on changes in citriculture).

those years as a possible locus for the emergence of a new, political counter-elite. With its strength significantly centered in Haifa, the Istiqlal was a conglomeration of the social elements created by the rapid socioeconomic changes of the Mandate, and was intimately connected to the economic renaissance. The party included young professionals, intelligentsia, and teachers and had ties to the Arab Communists and left-wing labor movements.[29]

After the war, during the period of impending crisis in Palestine, the emergent stratification patterns, characterized by the new urban economic elites and the growing nonagricultural labor force, had their effects on the political responses of the Arabs. Factionalism now spilled over from a purely intra-notable class framework to include some of the new urban forces. A stand-off between the weakened clans, with their many exiled leaders, and the rising new urban elite, mainly in the Istiqlal Party, led to a period of internal bickering about the composition of a new coordinating body for Palestinian politics.

Difficulties and slowness in getting themselves reorganized politically in this postwar era led to increasing involvement by the Arab League in internal Palestinian Arab politics. At first, the new Arab Higher Committee consisted of predominantly Husayni and Istiqlal forces. But the Husaynis expertly used cleavages within the Arab League and the British desire for a return to strong Palestinian Arab leadership as critical resources in eliminating their competition for leadership positions.

The Mufti was not allowed to return as a free man to Palestine, but, with the support given by the Arab League, he was able to direct the affairs of the Palestinian national movement from his base in Egypt. The potential of that leadership, however, was greatly diminished by the increasing gap between the social sources of the Husaynis' power and the new realities of Palestinian social and economic life. Fragmentation in Palestinian society meant that groups could no longer rule based on a convergence of social and political power. Fragmentation led to a pattern of politics that would carry through the next three decades: political maneuvering and power no longer stemmed most importantly from one's control of local resources but from one's relationship to powerful exogenous forces.

[29] Hurewitz, *The Struggle for Palestine*, pp. 116 and 62-63. He states that three members were on the board of directors of the Arab National Bank and one of these was the chairman of Haifa's Arab Chamber of Commerce. It should be noted, however, that an important role in the party was played from the outset by the Nablus notable family of 'Abd al-Hadi. Also, see Arnon-Ohanna, "The Internal Political Struggle." The best recent work on the changes in Palestinian politics late in the mandatory period, and especially on the growth of the Istiqlal, is Joseph Nevo, "The Political Development of the Palestinian Arab National Movement, 1939-1945," unpublished Ph.D. dissertation, Tel-Aviv University, May, 1977 (Hebrew).

The social fragmentation of Palestine that had been so magnified during World War II led after the war (as already had been seen in 1937-1939) to politics of intimidation and retaliation among themselves. Assassination and the threat of assassination characterized the political climate of those last few critical years before 1948. New economic resources and new prosperity did not bring social integration in their wake. And so at the most critical moment in their history, the Palestinians found themselves without a strong, dominant class to lead them, without leadership capable of mobilizing them into an effective political or military force. Table 5 on the following page summarizes the regime policies and changes in Palestinian society that underlay the political weakness manifested in the 1948 War.

Table 5

Effects of British Policy on Patterns of Stratification and Population

Type of Policy	Stratification Patterns	Population Patterns
Investment	Large Jewish and British (esp. in WW II) investments led to decreasing dependence on landowning notables; growth of new urban elite, but one with only limited social control over workers moving out of agriculture	British, Zionist, and other outside investments led to a movement westward and urbanization; Haifa & Jaffa gained relative to Jerusalem
Alliance	British offered legitimacy, institutions, and revenues to notables, solidifying the latter's hold on Arab political leadership	Alliances with Jerusalem notables maintained Jerusalem as most populous and central Arab city in early Mandate
Security	Dual effects of increased physical security and tenant security laws: (a) increased mobility and land security led to decreased dependency, but (b) lack of enforcement and land pressure led to increased dependency on notables	Increased security, especially public health, for most of Mandate led to population explosion (increases averaged 5%/year)

CHAPTER 3

Dispersal and Annexation:
Jordanian Rule

Diminishing Bases of Society-Wide Social Control

The period of violence that began in 1947 and culminated in the 1948 Arab-Israeli War was a major turning point for Palestinian Arab society; and, yet, there were critical elements of that society that displayed surprising continuity in the following decades, despite the massive upheaval. Given the challenges Palestinians were to face in the post-1948 era, the most notable among the continuities was the persistent social fragmentation.

Since the latter part of the nineteenth century, Palestinians had been experiencing an increasingly interactive society. Village autarchy and inward-oriented peasants had been fading into history. Despite the new socioeconomic ties forged in the first five decades of the twentieth century, however, a coherent pattern of stratification did not develop. All the new bonds were not adding up to a social structure marked by a degree of homogeneity sufficient to produce a fairly unified leadership—a social class that could at least agree on the rules of the game and the institutions to guard those rules.

Without that minimally common language of the rules of the game, politics does not become a coordinated joint venture by those controlling crucial resources. Instead, political power becomes a venture in denying others preeminent positions. As long as no leadership is sufficiently entrenched so as to mobilize power in exchange for the social resources it can offer, politics is marked by factionalism and attempts at intimidation. And such circumstances mean political weakness in confronting outside forces. In the years after 1948, the previous failure to overcome social and political fragmentation was to continue to plague Arab politics. Without the means of a state or a geographically unified population, there was little that could be accomplished after the mandatory period to overcome such fragmentation on the structural level.

Why were the new urban elites unable to crystallize into a unified social class and establish a new coherent pattern of stratification and cohesion on their terms? One simple explanation is that there simply

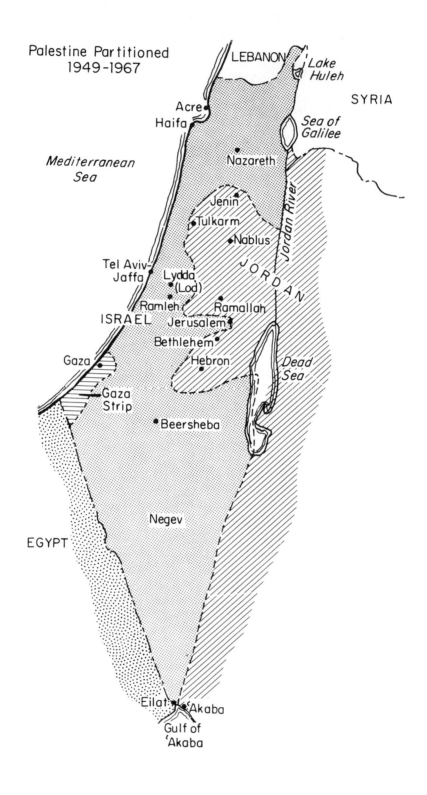

Palestine Partitioned
1949-1967

LEBANON

Lake Huleh

SYRIA

Sea of Galilee

Acre

Haifa

Mediterranean Sea

Nazareth

Jenin

Tulkarm

Nablus

Tel Aviv-Jaffa

JORDAN

Lydda (Lod)

Jordan River

Ramleh

Ramallah

ISRAEL

Jerusalem

Bethlehem

Gaza

Hebron

Dead Sea

Gaza Strip

Beersheba

Negev

EGYPT

Eilat 'Akaba

Gulf of 'Akaba

was insufficient time between the beginning of the boom years in the early 1940s and the 1948 War to complete so mammoth a task. Two additional factors probably also played a part during the Mandate. First, the presence of both the British and the Jews impeded the un-fettered development of a large, strong Arab middle class. The more highly developed economic institutions of the British and, less so, of the Jews and of foreign companies attracted Arab workers by offering relatively high wages and hindered the development of competitive Arab firms. Arab companies were encouraged to develop in order to service the larger, more sophisticated non-Arab enterprises. There was no class of Arabs that controlled urban resources critical to the Arab worker. Instead, Arab workers were feeding into a number of diverse, competitive institutional settings controlled by the British and the Jews, as well as by a relatively small number of Arabs.

A second factor inhibiting the new urban elites from establishing a coherent pattern of stratification was the *political* aspect of British rule compounded by the *political* challenge of the Jews.[1] The response of the Arab notables was to direct all political efforts toward the issue of British rule and its sanctioning of Jewish settlement. By doing this, the leadership was able to focus on an issue on which there was high consensus among the various local groups and, simultaneously, make it illegitimate for any other groups to raise the internal issue of changes in the basis of *Palestinian Arab* politics. Through co-optation of the issue of imperialism and Jewish presence, especially with a stand marked by extreme militancy during the late 1930s and 1940s, the Mufti succeeded in directing all politics to the larger communal and international issue. Those seeking a different basis for Palestin-ian politics faced accusations that they were traitors to the Pal-estinian people in their struggle against outsiders.

The 1948 defeat at the hands of the Jews further undermined both the basis of social control and the legitimacy of the notables. By then, however, it was too late for an urban elite to substitute itself. The fledgling economic and social infrastructure the new elite had built in the coastal areas was also destroyed as a result of the war. In addition, the 1948 War reversed two trends that had characterized Palestinian Arab society for three-quarters of a century, the movement from east

---

[1] The growth in Jewish numbers alone was shocking to Arab leaders, and an end to Jewish immigration was a prime demand throughout the period. Jews made up 11 per-cent of the population in 1922; 29 percent in 1936; and 32 percent in 1947. On the reaction to this growth, see the short, readable history by Edmond Bergheaud, *Les Palestiniens* (Paris: Bordas, 1972) in the Collection Bordas-Connaissance, Série Infor-mation, ch. 8. Also, see Janet L. Abu-Lughod, "The Demographic Transformation of Palestine" in *The Transformation of Palestine*, ed. by Ibrahim Abu-Lughod (Evanston, Ill.: Northwestern University Press, 1971), p. 151.

to west and urbanization. With the flight eastward of the refugees and with the dismantling of Arab urban institutions on the coast of Palestine, the society was left without a single social group capable of tackling the abiding problem of social fragmentation. Palestinian society was now spread over several different countries, with the majority living in the Jordan-ruled parts of Palestine.

The Incorporation of the West Bank into Jordan

Within this context King 'Abdallah set upon his course of incorporating the majority of the Palestinians into a Jordanian framework. Only days after the May 15 beginning of the 1948 War, King 'Abdallah established a military administration in Arab-controlled territories west of the Jordan River. His purpose was to prevent the Arab Higher Committee under the direction of the Mufti from establishing a civil administration in these areas. At that point 'Abdallah started his successful policy of reward and punishment in incorporating Palestinians into his regime. All the king's district military rulers in the newly occupied lands were of Palestinian extraction, but most key senior positions were in the hands of Jordanians.[2]

'Abdallah's anti-Husayni posture sounded the death knell for an independent political role for the old notable families. The Mufti did set up the Arab "Government of All-Palestine" in Gaza in the fall of 1948, but it soon proved to be nothing more than an organization on paper.[3] Late in 1948, two Palestinian congresses met under 'Abdallah's inspiration, condemning the establishment of the Government of All-Palestine and opening the way for the annexation of Arab-controlled Palestine to Trans-Jordan. In December 1948, the annexation was ratified by the parliament, and the new Arab Hashemite Kingdom of Jordan now consisted of two banks on either side of the Jordan River. The already greatly weakened opposition among the notables (Nashashibis and allies) also lost its independent political role as it was absorbed by the Jordanian regime.

Most significant of all the appointments involved in the absorption process was that of Raghib Bey al-Nashashibi as military governor of the West Bank. Later, he and other notables joined the Jordanian cabinet. Throughout the Jordanian period, a small number of Pales-

---

[2] See Shaul Mishal, "The Conflict between the West and East Banks under Jordanian Rule and its Impact on the Governmental and Administrative Patterns in the West Bank (1949-1967)," unpublished Ph.D. dissertation, Hebrew University, December, 1974, p. 99 (Hebrew). Also see Shaul Mishal, *West Bank/East Bank* (New Haven: Yale University Press, 1978).

[3] The Government of All-Palestine lasted formally until 1959 but was almost totally inoperative by 1952.

tinian leaders served as senior officials, ambassadors, and cabinet members. Nevertheless, although within Jordan these Palestinians had the form of power, the content remained firmly embedded in the East Bank of Jordan.

Palestinian Localism

Just as significant as 'Abdallah's co-optation of diminished notables into state-level positions was his policy of political alliance on the local level. As we saw, since the latter part of the nineteenth century, both the Ottomans and British had chosen to focus their political alliances on a society-wide leadership. Britain's elevation of the status of the city of Jerusalem was, in part, an attempt to establish it as a base for the recognition of such a society-wide leadership, specifically, men of prominent families that had extensive landholdings and often filled important religious posts. Until the late 1930s, this policy coincided fairly well with the structure of the society, a rural-based population with growing intervillage and interdistrict ties.

'Abdallah's aim through his policy of political alliances was to stem centralizing tendencies in Palestinian society. He sought to insure fragmentation as a means of denying the Palestinians a potential all-West Bank basis for mobilizing against his regime. The focus of his policy of political alliances harked back to the earlier Ottoman policy of alliances with local shaykhs. The central role of Jerusalem was greatly reduced through purposive policy, diminishing its potential as a base for the growth of an all-Palestinian leadership.

In addition, 'Abdallah was quick to note that there were very few Palestinians, including notables, who retained a society-wide constituency. Those chosen as municipal leaders were precisely those Palestinians who had little potential to become national leaders.[4] Even the most prominent of the West Bank mayors, Shaykh Muhammad 'Ali al-Ja'bari of Hebron, had little base of support or power outside his own district. Ja'bari was the prototype of the Palestinian leader 'Abdallah sought out. The Hebron leader acted in 'Abdallah's behalf in the important Second Palestinian Congress in Jericho that set up the annexation of the West Bank and gave 'Abdallah the right to solve the Palestinian problem. The payoff to the municipal leaders was the positions they were given, but real power was not so quickly dispensed. Municipal departments, for example, were often run directly out of Amman.

Changes resulting from the 1948 War reinforced 'Abdallah's move

[4] David Farhi, "The West Bank: 1948-1971—Society and Politics in Judea and Samaria," *New Middle East* (November, 1971), 34.

to establish a more localistic leadership and to fragment Palestinian society. Most important was the physical and geographic fragmentation that occurred in 1947-1949. Besides the Arabs in Israel (150,000), Palestinian refugees were now dispersed among Lebanon (100,000), Syria (83,000), and the Gaza Strip under Egyptian rule (200,000). In Jordan itself, not only was the West Bank population of 450,000 annexed, but an additional 450,000 refugees were scattered among twenty-nine camps and numerous communities.[5]

The physical and geographic fragmentation contributed to added social fragmentation. Rapid urbanization and social change in the latter years of the Mandate may have brought a weakening of the old clan (hamula) system. Following the 1948 War, scattered (and, to date, inconclusive) evidence seems to indicate a return to greater familism—a reliance on the hamula as the only steadfast institution at a time when Palestinians' more central institutions had totally disintegrated.[6] Palestine, as a unified country, no longer existed, and the Jordanian regime even banned the use of the term Palestine from official documents after March 1, 1950. Under these circumstances and given that they tended not to identify as Jordanians,[7] Palestinians looked to those local institutions or leaders that survived the trauma of flight and social dismemberment.

Jordanian Security and Investment Policies

The diminution of the old leadership over time did not mean that no new leadership arose. The basis for the new leadership was education. "Education, probably seen as the only tangible investment for the future," writes Fawaz Turki, "became to a Palestinian family the most crucial and the most momentous accomplishment ever."[8] Although such a leadership lacked the critical resources and concomitant social

[5] On the dispersal of the refugees from 1947-1948, see Don Peretz, *Israel and the Palestine Arabs* (Washington: The Middle East Institute, 1958), pp. 6-30. There are raging debates about the exact numbers of refugees. The Clapp Mission in 1949 found 726,000 refugees and more than one million receiving relief (Peretz, p. 30). There have been estimates of the influx into Jordan ranging from 350,000 to 450,000.

[6] Very little first-quality anthropological research on Palestinians has been undertaken. See Abner Cohen, *Arab Border-Villages in Israel* (Manchester: Manchester University Press, 1965), pp. 2, 9; and Abdulla M. Lutfiyya, *Baytīn, a Jordanian Village* (London: Mouton, 1966).

[7] See Lutfiyya, *Baytīn*, p. 87; and Daniel Lerner, *The Passing of Traditional Society* (New York: The Free Press, 1958), p. 304. My own interviews among nonelites in the West Bank in 1973 overwhelmingly confirmed the denial of a Jordanian self-identity.

[8] Fawaz Turki, *The Disinherited* (New York: Monthly Review Press, 1972), p. 41. He estimates that 64,000 university graduates were trained between 1948 and 1967 (only 3,000 less than in Israel).

control to give the Palestinians structural cohesion, the young teachers and professionals did, nevertheless, pose a threat to the Jordanian regime by their potential to elicit ideological unity of an anti-Jordanian variety. King Husayn, who ascended the throne after the assassination of his grandfather, 'Abdallah, and the incapacitation of his father, Talal, and who grew more powerful from the late 1950s on, adopted a two-edged policy towards the new, young leaders. Many young university graduates were absorbed into the regime as civil servants. More dissident leaders, however, were dealt with severely by the regime's security policy, which included arrest and imprisonment for years without a trial.[9]

Jordanian investment policy coupled with the existing economic strain of the years immediately following the 1948 War also furthered Palestinian social fragmentation. Once again, the Jordanian regime's goal was to prevent the growth of a West Bank infrastructure capable of serving as a basis for the development of a coherent, society-wide stratification pattern. Jordanian policy was clearly one of preferential treatment for the East Bank in capital investment.

Despite having a more literate skilled population, the West Bank stagnated compared to the East Bank. The East Bank had almost no industrial base and had the smaller population in 1948; yet, by 1965, three-quarters of all industrial output in Jordan (and a bit more than 50 percent of the population) were in the East Bank. Industry contributed only 6.6 percent to the gross domestic product (GDP) of the West Bank, while agriculture and services accounted for about 85 percent of its GDP. The gross product of the West Bank was only one-third of the total GNP for Jordan in 1966 while its population was almost half the total. There was a continuously negative trade balance with the East Bank. And in 1961, per capita income was half that of the East Bank.[10]

The West Bank economy reverted to one very much based on self-subsistence and service. Ties to an urban infrastructure were broken, since the West Bank's trade outlet before 1948 (and, incidentally, the East Bank's as well) had been via the coastal cities of Palestine. Imports in 1965 were twice as large as exports, and exported goods from the West Bank amounted to only 3.5 percent of GDP. The economy came to survive on four main pillars: agriculture, tourism, payments from the United Nations Relief and Works Agency (UNRWA), and

[9] Some of the documents captured by the Israelis in June 1967 relate to the harsh Jordanian security policy. See Israel Ministry for Foreign Affairs, "The West Bank" (Jerusalem, n.d.).

[10] Israel, Prime Minister's Office, Economic Planning Authority, *Economic Survey of the West Bank* (Summary), Jerusalem, December, 1967, pp. 7 and 26.

transfer payments from individuals' earnings outside the West Bank.[11]

Effects of Jordan's investment policy—preferential treatment of the East Bank—were compounded in the years immediately following the partition of Palestine by a severe economic depression. Trans-Jordan's population prior to 1947 was nearly 400,000. After the war, its population more than tripled. The loss of land and private sector jobs in the territory controlled by Israel, the loss of village lands for Arab border villages in the West Bank, and the reduction in the total number of public sector positions, all led to harsh economic crises and downward mobility for Palestinians. Hardest hit, of course, were the refugees, but other Palestinians were also deeply affected. In fact the heightened competition for many fewer employment opportunities led to recurring, small-scale tensions between the settled West Bank population and the newly arrived refugees.[12]

As for population patterns, the Jordanian investment policy and the harsh economic conditions led to both temporary and permanent out-migration from the West Bank. Jordanian authorities often aided out-migration through measures such as securing visas. An agreement was reached between Jordan and Iraq, for example, allowing the entry of Jordanian citizens into Iraq.[13] From Iraq, many went on to labor-scarce Kuwait. No exact statistics on total out-migration are available, but some estimates range between a third of a million and upwards of half a million emigrants from the West Bank during Jordanian rule.[14]

[11] See Brian Van Arkadie, *Benefits and Burdens* (New York: Carnegie Endowment for International Peace, 1977), pp. 22-28; and James Baster, "Economic Aspects of the Settlement of the Palestinian Refugees," *Middle East Journal*, 8 (Winter, 1954), 28-30. Baster writes of UNRWA, "It not only supports the Jordan balance of payments and the local wheat market but is also the largest local employer (there are some 2,500 people on the Jordan payroll) and the largest supplier and distributor in the country" (p. 30).

[12] Interviews in village of Khirbet Carma, Hebron, September 28, 1973.

[13] Jordan was the only country that attempted to assimilate large numbers of Palestinians and thus was the only one to grant citizenship (and, importantly, the right to secure a passport) en masse.

[14] Jon Kimche, *The Second Arab Awakening* (London: Thames and Hudson, 1970), p. 251, estimates an annual out-migration of 50,000 between 1956 and 1966. Jamil Hilal, "Class Transformation in the West Bank and Gaza," reprinted in "Views from Abroad," *Journal of Palestine Studies*, 6 (Winter, 1977), 167, estimates that 375,000 people left Jordan between 1950 and June 1967 and at least 170,000 of those were from the West Bank. Eliyahu Kanovsky, *The Economic Impact of the Six-Day War* (New York: Praeger, 1970), p. 365, working with data based on computations using World Bank and Jordanian census figures, found that 250,000 West Bankers left the West Bank between 1949 and 1961. The 1961 census reported over 60,000 Jordanians living abroad—a very low estimation—and 80 percent of these were from the West Bank. Fully half of the out-migrants reported were living in Kuwait. Jordan, Department of Statistics, *First Census of Population and Housing*. The Jordanian census excludes most

Whatever the exact number, several patterns can be seen. Palestinians began to leave the West Bank in significant numbers after annexation. In the almost twenty years of Jordanian rule, a period in which we would have expected the West Bank population almost to double given the Palestinians' previously high rates of increase, the West Bank numbers remained fairly stable at between 800,000 and 900,000.[15] Migration continued at high rates even after the Jordanian economy as a whole began to grow very rapidly (the average yearly rate of growth for GNP between 1960 and 1967 was over 10 percent).[16] The greatest share of migration was to the East Bank, but, as early as 1953, skilled and educated Palestinians began migrating to the oil states (particularly, Kuwait) and to countries outside the Middle East. Less skilled and less educated Palestinians followed. Often, husbands or sons would work abroad for several years and leave their families behind. The money sent from abroad made up a significant proportion of the total West Bank income.[17]

In sum, the period of Jordanian rule of the West Bank brought some significant departures from previous patterns of change, but social fragmentation and difficulty in achieving a coherent pattern of stratification with a unified social class at the top of the social ladder continued to characterize Palestinian society (see Table 6). The great changes came in population patterns, particularly population movement. After almost a century of steady movement westward and growing urbanization within Palestine, Palestinians now began to migrate eastward (first the flow of refugees and then the movement to the East Bank) and emigrate from the country altogether. The Jordanian regime's investment policy, particularly its preferential treatment of the East Bank, served to fuel these population movements.

Another significant change was in the nature of the policy of political alliances. Whereas the British and even the Ottomans in the latter

entire families that emigrated. It has also been estimated that 120,000 refugees emigrated from Jordan. *Economic Survey of the West Bank*, p. 4. None of the above sources estimates return rates of out-migrants to the West Bank.

[15] From 1952-1961, the West Bank population grew at an average rate of 0.85 percent, compared with 2.84 percent for all Jordan. The Palestinian rate of natural increase was probably of the order of 3 percent. Israeli sources estimated that migration from the West Bank was at even higher rates after 1961. *Economic Survey of the West Bank*, p. 3.

[16] On the outstanding growth of the Jordanian economy, see Richard J. Ward, "Jordan's Pre-1967 Economy and Prospects" in *The Palestine State*, ed. by Ward, Don Peretz, and Evan M. Wilson (Port Washington, N.Y.: Kennikat Press, 1977), pp. 107-13. It should be added, however, that labor force participation was extremely low and unemployment remained relatively high (officially, 7 percent; in fact, probably higher). *Economic Survey of the West Bank*, pp. 4-5.

[17] A little more than 10 percent of the gross product of the West Bank in 1966 came from money earned abroad. *Economic Survey of the West Bank*, pp. 7 and 27.

Table 6
Effects of Jordanian Policy on Patterns of Stratification and Population

Type of Policy	Stratification Patterns	Population Patterns
Investment	Preferential treatment to East Bank led to stratification patterns marked by Palestinians' serving as workers and managers in offices and enterprises which had non-Palestinians at the top	Preferential treatment to East Bank led to high out-migration from West Bank to East Bank and to other Middle Eastern countries
Alliance	Alliances with municipal leaders and mukhtars and not with potential national leaders; stratification patterns tended to be localistic and fragmented	Mobility patterns were highly limited by alliances with traditional leaders; high out-migration of young men
Security	Harsh security measures helped prevent new leadership patterns from emerging or becoming institutionalized on a national level	Harsh security measures led to out-migration of many of the newly educated youth

part of the nineteenth century had encouraged the emergence of a unified class at the pinnacle of Palestinian Arab society, the Jordanians set out to create a fragmented, localistic leadership. Through their harsh security policies, they also attempted to preempt the development of any new groups aspiring to national or all-West Bank leadership. The effect of these policies was to continue the social and political fragmentation that beset the Palestinians from the late 1930s on. Just as in the Mandate, there was no single social group that combined cohesiveness with control of resources crucial to the survival of large segments of the Palestinian population. The difference is that in the Mandate two groups were strong enough, at least, to aspire to such domination—the landowning urban notables and the new coastal entrepreneurs—while in Jordanian times no group emerged that could even aspire to this role. Jordanian policy insured that.

As during the Mandate, social mobilization remained high. But unlike the mandatory period, the social mobilization was not channeled—even partially—to a new urban infrastructure. Instead, it was characterized by rapid increases in educational levels coupled with migration from the West Bank. A new leadership did begin to emerge, but it was marked by two important characteristics that prevented it from establishing *social* power on a day-to-day basis. First, it was a leadership whose main resource was education. It lacked control over any social resources critical to the survival of large elements of West Bank or all-Palestinian society. Second, it was a leadership based outside the West Bank—in fact, outside most of the major Palestinian population concentrations. What this new leadership did begin to forge was a basis for a new *ideological* unity regarding the nature of the Palestinian problem.

After the June War in 1967, this new leadership was able to establish a firm organizational base by gaining control of the PLO. Since that time—with some notable ups and downs—the PLO has gained increasing support among Palestinians and increasing international recognition. For the first time in more than a generation, Palestinians had a *Palestinian* leadership capable of dealing with national issues. Once Israeli rule was established, however, the problematical nature of that leadership—its lack of social resources and its physical absence from Palestine—became even more apparent to West Bank Arabs.

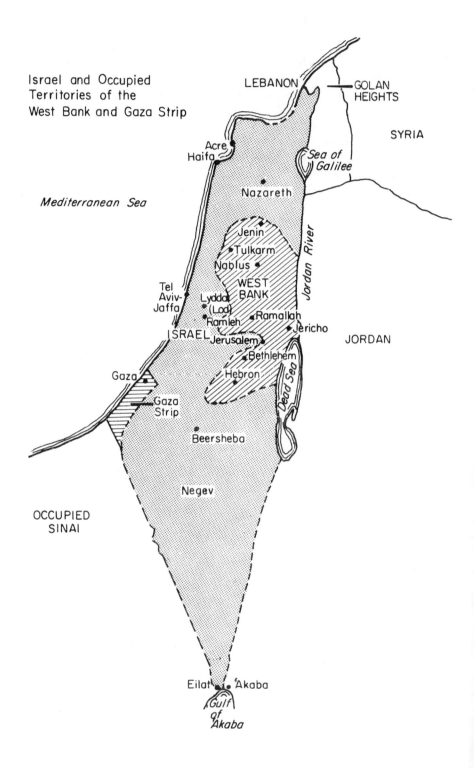

Israel and Occupied
Territories of the
West Bank and Gaza Strip

LEBANON

GOLAN
HEIGHTS

SYRIA

Acre
Haifa

*Sea of
Galilee*

Mediterranean Sea

Nazareth

Jenin

Tulkarm

Nablus

WEST
BANK

Tel
Aviv-
Jaffa

Lydda
(Lod)

Ramleh

Ramallah

Jordan River

Jericho

JORDAN

ISRAEL

Jerusalem

Bethlehem

Hebron

Dead Sea

Gaza

Gaza
Strip

Beersheba

Negev

OCCUPIED
SINAI

Eilat

'Akaba

*Gulf
of
Akaba*

CHAPTER 4

Israeli Military Rule:
Continuity at the Macro-Level

Israel's Occupation: Investment Policies

As in 1917 and in 1948, war brought social and personal trauma to the Palestinians, as well as a new and uncomfortable political status. Although military operations were minimal in the West Bank during the June 1967 War, a new refugee problem was created during and immediately following the fighting. Again, estimates of the actual numbers fleeing the West Bank vary widely, but we can say that roughly 200,000 people left during and just after the War. It is clear that the West Bank population was reduced substantially, probably by between one-quarter and one-fifth to a total of about 665,000.[1] Subsequently, only a relatively small percentage was permitted by Israeli authorities to return on a permanent basis, so the problem of physical dispersal of Palestinian Arabs was all the more intensified.[2] In fact, probably less than half of all Palestinians now live in historic Palestine (Israel plus the territories captured in 1967).[3] And the personal tragedies of homelessness and separated families have been compounded by the stark reality of Israeli military occupation for those who did not flee.

[1] Israel, Central Bureau of Statistics, *Census of Population 1967* (Jerusalem, 1967). The census excluded East Jerusalem, which was incorporated into Israel proper, and thus gave the population as 598,637. The population of East Jerusalem was 65,857. About a fifth were refugees and more than two-fifths of the refugees were in camps. A bit more than 5 percent were Christians.

[2] *Census of Population 1967* showed that one-third of all households had offspring living abroad (a total of 77,463 abroad). This figure, of course, did not include whole families or heads of households abroad. More than two-fifths of the offspring were in the East Bank and another one-third in Kuwait.

[3] There are probably more than three million Palestinians today with the major concentrations distributed roughly as follows:

> one million in occupied territories
> 850,000 in Jordan
> 450,000 in Israel
> 300,000 in Lebanon
> 160,000 in Syria
> 80,000 in Kuwait
> 50,000 in Iraq

The occupation itself turned out to be more benign than the Palestinians I interviewed dared hope in the early days of June 1967. Palestinians have found that Israeli policies—in investments, political alliances, and security—have not been very different from those of the Jordanian regime. The effect of these policies, too, has been to prevent the emergence of unified leadership and of cohesion. Without a comprehensive pattern of stratification, the society continues to be characterized by social fragmentation.

Just as King 'Abdallah and King Husayn had adopted an investment policy that accentuated Palestinian fragmentation, so did the Israelis. The basic constraints placed on the West Bank economy by Israel have been summarized by Brian Van Arkadie: "Israel channeled and controlled the basic market forces while, at the same time, limiting severely the role of public investment and comprehensive development programs in the territories. Political and business factors, furthermore, operated to limit Israeli private investment in the territories."[4]

What were those Israeli policy decisions that "channeled and controlled the basic market forces?" First, the Israelis opened up their economy to Arab labor. Second, they utilized the West Bank as a market for Israeli products. Third, they gradually opened Israel to most West Bank products. And, fourth, they adopted the "Open Bridges" policy that allowed for an exchange of products between Jordan and the West Bank.

The effect of these decisions was a tremendous economic boom for the West Bank, at least until the 1973 War, but a boom that had a very specific character. Overall growth rates were outstanding, bordering on what Van Arkadie terms the "economic miracle" class.[5] In addition, there were more jobs in more diversified fields bringing in higher incomes.[6] This economic growth, however, was not creating an

[4] Brian Van Arkadie, *Benefits and Burdens* (New York: Carnegie Endowment for International Peace, 1977), p. 38.

[5] Ibid., p. 118. The Bank of Israel estimated growth of GNP in the territories to have been an amazing 18 percent per year between 1968 and 1973, and the growth of per capita product to have been 15 percent per year. Van Arkadie tones down these figures to 9 percent and 6-7 percent respectively (pp. 116-19). Vivian A. Bull, *The West Bank—Is It Viable?* (Lexington, Mass.: Lexington Books, 1975), pp. 37-42, accepts the Bank of Israel figures.

[6] Between 1968 and 1973 the average annual increase of employed persons was 6 percent. Bull, *The West Bank*, p. 39. Also, see Van Arkadie, *Benefits and Burdens*, ch. 3. Between 1969 and 1973, wages rose 127 percent, while the consumer price index rose 107 percent. There was a vast increase in consumer durables, such as television sets and refrigerators. The number of agricultural workers fell from approximately 48,000 prior to 1967 to 7,300 in 1973 (3,400 of whom worked in Israel). For a summary of many of the economic changes, see Jamil Hilal, "Class Transformation in the West

indigenous West bank economic infrastructure outside the agricultural sector. Investment, per se, did increase substantially, with gross domestic fixed capital rising by a factor of eight between 1968 and 1973 and continuing to grow into 1974. The nature of that investment growth, however, was limited; it took place primarily through an increase in vehicles and in houses,[7] rather than in capital fixtures that could greatly expand the West Bank's own productive capacity.

Contact with the Israeli economy led to West Bankers' serving as a labor reservoir (over 40,000 workers daily by 1974, half of the West Bank's wage laborers) for the more sophisticated Israeli industrial, construction, and agricultural enterprises. By 1978, 5 percent of Israel's work force came from the occupied territories, mostly the West Bank.

Participation in Israel's economic spurt after 1967 did not translate into an indigenous West Bank economic growth that could serve as the focal point for a comprehensive, Palestinian pattern of stratification. Instead, stratification came to be characterized by a high-technology, managerial group (Jews) hierarchically situated above a less developed, working group (Arabs). Income earned in Israel reached 35 percent of the total income of the territories, according to Arye Gur-El, director-general of Israel's Labor Ministry. New vocational schools were established that tended to reinforce the stratification pattern.[8] Twenty-seven vocational schools trained workers in trades connected to the building and metal industries and the services.

The pattern is reminiscent of the Mandate: a high rate of social mobilization involving a stream of workers to the coastal areas engaged in new occupations. As in the Mandate, villages went from having labor surpluses to labor shortages. Landowners in the territories, for example, asked the minister of agriculture to halt labor movement from the West Bank to Israel.[9] This village labor shortage took place in a period of great agricultural growth, when West Bank farm products were in demand in Jordan, Israel, and the West Bank itself. Downward mobility associated with the early Jordanian period faded in favor of a rapidly rising standard of living suggestive of the Mandate.

Bank and Gaza," reprinted in "Views from Abroad," *Journal of Palestine Studies*, 6 (Winter, 1977).

[7] Van Arkadie, *Benefits and Burdens*, pp. 107-109.

[8] Israeli politician Arie Eliav notes the Israeli training of Palestinians and poses the moral question of whether such training should be and will be utilized for Israel's own needs or for the growth of the Arabs' own economic infrastructure. Arie Lova Eliav, *Land of the Hart* (Philadelphia: Jewish Publicaton Society, 1974), p. 130.

[9] *Ma'ariv*, September 17, 1972, p. 29.

Unlike the mandatory period, however, there has not been even the semblance of an Arab coastal infrastructure. The resumption of the old westward flow of Arab labor has been mitigated by the fact that workers have returned eastward in the evenings or at the end of the week.[10] All the most efficient and most competitive industries, construction firms, and farms have been in Israeli hands. The West Bank has become a lodging place for many, while the economic resources and relationships critical to their survival lie outside that area. An important result has been social weakness—portrayed by Van Arkadie in his likening of Israeli-territories economic relationships to classic developed economy-poor economy relationships.

> But the poor economy also finds itself operating as a captive market for the industrial products of the more developed one. Its agricultural products receive little protection or subsidization; its workers are the most vulnerable group in an otherwise highly organized labor market; and what investment opportunities emerge for the investors of the poorer economy are largely in a limited range of activities that play a complementary role to the more experienced and better-organized business of the richer economy.[11]

Political Alliance and Security Policies

Israel's political security and alliance policies also followed in the path of the former Jordanian policies. Even more explicitly than with investment policies, the goal has been to prevent new forms of Palestinian social and political cohesion. As with the Jordanians, the Israelis adopted security policies that would preempt any movement towards the establishment of a greater than local-level leadership.

Harsh Israeli retaliation to a wave of unrest and terrorism in the territories was carried out in 1968 and 1969. Arrests (including periods of detention without bringing charges), deportations, and demolition of houses were the three primary methods used to prevent anti-Israeli actions.[12] These tactics were used most often against the new

[10] Even overnight residence at places of work in Israel is illegal for West Bank residents, but the law is widely flouted (as is the requirement for an Israeli labor permit) so that many stay within Israel during the work week.

[11] Van Arkadie, *Benefits and Burdens*, p. 45.

[12] Predictably, Palestinian publications outside Palestine have emphasized these aspects of Israeli policy. See, for example, Michael Adams, "Israel's Treatment of the Arabs in the Occupied Territories," *Journal of Palestine Studies*, 6 (Winter, 1977), esp. pp. 34-39. Adams claims that upwards of 15,000 houses were destroyed in the decade following the 1967 War. Accusations against Israel have also included torture. See *The Sunday Times of London*, June 19, July 3, and July 10, 1977, for such accusations and the Israeli reply.

socially mobilized youths, who were usually associated with one group or another in the Palestine Liberation Organization. Here, Israeli policy emerged from the government's direct concern with national security and the immediate safety of its population. The same methods were also used, at times, against established mayors and mukhtars who gave signs of overstepping the limits placed on their roles by Israeli policy. In short, Israeli security policy was used as both deterrent and punishment to maintain the fragmentation that already existed in Palestinian society.

Israeli alliance policies evolved in a much more ad hoc fashion, but ultimately they too served to stem political cohesion among West Bank Palestinians. International political constraints and hopes for an early trade of territory for peace led the Israelis to change very little in the captured territories in the aftermath of the June War. The establishment of rule under a military commander was intended to imply a lack of change in the political status of the area. Jordanian law was left, for the most part, intact, as was the Jordanian administrative apparatus.[13]

Part of Israel's initial laissez-faire approach stemmed from the contingencies of the moment during the war itself. With the withdrawal of the Arab Legion across the Jordan River, Israeli battalion leaders were pressed to find someone who could surrender to them. The officer who captured Hebron knew that Israeli army ". . . doctrine made no mention of surrender documents or ceremonies with mayors." But he ". . . had not yet met a single local inhabitant and was wondering what to do. He had no administration unit—it was still in Jerusalem. He thought he had better get an official surrender of the town and went in search of the Mayor."[14] And so Shaykh Ja'bari passed easily from being the vital link of the Jordanians to the population to playing the same role for the Israelis. Similarly, the Israeli commander who captured Nablus sought the Jordanian military governor for the official surrender. When informed there was no military governor, he established his tie to Hamdi Cana'an, the mayor.

Israeli doctrine later followed the practices established in June 1967. Without an all-West Bank leadership to whom to turn, the mili-

[13] A number of changes in administration were made because each of the three West Bank districts—Jerusalem, Nablus, and Hebron—had been administered separately from Amman. Each had a Commission appointed in Amman. The major change instituted was a system of all-West Bank offices for such services as agriculture, commerce and industry, etc. See Shabtai Teveth, *The Cursed Blessing* (London: Weidenfeld and Nicolson, 1970), p. 286. It was difficult to reconstitute Jordanian administration because so many officials fled to the East Bank at the outbreak of war. Nimrod Raphaeli, "Military Government in the Occupied Territories: An Israeli View," *Middle East Journal*, 23 (1969), 186.

[14] Teveth, *The Cursed Blessing*, pp. 63 and 61.

tary administration adopted a system of political alliances with town mayors and village mukhtars. And the Israelis, after toying briefly with the idea of establishing a Palestinian entity on the West Bank, found the arrangement comfortable. With the municipality, or at most the district, as the outer limit of any Palestinian leader's influence, the Israelis quickly discovered the advantages to an occupying army of the absence of a united and unifying leadership. The fragmentation inherited from Jordanian times served the Israelis equally well. From 1968 on, the Israeli government was firm in denying mayors or others the right of association on a greater than local level for political purposes. Only a decade later did the Israelis become less stringent about such meetings.

The Embattled Role of Mukhtar

The policy of restricting local leaders, on the one hand, and of singling them out as go-betweens for the Israelis to the West Bank population, on the other hand, put these leaders into very difficult predicaments. This situation was particularly hard on village mukhtars, whose positions over the years had already diminished considerably to a near functionary role in the Jordanian administrative chain of command. Even under Jordanian rule, however, the existing norms had given the mukhtars some special status and special privileges.

After 1967, these norms clashed with those of the Israelis. Part of the respect and influence enjoyed by many mukhtars during the period of Jordanian rule had come from their easy, informal access to government offices. With the culturally alien Israelis, mukhtars have discovered that the result of serving as the link to government officials has been their humiliation in the eyes of their fellow villagers.[15]

In Jordanian times, stated one young man critical of his mukhtar, the mukhtar could meet the governor any day, not just once a week. Now his relations with the authorities are much more formal. The mukhtar, in a separate interview, confirmed the difficulty. Now if he goes to see the military governor, he said, the person sitting at the door does not let him in.[16] At times, even when summoned, he must wait for hours outside the office of the military governor. He complained of the indignity of being summoned to meetings at only 24 hours' notice and the relative importance placed by the Israelis on *his* being exactly on time. The precision of Israeli demands upon the

[15] One mukhtar stated, "It is difficult dealing with the Israeli authorities. The Jordanians are Muslims. Israel is ruled by Jews, so all we can do now is to live obediently." Interview, El-Wassifiya, Bethlehem, September 20, 1973.

[16] Interviews, Ummalas, Hebron, September 14 and 16, 1973.

mukhtar also reinforces the view of young villagers of his obedience to the occupying authorities.

The economic changes in village life brought about by Israeli rule, which will be discussed in the next chapter, have also diminished the mukhtar's stature. With the rising incomes of traditionally low-status groups in the village and uncertainty over the appropriateness of the old rules of behavior in the face of rapidly changing social conditions, a certain degree of confusion has appeared over questions of status. A mukhtar in the village of Janiya, 43 years old, vividly portrayed this confusion over old norms and new resources.[17] He feels that as mukhtar and as a member of a respected village family, he cannot simply hop on a pick-up truck each morning to work in Israel and still maintain the respect he has come to expect. Since his son is still too young to work or travel abroad, he finds his position slipping relative to others working in Lod or Jerusalem. "Money makes changes," he states. Previously, all men sat on the floor at the mosque. Now, those earning money outside the village buy rugs and chairs to sit on, while he must continue to sit on the floor.

In some ways, status can be bought. Many mukhtars have thus been in the difficult situation of being caught between the need for the resources to maintain the respect they had received in the past and the belief that the way to get such resources, to work in Israel, would in any case undermine that respect. Several of those interviewed sent their sons to work in Israel to bolster family income, but then discovered that this had the unanticipated effect of increasing the independence of their sons and thus somewhat undermining their familial authority in the eyes of the village.

Increased mobility and sophistication on the part of the villagers, together with less personalistic and more bureaucratic procedures on the part of the Israelis, have also served to undermine the brokerage function of the mukhtar. Some villagers reported that they now bypass the mukhtar altogether and, whenever possible, go directly to governmental offices to make their requests. Others contrasted the services of the mukhtar with those of the young educated civil servants in the village. One teacher reported, for example, that since the war he has increasingly been called upon as a broker. "The mukhtar is the formal head of the village," he says, "but if someone needs a letter the mukhtar does not know how to write. So people do not go to him."[18] Other villagers confirmed the teacher's assessment, some reporting that they prefer those "who know more" to mediate their disputes instead of the mukhtar. One man openly resented the con-

---

[17] Interview, Janiya, Ramallah, September 1, 1973.

[18] Interview, Ummalas, Hebron, September 18, 1973.

tinuing practice of the mukhtar's demanding payment for settling a dispute, as opposed to the more informal techniques of mediation by the educated villagers.

Despite the beleaguered position of mukhtar, the role itself is unlikely to disappear in the immediate future. Whatever regime has ruled the area has relied to some degree on the village mukhtar as a means to insure rural stability. The Israelis, in particular, have preferred to deal with a prior, established, older leadership.

Another factor also continues to reinforce the established mukhtar's claim to leadership. Whether the young educated men are abroad, working in Israel, or working in West Bank towns, they are typically not in the village during a great part of each day. In fact, often the only educated person spending his day in the village itself is the teacher—and, in many cases, he is not even a resident of the village. As one young man in the village of Khirbet Carma put it: "It is true the educated young men have schooling, but they don't understand traditional problems of large families, and they don't exert influence."[19] If something happens in the village, he asserted, the young are not on hand at all times and thus their mediation efforts might be rejected by one party or another. In short, the mukhtar's position continues to enjoy some legitimacy because the mukhtar is a man *of* the village at all times. Even though the village is the place of work for fewer and fewer village men, the appropriateness of young people who work outside the village serving as village leaders is still brought into question.

The fact that there is little alternative for Palestinian villagers to the continued leadership role of the mukhtar reinforces Israeli alliance policies. Like the clusters of investment and security policies, these alliance policies have promoted localism at the expense of all-West Bank integration. Table 7 summarizes the effects of the three clusters of Israeli policy on stratification and population patterns of the West Bank.

[19] Interview, Khirbet Carma, Hebron, October 1, 1973.

Table 7
Effects of Israeli Policy on Patterns of Stratification and Population

Type of Policy	Stratification Patterns	Population Patterns
Investment	Use of West Bank as a labor reservoir for Israel led to a stratification pattern marked by a layer of Israeli managers and entrepreneurs over a layer of skilled and unskilled Palestinian workers	Use of West Bank as a labor reservoir for Israel led to resumption of movement to coast, but now only on a commuting basis
Alliance	Alliances with municipal leaders and mukhtars and not with potential national leaders; stratification patterns continued to be localistic and fragmented	—
Security	Harsh security measures helped prevent new leadership patterns—new links or new groups—from emerging or becoming institutionalized on a national level	Harsh security measures led to some voluntary out-migration and to deportations; improved public health maintained high rate of natural increase

CHAPTER 5

The Impact on Stratification of Employment
in Israel: Change at the Micro-Level

Introduction

By 1967, an apparent contradiction had come to characterize Palestinian society on the West Bank. Despite increasing physical mobility and
higher levels of education[1]—qualities often associated with a rapidly
developing society—West Bank economic life was still that of a primarily low-technology, agricultural society. Agriculture was the sector of
direct employment for about half the population, and another fifth
worked in agricultural services and trade. Even in those areas of the
West Bank that were classified as urban, one-fifth of the households
engaged in farming.[2] In 1967, for example, Nablus, the city with the
highest standard of living in the West Bank and with a long history of
local industry, was still a permanent home for many who continued to
till the soil.

Farming (and particularly village farming) was the dominant mode
of life among West Bank Palestinians, but agriculture also turned out
to be as confining as a straitjacket for people experiencing rapid social
mobilization in other spheres of their lives. Although half the population was engaged in farming, the agricultural sector accounted for
only one-quarter of GNP. The average income in agriculture was only
60 percent of that in other sectors. Almost 85 percent of the farms
were under 25 acres, but these small farms accounted for only about
35 percent of the total cultivated land. Almost a third of the farmers
did not cultivate their own lands but were tenants. In short, there
were few employment opportunities outside agriculture. Farming was
how most West Bank Palestinians earned their livings, but its low-

[1] By the 1960s, the rate of migration to the East Bank and to other countries reached
2.6 percent per year. In 1961, less than 14 percent of boys between 10 and 19 had no
schooling at all. For girls, however, the figure was still close to half. See Israel, Economic
Planning Office, *The West Bank Economic Survey* (Jerusalem, 1967), pp. B-14 and B-23
(Hebrew).

[2] See Israel, Central Bureau of Statistics, *Survey of Housing, Household Equipment, Sup-
port and Farm Cultivation in the Occupied Areas* (Jerusalem, 1967); also, Aryeh Sheskin,
"The Areas Administered by Israel: Their Economy and Foreign Trade," *Journal of
World Trade Law*, 3 (1969), 522-52.

technology, small-plot character meant it could offer little more than subsistence at best.

Even the physical constraints of the land prevented farming from being a viable means of social mobility. The soil is mostly rocky, and its potential to deliver high yields through intensive agriculture is limited. Only 5 percent of the cultivable land was irrigated, and conditions are not suitable for extensive irrigation projects. With the very limited economic alternatives in the West Bank, numerous families opted for one (or both) of two alternatives: long-term migration from the West Bank, or "making do" in farming. "Making do" usually involved utilizing the rocky soil for what it produced best, fruit-bearing trees—particularly olives. The stagnation of the main economic sector, agriculture, also helped maintain stagnation in stratification patterns on local and all-West Bank levels. Most social mobility came to involve at least some family members leaving the West Bank altogether.

As we saw in Chapter 4, the new Israeli military rule was intent on not disturbing overall stratification patterns. Policies of political alliances, investment, and security had the effect of discouraging ties beyond the level of the local community and of preventing the rise of a new social or political leadership. Localism was fostered. Major economic activities and infrastructural growth that affected the economy of the West Bank took place in Israel so that no Palestinian group could gain control over resources crucial to a significant portion of the West Bank population. No coherent all-West Bank pattern of stratification emerged.

Israeli policies, however, did foster important and unanticipated changes in stratification on the local level. These changes came about as a result of one aspect of the cluster of Israeli investment policies. Work opportunities opened in Israel, and by 1973 more than 40,000 laborers (one out of every three to four workers on the West Bank) commuted to work there. The straitjacket imposed by West Bank agriculture was removed. The new jobs meant that for West Bank Arabs viable economic alternatives were created west of the Jordan River for the first time since before 1948. This chapter looks at changes in Palestinian society at the micro-level stemming from Israeli investment policies. It analyzes the impact on West Bank village society of the opening of these new opportunities, especially in light of the out-migration that has characterized the West Bank for the last generation. Most of the Palestinians working in Israel come from villages and not from cities or towns. Because there has been no overall coherent pattern of stratification, the various parts of the West Bank expressed the effects of these changes somewhat differently, manifesting different types of cleavage and conflict. To simplify matters somewhat, we can classify the West Bank into three regions—Jerusalem-Ramallah, Nablus, and Hebron—based on the three Jordanian administrative districts.[3] In the next section, we will look at some of the major, gross differences that already existed among these areas prior to the advent of Israeli rule in 1967.

West Bank Variability

During the period of Jordanian rule, the rural population growth rate was higher than that of the urban population—a pattern opposite to that of the Middle East as a whole, where city growth rates were more than double the rate of total population growth.[4] After 1948, cut off from their former economic centers and conduits to the world economy on the Mediterranean coast, and faced with Jordanian policy that purposely diminished the political centrality of Jerusalem, Palestinians in the West Bank turned to the village and their main kinship groups as the most stabilizing forces in their lives. Palestinian social relations were, in great part, within the frameworks of agriculture, village, and the dispersed-extended family.

The approximately 400 villages have varied considerably in size, ranging from less than 100 inhabitants to over 5,000 (see Figures 1 and 2). Most commonly, villages have had between 100 and 200 people, but the average number of inhabitants for all villages in 1967 was about 875. The more fertile subdistricts of Jenin and Tulkarm in the Nablus District had villages of noticeably larger average size (919 and 1,026 respectively), with 15 large villages of over 2,000 people bringing up the average considerably, while the desert dominated subdistricts of Bethlehem and Jericho in the Jerusalem District had smaller villages (averages of 692 and 167 respectively).[5] Poor land conditions are among the most important constraints on population density; nevertheless, the density of the West Bank as a whole in 1961 was 143 people per square kilometer compared to only 19 for the East Bank, which is largely desert.

[3] Two of the Jordanian districts had a number of subdistricts: the Jerusalem District included the subdistricts of Jerusalem, Ramallah, Bethlehem, and Jericho—total population in 1961 of 344,270; the Nablus District included the subdistricts of Nablus, Jenin, and Tulkarm—total population in 1961 of 341,748; and the Hebron District had a total population in 1961 of 119,432.

[4] On the changing nature of Palestinian population, see Elisha Efrat, "Change in the Order of Settlements in Judea and Samaria, 1947-1967," *Hamizrah Hehadash* (The New East), 23 (1973), 283-95 (Hebrew).

[5] For a fuller discussion of village size, see Elisha Efrat, "The Distribution of Settlements in Judea and Samaria," *Hamizrah Hehadash* (The New East), 20 (1970), 257-65 (Hebrew). Our data are computed from Israel, Central Bureau of Statistics, *Census of Population 1967* (Jerusalem, 1967).

Hebron District

All we have said about the constraints of peasant agriculture and the absence of local economic alternatives applies to the Hebron region, only more so. The Hebron region has been a traditionally conservative, religious Muslim stronghold, with an overwhelmingly agricultural economy characterized by overall low technology. This region was different from the districts of Jerusalem and Nablus during the Jordanian period, its population having markedly lower levels of skills and education. Its more traditional character was reflected in 1961 in the more than 75 percent of its population over 15 with less than four years of formal schooling—a proportion about 5 percent higher than for the West Bank as a whole.[6] Less than one-quarter of the population were literate compared to more than one-third in the rest of the West Bank. Of course, the rural population had even lower levels of education; in Hebron District, outside the city itself, almost 90 percent of the population did not have even a primary school education.

In other aspects as well, Hebron District's lack of development was evident. For example, it had one doctor for each 10,600 inhabitants compared to one for about 3,700 in Jerusalem District and 7,500 in Nablus District. None of the eight welfare institutions for youths and the elderly was located in Hebron District.

For the region of Hebron then, agriculture was even more of a straitjacket than for the other regions of the West Bank. It lacked both the relatively large variety of economic sectors characteristic of the Jerusalem region and the suitable conditions for relatively more intensive agriculture that characterized the Nablus region (particularly around Jenin and Tulkarm). Because of the more severe economic constraints, migration from the Hebron region during Jordanian rule was the highest on the West Bank. From 1952-1961, the entire West Bank had a net migration of −20 percent to the East Bank. For the Hebron region, the figure was −33.3 percent. It had the lowest rate of population growth of all areas in this period, −4.9 percent. In contrast, the more economically developed districts of Nablus and Jerusalem grew in population by 8.4 and 14.2 percent respectively.

Hebron region's net migration of its rural population to the East Bank was a whopping −37.4 percent. Jerusalem District had almost no net out-migration of rural population to the East Bank, while Nablus District had a net rural migration to the East Bank of −23.7 percent. As we shall see below, the heavy migration from Hebron region villages to the most accessible areas, the East Bank and Kuwait, re-

---

[6] The data in this section come from two principal sources: Jordan, Department of Statistics, *First Census of Population and Housing*; and the previously cited *The West Bank Economic Survey*, which is a compendium of numerous Jordanian statistics and surveys.

Figure 1:
Distribution of Villages Up to 1500 People by Population Size

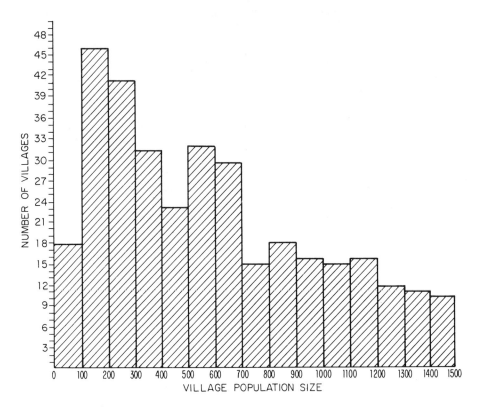

sulted in flows of cash from the outside to people in diverse social
strata. By 1967, then, these Hebron villages were already showing
signs of having somewhat more fluid social structures.

Jerusalem District

Even with the purposeful de-emphasis of Jerusalem in all-West Bank
affairs during the Jordanian period, the Jerusalem District continued,
to a degree, to retain a distinctive status. For example, it had the highest levels of schooling and literacy in the West Bank, and even its rural
men and women had more years of formal education than their rural
counterparts elsewhere in the West Bank. Also, as we saw, it had the
lowest number of people per doctor. Almost 70 percent of the population were wage earners (a high proportion in handicrafts and production) compared to only half in Nablus and Hebron. A smaller
proportion of the population was in agriculture compared to the rest

Figure 2:
Distribution of Villages of More than 1500 People by Population Size

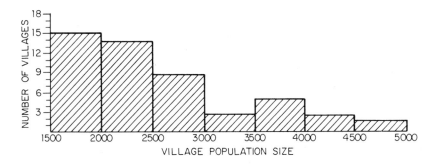

of the West Bank.[7] More than half of all West Bank industry was located in the Jerusalem-Ramallah region, while less than 10 percent,
for example, was in Hebron District.

Not surprisingly, then, the Jerusalem District had the most bal-
anced net migration with the East Bank between 1952 and 1961,
−14.2 percent, with a net rural migration of only −0.4 percent. When
village sons did migrate, they were less likely than those in Hebron
and Nablus to travel only to accessible sites in the Middle East. Those
with sufficient means, the sons of village landowners, often went as far
as North or South America. As we shall see, the money they sent back
to their families in the village often reinforced old status cleavages.
The higher urban out-migration may reflect the region's relatively
high proportion of Christians, who have long been more likely to
migrate.

Nablus District

The Nablus region developed a distinctive character that included
both some of the Jerusalem-Ramallah and some of the Hebron traits.
It became a center of urbane political and social culture as well as the
most agriculturally productive area. Among the regions of the West
Bank, it contained the largest proportion of rural population, about
three-quarters of the district's inhabitants, and the highest average
rainfall. The farmers in the villages around the towns of Nablus,
Tulkarm, and Jenin consistently had the highest yields per acre (often
twice those in the Jerusalem-Ramallah region).

The town of Nablus itself, on the other hand, had the highest percentage of all West Bank towns of workers in industry (more than

[7] The percentage of rural population in Jerusalem was not very much less than the
average for the whole West Bank (60.4 percent versus 67.6 percent).

one-quarter) in 1961. Proportionately, out-migration from the region's villages was less than that of Hebron region to accessible areas in the Middle East and less than that of Jerusalem-Ramallah to the lucrative West. Those who did travel within the Middle East, however, were more likely to gain some higher education than migrants from the Hebron region, and they were more likely to return to the village to make an impact than migrants from the Jerusalem-Ramallah region who were educated in the West.

In sum, the West Bank in 1967 was an area with few economic or political links among its regions and with limited opportunities for mobility within each region. Hebron District had the fewest human or capital resources outside agriculture and the strictest adherence to traditional socioreligious tenets. The principal changes that had occurred there were those involving "exit," out-migration from the West Bank to wealthier areas in the Middle East.[8] The resources that migrants injected back into the villages had an important effect on local status patterns. The Jerusalem-Ramallah region differed in a number of ways, having more industry and a more skilled and educated population. Jerusalem, however, was also suffering from a drive on the part of Amman to "equalize" it, that is, to give it a more provincial, rather than a more metropolitan flavor. The influence of notable families had declined markedly. The district's status as the social and political pacesetter of the West Bank was hurt even further in 1967 by the annexation of the city itself to Israel immediately following the war.

If there was an heir to this pacesetter role, it was the Nablus region, which was reemerging as a center of political discontent and unrest. A relatively large number of merchants, entrepreneurs, teachers, and clerks became concentrated in the city of Nablus and in the villages as well. But the district as a whole was something of an anomaly, with its combination of urban character and large farming population. The "triangle" area of Tulkarm and Jenin, in particular, had a heavily agricultural economic base. In some ways, then, Nablus District was more sensitive than the Jerusalem-Ramallah region to the needs and problems posed by agricultural life and to the constraints imposed, especially for those with limited resources, by the agricultural straitjacket.

[8] On the concept of exit, see Albert O. Hirschman, *Exit, Voice and Loyalty* (Cambridge, Mass.: Harvard University Press, 1970). It has been reported that Hebron's slower rate of change was attributable to out-migration to Jerusalem as well. See David Farhi, "The West Bank: 1948-1971—Society and Politics in Judea and Samaria," *New Middle East* (November, 1971), 33.

New Outlets: Post-1967

The immediate result of the 1967 War was that Palestinian society on the West Bank suffered a series of convulsions. There was some suffering due to the fighting itself. One survey found that 12 percent felt a direct, profound impact from the war (e.g., wounded, endured death of a relative, had house destroyed), while 59 percent reported an indirect or less profound impact (e.g., hurt economically, wounded national pride).[9] As noted in Chapter 4, probably as much as one-quarter of the prewar population (about 200,000 people) crossed to Jordan during and immediately after the hostilities. One source reports that almost all senior officials crossed to the East Bank, making it difficult (relative to the situation in Gaza) to reconstitute civilian administration. Banking, public services, and tourism were all disrupted for varying amounts of time.[10]

Israeli commanders made prompt efforts to normalize the situation. By June 8, for example, in the middle of the war itself, the Israeli Ministry of Agriculture began providing services to West Bank farmers in order to prevent crop failures and cattle deaths.[11] Although each of the districts established by the Israelis (Bethlehem, Jericho, Ramallah, Nablus, Tulkarm, Jenin, and Hebron) has been ruled by military governors responsible to the military commander of the West Bank, civilian staff officers were brought in to help the military with skills and services. These civilian staff officers have been responsible to both the head of the civil affairs administration (a military officer) and professionally to their civilian ministries. Most active among the ministries has been the Ministry of Agriculture, with the provision of training centers, demonstration plots, and professional agronomists.

An immediate effort was also made to recruit local Arabs to work on a district basis for the civilian staff officers. During the period 1967-1968, over 6,500 Arabs worked in these capacities in the West Bank.[12] By 1969-1970, over 8,000 were employed (about three-quarters of

[9] Y. Peres, "Attitudes and Values in the West Bank," unpublished research report presented to the Committee for the Affairs of the Occupied Territories, p. 28 (Hebrew).

[10] Nimrod Raphaeli, "Military Government in the Occupied Territories: An Israeli View," *Middle East Journal*, 23 (1969), 179, 180, and 186.

[11] Israel, Ministry of Agriculture, *Activities in Judaea and Samaria—June 1967-January 1970*. On the establishment of military rule and its later structures and policies, there is an article by the army general responsible for that rule: S. Gazit, "The Administered Territories—Policy and Action," *Ma'arachot*, 55 (1970), 24-39 (Hebrew).

[12] See Israel, Ministry of Defence, Coordinator of Government Operations in the Administered Territories, *Four Years of Military Administration, 1967-1971*; and Raphaeli, "Military Government in the Occupied Territories," 188-90.

them in the education sector), and payments were made to over 750 mukhtars.

The more profound impact on Palestinian social patterns, however, came neither as an immediate outcome of the fighting nor as a result of prompt establishment of Israeli administration. Rather, change came slowly as a result of the breakdown of the economic barrier between the West Bank and Israeli economies. One Ministry of Defence publication states, "The Six Day War abolished to all intents and purposes the 'green line' that in the past demarcated the Israeli sector from the administered territories. Naturally and unavoidably, these areas are becoming dependent upon Israel for all their economic and service needs."[13]

From September 1968 through September 1971, there was an almost sevenfold increase in the number of West Bankers employed in Israel (from 5,000 to 33,400), and a more than 20 percent additional increase up to the 1973 War. More than half worked in construction, and others were employed in the agricultural, industrial, and service sectors.[14] Per capita private consumption rose in the West Bank in those initial years after the war from I£668 in 1968 to I£807 in 1970.[15] By 1970, there was full employment in the West Bank (except in the Hebron region).

Employment in Israel was secured on an informal basis after the war through labor contractors and interested Jewish entrepreneurs. In November 1968, the Israeli government attempted to regulate the flow of labor formally through the establishment of government labor exchanges (by 1970 there were twenty such employment offices), but these were successful in registering only about half the workers who crossed into Israel daily.[16]

Shifting Village Conflicts and Cleavages

On the basis of my field research in the West Bank in 1973, including forty-five lengthy, in-depth interviews in ten villages (on methodology, see Appendix, "Field Research in an Occupied Territory"), I found that there were two major cleavages in the villages, a status cleavage and a generational cleavage, and that both were greatly affected by the outflow of workers to Israel. Moreover, these cleavages differed significantly among the areas of the West Bank, and thus the

[13] *Four Years of Military Administration*, p. 8.

[14] By 1977, the figures were 40 percent in construction, 25 percent in industry, and 35 percent in services.

[15] *Four Years of Military Administration*, pp. 16-21.

[16] A Ministry of Labor official took issue with this estimate in an interview, stating that 80 percent of all workers from the territories had secured the proper licenses.

changes wrought by Israeli employment opportunities were far from uniform from region to region. In the Jerusalem-Ramallah region, in which the largest village population was now in the Ramallah area, the most salient cleavage was that of status; in the Hebron region, the generational split was most evident; and in the Nablus region, the two cleavages took somewhat different forms but were not as sharp or intense as the major cleavage in each of the other two regions.

Signs of newfound Palestinian prosperity could be found throughout the West Bank in the early 1970s. In village homes, chairs were rapidly replacing pillows, and beds were replacing mats. Electrical lines and water pipes into houses, private vehicles, wristwatches, television antennas, and new clothes were all outward signs of the new prosperity. Many families were eating meat several times a week rather than once a week or less. In the villages of the Jerusalem-Ramallah region, the changes from the economically depressed period following the 1948 War were most obvious. It was there that one could see the most important symbol of new wealth, newly built homes, in its most lavish form. Formidable and beautiful houses, built of finely cut, white Jerusalem stone, dotted the landscape of numerous villages in the area (particularly those villages closest to towns).

By the middle of the Jordanian period, three modes of investment by Palestinian villagers had come to demonstrate a family's high status or upward mobility and claims on higher status: purchasing land in the village, building big new homes, and sending sons to foreign universities. The importance of owning significant amounts of land in their villages was reiterated by respondents time and again in interviews. Land ownership (understood in somewhat different terms from those in the West) had been a symbol of status and one's own self-worth for centuries, but it became even more important in Palestinian life after the creation of the refugee problem and the loss of lands in Israel during and immediately after the 1948 War.

Abdulla M. Lutfiyya, who undertook one of the few major anthropological surveys of a Palestinian village in Jordan, wrote on the meaning of land ownership,

> As in all landed societies there is a strong attachment between the villager and the land he owns. The land is much more than just a source of income: it is a status symbol. The land is also a sacred bond that links the villager with the past and the future. He inherits the land from his ancestors and expects to pass it to his own children. . . . Land is the most coveted kind of property in the community. The villager, regardless of his occupation or station

in life, seldom hesitates to invest any money he has or gets in a few more acres of land.[17]

With the unfavorable man-land ratio that existed following the doubling of the West Bank population in the years surrounding the 1948 War, land became even more valuable and took on heightened importance as a sign of social mobility. As numerous Palestinian villagers migrated to the East Bank, the Persian Gulf, and to the West, they sent money back to their families or returned with money and immediately invested that money in village land.

The following case exemplifies the seriousness with which Palestinians pursued the acquisition of land. One villager from Baytin (Ramallah District), now the owner of the largest house in the village, left his young wife in 1928 to travel to the United States.[18] He opened a hardware store in a southern American city and began saving for his eventual return to the village. He was able to return once, in 1947, to see his wife for an extended period and then left again until his final return in 1958. Between 1955 and 1958, with the money he had earned in the United States, his family bought 75 acres of land in his name to add to the 25 he had inherited from his father. In 1962, he capped his success with the completion of his new house.

Another villager in Baytin emphasized the continuing importance of land into the 1970s.[19] He is currently a bus dispatcher in Jerusalem for Egged, the Israeli bus cooperative, and his family's wages are among the highest in the village (more than I£2000 per month in 1973). Prior to the 1967 War, however, his income was only approximately I£60 per month since he had no land and worked simply as a watchman in other people's fields. The coveted job in Jerusalem was secured through personal contacts made by his son on another job, and a sign of its high desirability is his willingness to leave his house at 4 a.m. to take four buses to work each morning. Despite his gain in standard of living, he says, "I would prefer being a farmer with land in the village to making even I£10,000 per month." His status within the village does not reflect his high income, since he has not saved enough as yet either to buy land or build a new house. In fact, his definition of the "lower class" of the village was those who neither owned land nor had relatives abroad.

The centrality of houses as a mode of investment in Palestinian life was already documented in the nineteenth century. One observer wrote in 1881:

[17] Abdulla M. Lutfiyya, *Baytīn, A Jordanian Village* (London: Mouton, 1966), p. 102.
[18] Interview, Baytin, Ramallah, September 8, 1973.
[19] Interview, Baytin, Ramallah, August 25, 1973.

The erection of a new house is always a great event in the village; the man about to build it thinks of nothing else. As soon as the plans are drawn and the foundations commenced, he sits down beside his architect, foreman, and builder (one and the same person) and calmly smoking his pipe, follows the whole process with the greatest interest, occasionally signifying his approval by giving advice or urging on the work. When it is a Sheikh's or some other village potentate's house which is being built, the celebrities of the place, priests, elders, etc., join him in order to show their interest in the important event.[20]

The post-1967 era has greatly intensified a building boom that started in Palestinian villages in the early 1960s. The incomes sent from abroad and poured into house construction have created some local employment. In several villages in the Jerusalem-Ramallah region, for example, a number of small landowners have been able to supplement their incomes by quarry work or stonecutting, and others have worked full time in such jobs. A new house has taken on such importance as a cultural symbol among West Bank Palestinians that, at times, other values have simply fallen away in its wake. In the villages of Wassifiya and Khirbet E-Deir (Bethlehem District), for example, villagers have made the transition from nomadic life to settled village life within the last quarter century. Not one respondent expressed any regrets about giving up the life of the tent for the life of the house. Quickly, status in the two villages came to be determined by the size and quality of one's house.

Jerusalem-Ramallah Region

During the Jordanian period in the Jerusalem-Ramallah region, the old differentiations in village status, especially the division between those who did and did not own cultivable land, were used to create a new basis for status differentiation. As we saw above, this region, with its rocky Ramallah hills and arid Bethlehem and Jericho climate, was the least viable agricultural area in the West Bank. With farming affording little basis for future mobility, the village landowners, especially in the villages close to the cities of Jerusalem and Ramallah, used their wealth to place their sons in the West. Although many emigrants simply took jobs in the West or became small merchants, the highest source of status in the village was to have a university-educated son or, even better, one with a graduate degree.

What Fawaz Turki writes of Palestinian refugees is true as well for

[20] Rev. F. A. Klein, "Life, Habits and Customs of the Fellahin of Palestine," *Palestine Exploration Fund Quarterly* (April, 1881), 115.

West Bankers who had the means to finance Western university edu-
cations: "Education, probably seen as the only tangible investment
for the future, became to a Palestinian family the most crucial and the
most momentous accomplishment ever."[21] Some villages in the
Jerusalem-Ramallah region, such as Baytin and Bitunia, were literally
emptied of young men who were the sons of landowners. Besides the
status landowners gained by having a son studying or working in the
West, remittances from abroad also reinforced their positions in the
villages by giving them the means to increase their holdings and to
build new houses. The additional land acquired meant hiring poor,
low-status villagers as tenants and agricultural laborers, and thus increasing the bonds of dependency within the village.

Long-distance family ties have been a prominent mainstay of Palestinian social structure since the 1950s. As a result, events occurring in
such distant places as Caracas, Venezuela, or Detroit, Michigan, have
had important and immediate effects on Palestinian village social patterns.

One can only speculate about the reasons for the enduring strength
of these extended family networks relative to that of other nationalities. The steadfastness of fairly extended kinship relations over great
distances for considerable periods of time may be related to the destruction of Palestinian centers in Jerusalem and in the coastal cities in
1948 and to the inability of the West Bank towns to develop as new
centers. The lack of centralized bases, one can hypothesize, has forced
Palestinians to build strong local institutions, particularly family networks, to provide needed security and identity to individuals.[22]

The migration from Palestinian villages is distinctive in that it often
does *not* take place in stepwise fashion, first to small cities and then to
major national or foreign centers. Many villagers from the Jerusalem-Ramallah region have migrated directly to major Western cities,
without intermediate steps, using family funds and ties as their basis
for mobility. Once in the West, they are greeted by relatives and native village organizations that aid in their integration into the new setting.

By 1967, then, villages in the Jerusalem and Ramallah region were
dominated by an older landowning group whose status was being
reinforced by the remittances and local social standing of their sons
abroad. This landowning group dominated village affairs and exer-

[21] Fawaz Turki, *The Disinherited* (New York: Monthly Review Press, 1972), p. 41.

[22] S. N. Eisenstadt, "Prestige, Participation and Strata Formation" in *Social Stratification*, ed. by J. A. Jackson (Cambridge: Cambridge University Press, 1968), pp. 62-103,
has developed an hypothesis that the strength of local institutions, such as families and
clans, is inversely proportional to the strength of a country's major center.

cised considerable control over the landless workers, many of whom were without a viable alternative to offering themselves as tenants or agricultural laborers to the landowners. If this situation was resented by the land-poor or totally landless, their resentment was muted.

After the Israeli military victory, new means to much higher incomes became available. Israeli wages were huge compared to the former earnings of low-income groups and even compared to the income of the wealthier villagers. The new wages had a profound effect on social status in the Jerusalem-Ramallah villages, making it possible for the lower status groups to close the income gap considerably between them and their former landlords and employers.

This situation was unlike any other in recent Palestinian history. For the first time, the means to new status were not accessible first and foremost to the already relatively rich and powerful. Because employment in Israel was ideologically tainted and because it usually involved hard physical labor, it was shunned by the higher status (and, at first, middle status) village groups.

The old bonds of dependency were broken. With the narrowing of the income gap came new claims to status on the part of those working in Israel, as well as new resentments in village social life. Additionally, Israeli policy blocked the return of the vast majority of those villagers not in the West Bank at the time of the 1967 census right after the war. Often those prevented from returning were precisely the landowners' sons who would have been the inheritors of the dominant roles in village affairs. In fact, among village landowners, it was the Israeli policy of not sanctioning mass returns of village residents that elicited the most comment and bitterness concerning the military occupation.

Landowners were vociferous in the interviews in claiming that high Israeli wages for West Bank workers were undermining the viability of local agriculture. The landowners simply could not compete with the higher wages (much like the larger landowners during the latter years of the British Mandate) and were thus forced to abandon cultivation on large tracts of their land. A mukhtar in Baytin for example, claimed that only 7.5 of his 50 acres were cultivated in 1973.[23] This landowning group felt overwhelmingly that its standard of living had not risen during the Israeli occupation. An owner of 25 acres in Jamalah claimed that he was able to maintain his former level of yields (and thus not take a drop in his standard of living) only by using new agricultural technology, though he now cultivates only one-fifth of his total acreage.[24] The agricultural growth that has occurred during the

[23] Interview, Baytin, Ramallah, August 16, 1973.
[24] Interview, Jamalah, Ramallah, August 22, 1973.

years of Israeli occupation has generally been associated with new technology and capital intensification.

Surprisingly, most explicit resentment toward others within the village was shown not by those whose position was somewhat threatened, but by those who had managed to move up in status and close the rich-poor gap. Their new upward movement on the income ladder and their decreased dependency on the landowning group have made those working in Israel more outspoken about status differences in the villages. With new resources available and with relative incomes changing rapidly, the issue of status is constantly in the forefront of village discussion and affairs.

Resentment against high-status groups by those at the bottom of the status ladder was portrayed in an interview in Bitunia with the son of a refugee (refugees are at the very bottom of Bitunia's social hierarchy). His family is earning more now than ever before through his and his father's employment in Israel, yet he felt resentful of the elderly landowners who constitute the village leadership. Specifically, he complained about the leadership's penchant for counting villagers abroad as part of the current village population. Low-status refugees working in Israel now form the majority of the adult male population in the village, but, of the seven members on the village council, none is a refugee, and, since the council was formed, only one refugee has served on it.[25]

In Baytin, the former watchman of villagers' crops and current Egged bus dispatcher is now the head of one of the highest paid families in the village. He, too, was quite bitter about the continuing closed networks of power and connections that operate despite the new claims of those working in Israel. Segregated marriage patterns continue to exist, he said, and low-status males are forced to seek wives among other low-status families. His harshest criticism, however, was for those who reinforce their positions by sending their sons to "Nixon's America." He felt that sending sons abroad is tantamount to treason against the Palestinian nation. The sons, he said, return to the village "stupid and forget who they are and their homeland." He was particularly bitter because his own sons' applications to the United States consulate for a visa had been turned down. Excluded from the village network of crucial connections, he found that other villagers' sons abroad would not sign the necessary affidavits of financial guarantee for his family members so that they would be eligible for the coveted U.S. visa.

Resentment, then, seems to come from both those with new, higher incomes and those whose position has been endangered by the recent

---

[25] Interview, Bitunia, Ramallah, August 25, 1973.

changes. Despite the feelings on both sides, however, there seems to be little group consciousness or overt intragroup organization within the village. At times, the cleavage was talked about in we-they terms, referring to village status groups, but, nevertheless, most issues of status continue to be thought of in highly personal (or, more proper- ly, familial) terms.

Moreover, the rapidly changing social conditions have pointed to differences within each group, in addition to those between the groups. Within the group working in Israel, for example, new pat- terns of status differentiation have appeared that may well block the solidarity necessary for this group to demand status recognition in the village collectively. There is a distinction, for example, between those who can afford to learn a skill to use in Israel, particularly in the con- struction industry, and those who have remained unskilled. The skilled can usually earn twice as much as the unskilled in Israel.

Also, village social networks and connections are important among those working in Israel, just as they are among the landowners. Labor contractors can assign the most prized jobs to their relatives or to those who can offer them something in return. Those who were most destitute in the village prior to 1967 very often have ended up with the most menial and lowest paying jobs in Israel, sometimes earning as little as I£10 per day in 1973 compared to I£30-50 for most un- skilled workers and up to I£100 for skilled workers.

In many of the villages of the Jerusalem-Ramallah region, the Israeli-employed workers' new claims to status have brought a change in the nature of village leadership. As incomes of formerly low-status groups rose, the old leaders increasingly began to deny wealth as the basis for village leadership. I. Stockman has identified the emerging leaders as those, defined by villagers, "who know more."[26] The land- owning group in these villages has asserted that those "who know more" are their sons educated abroad, unable to return and assert their rightful roles because of Israeli military occupation.

As the Mufti and his fellow landowners did on a society-wide scale during the Mandate, the village landowners have used the larger political situation as a conservative tool, making any new claims to vil- lage leadership illegitimate for the duration of the occupation. Ques- tions of power in the village are thus in abeyance until the national question is resolved—the delay, of course, is used to keep the up- wardly mobile villagers working in Israel at bay. In the meantime, the landowning group continues to dominate village affairs, acting as self-defined caretakers for their educated sons and reinforcing their

[26] I. Stockman, "Changing Social Values of the Palestinians: The New Outlook of the Arab Peasant," *New Middle East* (June, 1969), 21.

conservative position by taking advantage of the Israeli policy of dealing with the old leadership. Israeli investment policy, ironically, has
given the low-status groups in the Jerusalem-Ramallah region the resources to claim a greater role in local affairs, while, at the same time,
denying them the legitimacy and recognition they need to make those
claims yield anything more than smoldering resentment.

Hebron Region

Resentments and conflicts resulting from economic status exist in the
Hebron region as well, but play a much less prominent role in village
affairs there than do those stemming from cleavages along more
strictly generational lines. The proportion of migrants who traveled
to the West from the Hebron area is much smaller than from the
Jerusalem-Ramallah region. Hebron villagers, faced with overex-
tended land resources, were most likely to migrate to areas that were
less expensive to reach and with which they felt some cultural affinity.
Many went to the East Bank or to Kuwait during the period of Jordanian rule. One explanation for the more daring migration of villagers
from the Jerusalem-Ramallah area is their long history of migrations
to America dating back to 1876. Christians were particularly important in such migrations, and they are found in much larger proportion in the Jerusalem-Ramallah area. Another factor is the greater
need to be innovative in villages around Jerusalem and Ramallah because of the poor quality of the land relative to the Hebron or Nablus
regions.

   Some existing differences in wealth were reinforced by the eastward migration of Hebron region villagers. In large part, however,
the greater accessibility and smaller fortunes associated with migration within the Middle East resulted in income gaps and status patterns different from those associated with Baytin or Bitunia near
Ramallah. Even nonlandowners were able to finance the sending of
their sons abroad or, more often, to the East Bank, as evidenced by
the statistic mentioned above of Hebron District's high net rural migration with the East Bank from 1952-1961, −37.4 percent.

   The opening of job opportunities in Israel, then, did not radically
alter the existing pattern in the Hebron region. There continued to
be continuous movement up and down the status ladder. It has remained possible for a low-income villager with several sons working in
Israel to bridge the income gap fairly rapidly. One villager from the
Hebron region stated that the aftermath of the 1967 War did not
greatly change his village, since there had been ways of earning
money for someone without land even before.[27]

---

[27] Interview, Ummalas, Hebron, September 14, 1973.

Those with money from abroad are not necessarily the wealthiest in the village, and it is not necessarily the wealthiest who send their sons abroad. The impact of Israeli rule has been to raise the standard of living generally but not to alter radically the pattern of stratification or the basis for achieving status. Several interviewees stated that since Jordanian times wealth has depended on the number of sons one has rather than on one's previous economic situation. Most recently, it has been those who have several sons working in Israel who have been building the new houses in the villages.

Our division of the West Bank into three regions does not strictly hold for analytical purposes. Some more remote villages in the Ramallah and Bethlehem districts, such as Janiya (Ramallah District) and Khirbet E-Deir (Bethlehem District), more closely resemble villages in the Hebron region, in their attenuated status cleavage, than they do villages such as Baytin. The social structures of these communities have also been more fluid. For example, in Janiya, an out-of-the-way village without an all-weather road, the previous social structure was not nearly as stratified as in the more cosmopolitan villages in the Jerusalem-Ramallah region. Very few families had the connections, resources, or initiative to send their sons to the West. Consequently, the closing of the income gap has happened much faster, and some landowners, including the two mukhtars, have quickly found themselves among the poorer groups of the village.

The rapidity of change in Janiya resembles the Hebron pattern. It is similar, for example, to the situation reported by a teacher in the village of Ummalas (Hebron District). He said, probably with some exaggeration, "Previously those who had land were the rich, and those without were poor. Now the situation is reversed."[28] In Khirbet E-Deir, a community of former Bedouins, none of the sons has migrated to the West, and there, too, the village is not highly stratified. One landowner in Khirbet E-Deir complained of the deterioration in his position since 1967.[29] Whereas previously he had one of the nicer homes in the village, he now cannot afford the chairs and radios bought by those working in Israel. "They have become better than we," he stated.

Although there has been some resentment in such villages on the part of those whose position has slipped in recent years, such resentment based on status gaps and changes has not been nearly as overt as in the villages with landowners' sons in the West. In El-Wassifiya (Bethlehem District), for example, work in Israel has merely served to extend patterns begun during Jordanian rule and has created few

[28] Interview, Ummalas, Hebron, September 18, 1973.
[29] Interview, Khirbet E-Deir, Bethlehem, September 20, 1973.

new conflicts. The new houses in the village have been built by men who went to Kuwait starting in 1955 and, more recently, by those working in Israel. The trips to Kuwait were financed by those willing to abandon the nomadic life and sell their flocks of sheep for the capital to finance the move. Those who could not or would not gain prosperity through long-term migration have succeeded in staying in step through daily commuting to Israel.

Much more salient than the status cleavage in the villages of the Hebron region has been the generational cleavage. In an area noted for its religiosity and conservatism, the introduction of Hebron region's young workers to Israel's highly technological, secular society has been unsettling to village life. It is important to note the youth of the workers. For the occupied territories as a whole, the laborers who work in Israel are younger, on the average, than those who work in the territories. In 1977, for 55 percent of those working in Israel, their job was their first employment opportunity.[30] As young West Bankers have become more educated and have been exposed to the technological and social phenomena in Israel, they have begun to view the old generation as an obstacle to modernity.

Interviews in the Hebron region, unlike those anywhere else in the West Bank, were marked by hostility and clashes between the generations. In the village of Ummalas, for example, one discussion was punctuated by the following exchange:

Old man: "Everybody must depend on God."
Young man: "Do you think if you stay at home and not work,
                   God will give you what you need?"[31]

Another young man showed open derision as the mukhtar and several elders sat in a circle listening. "The old people," he said, gesturing at the elders, "don't believe that people actually walked on the moon or that there is such a thing as skylab. They say it is against God." An older man then responded that such events signify the end of the world. The young man went on to say that the older generation is old-fashioned, and the old people don't know anything. Some can be convinced, he stated, but many have very antiquated ideas they hold on to.

In these villages, there is no large group of young people being educated abroad. The percentage of villagers who have gone beyond secondary school is much smaller than in the Jerusalem-Ramallah or Nablus regions. Those who have been educated frequently live in the village. The older generation does not pretend to be a caretaker lead-

---

[30] *Jerusalem Post*, May 1, 1978, p. 13.
[31] Interview, Ummalas, Hebron, September 14, 1973.

ership but claims to be the only legitimate village leadership. But because their roles are sanctioned by the Israelis, the elders experience additional derision from the young because of their "obedience" to the occupiers. In the village of Khirbet Carma, for example, a young man interrupted the mukhtar and derided him for his continuing deferential behavior to the Israeli authorities.[32] "The Israelis never send good replies to our applications," he said. "They give the mukhtar a cup of coffee and that's all."

In another interview in Khirbet Carma, a young man asserted that the mukhtar is the formal leader of the village, but he is only a figurehead.[33] The younger, more educated men have taken an active role in village affairs. He stated that in Dura, a neighboring village, the mukhtar has blocked villagers from applying for an all-weather road by refusing to pass on their request to Israeli authorities. In Khirbet Carma, the young have worked to overcome the older generation's resistance to running water and electricity. Additional conflicts have arisen, however, over such issues as birth control, marriage age, polygamy, and freedom to choose one's own bride.

Once again, as in the villages of the Jerusalem-Ramallah region, overt challenges to leadership are constrained by Israeli preference for dealing with the old leadership. But the young in a number of villages in the Hebron region have nevertheless not shunned confrontation and conflict with the older leaders. As in Khirbet Carma, those with more than secondary school education have appropriated informal leadership roles. Where there have been new institutions established since 1967, such as the regional council to which Ummalas sends representatives, these institutions are often dominated by the young. (The regional council consists of three mukhtars plus six additional representatives—all youths. It is these six who are the most vocal members of the council.)

Nablus Region

Since the 1950s, Nablus has been reemerging as a cultural and political focus for Palestinians throughout the West Bank and possibly even beyond the West Bank. Since the 1967 War, the villages in this region have not been as wracked by intense conflicts, resentments, and divisions as the other regions have been. Many Nablus villages have been free of the deep status cleavage caused by sending sons to the West. The substantial out-migration of Nablus area villagers during the period of Jordanian rule was to the Middle East, in a pattern similar to that in the Hebron region. The statistics cited above indicate the

[32] Interview, Khirbet Carma, Hebron, September 30, 1973.
[33] Interview, Khirbet Carma, Hebron, October 1, 1973.

much greater net rural out-migration from these areas than from the Jerusalem-Ramallah region. Rural migrants to Western Europe or the Americas were simply not sufficient in number to create or reinforce a strong basis of cleavage in Nablus region villages. Consequently, employment elsewhere in the Middle East was almost as readily obtained by sons of nonlandowners and even sons of refugees as by sons of landowners. The money sent back to the villages created a more fluid and less stratified social structure for many communities around the cities of Nablus, Jenin, and Tulkarm than for their counterparts around Jerusalem-Ramallah.

Also, the Nablus villages, for the most part, were free of the intense generational cleavages found in the Hebron area. The youth in the Nablus region villages in many cases did not view the old generation as an obstacle to achieving modernity. By the same token, the older generation was often both more open to technological change and more willing to accept new types of political organization than was the more conservative older generation in the villages around Hebron.

The absence of intense, new conflicts and resentments in the Nablus region does not mean that there were no substantial changes in the village caused by the opening of employment in Israel. As in the other regions, particularly Hebron, employment in Israel undermined the already weakened power of landowners. Moreover, the rapid shifts in status after 1967 created a certain degree of questioning and bewilderment about old standards and modes of behavior. One landowner and village merchant, for example, stated that previously his position in the village had made it unnecessary for him ever to do any physical labor, and now he felt it was still inappropriate for him to work in Israel.[34] At the same time, however, he complained that "those who go to work in Israel are now rich and before they were poor." Previously, they were his workers and dependent upon him, and now "they have televisions and I do not."

Rather than confrontation with the upwardly mobile or the young, the pattern has been for the landowning leadership in numerous villages in the Nablus region to adopt a policy of accommodation and co-optation. Serious efforts have been made at accommodating new demands for recognition on the part of the former low-status people who now work in Israel. The mukhtar of Kafr Zibad, for example, reports that two out of the seven members of the village's electricity cooperative are workers in Israel.[35] "We are now trying to encourage them to be part of village life," he says.

Nevertheless, notes of strain and condescension do filter through. The mukhtar is bitter that two-thirds of his large 150-acre holding are

[34] Interview, Kafr Zibad, Tulkarm, September 24, 1973.
[35] Interview, Kafr Zibad, Tulkarm, September 25, 1973.

now uncultivated because he cannot compete with prevailing Israeli wages. Also, the village had experienced a building boom after 1955, with new house construction led by the village landowners and merchants and followed by others receiving money from Kuwait. After 1967, the mukhtar, a strong personality and powerful leader, declared a ban on building houses as a sign of protest against Israeli rule. The result is that those low-status people in the village whose first access to new wealth was through Israeli employment and whose income since 1967 has risen most rapidly have remained with clearly inferior housing.

Another potentially problematical group in village life in the Nablus region consists of the young, educated men, mostly sons of landowners. The villages here are unlike villages in the Jerusalem-Ramallah region where the most educated have been trained in the West and large numbers continue to send money from abroad. In the villages around Jenin, Tulkarm, and Nablus, a sizable proportion of the educated youth has been trained in Middle Eastern universities and is now living in the village. These villages are also unlike those in Hebron because of the higher proportion of young men with more than secondary education.

Many of the educated people are teachers and lawyers who initially went on strike in the summer following the 1967 War. They and other young educated men shunned work in Israel or jobs under the military government in the West Bank. As low-status families vastly increased their incomes with several members drawing wages in Israel, the more educated felt their status in the villages threatened. Even after the strike ended and West Bank civil servants were drawing double salaries (from the Israelis and the Jordanians), they were still earning less than most people working in Israel. These tensions were felt throughout the West Bank but were particularly intense in the Nablus region because of the higher proportion of educated men there.

For some, the pressure to maintain their status and the lure of higher salaries induced them finally to take employment in Israel; for a whole middle-level stratum of village life, the self-imposed barriers against work in Israel crumbled between 1968 and 1973. In one way, the willingness of people in the middle stratum to perform tasks associated with lower-status groups (physical labor in Israel) in order to maintain their status helped to break down old status barriers in the village all the more.

Other educated young men have withstood the prospect of a higher income to remain in civil service or other jobs on the West Bank. A teacher in Kafr Zibad, 36 years old with twenty years of education, earned I£780 per month in 1973, the equivalent of the income of the unskilled working in Israel. In Jordanian times, he had been one of the few villagers with a car. Now, despite his relative decline in income, he states that he feels it his duty as an Arab not to work in Israel—even if he were to starve.[36] He voices resentment, however, that the educated, the people's natural leaders, are humbled by receiving such small recompense compared to the workers who travel daily to Israel.

Some village leaders in the Nablus region have coped with the problem of the resentment generated by the relative decrease in wealth of these educated young men by responding to their claims on leadership roles. The older leaders have not relinquished their sources of power and influence in the village, but they have, in many cases, given both formal and informal positions of leadership to the young. The teacher in Kafr Zibad, for example, has been appointed (through the insistence of the mukhtar) as secretary of the electricity cooperative, and the cooperative's accountant is also a university graduate.

The presence of the educated younger generation in the villages of the region—as opposed to its absence in many Jerusalem-Ramallah region villages—makes its claims on leadership, as those "who know more," quite compelling. As one educated young man in Tulkarm District stated, the solution in the villages of that area has been for "young and old to go together." In 1973, however, the situation generally remained that the young served at the behest of the entrenched, older village leadership.

Conclusion

New conditions after the 1967 War brought an end to the either-or choice that had confronted many Palestinian villagers, particularly the poorest, during the period of Jordanian rule: either accept the straitjacket of the low technology, mostly agricultural economy, or resort to relatively long-term migration from Palestine. At the micro-level, Israeli investment policies gave poorer, low-status families in villages the opportunity to close the income and status gaps quickly. The effects of employment in Israel on village social structure have varied from place to place, but three distinct patterns can be discerned. These patterns are based on two variables, the previous social structure and the village leadership's openness to technological and social changes.

In the first pattern, the village was already highly stratified, and old cleavages were reinforced by sending sons to the West; many of the educated sons continue to reside in the West; and leaders have been

[36] Interview, Kafr Zibad, Tulkarm, October 2, 1973.

open to certain kinds of technological and social change. This pattern was found most often in villages of the Jerusalem-Ramallah area. Here, the upward mobility of those working in Israel has led to overt mutual resentment by formerly high- and low-status groups. Leaders in these villages have chosen *deferral* and *caretaking* as their means of dealing with new claimants to recognition and leadership.

In the second pattern, the village was not highly stratified and had displayed some prior fluidity of social structure; the number of educated young men either in the village or abroad was limited; and leaders have been relatively closed to change. This pattern characterized many Hebron region villages. Here, clashes and conflict have been based more on generational differences than on former differences in status. Village leaders have often chosen *confrontation* as their means of dealing with new claimants to leadership.

Finally, in the third pattern, the village was not highly stratified and had displayed some prior fluidity of social structure; a substantial number of educated young men resided in the village itself; and leaders have been open to certain kinds of technological and social change. Such conditions were frequently found in many Nablus region villages. Here, homogenization of social structure has been most rapid, and conflicts based on status and generational cleavages have stayed at much lower intensity. In such villages, older leaders have frequently chosen *accommodation* and *co-optation* as their means of dealing with new claimants to recognition and leadership.

Conclusion

The Content of Change

In a world that has increasingly valued "political centralization" and "national integration," Palestinian society has remained diffuse and fragmented. "The Palestinian Arabs, especially villagers and small-town dwellers," write Dodd and Barakat, "are person-oriented, and community-oriented, and family-oriented. Outside these spheres, they feel lost." They add, "As a result, in time of disaster, there is no other decisionmaking group except the family."[1]

Much of the diffuseness and fragmentation has stemmed directly from dispersal and statelessness since 1948, but these characteristics were already evident during the struggle for independence and against partition during the Mandate. A strong, centralized, and integrated society, based on high social cohesion, is not the only possible result of the process of change in an industrial world. Changes that have been induced in non-Western societies by the spread of capitalism from the West have taken a number of distinct routes. Those routes are very much determined by the interaction of the pressures generated by capitalism with the specific policies adopted by the state, and with the structure of the society at the onset of the penetration of the new forces. (Palestine was an agricultural, predominantly Muslim society, with local power exercised by urban notables and rural shaykhs.)

By the end of the eighteenth century, capitalism had already begun to affect the lives of the fellahin. New demands and pressures were exerted upon them by shaykhs who had connections with French merchants. Suddenly, the fellahin were growing crops, such as cotton, that were to be shipped to distant Europe rather than to be consumed in the village itself. By the latter half of the nineteenth century, the spread of the worldwide market economy was leading to changes in where peasants lived, what they produced, whom they paid deference to, what their tenurial rights were, and how their surplus was extracted.

Many of the new pressures and demands made themselves felt

[1] Peter Dodd and Halim Barakat, *River without Bridges*, monograph series no. 10 (Beirut: The Institute for Palestine Studies, 1968), pp. 33 and 51.

through changes in regime policies. The Ottomans, searching for ways to get more surplus to the center, adopted new allies at the local level, subdued the shaykhs and Bedouin, changed land registration procedures, sought taxes in cash, provided new banking services, and more. There were new constraints on people's behavior as well as new opportunities. How those constraints and opportunities worked themselves out in Palestinian society depended partly on who was in an advantageous position and who was not, that is, the content of change was determined partly by the existing social structure.

In brief, Book I has traced certain developments in Palestinian society from the time of the broad penetration of capitalism into the Middle East in the latter half of the last century to the present. The aim has been to understand those changes that lead to political centralization and national integration through increased social cohesion, on the one hand, or to political diffusion and social fragmentation, on the other. I have argued that we can best understand the specific content of the process of change in Palestine by classifying regime policies into three categories. Through these categories, we can better comprehend the impact of forces as diverse as Zionism and the end of the musha'a land tenure system on Palestinian society and politics.

Regime Policies and Social Cohesion / Fragmentation

The Palestinians present an outstanding opportunity to study the effects of regime policies on a comparative basis, since there were four different regimes in Palestine in half a century. Political alliance policies are the first category of regime policies affecting possible movement toward a more centralized and integrated society. We can hypothesize that when the regime opts for alliances with a fairly homogeneous, unified group possessing resources critical to the survival of large segments of the society, then some necessary (but not nearly sufficient) conditions for the emergence of a comprehensive pattern of stratification have been met. This was true of the Ottoman and British alliances with the urban, landowning notables from the middle of the nineteenth century until the late 1930s (and revived shortly after World War II).

A related hypothesis involves the case where the regime is bent on a policy of alliances with leaders who have little social power beyond a narrowly circumscribed, local base. In such cases, structural impediments act against the emergence of a unified class leadership and of a comprehensive pattern of stratification. This type of policy was adopted by the Ottoman Empire prior to the mid-nineteenth century and by the Jordanians and Israelis after 1948.

Investment policy, the second category of regime policies affecting the ability of the indigenous society to achieve a coherent pattern of stratification, is often intertwined in complex ways with alliance policy. Where investment policy is directed towards the growth of an indigenous infrastructure absorbing the society's laborers, and where that policy is directed at fostering at the top of that infrastructure those with whom the regime has forged political alliances, then we can expect movement towards a coherent pattern of stratification. In the late nineteenth century, Ottoman investment policy was geared towards advancing their chosen allies, the urban notables, by placing at their disposal huge tracts of land in what was an almost totally agricultural society.

Investment policies, however, can also act counter to the policy of political alliances. Where investment policy encourages the development of an infrastructure that promotes new elites other than the regime allies, and promotes growth and movements of population that feed people into that new competing infrastructure, we can expect fragmentation at the elite level (horizontal fragmentation).

Also, where investment policy leads to the introduction of more highly developed (often foreign) infrastructures, we can hypothesize the result will be fragmentation marked by an inability of elites—*any* indigenous elites—to control the resources crucial to the survival of large segments of nonelites (vertical fragmentation). With vertical fragmentation, elites are rarely able to gain widespread compliance in the society on a sustained basis. British investment policy caused modified forms of both horizontal and vertical fragmentation among Palestinians. The British created the conditions for the development of a new Arab coastal infrastructure, but simultaneously kept that infrastructure's role subsidiary to British and Zionist institutions. Both the Jordanians and Israelis devised investment policies that insured continued vertical fragmentation.

Security policy is the final category we examined that affected social cohesion / fragmentation. Like investment policy, security policy can either reinforce or counteract the regime's political alliance policy. Increased physical and social security, after a period of insecurity, leads to both great increases in the size of the population and to much greater mobility for the population. These changes put tremendous stresses on old institutions and patterns (e.g., land-man ratios and local patron-client ties). Where those elites which are creating new institutions to cope with problems arising from population growth and movement are the same elites with which the regime is allied, then we can expect growing social cohesion. In cases where the new institutions are controlled by counter-elites or exogenous forces, then we can expect horizontal or vertical fragmentation respectively.

In Palestine, physical and social security for most of the population have been increasing in an almost linear fashion (with certain definite backslides) since the mid-nineteenth century. As long as land remained the key resource, the landowning notables were able to use population changes to solidify their position and foster social cohesion. Once alternative economic means were open, population movements aided a Palestinian counter-elite, but, more importantly, they aided the British and the economic and political elites of the East Bank, Israel, and Kuwait.

In addition to its importance as a cause of population changes, security policy is also used as a deterrent by regimes to reinforce their political alliance policy. Both Jordan and Israel, as we have seen, used harsh security measures to prevent the development of new elite configurations.

Finally, where regimes provide a secure environment for innovative social or economic behavior, free from retribution by the regime or the existing social elite, it is possible for new cohesive elite groups to emerge. Only in the 1940s did Palestinians enjoy conditions that encouraged the complex process of combining new social behavior and new social ties to create a new cohesive elite group. (The effects of the three categories of regime policies on social cohesion / fragmentation among the Palestinians are summarized in Table 8.)

Change and Continuity at the Micro-Level

Regime policies do not always work in concert. Israeli aims after 1967 were to maintain Palestinian social fragmentation and to preserve existing patterns of stratification in the West Bank. Despite these goals and the effects of alliance and security policies and also of some investment policies, there has been considerable change in stratification patterns at the micro-level of village society. Many of these changes have come from other Israeli investment policies (specifically related to employment) and have weakened the position of precisely those individuals and groups that the Israelis have, in other ways, sought to promote.

Two major cleavages have intensified as a result of the new opportunities for social mobility created by Israeli employment policy. The first split is based on income and status, and the second is a generational cleavage. Where each type of division has appeared and the degree to which it has caused significant tensions over questions of social and political leadership have depended on the village's social structure in 1967 and the openness of its leadership to innovation.

The interviews that uncovered these micro-level changes took place in 1973. Since the October 1973 War, dramatic changes have occurred in the political environment within which West Bank Palestin-

Table 8

Effects of Regime Policies on Palestinian Social Cohesion / Fragmentation

Type of Policy		Ottoman early 19th century	Ottoman late 19th century	British	Jordanian	Israeli
Alliance		fragmentation (local - shaykhs)	cohesion (central - notables)	cohesion (central - notables)	fragmentation (local - municipal & village)	fragmentation (local - municipal & village)
Investment		fragmentation (inward - oriented)	cohesion (Arab notables)	horizontal fragmentation (new Arab counter-elite); vertical fragmentation (competition of British & Zionists)	vertical fragmentation (preference to East Bank)	vertical fragmentation (infrastructure in Israel)
Security	*Societal Level* — internal mobility	NO	YES	YES	YES	YES
	population growth	NO	YES	YES	NO	NO (later, slightly)
	out-migration	YES	NO	NO	YES (about 2.6% yearly)	YES (high in 1967-1968 & then about 1% yearly 1969-1973)
	Elite Level	fragmentation (prevention of central leadership)	cohesion (undermining shaykhs & security for notables)	horizontal fragmentation (security for counter-elite)	vertical fragmentation (prevention of central leadership)	vertical fragmentation (prevention of central leadership)

ians exist. Even among the least educated people in the most remote villages, there is considerable sensitivity and sophistication concerning such events as the interim agreements between Israel and Syria and Egypt, the Lebanese civil war, Sadat's visit to Jerusalem, the Israeli-Egyptian peace treaty, and various other diplomatic maneuverings among Middle Eastern states and the superpowers. In the West Bank itself, the aftermath of the war and the diplomatic successes of the Palestine Liberation Organization prior to the Lebanese civil war brought heightened political awareness and activity, especially noticeable as riots and demonstrations wracked West Bank towns after 1975.

Despite the rapidly changing political situation, there has been a degree of consistency in the West Bank socioeconomic environment. West Bank Palestinians have continued to find their stratification patterns profoundly affected by their ties to Israel. Israel's economy worsened significantly after 1973—especially in relation to the unprecedented boom years from 1967 to 1973, when there was a tremendous demand for labor. Deterioration of economic conditions, however, did not greatly change the structure of Israel's economic ties to the West Bank. In 1973, the West Bank had a work force of 127,700 people, 99 percent of whom were employed.[2] Of this work force, 38,600 were employed in Israel. The 1976 statistics do not portray a very different situation. In that year the work force was about 131,000, with 98.8 percent employed, 37,500 in Israel. The consistency of these figures is all the more surprising given the widely held view prior to 1973 that any slow-down in the Israeli economy would result first in mass unemployment of West Bank (and Israeli) Arabs, reminiscent of the situation in the early 1950s.[3]

The economic environment back to which villagers bring their wages also remains much the same. Transfer payments from abroad, for example, have remained a fairly constant proportion of total GNP. Agriculture has boomed to a degree with increased capital expenditures, but not enough to overcome the vagaries of changing yearly rainfalls or to lure back a sizable proportion of landless villagers to work in the villages.

[2] These statistics and the ones following are taken from Israel, Central Bureau of Statistics, *Administered Territories Statistics Quarterly*, 6 (1976).

[3] For example, Van Arkadie has written, "Because the expansion of Palestinian employment in the Israeli economy took place during an upswing in the Israeli economy, the question arises whether there is likely to be cyclical change as that economy moves into recession. With heavy concentration in the construction industry and the more manual occupations, and with no organizational basis for bargaining, laborers from the territories would seem to be highly vulnerable, their unemployment levels probably magnifying Israeli economic fluctuations." Brian Van Arkadie, *Benefits and Burdens* (New York: Carnegie Endowment for International Peace, 1977), p. 63.

What did come into question after 1973 was the real and perceived
prosperity that had existed before the war. GNP for the West Bank
still continued to rise in 1974—a whopping 27 percent according to
the Bank of Israel—but, by 1975, it dropped 6 percent. In 1976, it
rose, once again, by more than 12 percent, but that part of the product coming from employment in Israel declined 7 percent (the overall
rise could be attributed, in large part, to an especially good yield of
olives). The unsettling effects of inflation, which had already been one
of the biggest sources of complaint before the war, were all the more
intensive after it. From 1968 to 1976, prices rose by an unprecedented factor of five.

Nevertheless, some of the signs of the new prosperous life, which
were so evident in the villages before 1973, have continued to exist to
some extent even in the years after the war. The gross product of the
building sector, for example, continued to soar (up by 35 percent in
1974 and 19 percent in 1975), especially in the area of construction of
private homes. Also, there was no resumption of mass out-migration
similar to that during the Jordanian period, despite the vast increase
in the wealth of the oil states after 1973. In fact, in 1975 there seemed
to be a small net in-migration to the territories under Israeli military
rule.

The Individual: Caught between Micro- and Macro-Change

Individual Palestinians in the West Bank have been faced since 1967
with difficult choices. Each must steer a careful course of action based
on values related to individual and familial status and mobility as well
as on values concerned with larger national questions—and all the
choices must be made within the constraints of Israeli military rule.
For the various groups in the village, Israeli rule has had different
kinds of impact on status and mobility.

Israeli economic policies, particularly the opening of job opportunities in Israel, have tended to benefit the formerly low-status, less educated village men (97 percent of the workers from the occupied territories are men). Larger landowners in the villages, on the other
hand, have found themselves either in the throes of downward mobility or, at the very least, in situations in which their relatively high local
status has been threatened. Others who have been adversely affected
by Israeli economic policies are the educated men of the villages. With
their slowly changing civil servants' salaries, they, along with those on
fixed incomes, have been particularly hard hit by the spiraling prices
generated by Israel's high-employment, high-inflation fiscal policy.

On the level of larger national goals, Israeli occupation is universally decried among residents of the West Bank. Also, from the point

of view of Israeli policymakers, it is ironic that military rule may well have exacerbated the strains in Palestinian-Jordanian ties as well as accelerated the widespread adoption of a Palestinian self-identity in place of other political or religious identities. In the interviews, each respondent was asked to choose the most important to him of five possible self-identities: Arab, Jordanian, a member of his village, Muslim, and Palestinian. Perhaps the most interesting pattern in the responses was the near-total rejection of the Jordanian self-identity among the villagers. Failure to adopt the Jordanian identity had been documented even prior to 1967,[4] but what was striking three years after the events of black September was the vehement insistence that the Jordanian option not be included on the list of possible identities.[5]

From our small sample, no one selected the Jordanian identity, only one chose the narrow village identity, and only four indicated the broad Arab identity. The remainder of those who answered were fairly evenly divided between the Palestinian (19) and Muslim (17) identities. Surprisingly, people over 40 years of age were even more likely to select the Palestinian designation (60 percent) than those under 40 (47 percent). In the Jerusalem-Ramallah region, the older "caretaking" landowners tended to choose the Palestinian designation more often than the young men working in Israel, whereas in Hebron the older generation was more likely than the younger to choose the Muslim identity.

Several times in the course of the interviews (see Appendix), the interactions among the villagers that the questions stimulated were more interesting than the formal responses. In two separate interviews with landowners in Baytin (Ramallah District), young women in the families were present throughout the interviews (all the young men of the families were abroad). In both cases, the young women sat silently through the long interview until the last question, the one concerning self-identity. And, in both cases, the young women cut off

[4] Abdulla M. Lutfiyya, *Baytin, A Jordanian Village* (London: Mouton, 1966), p. 87; and Daniel Lerner, *The Passing of Traditional Society* (New York: The Free Press, 1958), p. 304.

[5] Another observer also found deepened animosity to the Jordanian regime after its ineffectual defense of the West Bank in 1967. He wrote, "We know that the inhabitants of the West Bank hadn't particularly loved King Hussein's regime and this was often reflected in mass protest demonstrations. These talks, however, brought out the differences much more vividly." Amnon Kapeliuk, "Talking on the West Bank," *New Outlook*, 10 (July-August, 1967), 39. A survey taken shortly after the 1967 War also indicated ambivalence and confusion concerning the Palestinian links to Jordan. In that survey, 72 percent thought the West Bank *would* be returned to Jordan, and 58 percent indicated that it *should* be returned to Jordan. Y. Peres, "Attitudes and Values in the West Bank," unpublished research report presented to the Committee for the Affairs of the Occupied Territories, pp. 14-15 (Hebrew).

the older men before they could respond and answered for them, "Palestinian." In each case, the older man agreed, and one added, "Yes, we cannot deny what we are."[6]

For some in the villages, the two sets of values—of individual mobility and status and of national status—have not conflicted with one another. Israeli rule for many mukhtars, for example, has meant enduring personal *and* national humiliation. In their view, the shame they have had to endure in their official dealings with the authorities is representative of the national shame of the Palestinian people being ruled by the Israelis.

Much the same kind of self-perceived correspondence between individual and national values has been observed in those whose status has fallen as a result of village workers' traveling to Israel. This group includes many village landowners and educated young men. The two major problems that were mentioned time and again, the Israeli refusal to allow mass reentry of villagers abroad and the unsettling effects of inflation, have been viewed by these groups as problems indistinguishable on the personal and national levels. The split families and economic and social uncertainties these people have faced have been viewed in many cases as central national problems coming from a lack of self-determination. It was these problems that were far more often raised in the context of the national questions than such issues as repatriation of the refugees.

For others in the villages, particularly those who have gained handsomely in status and income during Israeli rule, the two levels of values exist in a much less comfortable relationship. The course they have to steer in attempting to maximize personal status while working towards the achievement of national goals is a much more difficult one. Open borders and a modicum of economic integration with Israel have afforded them access to resources that are largely inaccessible to the higher status groups in the village. For many villagers working in Israel, national humiliation has corresponded with unprecedented personal social mobility upward. They have had to face implicit and explicit taunts and threats. They have heard that their behavior is near-traitorous or have met the condescending attitude that they are too uneducated to understand how detrimental their actions are to the Palestinian national cause.

Their own responses indicated how aware they are of the clash of values. Much as their fathers and grandfathers confronted the dilemma during the Arab Revolt in 1936-1939, they have had to face the excruciating choices between individual and national ends. In the interviews, many were assertive in stating that the viability of a Pales-

---

[6] Interviews in Baytin, Ramallah, August 27, 1973.

tinian national entity in the future would depend on the open borders and economic integration that have been forged during Israeli rule. Others indicated that those who are too powerless to affect the political situation can only take advantage of the situation as it exists while hoping for political changes—even if they will mean economic hardship.

The years since 1967 have seen a continuation of some of the major social patterns established under the rule of the British and the Jordanians. Dispersal, fragmentation, and high social mobilization continue to characterize the Palestinians. There have also been changes. The struggle against the Israelis, for example, has intensified and included broader elements of the population, especially youths. Growing solidarity has been evident. Still, the factionalism and difficulties in achieving unified political leadership that William B. Quandt documents remain.[7] They are not based merely on immediate contingencies but are rooted in the history of the interaction of three forces: Palestinian society, Palestinian leadership, and the regimes ruling the Palestinians over the last century and more.

Even after more than a decade of Israeli rule and all the changes it has brought to this society already in flux, there remains a certain constancy and stability to Palestinian village life. The average size of villages, something over 800 people, has been the same for more than thirty years.[8] Household size, on the average, has hovered around five persons since the early decades of the century.[9] Family ties have remained very strong as the backbone of the society. In the face of overwhelming political, social, and economic uncertainties, West Bank Palestinians have held on all the more tightly to the security and stability of their local, kinship ties.

[7] William B. Quandt, Fuad Jabber, and Ann Mosley Lesch, *The Politics of Palestinian Nationalism* (Berkeley: University of California, 1973), pp. 79-80.

[8] A major change did take place between 1931 and 1945, the average village population rising by more than one-third during that period.

[9] In the 1967 census, village household size varied from 4.6 for Ramallah District to almost 5 for Hebron District. In 1931, it varied from 4.2 for Ramallah District to 5.7 for Bethlehem District. Also, see A. Granott, *The Land System in Palestine* (London: Eyre and Spottiswoode, 1952), pp. 164-65; and Government of Palestine, Department of Statistics, *Survey of Social and Economic Conditions in Arab Villages*, 1944, Special Bulletin, No. 21.

Field Research in an Occupied Territory

When, in 1972, I had finished the lion's share of the work on my first book, *Peasants, Politics, and Revolution*, I was still left with countless nagging questions about the processes of change in peasant villages in the Third World.[1] The opportunity to work in Israel's Tel-Aviv University and its supportive atmosphere led me to begin shaping a research project focusing upon change among Palestinian fellahin in the West Bank. Conditions there, I felt, would enable me to test some of the hypotheses I had developed in the peasants book. Research would also afford me an opportunity to specify and better understand some of the notions about social and political change that had remained vague and abstract to me.

I had written that the inducements for villages to move from an inward orientation to an outward orientation are family economic crises resulting from changing external forces. I summarized these outside forces as "imperialism"; others called them "capitalism." Whatever the catchword used, it connotes numerous processes and factors that remain hazy and undefined. Much more serious thought and careful analysis would have to sort out the variables making up "imperialism" or "capitalism" and the interaction among these variables. In too many recent studies, the effects of external forces on social and political life have been handled all too glibly.[2]

The Palestinians had experienced rapid changes in outside forces— four different external regimes, with varying economic and social policies, in the course of fifty years. There was a need to order the Palestinians' modern history into a comparative study that would look at different, specific applications of external forces and their effects on Palestinian society. I thus devised a dual research strategy. The first part involved historical sociology, synthesizing existing written sources to gain a comparative view of the processes of change since

---

[1] Joel S. Migdal, *Peasants, Politics, and Revolution* (Princeton, N.J.: Princeton University Press, 1974).

[2] For an interesting criticism of the reductionism in explaining politics and political change as functions of market situations, see Theda Skocpol, "Wallerstein's World Capitalist System: A Theoretical and Historical Critique," *American Journal of Sociology*, 82 (March, 1977), 1075-90.

the mid-nineteenth century. Here, the intended focus was the effects of changing market forces, working through specific regime policies, on the distribution of power and wealth among the Palestinians. Second, I decided it was important to probe in depth into how the villagers perceived their own situation and into the tenor of village social interactions. Because major changes had been so rapid and so recent in Palestinian history, the villagers could talk about how they viewed the resulting shifts in personal status and in local and national institutions.

Selecting Respondents

In the summer and early fall of 1973 (prior to the October War), I undertook a series of interviews in the West Bank. The timing of the interviews resulted in a particular tone to the responses. That period was probably the pinnacle of West Bank economic prosperity and the nadir of the Palestinians' political hopes. Because economic and political conditions have been changing so quickly since 1967, there probably has not been an ideal time to interview, and any other timing would have been, in all likelihood, similarly unrepresentative. Nevertheless, as a supplement to the historical materials, the interviews did provide an essential and rare glimpse into the lives of nonelites—peasants and workers—living under military occupation.

It is probably true that all types of conflict are exciting subjects for research. Conflicts are also subjects in which the evidence is frequently piecemeal and fragmented, the oral and written records are purposely distorted, and the inquiries are ill-timed. There is no doubt, for example, that British statistical records in Palestine, particularly the censuses, were distorted so as to better fit British political aims (but probably not enough to make them useless as historical guides).

Of course, there is no typical West Bank peasant or worker or even West Bank village. The best that could be hoped for was the selection of respondents and research sites similar enough to most others in the district so that some generalizations of value could be made. The first criterion for village selection, then, was that its inhabitants be preponderantly Muslim, which eliminates Christians from our generalizations. Palestinian Christians have been a distinct minority (they make up about 5 percent of the West Bank population), differing from Muslims in many social and demographic characteristics. Significantly, they have been an even smaller proportion of the Palestinian rural population. Second, villages selected were in the range of average-sized villages for the West Bank as a whole, consisting of from about 500 to 2,000 inhabitants. The sample, as a result, may not represent the populations in the smaller, modal villages of 100-300 people nor the few, but influential villages of over 2,000 people.

Third, geography was a consideration in village selection. Villages chosen were spread out over the entire West Bank, representing the Jerusalem-Ramallah, Hebron, and Nablus regions. Unfortunately, because of the October War, interviewing was not completed in the Nablus region. Also, villages were divided between those on main roads, accessible to more urban centers, and those more remotely located.

Fourth, no refugee camps were selected, but refugees in villages were included among those interviewed. The camps represent a whole different pattern of social life (as Shamir's article in Book II indicates) and demand a research project with their special situation in mind. Finally, within the villages selected, those interviewed were chosen rather unsystematically. Daily movement in and out of the village and longer-term migration patterns made the selection of a stratified, random sample all but impossible. The only guidelines used, then, were to select only males over 20 years of age and to try to approach the mukhtar(s) of the village first or at least very early in the interviewing.[3] Their formal positions of leadership and their continuing (though waning) influence necessitated showing them respect and winning their approval for the project.

Interviews in a Hostile Environment

American social scientists face substantial problems in conducting research in almost any part of the Third World. Myron Glazer writes of the situation of the field researcher from the United States, "As 'strangers,' they are lightning rods, often attracting free floating suspicion and hostility."[4] In the occupied West Bank, these problems of suspicion and hostility were only compounded. Military occupation could not simply be dismissed, and anxiety and fear were very real parts of the research process.

[3] In a review of Daniel Heradstveit's *Arab and Israeli Elite Perceptions*, William R. Thompson writes, ". . . Heradstveit interviewed a 'purposive sampling' . . . which often seems to represent a euphemism for talking to whomever one can. Given the difficulties of doing field research in the Middle East, particularly on this sensitive topic, this result may be about as much as can be realistically expected." *American Political Science Review*, 71 (September, 1977), 1295.

[4] Myron Glazer, "A Note on Methodology. Field Work in a Hostile Environment: A Chapter in the Sociology of Social Research in Chile" in Frank Bonilla and Myron Glazer, *Student Politics in Chile* (New York: Basic Books, 1970), p. 313. Glazer is one of the few who has dealt with the many-sided issues raised by field research. See his *The Research Adventure* (New York: Random House, 1972).

Despite the fears and suspicions, however, establishing the groundwork for successful research was possible. Glazer writes,

> This is not to assert that, at the outset, the researcher can expect to find only difficulty and resistance. On the contrary, as a foreigner, he is also the subject of curiosity and interest and his views are usually solicited on matters concerning his country and others. In addition, he is often able to obtain the cooperation which may be withheld from his local, professional colleagues as a result of the prestige which accrues from the more developed state of the social sciences in his country.
>
> What often develops, therefore, is an attraction-repulsion relationship and the social scientist will be compelled to make several basic decisions. These include how he will present himself, how he is to react to the activities of his government and embassy, and the manner in which he will respond to the just, as well as unjust, criticisms of his country.[5]

A first order of priority was to establish a milieu in which interviewer and interviewee could meet on some common ground, could share some common purpose. Interestingly, it was the villagers who offered that purpose. When I presented myself as an American scholar seeking to learn *and write* about them, they seized upon the writing as a function that could fulfill their own needs. Their perceptions of the United States were of a country that desperately needed to hear their point of view on the Arab-Israeli conflict.

President Nixon and other political leaders, they felt, were distorting the issues in a pro-Israeli way. Even Arab governments, some asserted, were pursuing their own interests at the expense of an honest presentation of the Palestinian issue. Many villagers thus took on the role of national spokesman in the course of the interviews and saw me as their conduit to the American public—a channel that would be independent of the biased leaders and media in the United States.

My protestations that American academics, unfortunately, reach only an infinitesimally small audience were barely heard after the respondents began to view me as a writer. Although I can hope that the present book's sales prove their perceptions better than mine, I do feel that the volume as a whole, and Chapters 4 and 5 in particular, speak for both my objectivity as a social scientist and the moral contract I entered into with them. That contract committed me, I believe, to put down in writing the feelings, attitudes, and dilemmas of these West Bank villagers. Certainly, their assumption of the role of national spokesman gave a particular hue to their responses. I would ar-

---

[5] Glazer, "A Note on Methodology," p. 314.

gue, however, that respondents always assume a particular role in their interaction with interviewers. In this case, I was fortunate to see that role so explicitly assumed.

I should note here that finding common ground with respondents in a hostile atmosphere presents the researcher with sticky, ethical issues. Although I deplore lying about who one is and what his or her overall purposes are in research, the question of deception arises in sins of omission. I could have volunteered the information that I was affiliated with Tel-Aviv University or that I am a Jew. I chose not to. If asked, I was forthright about these matters. But it was my feeling— although my rather uncomfortable feeling—that I could manage to present information about myself that would allow common ground to be established while still remaining within the bounds of an honest relationship.

Several small steps were taken in a further attempt to alleviate villagers' anxieties about my role and motivations. No recording device was used. In fact, I even experimented with not taking notes during the interview itself and instead simply reconstructing the interview on paper as soon as I was outside the village. Interestingly, the respondents seemed to be much more comfortable when I did write down their answers. Seeing me take notes during the interview, I imagine, made them more certain I was recording their views accurately.

Each of the interviews was conducted by me and my associate, Nicholas Saba, in translation between Arabic and English. Although translation certainly has its drawbacks, it did help us in our effort to create a very deliberate, slow-paced, and relaxed style and mood during the interview. Many villagers were insecure about the interview process—some felt they were being "tested," as in school—and the deliberate style helped alleviate their fears of being tricked into saying something that they would feel was personally damaging.

Creating a basis for dialogue and using interview techniques that were minimally threatening were not nearly enough to ensure the success of the research because of the suspicions and tensions among the villagers themselves. I am not speaking here of the local divisions and sensibilities to which every researcher must be particularly sensitive, but of the problems of a people living under military occupation—under a self-defined enemy. Stories, rumors, and charges abounded among the villagers of unjustified arrests and of the large numbers of Israeli agents within the villages. It was crucial to create a milieu in which neither we nor those seen talking to us would be thought of as Israeli agents.

Early in the research, two separate incidents underscored the fears respondents could have about us and about their fellow villagers. In one village, we interviewed the owner of a coffee-house, as we sat and

sipped coffee with him. The atmosphere was relaxed and congenial as
he spoke of village cleavages, his personal life, and the effects of Israeli rule. Near the end of the interview, however, he bolted from his
chair and begged us not to report to the authorities all that he had
said. Although, in fact, he had told us little that was potentially in-
criminating, his fears were very real. He felt that he had let down his
guard at a time when he thought many people on the West Bank were
being arrested on the slightest evidence of subversive activity. The
boundary lines separating subversive from legitimate behavior were
far from clear to him. Our assurances and promises of his anonymity
calmed him only partially.

The second incident grew out of a ride that we gave to a villager in
Bitunia (near Ramallah). After we had reached his destination in the
village, I presented myself as an American academic and asked if he
would be willing to be interviewed. As others, he seemed pleased, at
first, at having been chosen. As we sat in the car and talked, however,
he began to look anxiously around him. After only a few biographical
questions, he seemed to be gripped totally by fear and suddenly
opened the door and ran from the car. Clearly, his actions were a result of his imagining what others would think seeing him talking alone
to a non-Arab. He simply had no way of refuting any accusations that
might be raised against him.

It became necessary to find some way of conducting the interviews
so that the respondents would not be seen alone with us and so that
others could be certain of what was really occurring. Fortunately, the
outstanding hospitality we were offered, coupled with the friendliness
and curiosity we aroused, presented a ready-made solution—a solution that presented some pitfalls but also some extremely important
benefits. Interviewees almost always invited us into their courtyards
and homes where family members and neighbors would gather to sip
mint tea or coffee and listen to the interview. Invariably, comments
were interjected, and discussions within the small circle of people
were generated by both the questions and the answers of the main respondent. By having an "audience," the respondent could be certain
that the nature of his interaction with us could not be misconstrued by
fellow villagers.

The interview itself was semistructured, with both open- and
close-ended questions. Respondents' responses often gave rise to
numerous unscheduled questions, as we pursued their thoughts. As a
result, the interviews lasted anywhere from 45 minutes to several
hours. The major difficulty with the format, of course, was that because of the group interaction the interview answers were not totally
independent responses. Moreover, the respondent's self-image as national spokesman frequently took on an added dimension because he

was "performing," not only for me, but also for his relatives and neighbors.

Nevertheless, the group setting offered insights and dimensions that would have been closed to me had I undertaken a more traditional type of interview.[6] The interviews took on different styles and patterns of interactions in different parts of the West Bank, *even though the formal responses to questions were often very similar*. Differing types of interaction among those present in the group setting were particularly revealing about patterns of deference and conflict among the villagers.[7]

Most immediately striking were the contrasting styles of interaction between the generations in the different areas. Almost everywhere, young men *and* some young women displayed a greater confidence about their ability to deal with me and my questions, as well as a greater sense of efficacy in dealing with their complex environment, than did those in the over-40 age category. In Hebron, the younger men's sense of power in dealing with their immediate and larger environments was manifest in their disrespectful actions towards the older generation. Younger men frequently interrupted, argued with, and corrected the village elders. The group setting proved to be an outstanding vehicle for getting a quick reading of the strong intergenerational tensions.

In the Jerusalem-Ramallah region, generational interaction was quite different. There, young adults listened in respectful silence as the elders answered. When the young people felt a "wrong" answer had been given, their interjections followed, but they were low-keyed and respectful. Several times the older person was saved the embarrassment of a "wrong" answer by the younger person's interjection before an answer was given. Invariably, the older person agreed with the interjected answer.

[6] The group setting provided data that, strictly speaking, are outside the framework of the interview. "We are excluding . . . behavioral observation from consideration as interviews. . . . For example, observations of the verbal behavior of small groups holding discussions, or observations of a parent answering the questions of a child, are not considered interviews within the limits of our definition. In the interview, the verbal expressions of the respondent must be directed toward the interviewer, in response to the interviewer's questions or comments." Eleanor E. Maccoby and Nathan Maccoby, "The Interview: A Tool of Social Science" in *Handbook of Social Psychology*, Vol. 1, ed. by Gardner Lindzey (Reading, Mass.: Addison-Wesley, 1954), p. 449.

[7] In the foreword to A. R. Luria's book on cognitive development, Michael Cole writes, ". . . the inclusion of several people whose arguments among themselves become his data, [has] no parallel in the psychological investigations of our century." A. R. Luria, *Cognitive Development* (Cambridge, Mass.: Harvard University Press, 1976), p. xvi (also, see p. 16). The group interview approach among peasants has also been used in Bolivia. See Dwight B. Heath, Charles J. Erasmus, and Hans C. Buechler, *Land Reform and Social Revolution in Bolivia* (New York: Frederick A. Praeger, 1969), pp. 84-85.

The kind of personal respect and deference found between the generations in the Jerusalem-Ramallah region was in sharp contrast to patterns among its various status groups. Group settings in this region, significantly, usually did not cut across status lines, as they did in the Hebron and Nablus regions. Neighbors and relatives who gathered to listen were a rather homogeneous group. But in cases where status lines were crossed, divisions and conflicts were not hidden.

In short, I am suggesting that the interview process in social science may be used for more than soliciting attitudes, values, and opinions. Self-selection and dynamics in a group setting may expose important elements about patterns of deference and cleavage. They may also reveal in tone and style aspects of the interviewee's self-image, his image of others, and others' image of him that could not come through in isolated, independent interviews.

Such dynamics and revelations thrust the interviewer into the midst of these conflicts and cleavages. As hostilities are unmasked, different people use the "third party," the interviewer, as a source of authority or an audience for their abuse of others. In such instances, I always found myself extremely uncomfortable and walking a fine line, careful not to offend anyone or to be used as a tool against anyone.

A group-setting interview in India, which I conducted for a different research project, illustrates some of what such an interview exposes as well as the awkward position in which it can place the interviewer. After interviewing a number of high-caste villagers, who told me of the declining importance of status distinctions based on caste, I interviewed a member of the lowly washerman caste. As others from higher castes gathered around, the washerman himself assumed the role of buffoon, poking fun and directing insults at himself, while the others laughed and added to the atmosphere with their own comments making fun of him. He clearly was denigrating himself—and, probably more importantly, the perceived importance of his answers to me—in front of those whom he saw as more powerful than himself. The others were willing to "entertain" me by accepting the role the washerman assumed. I was in the difficult situation of trying to observe this interaction while still conveying to the respondent that I respected him.

In conclusion, research in an occupied territory was at once exhilarating and frightening. The drain on my emotions was enormous. But given all the difficulties in undertaking social science research, the setting proved to be as much a boon as an impediment. With flexibility and innovation, seemingly adverse conditions for research can be overcome and even used to advantage. In fact, if there is a lesson to be learned, I would say it is not to *over*estimate the difficulties. My own overestimation of the barriers demonstrates this point. At the start of my research, I began a long correspondence with Israeli military authorities as I sought to get permission to do research in the occupied West Bank. After months of letters back and forth, I finally received a definitive reply from the West Bank's military command spokeswoman: As the signs on every road into the West Bank make clear, anyone may travel and talk with people there during the day. Researchers are no exceptions. Please be careful!

Studies in Continuity and Change under Four Regimes

Introduction

Palestine has been in the grip of turbulent changes ever since the middle of the nineteenth century. These changes have come partly from the catastrophic wars that have plagued the country in the twentieth century, much as in the past. These recent wars, however, have taken place in the context of other powerful forces—the spread of capitalism from Western Europe, the clash of two nationalist movements, and the rule of four different regimes (five, counting Egypt's rule of the Gaza Strip) in this century alone.

The new forces of change have affected every aspect of Palestinian Arab life, but little has appeared about them in social science literature. There is a need for some intellectual ordering to help understand how these changes relate to one another. The essays in Book II begin to sort out the transformations that have occurred, as well as those aspects of Palestinian society that have endured. The eight articles were written independently of each other and of Book I and thus the interpretations and conclusions differ from each other and also, at times, from those in Book I.

Nevertheless, there is an important aim in bringing these essays together in this volume. That aim is twofold: to begin the important analysis of changes in Arab social life and how they have affected Palestinian politics; and the opposite, to analyze how changes in the Palestinians' politics have affected aspects of their social life. The articles point to the importance of powerful outside forces in both social life and politics.

Book II is organized into three parts. Each part views from a different vantage point the historical interaction of Palestinian society and politics. These three points are (1) the Palestinian village, which has included the large majority of the people; (2) the Palestinian urban elites; and (3) the nodes of interaction between the two—between these elites and the remainder of the largely rural population.

Although towns and cities played a role in pre-twentieth-century Arab life far more central than that of towns and cities in preindustrial Europe, the villages were (and, in many ways, continue to be) the numerous centers of Palestinian life. Two articles, by Gabriel Baer and Ylana N. Miller, focus on the changing features of village life. A third article, by Shimon Shamir, also focuses on nonelites but, in this case, on people who cannot return to their home villages, the refu-

© 1979 by Princeton University Press, *Palestinian Society and Politics*
0-691-07615-4/79/0099-02$00.50/1 (cloth)
0-691-02193-7/79/0099-02$00.50/1 (paperback)
For copying information, see copyright page

gees. These articles show the Palestinian rural population and institutions to have been changing significantly since the early nineteenth century. As regime policies and social life changed, Baer finds, powerful *shaykhs* gave way to less powerful village chiefs, *mukhtars*, and these, in turn, have in recent decades found their positions greatly undermined. Miller and Shamir show how changes outside cause the small community to be redefined. Miller's essay covers the mandatory period, while Shamir's is a snapshot of life in a refugee camp as seen by an Israeli historian at an important moment in Palestinian history, right after the 1967 War.

Different political, social, and religious elite groups have had varying ideas of how the society should be structured and how it should be led. To establish their leadership, elites have had to take account of changes at the base of society creating new resources, opportunities, and constraints, and have also had to face formidable barriers created by outside forces. They have attempted to take advantage of local-level changes in order to exercise leadership or to stop others from doing so. At the same time, however, they have come under close watch by the ruling regimes. As a result, the elites have had to be primarily reactive to changes in society.

This inability to shape the course of social change has led to several prominent elite characteristics, analyzed in Part Two. As Mark Heller shows in his essay, Palestinian elites have been highly adaptive in the face of the changing social and political environment. Old elite cleavages dating back to the nineteenth century and before, as Donna Robinson Divine indicates, have been surprisingly enduring. And elites have been highly dependent on resources and roles allocated by the ruling regime, as Shaul Mishal demonstrates in his essay on the Jordanian period.

The nodes of interaction between the elites and the rest of the population, as seen in Part Three, have altered in character several times during the last century and a half. As regimes and regime policies changed, so did the capabilities of Palestinian elites to exercise significant social control vary. The essays by Kenneth W. Stein and Rachelle Taqqu focus on nodes of interaction that were in the process of changing character under the impact of a specific environmental stimulus. In Stein's case, the stimulus was the land hunger of the Zionists; in Taqqu's case, it was the rapid economic expansion of the 1940s brought on by Britain's heavy wartime expenditures in Palestine.

Together the essays begin to etch a new picture of Palestinian society and politics. Leadership patterns become comprehensible by relating them to the society itself. And both leadership and society are seen as changing patterns that have resulted, in great part, from external forces.

PART ONE

The Palestinian Village

CHAPTER 1

The Office and Functions of the
Village Mukhtar*

by Gabriel Baer

The Legal Basis of the Office of Mukhtar

The office of *mukhtar* was first established by the Ottoman Law of
Vilayets of 1864.[1] According to this law, every group of people (*sinif*)
in a village was to elect two mukhtars, but a group of less than twenty
houses was entitled to elect only one. The term sinif does not specify
the character of these groups, which means that the Ottoman legis-
lator intended the existing traditional groups to be represented by the
holders of the new office. These were the *hamulas* (clans) and religious
communities. Though this was contrary to the territorial character of
the Law of Vilayets, the Ottoman government apparently was compelled, at that stage of the reforms, to base the administration partly
on traditional units, as it did in the towns with respect to the guilds. In
any case, the principle that mukhtars represent groups within the village continues to hold until today, though from time to time a tendency emerges to appoint only one mukhtar for the whole village as a
territorial unit. Thus, as early a law as the Law of Vilayet Administra-

*This paper is part of a longer study called *The Village Mukhtar in Palestine—A History
of his Position and his Functions*, published in Hebrew by the Harry S. Truman Research
Institute of the Hebrew University of Jerusalem. Permission to publish part of the work
in English in this volume is acknowledged with thanks. The study of the mukhtar, as
well as a series of other studies, resulted from a comprehensive research project on the
West Bank under Jordanian rule carried out by the Institute of Asian and African
Studies at the Hebrew University during the years 1967-1971. The material on the
mukhtars from the files of the Jordanian administration, now kept in the Israel State
Archives, was classified and arranged by Miss Rachel Simon, without whose assiduous
and conscientious work the study could not have been written. I am also grateful to Dr.
P. Alsberg, Director of Israel State Archives, and to his staff for their help.
    [1] *Düstur*, Vol. I (Istanbul, 1289), pp. 618-20; G. Young, *Corps de droit Ottoman*, Vol. I
(Oxford, 1905), pp. 42-44 (hereafter: Law of Vilayets).

tion of 1871 provided for the possibility that a village may have only one mukhtar if this was sufficient for its administration.[2]

The appointment of mukhtars made slow progress during the last third of the nineteenth century. By the beginning of the twentieth century the process had been completed in theory, but not in practice. The temporary law of general vilayet administration published by the Young Turks in 1913, as well as its amendment of 1914, repeated the stipulation that every village should have a mukhtar, and if there were different groups in the village each was entitled to a mukhtar of its own.[3] These laws were in force when Palestine was occupied by the British army and the British Mandate was imposed. In 1934, however, the Mandatory Municipal Corporations Ordinance repealed the Ottoman laws of local administration and left village administration without a legal basis. Though mukhtars continued to be appointed as if the Law of Vilayets were still in force, the enactment of a new law became necessary.

In 1940, the High Commissioner appointed a committee, which presented a detailed and extremely illuminating report in 1941.[4] Among other recommendations, the committee reiterated the suggestion to confine the number of mukhtars, if possible, to one for every village. According to data presented to the committee, villages of less than 1,000 inhabitants had in fact, as a rule, only one mukhtar, but villages between 1,000 and 5,000 had more than two, and villages with more than 5,000 inhabitants had from four to eleven mukhtars. A great number of mukhtars in one village, rather than satisfying rival claims, may result in keeping alive the flame of party rivalry, the committee asserted. Only in very large villages, or in places with different religious communities, did the committee consider the appointment of assistants to mukhtars justified, but nowhere of more than one major mukhtar.[5] A new mandatory ordinance to regulate village administration was finally issued in 1944, but it left things more or less as they were before: every village would have one or more mukhtars and assistant mukhtars, as required by the size of the village or other conditions.[6]

After the termination of the Mandate, the West Bank was annexed

[2] *Düstur*, p. 638, art. 59; Young, *Corps de droit Ottoman*, p. 59 (herafter: Law of Vilayet Administration).

[3] Palestine Royal Commission, *Memoranda Prepared by the Government of Palestine* (London, 1937), pp. 80-81 (hereafter: *Memoranda*).

[4] Palestine. *Report of the Committee on Village Administration and Responsibility* (Jerusalem: Government Printing Press, n.d. [1941]) (hereafter: *Report on Village Administration*).

[5] Ibid., pp. 17, 43.

[6] Art. 36 (1) of Village Administration Ordinance No. 23 of 1944, Supplement No. 1 to *The Palestine Gazette*, No. 1352 of 17th August, 1944 (hereafter: 1944 ordinance).

by the Hashemite Kingdom of Jordan, which replaced the 1944 ordinance by a new practically identical law of 1954. According to this law, too, the number of mukhtars in each village was flexible,[7] but the office of assistant mukhtars was no longer provided for. Instead, so-called "village committees" or "makhtara committees" were established to assist the mukhtar in the performance of his functions. Candidates for membership of these committees were to be named by the mukhtar and confirmed or rejected by the governor of the province (*mutasarrif al-liwa*), who also was to determine the number of the members of the committee (generally two to three). Whenever the government was reluctant to appoint additional mukhtars, the establishment of such a committee was recommended instead. It was a device to grant representation to various components of the village population without creating a top-heavy administration. The number of such committees in the West Bank, prior to 1967, amounted to more than thirty.[8] The tendency to organize village administration on a territorial base was, however, scarcely successful. In practically all villages that include more than one important hamula, each such hamula is represented by a mukhtar of its own.[9]

The Selection Process

A major innovation of the Law of Vilayets was the introduction of formal election of the mukhtar. According to that law the mukhtars were to be elected for one year (with the right to unlimited reelection) by males of their group over 18 years who paid more than 50 piastres as direct taxes. The authorities had only to confirm the election.[10] In fact, the mukhtar was rarely elected in this democratic fashion. True, evidence from the Jerusalem Sancak shows that late in the nineteenth and early in the twentieth centuries, elections for the office of mukhtar took place. But very few men participated in these elections, probably only the chiefs of the main families in the village.[11] Appar-

[7] Art. 22 (1a) of Law No. 5 of 1954 (hereafter: Law of 1954).

[8] See, for instance, governor of Hebron, February 1 and 6, 1962, Israel State Archives (hereafter: I.S.A.) 1160/4/1; director of police, Hebron, July 23, 1966, I.S.A. 826/12/8/11/33; governor of Hebron, November 12, 1958, I.S.A. 826/8/4/33, and April 10, 1954, I.S.A. 1318/27/8/33; letter of qa'imaqam Tulkarm, March 4, 1962, I.S.A. 1502/9; correspondence between governor of Nablus and the mudir of Salfit, September 1955, I.S.A. 771/23.

[9] See also R. Antoun, *Arab Village* (Bloomington: Indiana University Press, 1972), pp. 89, 91-92.

[10] Law of Vilayets (1864), arts. 54-55, 62-66.

[11] For a description of these elections, based on the minutes of the *Maclis-i Idare* of Jerusalem in the Israel State Archives, see Haim Gerber, "Ottoman Administration in the Sancak of Jerusalem, 1890-1908" in *Hamizrah Hehadash* (The New East), 24 (1974), 12-13 (Hebrew).

ently reality was less formal and nearer the following description given by the Committee on Village Administration: "In practice, however, election in the ordinary sense did not take place. They were in fact the nominees of the local administration, which, although account was taken of the wishes of the people when appointments were made, put the interests of the Government first, following the principle of direct control."[12]

As we have seen, the Law of Vilayets was in force up to 1934, and only in 1942 did the High Commissioner issue an order providing for the appointment of the mukhtar and his dismissal by the governor of the province, no mention being made of further elections. Few elections to the post of mukhtar seem to have been held in mandatory Palestine even prior to the new order. Usually the mukhtars were appointed and dismissed by the district officers, and if the latter took into account the view of the village notables, they did not do so in any formal way.[13] This situation was finally legalized in the 1944 ordinance, which did not provide for elections at all.[14]

Election of the mukhtar by male villagers over 18 years was reintroduced by Jordan. Regulations for such elections were to be issued by the governor, who also retained the right to dismiss a mukhtar if he had good reason to do so.[15] Such regulations were issued for both Nablus and Hebron provinces in 1955. They differed in one major provision: the governor of Nablus allowed village notables of this province to agree—according to a clearly defined procedure—on one candidate for the post of mukhtar and thus to make the election superfluous. In such a case, only the objection of more than a quarter of the adult male villagers would ensure the holding of elections.[16] In addition to this system of election by agreement, many mukhtars continued to be appointed by governors without election, as in mandatory times; but even in these cases the governors probably took into account the trends of village opinion.[17] This system seems to have been the prevalent one during Jordanian rule of the West Bank. A breakdown of election and appointment of new mukhtars in the files of the Jordanian administration of the West Bank shows the following distribution.

---

[12] *Report on Village Administration*, p. 7.   [13] Ibid., pp. 43-44.

[14] Arts. 36-39 of the 1944 ordinance.

[15] Law of 1954, arts. 22 (1b); 25 (1).

[16] See circular of governor of Nablus, n.d. [1955], I.S.A. 1160/9/1/.

[17] It is difficult to imagine how mukhtars functioned if indeed they were often "appointed by the *qā'immaqām* without any regard for the wishes of the *hamula*," as claimed by Lutfiyya with regard to Baytin, a village in the West Bank, under Jordanian rule. His statement that "the popular vote has not been officially accepted as the way in which such matters are to be decided" is also inexact. See A. M. Lutfiyya, *Baytin, a Jordanian Village* (London: Mouton, 1966), p. 79.

Table 9
Election and Appointment of Mukhtars in the West Bank, 1949-1967

Province	Total new mukhtars		Appointment w/o elections		Agreement w/o elections		Elections by majority	
	number	percent	number	percent	number	percent	number	percent
Nablus	49	100.0	25	51.0	17	34.7	7	14.3
Hebron	120	100.0	73	60.9	30	25.0	17	14.1
Total	169	100.0	98	58.0	47	27.8	24	14.2

It is remarkable that the percentage of mukhtars elected in Nablus and Hebron is practically identical. Thus it would seem that the option opened by the governor of Nablus—nomination through agreement by notables—substituted direct appointment by the authorities for elections by majority.

Village opinion was of course not the only consideration of governors who appointed or dismissed mukhtars. But among the reasons given for the dismissal of mukhtars in the West Bank between 1949 and 1967 the most frequent was disagreement between the mukhtar and his hamula (or most of its members) or deterioration of relations among the villagers.[18] Village opinion, then, had an important influence on the deliberations of the government in this matter. In many villages, however, the office of mukhtar was customarily inherited within a certain family.[19] In a memorandum submitted by the Bani 'Awda hamula from Tamun village in June 1955 to the prime minister of Jordan and many other addressees, they claimed that the backwardness of the village was due to the fact that the makhtara was inherited within one family who, in the view of the petitioners, were not interested in the welfare of the village.[20] In Surif the office of one of the mukhtars was held by one family (brothers and sons) for decades, a fact that was advanced as a strong argument by the nephew of a dismissed mukhtar who aspired after the office himself.[21] Often the son of a mukhtar officiated as acting mukhtar when his father became old or sick and was then appointed to the office when the father died.[22]

[18] See, for instance, for Surif in 1953 I.S.A. 1160/9/1 and 1318/18/1/16/10/1; for Tamun in 1955 I.S.A. 675/18; for Tamun in 1965 I.S.A. 4/1 and 3362/3; for Jab'a in 1958 I.S.A. 1318/27/8/33; for Samu' in 1962 and Idna in 1963 I.S.A. 1160/4/1.

[19] For instance, the al-Najjada family in 'Arab al-Ka'abina, I.S.A. 2865/11/19/33; the Abu Hamiyya family in al-Shuyukh, I.S.A. 2865/4/15/33; the Imtayr family in Zahiriyya, I.S.A. 2865/6; the 'Isa and Musa families in Bani Na'im, I.S.A. 2865/3/1; the 'Aql family in Sa'ir, I.S.A. 1318/2/1/13/10/1; the Darwish family in 'Asira al-Shimaliyya, I.S.A. 3362/3; etc.

[20] Bani 'Awda to prime minister and others, June 27, 1955, I.S.A. 675/18.

[21] "Ilman bi'anna al-makhtara al-shaghira mundhu al-qidam hiya li'a'ilatina. . . ." Letters to the governor of Hebron Province, May 1 and June 17, 1965, I.S.A. 2865/1.

[22] See, for instance, for Sebastiya, November 1966, I.S.A. 771/15; Qisra, May 1950 to

In addition to these considerations, the economic and social position of the mukhtar was taken into account, as well as his education.[23] Almost half of the dismissals of mukhtars in the West Bank between 1949 and 1967, however, were accounted for by administrative, political, and security reasons, such as lack of cooperation with the government, neglect of the functions of the office, danger to security, and shielding of criminals and smugglers. The best recommendation for an aspirant to the office of mukhtar was cooperation with the government, while any connection with "one of the parties" (which were all opposition parties) was explicitly given by the governor of Hebron as a good reason to reject a candidate.[24]

By and large, the stabilizing factors seem to have outweighed the motives for replacing mukhtars with others. In 89 villages of Nablus District there were, in 1957, 134 mukhtars of which only 23 (17.2 percent) were replaced by others in the course of the next eight years, while 111 (82.8 percent) remained in office. In 21 villages of Hebron Province, more than half the mukhtars retained their position from 1949 to 1960 (and almost half up to 1963), in spite of changes in the administration, innumerable complaints of mukhtars submitted to the Jordanian administration as the result of village conflicts, serious security problems, stormy political events, and natural mortality.[25]

Thus, the Palestinian mukhtar was the kind of office holder whose administrative functions were performed within a unit of traditional society, such as the hamula, the village community, or the professional guild. In order to guarantee its effective control, the government always retained the right to appoint and dismiss these functionaries.

Since it acted within a traditional framework, however, the government was compelled to consider the views of influential leaders of these units and the custom that the office of mukhtar was inheritable within specific families. The relative weight of these factors differed according to different conditions. The more remote a place was from the central government, the greater was the autonomy of traditional

November 1951, I.S.A. 785/25; Nuba, February to August 1952, I.S.A. 2865/14/21/33; Wadi Fuqin, September 1964, I.S.A. 91/5; as well as some of the instances mentioned in note 19. A field investigation by the author in the Tulkarm District conducted in April 1969 showed that this was common practice in that area.

[23] The economic and social position of the village mukhtar in Palestine has been dealt with by us in a separate paper published in Gabriel Ben-Dor (ed.), *The Palestinians and the Middle East Conflict* (Ramat Gan, Israel: Turtledove, 1978).

[24] Circular of governor of Hebron, 1955, I.S.A. 1160/9/1.

[25] Figures based on comparison of lists of mukhtars for Nablus District in 1957, I.S.A. 1502/9, with lists for June 1965, I.S.A. 771/14 and of lists of Hebron District in 1949, I.S.A. 1318/20, with similar lists for Hebron Province dated October 15, 1960 and August 7, 1963, I.S.A. 1318/3/7/1.

units and therefore the importance of social tradition and the influence of community leaders in choosing the administrative chief of the unit. In the appointment of the *umda* (village chief) in more centralized Egypt, the say of the government always was relatively more decisive than in the appointment of mukhtars in the hilly areas of the Fertile Crescent, where the hamula leaders had greater influence. Similarly, Westernization strengthened the central government: in Egypt, British occupation did away with the considerable autonomy rural notables had enjoyed in the time of Ismail, and mandatory rule in Palestine never acknowledged de facto, and after 1942 not even de jure, the principle that the mukhtar be elected by his village or hamula.[26] Finally, even where elections were held before the middle of the twentieth century, they were never formal popular democratic elections but rather informal consultations of notables with the aim of reaching agreement and electing a chief by acclamation.

Functions of the Mukhtar

Ever since the creation of the office of the mukhtar, one of his principal functions, if not *the* principal function, has been to maintain order and security in the village. The 1864 Law of Vilayets stipulated that the guardians of the villages, such as *bekci*s (field watchmen), *korucu*s (forest watchmen), and others, were subject to the orders of the mukhtar. In the Law of Vilayet Administration of 1871, the functions of the mukhtars were enumerated in detail. They were obliged to inform the Ottoman official in charge of a group of villages of any violent conflicts or murders in their villages and to assist in delivering the culprits into the hands of the government. In addition, they were to supervise the activities of the field and forest watchmen as well as other village guards appointed by the council of elders.[27]

As we have seen, these regulations remained in force until 1934 in theory, and in fact until they were replaced by the Village Administration Ordinance of 1944. Meantime, the security functions of the mukhtars were confirmed in several other mandatory laws, such as

[26] On the Egyptian village shaykhs and umdas see G. Baer, *Studies in the Social History of Modern Egypt* (Chicago: University of Chicago Press, 1969), pp. 30-61. On appointment and election of guild shaykhs, see G. Baer, *Egyptian Guilds in Modern Times* (Jerusalem: Israel Oriental Society, 1964), pp. 69-72, and *The Structure of Turkish Guilds and its Significance for Ottoman Social History* (Jerusalem: The Israel Academy of Sciences and Humanities Proceedings), vol. IV, no. 10, p. 17. The Iraqi Law of Village Administration of 1957 found a compromise: the government appoints the umda from among those recommended by the males of the village. See Muhammad Hilmi Murad (ed.), *Qawanin al-idara al-mahalliyya fi al-duwal al-'arabiyya* (Cairo: Arab League Publications, 1962), p. 511, article 3 of the law.
[27] Law of Vilayets, art. 57; Law of Vilayet Administration, art. 60.

the Police Ordinance, which reiterated the duty of the mukhtars, in conjunction with village notables, to appoint *ghafirs* (guards); the Ordinance of Criminal Procedure, which provided for the mukhtar to accompany police officers in the exercise of their duties in the village; or the Firearms Ordinance, which entitled the mukhtar to require the production of firearm licenses and of firearms and ammunition.[28] In this context, a passage from a report on the Palestine police force written in 1930 by H. L. Dowbiggin is of special interest. He said that "the police will . . . look to the Headman as their principal means for getting information as to what is going on in the village. . . . The inspecting officer should make a point of asking the Headman if the Police are treating them with every consideration and with the respect due to their rank. . . . The Headman, if questioned, may have some ideas as to how the patrol system might be organised to better advantage."[29]

The Village Administration Ordinance of 1944 again stressed the security functions of the mukhtar and did not leave any doubt that these were his major duties. Article 40, which deals with these duties, opens with his obligation to maintain order and security in his village; to inform the police about criminals, vagabonds, foreigners, or suspicious persons who are found there; and to relay any information about intentions to commit an offense that may come to his knowledge. It then goes on to state that it is his duty to send information as soon as possible to the nearest police station of every serious offense or accident or death due to unnatural causes occurring in the village, and also to report every case of the use of false weights or measures. The Jordanian Law of Village Administration of 1954 adopted these articles verbatim.[30] In addition, the Jordanian mukhtars were obliged, according to special legislation, to assist the attorney general.[31]

Additional responsibilities connected with security were imposed on the mukhtars of the West Bank during the period of Jordanian rule as the result of the special military situation of the kingdom. For guarding the villages, special police were appointed who were paid by the villagers.[32] But while the mukhtars were ordered to man and finance this unit, a military officer was appointed as actual com-

[28] *Report on Village Administration*, p. 50, arts. 3, 4, and 5.

[29] Ibid., p. 56.

[30] 1944 ordinance, art. 40, paras. 1, 2, 7, and art. 42; Law of 1954, art. 26, paras. 1, 2, 7, and art. 28.

[31] Law of Criminal Court No. 76 of 1951, art. 9, *Official Gazette* No. 1071 of June 16, 1951; Law of Criminal Court No. 9 of 1961, art. 9 (1), *Official Gazette* No. 1539 of March 16, 1961.

[32] See, for instance, governor of Nablus to mukhtars, February 28, 1965, and March 8, 1965, I.S.A. 771/14; also the whole file I.S.A. 1513/2.

mander of the guard, which frequently caused friction.[33] The mukhtars were also responsible for payments for arms supplied to the villages, for storing the arms, for preventing the inhabitants from going too near the border, and for fighting infiltrators, spies, and smugglers.[34] Various duties of a similar character were assigned to the mukhtars by the laws dealing with the National Guard and National Service.[35] In addition, the mukhtars were supposed to recruit villagers for public works with security implications, such as digging trenches, erecting fences, or paving roads,[36] but often the help of the police or the army was needed to put the plans into practice.[37]

All these duties were the result of external pressures, but internal security conditions occupied the attention of the mukhtars as well. Thus one of their concerns was to prevent fights between different villages. The mukhtar of Jab'a village, for instance, explained to the governor of Hebron in a memorandum dated January 21, 1957, that one of the reasons for the hostility against him that prevailed in his village was that he had taken severe measures against the time-honored custom of villagers raiding and plundering neighboring villages.[38]

It would seem, therefore, that the security concerns of the mukhtar were not only an important part of his functions, but that they increased and ramified under the different regimes. These duties confronted the mukhtar with difficult problems. Unlike the traditional village shaykh,[39] the modern mukhtar had neither the social prestige

[33] For instance: governor of Hebron Province to commander of Hebron Area, October 27, 1953, I.S.A. 1160/9/1; mukhtar of Jab'a to commander of Surif guard, August 15, 1953, I.S.A. 1318/27/8/33.

[34] See, for instance, commander of Tulkarm Area, August 5, 1956, I.S.A. 1426/1; Villagers of Jab'a, July 2, 1953, I.S.A. 1318/27/8/33; commander of Hebron District, September 2, 1962, and January 18, 1964, I.S.A. 1160/4/1; minutes of meeting of mukhtars on August 29, 1963, ibid.

[35] National Guard Law No. 7 of 1950, arts. 9 and 16, *Official Gazette* No. 1010 of February 9, 1950; Law of Compulsory National Service No. 102 of 1966, arts. 8 and 14, *Official Gazette* No. 1966, November 27, 1966; Temporary Law of Compulsory National Service No. 18 of 1967, arts. 45, 46, and 48, *Official Gazette* No. 1988 of March 1, 1967.

[36] Mukhtar of Kafr Sur to the qa'imaqam, October 7, 1955, and reply dated October 12, 1955, I.S.A. 1624/12; I.S.A. File 1566/19 dealing with the paving of the 'Azun-Kafr Tilth road in 1951-1952; I.S.A. File 1426/5 on paving the Dayr al-Ghusun-'At il-Baqa al-Sharqiyya road in the years 1950-1965; qa'imaqam of Tulkarm to mukhtars of 'Alar and Sayda, July 7, 1956, I.S.A. 1421/5; etc.

[37] Qa'imaqam of Tulkarm to police of the area, February 25, 1962, I.S.A. 1426/6; mukhtar of Shuwayka village to commander of Tulkarm Area, August 7, 1951, I.S.A. 1426/5.

[38] I.S.A. 1318/27/8/33.

[39] On the differences and relations between the mukhtar and the traditional village shaykh in Palestine, see my paper on the economic and social position of the mukhtar in Ben-Dor (ed.), *The Palestinians and the Middle East Conflict*.

and authority nor the armed retainers to enable him to maintain
order and to punish criminals. Since mandatory times, the complaint
has been voiced that numerous duties and functions are imposed on
the mukhtar, but that, in fact, he has no executive authority over the
village population.[40]

Apparently the 1944 and 1954 laws attempted to overcome this dis-
advantage by conferring on the mukhtar the authority of a police
officer, but it is extremely doubtful whether this measure achieved its
aim. The weakness and helplessness of the mukhtar in implementing
his authority has been described very well in Richard Antoun's study
of the Jordanian village Kufr al-Ma.[41] Antoun says that if members of
the clan refuse to pay their dues, the mukhtar is powerless to force
them to comply. Moreover, for social reasons, he is extremely reluctant to use the governmental authority vested in him against recalcitrant clansmen or even against other villagers. By virtue of his office,
he can call on the support of such government officials as subdistrict
officer or police chief, but he seldom does so. Antoun reports that in
the twelve-month period in which he stayed in the village (November
1959-November 1960), the mukhtar of Bani Yasin requested the intervention of government authority only twice; and in one case, when
the mounted police arrived, he apologized and told them that the dispute had been settled amicably by the villagers themselves. Similarly,
in the above-mentioned memorandum dated January 1957, the
mukhtar of Jab'a frankly admitted that he had concealed and hushed
up a murder case "in order not to arouse fraternal strife."[42] The
mukhtar fears both alienation of his hamula and any violation of the
prevalent conception that it is the village that is the proper framework
of social control, mediation, and punishment, rather than government administration, courts, and police.

Such attitudes, and sometimes perhaps also avarice and greed, gave
rise to frequent complaints that the mukhtars did not discharge their
security and police duties properly. In the files of the Jordanian administration of the West Bank, one can find many petitions accusing
mukhtars of having received hush money to disregard thefts, of having shielded relatives who had committed offenses, of having hidden
fugitive criminals, of having concealed murder cases, of having freed
persons who had been rightfully arrested, and the like.[43] Frequently,

[40] *Report on Village Administration*, p. 16.
[41] Antoun, *Arab Village*, pp. 92-93.   [42] See note 38 above.
[43] See, e.g., correspondence concerning the mukhtar of Qisra dating from the end of
1942 and the beginning of 1943, I.S.A. 786/14; Muhammad 'Abd al-Razzaq Musallam,
November 21, 1951, I.S.A. 1318/18/1/16/10/1; Sadiq Muhammad Ahmad Najib, December 19, 1961, I.S.A. 3369/24; commander of Hebron Area concerning mukhtar of
Halhul, August 29, 1963, I.S.A. 1160/9/1.

mukhtars were reported to have tried to delete names from the lists of military conscripts.[44] In all these respects, there was a remarkable similarity between the Palestinian mukhtar and the Egyptian umda.[45]

Nevertheless, concern for village security remained the main responsibility of the Palestinian mukhtar, as it did of the umda in Egypt. This function of the umda was later abolished in villages where police stations were established. In less centralized Palestine, that development has not yet taken place, but mukhtars have begun to voice demands that police stations be located in their villages.[46] This may be the first sign that in Palestine too, sooner or later, the office of mukhtar may disappear.

Though providing for security was the principal function of the mukhtar, it certainly was not the only one. When the office of mukhtar was created in the nineteenth century, the Ottoman administration intended it to fulfill an important purpose in its system of taxation. Prior to the era of reform, taxes were collected by the traditional village shaykhs who served as *multazims* (tax-farmers) or sub-multazims.[47] In replacing the village shaykh by the mukhtar as tax collector the administration intended to put an end to the practice of tax-farming, which was legally abolished in 1839 and again in 1856.[48] Indeed, in the 1864 Law of Vilayets, the mukhtar was explicitly made the agent of the government for the purpose of collecting taxes in the village, while the Council of Elders was to supervise the distribution of the tax burden among the villagers; and the 1871 Law of Vilayet Administration reiterated the duty of the mukhtars to collect taxes in accordance with the decision of the Council of Elders and government instructions.[49]

These laws alone, however, were not enough to bring about the desired changes in practice. Tax-farming persisted as the prevalent system of tax collection until World War I,[50] and the mukhtars generally did not collect the taxes.[51] It should be noted, though, that in the early

[44] Commander of Hebron Area, January 5, 1953, I.S.A. 1318/18/1/16/10/1; governor of Hebron Province, March 29, 1954, I.S.A. 1318/29/8/33; commander of Regiment 333, September 8, 1962, and commander of Hebron Area, September 17, 1962, I.S.A. 2865/3/1.

[45] Baer, *Studies in the Social History of Modern Egypt*, p. 46 and note 88.

[46] Mukhtars and notables of Mukhayyam 'Askar al-Jadid, August 19, 1965, I.S.A. 771/14.

[47] See Ihsan al-Nimr, *Tarikh Jabal Nablus wa'l-Balqa'*, Vol. II (Nablus, 1961), pp. 184-86, 233; Amnon Cohen, *Palestine in the 18th Century* (Jerusalem: Magnes Press, 1973), pp. 8, 50, 83, 123, etc.; Miriam Hoexter, "The Role of Qays and Yaman Factions in Local Political Divisions," *Asian and African Studies*, 9 (1973), 252-53.

[48] Baer, *Studies in the Social History of Modern Egypt*, p. 65.

[49] Law of Vilayets, arts. 56 and 59; Law of Vilayet Administration, arts. 60 and 108.

[50] Baer, *Studies in the Social History of Modern Egypt*, pp. 65-66.

[51] Gerber, "Ottoman Administration," p. 13.

years of the twentieth century, Ottoman administration in the Sancak
of Jerusalem made an attempt to do away with this system by encouraging the mukhtars to compete with the multazims at the auc-
tions of tax-farming and to farm the taxes themselves in the name of
their villagers. They were urged to distribute the tax burden among
the villagers, after which they or the villagers would sign a contract
stating the amount of taxes to be paid. These then would be collected
by the official in charge of the subdistrict.[52] According to another description, it was not the mukhtars but the village notables or the
Council of Elders who distributed the tax burden among the villagers,[53] as laid down in the Law of Vilayets. The laws of vilayet administration published by the Young Turks in 1913 and 1914 confirmed that this was the duty of the Council of Elders.[54] But whoever
distributed the tax burden, the Ottoman government in Palestine did
not succeed, before World War I, in abolishing tax-farming by substituting the mukhtars for the multazims.

The British occupation of Palestine did not do away immediately
with the collective responsibility of the village for the payment of
taxes. For some years to come, the mukhtars and the village elders
used to sign an obligation of the village as a whole and afterwards distribute the burden among its inhabitants. Only in 1922 was the collective tax liability of the village abolished, and taxes were levied from
then onwards on each peasant individually. The mukhtars became
the representatives of the regional tax authorities and collected the
taxes from the peasants according to individual assessments.[55] (A
similar change had taken place in Egypt seventy years earlier, in Said's
days, when new duties of the umda in the sphere of taxation replaced
the old function of distributing the tax burden.[56]) Thus, the mukhtar
was required (together with the village elders) to nominate candidates
for membership in the committee for tithe assessment and to inform
the government when the crops had been gathered and were ready
for assessment. He was also made responsible, together with the village elders, for the crops stored in the barn or the threshing-floor,
and if the committee for the assessment of the taxes did not act within
a time limit fixed by law, the mukhtar and the village elders were entitled to perform the assessment themselves.[57]

In addition, the mukhtars were required, according to laws promulgated in the 1920s and 1930s, to assist the government tax collectors

[52] Ibid., p. 31.
[53] C. T. Wilson, *Peasant Life in the Holy Land* (London, 1906), pp. 80-81.
[54] *Memoranda*, p. 83, arts. 16 and 27.
[55] A. Granovsky, *Das Steuerwesen in Palästina* (Jerusalem, 1933), p. 155.
[56] See Baer, *Studies in the Social History of Modern Egypt*, pp. 40-41, 45.
[57] Granovsky, *Das Steuerwesen*, pp. 152-54.

in sequestrations and confiscations, to certify the ability of tax de-
faulters to pay taxes due, to keep safe goods which had been confis-
cated, to certify statements of petitioners for exemption from rural
property tax, to prepare lists for collection of animal tax, to register
flocks exempted from payment of animal tax, to help in procedures
of confiscation in connection with the animal tax, and so on.[58]

There can be no doubt that these numerous and variegated functions in the sphere of taxation conferred on the mukhtar in the 1920s
and 1930s a central position in Palestine's village economy. But British mandatory administration tended, over time, to reduce this position and these functions of the mukhtar. After the British occupation
of Egypt in the 1880s, the Egyptian umda had been deprived of the
role of assessor and collector of taxes.[59] Similarly, the mandatory ordinance of 1944 did not any longer consider these activities to be the
explicit duty of Palestinian mukhtars. Among the manifold functions
of the mukhtar enumerated in article 40 of this law, tax collection is
mentioned only indirectly in paragraph 3 as follows: ". . . to assist the
officers of Government in the execution of their duty, including the
collection of revenue." The Jordanian law of 1954 adopted this provision word for word.[60] The assistance to government officials consisted, of course, mainly of securing information and registration.
Thus the mukhtars were required, under Jordanian rule as in mandatory times, to transfer tax assessments and demands to the taxpayers,
to keep registers of taxation of buildings, and to serve as memebers of
committees conducting livestock censuses for the purpose of taxation.[61]

In fact, however, the mukhtars did much more than just assist officials of the inland revenue department. They participated as members of the committees that assessed the property and solvency of the
villagers, and thus they took part in preparing the lists of persons who
were subject to taxation.[62] In the years 1944-1951, the mukhtars of
some villages prepared lists of villagers according to the following

[58] *Report on Village Administration*, pp. 50, 52 (the laws concerning animal tax had
existed in the Ottoman period as well).

[59] Baer, *Studies in the Social History of Modern Egypt*, pp. 42, 45.

[60] 1944 ordinance, art. 40 (3); Law of 1954, art. 26 (3).

[61] Law No. 57 of 1951, art. 6, *Official Gazette* No. 1062, April 16, 1951, p. 990; *Supplement to Official Gazette*, No. 1081/1, September 25, 1951, p. 276; Law No. 30 of 1955,
arts. 9 (2) and 10 (5), *Official Gazette* No. 1226, May 16, 1951, pp. 482 and 484; Law No.
42 of 1951, arts. 5 and 9, *Official Gazette* No. 1057, March 1, 1951, pp. 799-800; Law No.
5 of 1952, arts. 5 and 9, *Official Gazette* No. 1100, February 16, 1952, pp. 80-81.

[62] Correspondence between Mudir of Tubas and governor of Nablus, 1961-1963,
I.S.A. 741/15; petition of villagers of al-Majd al-Sharqiyya to governor, April 26, 1962,
I.S.A. 826/19/2/11/33; minutes of meeting of mukhtars on September 18, 1951, I.S.A.
1624/1.

classification: persons without property, persons with property who lived in the village, and landowners without houses who did not usually live in the village but were liable to taxation.[63] After the tax was assessed, the mukhtars had many ways of influencing decisions on exemption from taxation because of crop failure, animal diseases, loss of land, emigration, or just individual hardship.[64] All these practices naturally enabled the mukhtars to influence the actual burden of taxation imposed on individual villagers. Indeed, villagers frequently voiced complaints and accusations of discrimination and favoritism against mukhtars.[65]

But mukhtars also had other means to turn their offices to their own economic, social, and political advantage. At the time of Jordanian rule, for instance, the distribution of government aid and relief was added to their regular duties. This aid was of two kinds: development subsidies for afforestation, amelioration of land, and the like; and relief for refugees, poor people, and inhabitants of border villages. To judge by complaints found in the files of the Jordanian administration, it would seem that the mukhtars were able to benefit both from preparing the lists of villagers entitled to aid, and from the distribution itself. They were accused of deleting from the lists names of persons rightfully entitled to aid and adding names of their relatives or fictitious names,[66] of accepting bribes for including persons on the lists, and of preparing defective lists because of family strife.[67] Frequently, it was claimed that the money remained with the mukhtar and was not distributed at all, or that the mukhtar distributed reduced quantities of goods and food and mixed them with inferior materials.[68] Many such claims and accusations turned out to be false, but

[63] I.S.A. 1395/4 (Kafr Sur); 1395/1 (al-Nazla al-Sharqiyya); 1624/14 (Saffarin); 1566/12 (Shuwayka); 1463/12 (Khirbet Ijbara).

[64] Minutes of meeting of mukhtars, August 29, 1963, I.S.A. 1160/4/1; Mukhtar Iktaba, January 10, 1961, I.S.A. 1426/8; mukhtars of Bayt Lidd, March 17, 1951, February 23, 1952, November 23, 1952, I.S.A. 1395/8; mukhtar of Tira, October 8, 1949, I.S.A. 1395/5; Mukhtar Zibad, September 12-24, 1962, I.S.A. 1624/9; Mukhtar Fir'awn, May 20, 1962, I.S.A. 1395/12; villager of Baqa al-Sharqiyya, October 3, 1962, I.S.A. 1632/3; etc.

[65] Villagers from Iktaba, June 16, 1957, I.S.A. 1426/8; villager of Bayt Lidd, January 6, 1950, I.S.A. 1395/8; Ahmad Khalil al-Najjar, January 3, 1953, I.S.A. 1160/17/22; notables of 'Ashirat al-Sarratin in Bayt Ula, March 29, 1967, I.S.A. 826/8/4/33.

[66] Commander of Hebron District, October 24, 1963, I.S.A. 1160/4/1; notables of the Zaydat Hamula in Bani Na'im, September 1962, I.S.A. 2865/3; Muhammad Jibrin Mita, March 29, 1966, I.S.A. 2865/10; villagers of Bayt Ula, October 6, 1951, I.S.A. 826/4; Basma Abu Latif of Jab'a Village, October 6, 1951, I.S.A. 1318/27/8/33.

[67] Complaint about mukhtar of Bani Na'im, October 6, 1951, I.S.A. 1160/4/1; Muhammad 'Abd al-Razzaq Musallam of Surif, November 21, 1951, I.S.A. 1318/18/1/16/10/1; complaint about mukhtar of Jab'a, enclosed in report of commander of Hebron Area, December 15, 1956, I.S.A. 1318/27/8/33.

[68] Complaints about mukhtar of Surif, January 4, 1954, I.S.A. 1318/18/1/16/10/1;

they would not have been launched had it not been likely that the mukhtars were guilty to some extent. Opportunities to engage in such self-interested activities were one reason why villagers fiercely competed for the office of mukhtar, although the prestige attached to it had considerably declined. A similar situation seems to have existed in Turkey; it has been pointed out that the fact that the Turkish *muhtar* distributed government aid to villagers was the main reason for his high status among them and for the great demand for this office in Turkish villages.[69]

As against the mukhtar's functions in the sphere of taxation and as distributor of government aid, which entailed opportunities of making material and social profit, a large number of administrative duties was imposed on him which constituted a heavy burden with no attached advantages at all. Since the 1871 Law of Vilayet Administration, the mukhtar was supposed to transmit information from the government to the villages and vice versa. In his village, he was required to publish laws, regulations, and ordinances; to inform defendants that they must appear in court and the authorities when they would be able to appear; to inform the competent authorities of births and deaths in the village, in particular deaths of persons with heirs who were minors or absent; and so on.[70] In mandatory times, the mukhtar continued to serve as a source and a channel of information for the government on events in the village and for the village about the demands of the government. In this respect the 1944 ordinance adopted, with small changes, part of the provisions of the 1871 Law of Vilayet Administration, and the Jordanian law followed the former word for word.[71] Many Jordanian laws, especially those concerned with taxation and agriculture, mention the mukhtar as the conveyor of government instructions to the villagers. In addition, from time to time the mukhtars were supplied with official circulars containing such matters as conditions of loans to agriculturists and similar information.[72] In the past the mukhtar's position as the principal source of information in the village had considerably enhanced his prestige and social status. But the development of modern means of communication enabled a growing number of villagers to go to town and to obtain information through other sources, such as newspapers, radio, and television, and today a large proportion of villagers in Palestine are literate. The mukhtar continues, of course, to transmit

complaints about mukhtar of Jab'a, October 1956, I.S.A. 1318/27/8/33; villager of Habla, October 21, 1946, I.S.A. 1345/3.

[69] Richard B. Scott, *The Village Headman in Turkey, A Case Study* (Ankara: Institute of Public Administration for Turkey and the Middle East, 1968), p. 29, note 55.

[70] Law of Vilayet Administration, art. 60.

[71] 1944 ordinance, art. 40 (4), (6), etc.; Law of 1954, art. 26 (4), (6), etc.

[72] See, for instance, *al-Difa'* (daily), September 14, 1953.

government instructions to the villagers, but as a result of these developments, his position as a source of information has declined, and the prestige connected with this position has been severely damaged.

While the 1871 Law of Vilayet Administration required no more than periodical information about births and deaths, the mandatory government introduced the obligation of mukhtars to keep registers of births and deaths in the village.[73] The 1944 ordinance and the 1954 law did not specify the kind of registers the mukhtar was supposed to maintain, but the Personal Status Law of 1966 made it clear that the mukhtar's duty was to register births and deaths and even details about health conditions of the villagers.[74] Since it constituted a profitless burden for the mukhtars, they frequently neglected this duty. The files of the Jordanian administration include numerous memoranda requiring mukhtars to comply with instructions and accusing them of ignorance and obduracy for neglecting to do so.[75]

Other administrative burdens, too, were imposed on the mukhtar in the mandatory and Jordanian periods. The laws of 1944 and 1954 required him to do his best to guard railways, telegraph and telephone communications, roads, forests, and other government property, and to notify the government of any damage to such property. He was also required to inform the authorities about antiquities that were discovered in his village and to conserve them, as well as to maintain monuments and historical sites.[76] When the Hashemite Kingdom introduced parliamentary elections, the village mukhtars were required to participate in committees for preparing the lists of voters and to publish those lists. Similarly, they were supposed to prepare and keep lists for local elections.[77] Thus, with regard to the functions of the mukhtar, the mandatory and Jordanian periods correspond to the period of British domination in Egypt (1882-1922) in which many new duties were imposed on the umda as the result of the reorganization of the administration—including many of the same duties men-

---

[73] Cf. Public Health Ordinance of 1940, *Report on Village Administration*, p. 51, art. 10.

[74] 1944 ordinance, art. 40 (10); Law of 1954, art. 26 (10); Personal Status Law No. 32 of 1966, *Official Gazette* No. 1927, June 11, 1966, pp. 1012-15, arts. 27, 28, 34, 50, 55, 57.

[75] For instance: complaint of Tulkarm physician that mukhtars supply incorrect lists of births and deaths, May 17, 1953, I.S.A. 1581/2; qa'imaqam of Tulkarm, January 22, 1958, I.S.A. 1624/1; minister of health, June 23, 1958, I.S.A. 1502/9; commander of Nablus Province, March 8, 1961, I.S.A. 771/15.

[76] 1944 ordinance, art. 40 (8), (9); Law of 1954, art. 26 (8), (9).

[77] Temporary Electoral Law No. 24 of 1960, arts. 7, 10, 14 (c), 15 (b), *Official Gazette* No. 1494, June 11, 1960; superintendent of police, Nablus, August 16 and 22, 1966, I.S.A. 771/21; correspondence of commander of Nablus Area, mid-September 1965, I.S.A. 3362/3. Commander of Tulkarm Area giving detailed instructions on how to conduct the elections, October 25, 1965, I.S.A. 771/13.

tioned above.[78] It was felt in the latter part of this period that this burden surpassed the capabilities of the umda, and indeed, from the 1920s onward, many of these functions were transferred to the appropriate government departments.[79] This stage of development had not yet been reached in the West Bank when Jordanian rule ended in 1967.

There was, however, one administrative function from which mukhtars were able to derive considerable material and other profit, by legal means or otherwise. This was their authority to issue certificates and affidavits of various kinds. The first time this duty was mentioned was in the 1871 Law of Vilayet Administration, which entitled the mukhtar to issue affidavits for persons who had applied for transit certificates.[80] In mandatory times this authority of the mukhtar was also originally confined to the same purpose,[81] but the 1944 ordinance on village administration extended it and demanded that the mukhtar keep a seal to be affixed to all certificates and documents that required one. This provision, like most other provisions of this ordinance, was reiterated verbatim by the Jordanian law of 1954.[82]

The need to confirm certificates by affixing the mukhtar's seal and signature was indeed considerably extended in the Jordanian period, and villagers very frequently were compelled to have recourse to the mukhtar to verify their documents. For instance, without the mukhtar's signature and seal, no claim to an inheritance would be accepted by the shari'a court, since the mukhtar kept the registration of both personal status and landownership; and the final division of the estate again needed his signature.[83] The mukhtar's signature was required for marriage contracts, and for the issuing of identity cards and passports.[84] A certificate of character signed by the mukhtar was needed by villagers on innumerable occasions, such as enlistment in the army, any legal procedure, or any petition presented to the authorities.[85] Of particular importance was the requirement that the mukhtar's signature and seal be attached to documents concerning ownership of land and real estate.[86]

---

[78] Cf. Baer, *Studies in the Social History of Modern Egypt*, p. 43.

[79] Ibid., pp. 43-45, and table on p. 45.

[80] Law of Vilayet Administration, art. 60.

[81] *Report on Village Administration*, p. 52, art. 12.

[82] 1944 ordinance, art. 40 (5); Law of 1954, art. 26 (5).

[83] Qadi of Hebron, and governor of Hebron, November 28, 1961, I.S.A. 826/3 and March 8, 1965, I.S.A. 826/11.

[84] See, for instance, governor of Hebron Province to mukhtars of villages, December 11, 1964, I.S.A. 1160/4/1, etc.

[85] For a list of laws and orders including relevant provisions, as well as for many examples, see our full study.

[86] Ordinance of Land Registration No. 3 of 1952, art. 7, *Official Gazette* No. 1123, Oc-

This manifold dependence of villagers upon the good will of the mukhtar could of course be easily exploited by him for extortion and blackmail. Thus Hilma Granquist tells us in her book on 'Artas in the 1930s, that on the occasion of a procession to fetch the bride, people had to wait outside the bride's village. When asked why this happened, the bridegroom explained: "Because she [i.e., the bride] was young and the civil head of the village [the mukhtar] must give his stamp; we gave him sugar and coffee and money." In this way, explains Granquist, the mukhtar was bribed to give his permission, although the bride was only 11 years old, below the legal age to marry.[87]

In order to prevent such misuse of authority, the laws of village administration provided for legal fees to be collected by the mukhtar for confirming documents.[88] Nevertheless, villagers frequently complained that mukhtars refused to put their seals to documents for no good reason,[89] and a special circular was distributed among the mukhtars warning them not to misuse the seals.[90] But the temptation was too strong and the exertion of pressure on the villagers by the mukhtars too easy to be restrained by circulars. To cite only two instances from the Jordanian files: when the Red Cross began in 1948 to distribute relief to refugees in Taffuh, the mukhtar demanded £P1.50 (an enormous sum at that time) from every refugee to issue the certificate he needed to qualify for relief; and in 1954, the mukhtar of Tamun received 4 dinars per person from a group of people as a bribe to certify that they had not been in prison, though he knew well that the opposite was the truth.[91]

As against his manifold administrative duties, the Palestinian mukhtar lacked most of the social functions that had been performed by the traditional village shaykh and that were attached to the office of the Egyptian umda. The village shaykh in Palestine was the acknowledged arbitrator and judge of the villagers' conflicts and was entitled to fine and punish them in accordance with rural custom, called in

tober 1, 1952, p. 371; Law No. 42 of 1953, art. 8, *Official Gazette* No. 1134, February 16, 1953, p. 56. See also commander of Hebron Area, October 24, 1963, I.S.A. 1160/4/1; Hasan Mahmud Abu 'Ayyash of Bayt Umar, March 18, 1951, I.S.A. 826/3.

[87] H. Granquist, *Marriage Conditions in a Palestinian Village*, Vol. II (Helsingfors: Akademische Buchhandlung, 1935), p. 63.

[88] 1944 ordinance, art. 44; Law of 1954, art. 30; Payments to Mukhtars Ordinance No. 62 of 1964, *Official Gazette* No. 1803, November 1, 1964, p. 1565.

[89] See, for instance, Muhammad 'Awda Musa al-Hala'iqa from Shuyukh village, November 27, 1952, I.S.A. 2865/4/15/33; Muhammad Ahmad Sulayman from Taffuh, February 25, 1952, I.S.A. 826/24/6/22; letters from villagers of Salfit to governor of Nablus Province, January 22, 1955, February 11, 1955, and December 13, 1958, I.S.A. 771/23.

[90] Governor of Hebron Province to mukhtars, May 3, 1964, I.S.A. 1160/9/1.

[91] Elders of Taffuh Village, September 27, 1950, I.S.A. 826/24/6/22; mudir of Tubas, February 18, 1954, I.S.A. 675/18.

southern Palestine *Shari'at al-Khalil* (in the towns *Shari'at Muhammad* was in force).[92] Similarly, the Egyptian umda judged villagers who had committed certain offenses, fined them up to a certain limit, and arbitrated land disputes and other conflicts. His judicial functions were reduced in the 1890s after the British occupation, and abolished altogether in 1930; his role as an arbitrator of village disputes was not mentioned at all in the Umda Law of 1947. Actually he continued to perform these functions up to the middle of the twentieth century, though to a lesser extent than before. In contrast, the Palestinian mukhtar was never charged with these duties by law and did not exercise them in practice, except in limited periods and areas. Both the 1864 Law of Vilayets and the 1871 Law of Vilayet Administration considered arbitration of disputes among villagers as the province of the village elders, not the mukhtar, while trial and punishment were simply not mentioned in connection with any authority at the village level.[93] These principles persisted in later legislation concerning village administration. Thus the Young Turks' vilayet laws of 1913 and 1914 again charged the Council of Village Elders and the Nahiya council with arbitraton of disputes inside the village and between villages; mandatory legislation transferred this authority to the village councils, whose creation was planned from the early years of the Mandate; and the Jordanian law made no changes in these provisions.[94]

The reason for this difference between the authority of the Palestinian mukhtar and the Egyptian umda was their differing historical backgrounds. The office of the Egyptian umda developed from the position of the traditional shaykh, whose social functions the umda inherited together with his other duties and powers. Gradually the umda was absorbed into the modern network of administration, which attempted to introduce the principle of division between the judicial and the executive power. The office of the Palestinian mukhtar, on the other hand, was created as a counterweight to the position of the shaykh, with the aim of weakening his position or

[92] Cf. Mrs. Finn, "The Fallahheen of Palestine—Notes on their Clans, Warfare, Religion, and Law," *Palestine Exploration Fund Quarterly Statement (PEFQS)* (1897), 38-39, 44-45; Yūsuf Jirjis Qaddūra, *Tārīkh Madīnat Rāmallah* (New York, 1954), pp. 29, 40; *Report on Village Administration*, p. 6; James Finn, *Stirring Times* (London, 1878), Vol. I, pp. 216-20; P. Baldensperger, "The Immovable East," *PEFQS* (1906), 15; al-Nimr, *Tarikh Jabal Nablus*, p. 185.

[93] Law of Vilayets, art. 59; Law of Vilayet Administration, art. 107. It is interesting to note that, corresponding to these Ottoman reforms, Ismail decreed in Egypt in 1871 the establishment of special "Judicial Councils" in large villages to take over the judicial functions of the shaykhs; but apparently the implementation of this decree was rather limited. See Baer, *Studies in the Social History of Modern Egypt*, p. 41, note 66.

[94] *Memoranda*, p. 83; 1944 ordinance, part IV, arts. 31-35; Law of 1954, Part III, arts. 18-21 (art. 35 of the 1944 ordinance was deleted in the 1954 law).

evading him. From the beginning, it was part of the administrative structure of the Ottoman reform period, and therefore the mukhtar was charged with executive duties, but not with judicial powers. Traditional arbitration, which could not be abolished by decree and which had its advantages even in the new context, was left in the hands of the Council of Elders—an established institution with sufficient prestige to perform this function, as it had done, at least partly, in the past. But the traditional shaykhs were explicitly deprived of their judicial authority, including arbitration, in order to undermine the autonomy of the influential chiefs of powerful families.

In fact, it would be an exaggeration to claim that the village mukhtar in Palestine had nothing to do with arbitration among villagers. There were, of course, strong and prestigious mukhtars whom villagers asked to settle their disputes, even without legal authority to do so. However, it certainly is not coincidental that in the files of the Jordanian administration such cases appear in the southern parts of the Hebron hills only, an area with strong tribal traditions. Thus the mukhtar of Dura was appointed as arbitrator in a quarrel between two Dura villagers about a plot of land.[95] Occasionally, mukhtars were appointed arbitrators, or at least they named arbitrators, in arguments between different villages. For instance, in December 1954, the mukhtar of Halhul was appointed to arbitrate a dispute about lands between Khirbet Jala and Bayt Umar; and in January 1961, the mukhtar of Dura settled a similar dispute between Halhul and Bayt Kahil.[96] Because of the unofficial character of such activities, they are of course reflected only very sparely in the official correspondence. When the mukhtar performed arbitration, he usually did so in cooperation with other persons in the village—notables of various families, religious functionaries, and others. In the only case of arbitration in Kufr al-Ma recorded in Antoun's book in which the mukhtar played any role, he did so together with the *imam* (religious functionary) and one of the hamula elders.[97]

Another function of mukhtars in Palestine, as in Egypt, was that of extending hospitality to foreigners passing through the village and especially to government officials. This duty was not established by law either. It resulted from a tradition born at a time when the village shaykh was the richest and most influential person in the village, controlling the *madafa*, the place where strangers were accommodated. The Egyptian umda inherited this function from the village shaykh and was responsible for offering hospitality to all strangers who hap-

[95] Governor of Hebron Province to mukhtar of Dura, April 16, 1963, I.S.A. 2871/22.

[96] Instructions of governor of Hebron Province, December 30, 1954 and January 23, 1962, I.S.A. 2871/1/13.

[97] Antoun, *Arab Village*, pp. 66-68.

pened to come to the village, until in the later period his material position deteriorated to such an extent that he could no longer perform this duty properly.[98] The Palestinian mukhtar was supposed to entertain, in particular, government officials (usually not overnight) and was helped in performing this duty by the members of his hamula.[99]

Conclusion

One of the principal changes in the position of the mukhtar brought about by the British Mandate stemmed from the abolition of the collective responsibility of the village for paying the taxes, thus depriving the mukhtar of the job of distributing the tax burden among the inhabitants of the village. In addition, the administration was gradually organized according to modern principles, and thus the collection of taxes, formerly the function of the village shaykh and the mukhtar, became the duty of officials specially appointed for this purpose. On the other hand, the mukhtar was charged, during the Mandate, with a large number of duties that constituted a heavy burden without conferring on him effective executive authority and without rendering any equivalent personal or material profit.

Generally speaking, growing efficiency in government administration over the course of two hundred years left the mukhtar with fewer opportunities to turn the office to his personal profit. Some of his new duties, however, reinforced his position and enabled him to derive advantage for himself. Among these were the preparation of lists of villagers' property and the distribution of government aid. In particular, the increasing ties of the villagers with the outside world and with the authorities increased their need for all kinds of documents and verifications of their identity, their personal status, their integrity, their property, their inheritances, and the like. The responsibility of the mukhtar to supply these documents was a source of considerable power, a fact that became more and more noticeable during Jordanian rule of the West Bank. But this, no doubt, was only a period of transition. The establishment of village councils and the continuing integration of villages into a centralized administration will certainly strengthen government control over the mukhtar and thus complete his transformation into a regular government official of the lowest grade.

[98] See Baer, *Studies in the Social History of Modern Egypt*, pp. 39, 46, 52-53.

[99] Cf. Antoun, *Arab Village*, pp. 91-92. In Palestine the madafa was usually maintained by the village or the hamula, while in Egypt the umda himself used to keep the madafa on behalf of the government. For details and sources, see G. Baer, *The Arabs of the Middle East* (Tel-Aviv: Hakibbutz Hameuchad, second edition, 1973), p. 180 (in Hebrew).

Administrative Policy in Rural Palestine: The Impact of British Norms on Arab Community Life, 1920-1948

by Ylana N. Miller

Introduction

In 1920 the League of Nations Mandate for Palestine gave international recognition to the British presence in that country. It also formulated contradictory imperatives that would hamper the development of a unitary state and lead to severe imbalances in communal
growth. The difficulties were partially inherent in the mandate system
itself and thus were shared with other countries in the Fertile Crescent. In part they were peculiar to Palestine, which was singled out as
the site of a Jewish national home.

Palestine entered the Mandate with a history and demographic
character that resembled those of surrounding areas. Its population
underwent changes comparable to those of the Lebanese or Syrians
under French rule, yet Palestine was the only mandatory territory
that never fully made the transition to independent statehood. A partial explanation of this phenomenon lies in its original definition. The
Palestine Mandate was unique in its inclusion of the promise first
made in the Balfour Declaration of 1917. It therefore differed substantially from all other mandates because it introduced a third element into the relationship between an Arab population and a European government.

Articles 2, 6, and 11 of the Mandate required the British to facilitate
Jewish immigration and settlement on the land. In this way, they
specifically encouraged a social transformation not anticipated in any
of the other mandates. Although all provisions included a clause to
protect the existing Arab population, the thrust of the Mandate was to
support measures that would place the country "under such political,

administrative and economic conditions as will secure the establishment of the Jewish national home."[1]

Much of the literature on Palestine has dealt with the contradictions
of British policy in the Middle East during World War I.[2] British efforts to reconcile their commitment to Jewish settlement with their obligation to protect the Palestinian Arab community ultimately proved
fruitless. The nationalist conflict that engulfed Palestine throughout
much of the Mandate has been presented from many points of view.
The apparent logic of Arab-Jewish struggle over Palestine often
seems to need little explanation. Most evaluations of British policy in
this period thus deal with the efforts to arbitrate between the competing communities. Partisans of each side have accused the mandatory
authority of bias in its implementation of the Jewish national home
policy at different times. Rarely has anyone examined the direct impact of British government on the communities themselves.

The existence of a Palestinian administration under British mandate in itself permanently altered all aspects of Arab life. The drawing
of new territorial boundaries enclosed a particular population and
subjected it to a specific set of regulations. The development of a
Jewish national home must be set within this framework and understood as part of a process that brought Palestine into an international
arena of political and economic relationships. The Jewish immigration that followed establishment of the Mandate had a direct effect on
the Palestinian Arabs and helped differentiate them from the surrounding areas. Exposure to an activist nationalist movement intensified Palestinian Arab self-consciousness and stimulated political
organization. Economic development, fueled by the importation of
capital and resulting in an active land market as well as rapid urbanization, affected the Arab population in a variety of ways. Regulation
of this interaction was left in large measure to the British government.
Its actions or failure to act helped to define the terms of Arab-Jewish
interchange.

The Mandate imposed dual obligations on the Palestine government, but from the beginning of the Mandate its responsibilities were
not equally divided. Whereas the Jewish community was skilled,
well-organized, and had access to independent sources of income, the

<hr>

[1] *The Mandate for Palestine*, July 24, 1922. Great Britain, *Parliamentary Papers*, Cmd.
1785.

[2] See e.g., Elie Kedourie, *England and the Middle East* (London: Bowes and Bowes,
1956); Elizabeth Monroe, *Britain's Moment in the Middle East* (London: Chatto and Win-
dus, 1963); and Leonard Stein, *The Balfour Declaration* (New York: Simon and Schuster,
1961).

Arab population possessed none of these advantages. Its dependence on the government consequently grew in conjunction with the expansion of public activity in all areas. Although the British were strongly committed to preserving the traditional structure of Arab life, their presence and policies made this goal a contradiction in terms. The interaction between government officials and Arab villagers shows us precisely why this was the case and how the implementation of policy generated defined patterns of reaction. While the British sought to protect a traditional elite and to preserve village life, the administrators themselves required a legal framework. Even an innovation that was as limited and as carefully contained as the creation of a new set of laws had implications for the character of Arab community existence. The formality of legal authority was not rendered significant because of its prescriptions or assumed rationality. It was important because it made customary behavior appear irrational to its adherents.

It is my contention that below the surface of nationalist politics and government policy in Palestine lay an unarticulated but fundamental crisis. This crisis was the progressive erosion of a longstanding definition of community based on unquestioned norms of human behavior. Community in this context refers to the way in which individuals draw their social boundaries. In order to be meaningful, communal boundaries must reflect a generally accepted view of power within a defined social group. Those who consider themselves members of the community share a set of norms that regulate their relationships and the ways in which they handle conflicts. Such norms are not taught or explained; they are assimilated through example, and act as an unconscious source of action.

The unarticulated basis of peasant community life has given it stability over the centuries and rendered it vulnerable to collapse in recent times. It is true that, apart from a small minority, the Palestinian Arabs had no clearly articulated view of themselves as a separate people before 1918. This does not mean that the Palestinian villager had suffered from a lack of social integration. On the contrary, the ties of family, religion, and region had been important sources of security; these ties, moreover, had been comprehensibly related to both notable groups and to the larger Ottoman Empire.

This structure of relationships was drastically altered by the imposition of new governments in the Middle East. British use of administrative authority in Palestine was one aspect of a development that led many Arabs to believe that autonomy depended upon control over an independent state. Jewish organization of quasi-governmental institutions reinforced this belief. It is in this context of forced adjustment to a new political order that we must place any evaluation of Palestinian strength or weakness under the Mandate.

The Palestinian experience suggests that the creation of a new state system, even when viewed as illegitimate by those who are ruled, has direct repercussions for them. Such effects are not merely external; they penetrate and alter intracommunal relationships. The evidence presented here was chosen to illustrate some of the implications of a new governmental system for villagers. When I discuss village response to British policy, it is to show that Palestinian Arabs were constantly seeking to control the degree to which their lives were changing. Policy is therefore not to be viewed as a determining factor, much less the major cause of social change. It is simply one part of an interaction that helped to shape Palestinian self-consciousness.

Rural Society: Structure and Problems

The population that came to be defined as Palestinian was located mainly in village communities. In 1922, Jews constituted a little over 10 percent of the population, and, among the Arab sector, 71 percent were classified as rural. Despite important demographic changes in the composition of this population, a significant majority of the Arab community continued to live in villages and to support itself by agricultural occupations during the course of the Mandate. Although the rate of urban growth was high, it primarily reflected Jewish immigration and only to a lesser extent migration due to population pressure on the land. The result was that while the context of Arab village existence changed dramatically (with Jews forming one-third of the total Palestinian population by 1946), the proportion of Arabs tied to village society remained substantial.[3]

In the early years of the Mandate, the controlling force in all Palestinian villages was the extended family and its system of alliances. Each village was divided into two or more clans (*hamulas*) whose elders dominated the political and economic life of the group. Kinship affiliation guaranteed the individual concrete support and the protection of the society within which he operated. In return, he observed its customs, which gave priority to the family rather than any territorial unit.

British administrators recognized that this social order was based on rigid adherence to the rules of collective expression. In 1921, the governor of Tulkarm subdistrict discovered that when villagers could

---

[3] Palestine Government, *Report and General Abstract of the Census of 1922* by J. B. Barron (Jerusalem, 1922); and *A Survey of Palestine* (Jerusalem, 1946), Vol. I.

visit him in secret they would complain freely, but when he visited the villages themselves, he noticed that "notables in villages frighten the villagers into silence. . . ."[4] It became British practice to respect this hierarchy as much as possible throughout the Mandate.[5]

The place of the elders or notables in village life was pivotal. They were the personalized representation of a commitment to unity of values—kinship, religion, and politics were intertwined in their style of leadership. Individuals were always subject to challenge and different families might vie for control, but the underlying consensus on values remained.

The dominant concerns of village society were expressed in a periodic alternation between unity and division within this leadership. Its position might be generally recognized, but there was a constant tension between families that frequently manifested itself in feuds. Such conflicts generally erupted over land or personal relationships. For the outsider, the substance of these conflicts is less important than the function they performed in periodically mobilizing the social forces available to each village faction. Customary means of arbitration controlled but never destroyed this pattern. Throughout the Mandate intrigue and the traditional alliances of rival family groupings remained constant factors in village life.[6]

Village organization along hamula lines used kinship as the primary basis of identity, but it was also responsive to economic power and religious authority as legitimate instruments of control. In villages composed of several religious groups, the dominant cleavages followed sectarian lines. Where absentee landlords owned significant portions of village land, their representatives held correspondingly important positions in the local distribution of power. As the economy of Palestine began to change in response to Jewish immigration and the consequent growth of capitalist enterprise, existing patterns of village leadership based on family ownership of land were exposed to substantial threats.[7]

[4] Subdistrict governor, Tulkarm to governor, Jaffa, July 28, 1921. Israel State Archives (ISA) 2/67.

[5] Palestine Government, Department of Statistics, *General Monthly Bulletin of Current Statistics* (July, 1945), p. 429.

[6] Intravillage feuds were common. Conflicts over land or family honor were a frequent source of tension. Ya'acov Shimoni, *Aravei Eretz Israel* (Tel-Aviv: Am-Oved, 1947) (Hebrew) gives an excellent description both of village structure (pp. 157-82) and of the important families throughout Palestine (pp. 206-39). For a precise description of family control over the threat of conflict in one village, see R. Antoun, *Arab Village* (Bloomington: Indiana University Press, 1972), pp. 103-13.

[7] Two sets of police reports provide insight into government classification of notables. See "Information: Mukhtars and Notables, Lydda Police Station Area," ISA 65/2216 and a police report on Nazareth District ISA 65/2533. Another, less extensive list made by the district commissioner, Galilee, is in ISA 27-2640/G607. A series of village

The advent of British government and large-scale Jewish colonization in the critical period following World War I inevitably affected
property relations within many villages. Land and the standardization
of legal procedures affecting it commanded the attention of the Palestine administration from the beginning. The obligation to facilitate
land purchase by Jews certainly played a role, but also significant was
the desire to order the financial affairs of Palestine. Only the registration of land (with the concomitant regularization of taxes) and an increase in production could provide the basis for a growing economy.[8]

From the beginning of the Mandate, government policy toward the
villages aimed at achieving administrative stability without altering
existing social relationships. The British limited their objectives in
rural areas to the minimum they associated with responsible government. Priority was given to public order and efficient collection of
taxes. The expansion of services and development of the agricultural
economy remained secondary, in part because they were dependent
on the generation of adequate revenue.

In theory, the Palestine government resisted innovation. Whenever
new legislation was considered, Ottoman precedents served as the
basis for discussion, and British officials sought to formulate their policy in accordance with these norms. There were several fallacies in
this approach. Ottoman laws had rarely been implemented on the village level. Moreover, the Ottoman political system bore little re-
semblance to that of the Mandate. The former had been formulated
to govern a substantial area in which most social groups remained distant from the center of power. The latter was territorially limited and
sought to establish closer administrative control. Inevitably, therefore, the British or Arab officers who applied laws under the Mandate
introduced new expectations. Their judgments respected local custom where possible, but customary procedure was now integrated
into a larger system based on Western legal concepts. Custom was no
longer an inherently legitimate source, but had to be rendered compatible with externally imposed standards. The interaction between
administrators and villagers was consequently impeded by an unac-
knowledged barrier of conflicting expectations. British officials assumed that the state and its legal system were impersonal mechanisms

history sheets includes data on important families. See ISA 27 Files 71/3/20; 71/3/37;
71/3/38.

[8] Avraham Granovsky (Granott), *The Land System in Palestine* (London: Eyre and
Spottiswoode, 1952); Kenneth Stein, "The Land Question in Palestine, 1920-36," unpublished dissertation, University of Michigan, 1976. A report written in 1922 on the
estimation and collection of tithes, along with related correspondence between the
High Commissioner and the Colonial Secretary may be found in PRO CO 733/20/167-
306.

with inherent legitimacy. Villagers viewed both as suspect and extended recognition only when it was forced on them.

The legal framework for administration of rural areas was developed gradually in response to need. It embodied no general policy, but was at all times governed by the desire to avoid unnecessary changes. Consequently, principles of collective responsibility and control were retained. The government accepted *mukhtars* and notables as village representatives on their own terms. No effort was made to standardize their bases of authority until late in the period.[9]

Rural Administration, 1920-1936

The first mandatory law that had granted some governing power to local bodies was a short, rather vague provision entitled the Local Councils Ordinance, 1921. The general terms were formulated to provide maximum flexibility for the creation of councils in distinctive town quarters as well as in large villages. A second, clarifying ordinance was published six months later. The two ordinances constituted enabling legislation that required specific orders for their application in any given instance.[10]

By the terms of these laws, the High Commissioner could (on the recommendation of the district governor) declare that a large village, a group of villages, or a distinctive quarter should be administered by a local council. Such a council would then have the right to impose taxes, raise loans, enter into other contracts or pass bylaws to secure order. The council's budget was to be subject to approval by the district governor and, in appropriate cases, the relevant municipality. All other functions and the composition of the council were to be specified in the particular order required for each case.

Although, in theory, the Arab community might have gained both experience and self-confidence through participation in such bodies, this promise was largely unrealized. The inherent obstacles to villagers' utilization of local councils, particularly in the first fifteen years of the Mandate, counteracted any incentive they might have offered. Extensive rural poverty prohibited villages or small towns from undertaking significant projects by themselves. The supervisory power of district commissioners (defined in each order applying to Arab villages) also deprived the councils of full responsibility for their actions.

[9] The Municipal Ordinance of 1934 inadvertently rescinded all previous laws dealing with local administration. Discussions on new legislation to permit the appointment of mukhtars may be found in ISA 4 550 Y/150/37, 551 Y/7/38, and 27-2612/G19. The Mukhtars (Appointment) Ordinance, 1942 was published in the *Palestine Gazette*, Supplement No. 1 (June 25, 1942).

[10] Local Council Ordinance, 1921, *Palestine Gazette* (May 1, 1921).

Villages were generally dominated by a small set of competing leaders, and the decisive role of an outside authority only strengthened their tendency to rely on manipulation rather than compromise to retain control.[11]

In the first few years after the enactment of the Local Councils Ordinance, 1921, approximately twenty councils (Arab and Jewish) were established.[12] Most of the orders creating Arab councils provided for a limited franchise, restricted prerogatives, and carefully controlled access to office. The cases of Tantoura and Tira (both in Haifa subdistrict) illustrate the fate of some of the councils. Both had councils for short periods of time, but they were "abolished owing to dissension and quarrels amongst the members and the various families."[13]

Failure to establish a comprehensive structure of representative institutions caused the government to seek other ways to support village services.[14] In 1926, the Village Roads and Works Ordinance was promulgated. It was based on Ottoman provisions and incorporated the principle that villages were responsible for financing local projects. Every male villager between the ages of sixteen and sixty could thereby be required to contribute either a tax or labor for the construction of roads or sanitation works. Village leaders were made nominally responsible for outlining a program of works, but their primary responsibility was to furnish a list of those liable to the tax. The district commissioner retained the power to authorize work that he considered necessary; he also determined the amount of tax to be paid.[15]

The ordinance was expanded and amended several times to broaden its area of jurisdiction. Although limited progress was made, the financial position of most villages did not permit extensive projects until the 1940s. The rural community was left largely to itself in this regard. The result was that despite the general expansion of roads in the country, many villages remained relatively isolated and accessible only on horseback.[16]

[11] The Peel Report dismissed local councils as "more an instrument of the Central Administration than a real organ of local self-government." Great Britain, *Parliamentary Papers*, Cmd. 5479. *Report of the Palestine Royal Commission* (Peel Report) (London, 1937), p. 257.

[12] *Survey of Palestine*, p. 128.

[13] "History of Tira," ISA 27 71/3/38; "History of Tantoura," ISA 27 71/3/37. For similar cases in other districts see ISA 3885 T/41/9/3 and 27-2578 A 283.

[14] Earlier discussions on a comprehensive scheme for local government had resulted in a report, but the recommendations it contained were never implemented. For a full transcript of the discussions and the reports, see ISA 2/132-34 and 65/86.

[15] *Palestine Gazette* (December 1, 1926), pp. 626-27. Correspondence regarding the formulation of the ordinance is contained in PRO CO 733/113/53-65.

[16] For information on roadbuilding, see Palestine Government, *Annual Reports to the League of Nations*.

The nature of village communities also created problems in regulating crime. Since feuds were the product of a strong collective identification, it was difficult to apply personal sanctions. The Collective Punishment Ordinance of 1925 sought to deal with this problem. It became an important foundation for the control of criminal behavior (both personal and political) in the villages. The law recognized the strength of a social system based on mutual protection rather than justice. An entire village could therefore be held responsibile for damages inflicted by one of its inhabitants. It was assumed that local notables knew in most cases who was responsible, and their unwillingness to share such information was now turned against them. Although village leaders thus retained the power to allocate fines, they also bore the onus involved.[17]

The difficulty of applying the Collective Punishment Ordinance to ordinary crime in isolated villages became apparent by 1930. A report from the administrative officer in Nablus details the difficulties of containing the agrarian crimes and murders that frequently accompanied family feuds. Often mukhtars who knew the responsible party did not want to expose themselves to reprisals by cooperating with an investigation. The local officials responsible for order therefore suggested that such incidents be dealt with immediately "by an officer with knowledge of the facts and persons as it is in no way a judicial proceeding."[18] The reports also suggest banishment as an effective punishment.

Cases of this nature offer one example of the confrontation between village society and representatives of outside authority. Officials who sought to enforce the law inadvertently helped to undermine it. The apparent advantages of respecting local leadership led them to reinforce its monopoly over access to government power. The desire to be effective, however, created frustration with local custom and led to efforts to circumvent it. Resorting to administrative hearings rather than regular trials was an unhappy compromise. The personal knowledge of district officers replaced that of mukhtars, but the older system continued to exist in the guise of more impersonal mechanisms for administering justice.

Evidence on the operation of local councils in Arab villages substantiates the impression that the attempt to incorporate existing social relationships into new institutions only served to undermine both. By 1933, fourteen Arab local councils were functioning, but ten years later the number had decreased to eleven. Three out of the nine vil-

[17] *Palestine Gazette* (1925). Correspondence on the law is contained in PRO CO 733/98/690-702.

[18] District commissioner, Haifa to chief secretary, March 23, 1920, ISA 4 546 Y/141/31.

lage local councils that existed in 1945 were in purely Christian areas, while one had a Christian minority. This number was decidedly out of proportion with the ratio of Christian villagers to Muslims (there were only nine entirely Christian villages in all of Palestine in 1941). It is clear, therefore, that Muslim Arab villagers benefited only marginally from the existence of local councils.[19]

The difficulties experienced by both government officials and the rural population in creating representative institutions were not only technical. They reflected a wide gap in the assumptions made about decision-making processes. To be successful, the new concept of electoral politics required an appropriate social context. This context was generally lacking in Arab villages and was unlikely to develop without economic changes.

In a community governed by patriarchal authority, the natural role assumed by leaders in a village is that of mediators between a personal "constituency" and superior authorities. Elected councils normally make quite different demands on their membership. Such bodies require individual decisions, the compromise of concrete interests, and identification with the representative institution as well as with a particular sector of those represented. There is an appreciation of politics as a distinct arena of relationships governed by separate rules of behavior.

The dissolution of nonfunctioning village councils on the grounds of family dissension was therefore simply an official admission that the new structure could not be successful without a simultaneous reformation of its social and cultural base. Those councils that did maintain their existence did so by assimilating theoretically innovative institutions to established conceptions of authority. There was continued predominance of hamula divisions; and one of the most important functions that local councils chose to perform, particularly before 1936, was that of presenting village needs to governmental authorities. In this way, they retained a familiar mediating position. For the most part the few councils that functioned remained the preserve of existing leadership.[20]

Petitions, one of the most common channels of communication used by the villagers, were often addressed by local councils to the

---

[19] In 1933, the High Commissioner declared fourteen Arab local councils to be local education authorities under the new Education Ordinance. See *Palestine Gazette*, Supplement No. 2 (May 4, 1933), p. 267. On the number in 1944, see *Survey of Palestine*, Vol. I, p. 129.

[20] President, local council of Rameh to officer administering the government, October 7, 1933; and district commissioner, northern district to chief secretary, November 5, 1933, ISA 4 207 G/110/33. Speech by president local council, Bira, received in chief secretary's office, November 1, 1934, ISA 4 G/162/34.

High Commissioner. These appeals sought to circumvent district administrators and to apprise the highest authority of the peasant's
plight. These appeals commonly contained requests for services, such
as the extension of educational facilities, the installation of tele-
phones, or economic aid of various sorts. The petitions reflected the
wide range of social and political conditions obtaining even within
Arab communities that could be brought under the umbrella of the
Local Councils Ordinance of 1921.

By 1935, Palestine was still devoid of an integrating political structure. The Jewish community was effectively organized, but the Arab
population remained divided. The slow growth of a government bureaucracy only produced a parallel set of authorities without taking
into account the impact of the new authorities on existing power relationships.[21] In that year a new British report was issued, but it simply
confirmed that the British were seeking a solution that would ensure
support for public works without any definitive transfer of power
from the district commissioners to village councils.[22]

Reports issued in the early 1930s had indicated clearly the need for
greater development of the Arab economy. The central government
was neither prepared nor able to finance the necessary undertakings,
and the result was the district administrators were forced to depend
largely on local sources for funds. Popular resistance to taxation and
endemic feuding, however, reinforced their inclination to mistrust
any solution that involved genuinely autonomous local government.
Village notables often supported this attitude at least indirectly. Their
position normally depended on the ability to play a mediating role,
and the notables preferred not to burden themselves with the responsibility for imposing taxes unless it carried reasonably extensive powers of control as well.[23]

Rebellion, 1936-1939

There was no single cause leading to the general strike and rebellion
that began in April 1936. For our purposes, one of the central problems raised by the Arab Revolt was the breakdown in Arab communal

[21] "Local Government Commission Report," February 24, 1925, ISA 2/133.

[22] This report, known by the name of the chairman as the Campbell Committee Report, was presented to the High Commissioner on January 16, 1935. See "Report of
Committee on Village Organization, Part XIV of the (old) Local Government Bill," ISA
4 548 Y/196/33.

[23] Great Britain, *Parliamentary Papers*, Cmd. 3683-3697. *Report on Immigration, Land
Settlement and Development by Sir John Hope Simpson* (London, 1930). Palestine Govern-
ment, *Report on Agricultural Development and Land Settlement in Palestine by Lewis French*
(London, 1931).

relationships. By 1936, the Arab population was becoming part of a larger economic and social environment. Jewish settlement had stimulated the development of an active land market, internal migration, and population growth among villages, all of which affected Arabs in varying ways. The resulting divisions within the Arab community strained the ties of a common lifestyle and gave rise to internal tension. The lack of institutions that could connect villagers to the state contributed to a growing imbalance.

The outbreak of violence throughout Palestine in the late 1930s demonstrated the weakness of government control over large portions of the population. The rebellion underlined the limitations of a policy based on British willingness to accept factional disputes as a legitimate basis for political control. By this time the internal divisions within the Arab community were no longer based on one accepted view of how social life should be ordered. The breakup of communal land tenure, coupled with increased land sales by smaller owners, deprived some families of a secure income while increasing opportunities for others. The agricultural depression of the early 1930s occurred during a time of intensified Jewish settlement and added to the growing pressure for the development of resources available to the Arab population.

The influx of capital that contributed to expansion of the Palestinian economy took place without any substantial change in political institutions. In the political chaos that developed, officials showed renewed awareness of the confused nature of local government. Widespread popular participation in militant actions helped to stimulate government initiatives to resolve the problems created.

The High Commissioners, Sir Arthur Wauchope and Sir Harold MacMichael, were particularly interested in building village institutions. Their concern was instrumental in generating new discussions among district administrators. The convergence of economic and political changes within the Arab sector encouraged the search for a more coherent way of gathering and using revenues at the local level.[24]

The height of confusion in these matters was reached when the Palestine government tried to consolidate effective legislation for rural government in the midst of the rebellion. Historical factors had led to a muddled situation in which some Arab municipalities were little more than large villages, local councils often ceased functioning, and village government by elders or mukhtars had only a customary, not legal, basis for existence. Most Jewish settlements remained organized as local councils despite their growth. The reality of local

[24] G. H. Hall to acting chief secretary, February 16, 1936, ISA 4 210/G/96/35.

government therefore had little to do with theoretical provisions. Nevertheless, the fiction of providing a uniform set of regulations for Arab and Jewish settlements was maintained. A scheme for the creation of rural local councils is a clear indication of this fruitless approach. In 1937 and 1938, ordinances designed to encourage more effective councils were enacted, but they appeared during a period marked by the frequent substitution of nominated for elected councils because of the rebellion.[25]

Tension between the maintenance of custom and the introduction of a rational legal system was also heightened by the extraordinary measures taken during the rebellion. In the years prior to 1936, the village population had become accustomed to government as an arbitrator among factions rather than an impersonal authority governed by an independent ethical standard. The legal system came to be perceived as an instrument of this arbitrating power with little inherent legitimacy. This view was naturally reinforced by the imposition of numerous emergency regulations.

In 1936, a new Collective Fines Ordinance was promulgated. It retained the concept of communal responsibility for crime, but, in one important respect, the new law sought to establish a new principle. Whereas the Collective Punishment Ordinance had imposed penalties for intercommunal conflict and permitted the use of fines for compensation of damage, the new law was aimed at offenses against the state. The fines were therefore forwarded to the central government and not retained by the locality. Although the logic of this position is clear, its implementation suffered from the ambiguity that continued to plague the relationship between state and community. The Palestinian government had become a concrete presence, but this did not mean that either sector of the population, Jewish or Arab, identified its interests with state policy. Instead, each was now seeking to capture the state.[26] In the interim, the line between intercommunal conflict and antistate actions was not always clearly drawn. The violence of this period caused personal feuds to be interpreted as political opposition, just as earlier acts of nationalist assertion had often been seen as purely personal.

The breakdown of order on a large scale brought to light the conflicting mechanisms available for social control. In the town of Shefa Amr, Muslims and Druzes had engaged in bitter feuding as a result of

[25] The model order for rural councils is in ISA 4 210 Y/196-33. Assistant district commissioner, Safed to assistant district commissioner, Galilee, September 3, 1937, "Note on Rural Councils in Arab Areas," ISA 27-2641/G625.

[26] Acting district commissioner, Galilee to chief secretary, September 20, 1937, ISA 26-2642/G665.

the general disturbances. To resolve the conflict government officials initiated a traditional process of arbitration. The two parties arrived at a peace settlement that included the stipulation that no more Muslims would be tried for crimes arising out of the dispute. Despite government involvement in this *extralegal* procedure, charges continued to be brought. Mukhtars of villages throughout the area protested these acts, which seemed to be arbitrary violation of the agreement. The acting district commissioner for Galilee proposed that

> the petitioners be informed that in such cases a third party is also concerned, namely that which is reponsible in the interest of law and order for the administration of justice. Hence in the case of serious offense, although the parties may come to settlement, it is still necessary to vindicate the law lest others be encouraged to similar deeds to the detriment of the State.[27]

The primacy of personal relationships was giving way in the minds of officials to the concept of an abstract state.

After 1937, the earlier semblance of cohesion dissolved into conflict among competing Arab groups. For many villagers, the government became only one claimant in the competition for followers and often it was not the strongest one. Inability to collect more than one-third of the fines imposed in 1936 and 1937 testifies to the legal impotence of the Palestine government. The proliferation of rebel courts as a response to military courts created conflicting systems of justice.[28]

Superior British forces and the political concessions of 1939 finally succeeded in restoring order in Palestine, but obedience to power does not always reflect respect for the law. Earlier failure to bring villages within the purview of a rational legal system was compounded by the introduction of extraordinary measures during the rebellion. The absence of effective institutions acting on behalf of the rural population deprived the legal system of a concrete base and created a situation in which law was rarely seen as protective. In most cases, it had come to be intrusive or at best irrelevant.[29]

---

[27] Acting district commissioner, Galilee to chief secretary, April 25, 1940, ISA 27-2629/G343.

[28] On the development of rebel courts, see Yuval Arnon, "Fellahim Bamered Ha'aravi B'Eretz Yisrael," unpublished M.A. thesis, Hebrew University, 1970, pp. 73-74; *Criminal Investigation Division News Bulletin*, September 6, 1938 to September 13, 1938, in the Tegart Papers, Box I, File II; and H. M. Wilson, "School Year in Palestine, 1938-39," both at the Middle East Centre Oxford, England. For the proportion of fines actually collected, see chief secretary to all district commissioners, May 3, 1938, ISA 27-2642/G665.

[29] Great Britain, *Parliamentary Papers*, Cmd. 6019.

Restoration of Order

As the Palestinian government regained control over the country, a new set of relationships between government and society began to emerge. The end of the rebellion left Arab society not only exhausted but internally fragmented and far more vulnerable. The emergence of a broader communal consciousness less limited by regional differences had not produced effective leadership. Many national leaders were no longer in Palestine, and the state now began to replace communal organizations as the only concrete source of authority.

The transition was marked by a renewed consideration of alternatives in local government; the discussion begun in 1938 took on a more definite and viable form in the early 1940s. By this time, the general inadequacy of Arab local councils was recognized. Although such existing councils continued to function, no new ones were added. Instead the administration turned to legislation designed specifically for villages.[30]

Wauchope had first made the decision to reactivate village organization in 1935, but no consistent approach to the issue materialized until the end of 1938. By this time, the new High Commissioner, MacMichael, had lent his support to the plan for reorganization. Both High Commissioners were particularly interested in the development of village government as proof of the integrity of British mandatory policy. They realized also that rural disruption had destroyed an increasingly tenuous stability and that the government therefore had to re-create connections with the villagers. The outbreak of war in September of 1939 gave further impetus to this effort by stimulating the drive for effective mobilization of the population. In 1940, MacMichael therefore appointed a committee to develop a legislative proposal for the revival of village institutions.[31]

The Bailey Committee Report on Village Administration was submitted on October 2, 1941. It stresses the continuity that British officials persisted in attributing to rural society despite their own accurate analyses of the changes that had occurred. The introduction to the report summarizes the history of village organization under Ottoman government and states that since 1934 "neither the council of elders nor the office of mukhtar has had any legal existence, although

[30] Assistant district commissioner, Tiberias to district commissioner, Galilee and Acre, September 9, 1939, ISA 26-2741/G625. M. Bailey to Keith-Roach (personal), December 1, 1938, ISA 27 71/2-1. District commissioner, Galilee, to district commissioner, Jerusalem, August 15, 1939, ISA 27 71/2-1.

[31] "Note" by High Commissioner, September 23, 1940, ISA 27 71/2-1. Palestine Government, *Report of the Committee on Village Administration and Responsibility* (Bailey Committee Report) (Jerusalem, 1941).

mukhtars have continued to be appointed. . . ."[32] According to the authors, lack of government support had contributed to a decline in the authority of village elders. Advances in self-government were limited and confined to urban areas; no steps to develop local autonomy had been taken in the 1,000 villages that contained 50 percent of the Palestinian population. The current situation in rural areas is summarized. The description points to the absence of any legal foundation for village authority. Although councils of elders, committees of arbitration, and mukhtars continued to function, they had no legal status.[33] The bulk of the report that follows this introduction consists of suggestions for the revival and formalization of the prerogatives customarily ascribed to village leaders.

The report cites the case of Anebta (Tulkarm subdistrict) as proof of the need for new legislation to support existing practices. In this village, a Council of Elders had continued to meet regularly despite the existence of a local council. The authors thus agreed with the Peel Commission that meaningful development had to utilize "such inherent self-governing impulses and institutions as the people possess."[34] The committee therefore proposed that village councils with executive and in some cases judicial functions be established. That such administrative initiatives and legal provisions tended to lag behind actual practice becomes evident in the section dealing with arbitration. The writers recommended that the system of village councils and courts first be applied to a few "enlightened" villages. The system would then be extended "only in response to demand and in the light of experience gained."

The Bailey Committee Report's basic thrust, then, was to place the rural sector within a national legal framework by legitimizing existing institutions. The law also provided for greater specificity in the powers and responsibilities of officially recognized village councils. Nevertheless, these councils were to remain under close supervision by district commissioners.[35]

It is natural to ask why it suddenly became necessary to reinforce organizations or customs that were presumed to be "inherent" and stable: that is, to make explicit village power relationships that were previously unquestioned. In the case of Palestine, the answer seems clear. The evidence strongly suggests that traditional leadership and institutions had been weakened by severe pressures during the previous decade; consequently, government officials had to choose between an overt commitment to this structure and a decision to permit its dissolution. Earlier dependence upon notables for effective control

---

[32] Ibid., p. 7.
[34] Ibid.

[33] Ibid., p. 8.
[35] Ibid., pp. 21-33.

and the decision (made in 1939) to prepare Palestine for a form of self-government helped to determine the outcome of this choice. It is difficult to judge the effects of the new legislation because the Mandate came to an end three-and-a-half years after it was promulgated. It remains necessary to examine the significant alteration in peasant attitudes toward government and toward official village administration that took place in the 1940s.

Initiatives in the 1940s

It is not hard to find evidence for the expansion in village interests that went on during the years of World War II. Movement occurred at all levels of local government and administration. The motives for this surge of activity were numerous. A comparative survey of local budgets clearly shows the increase in financial resources that accompanied the war. In the villages, government-sponsored organizations controlled and allocated food production. Wartime requirements stimulated efforts to mobilize the entire population of Palestine within a more rational administrative structure. At the same time, there was increased generational and social change.[36]

Between 1943 and 1947, village procedures began to acquire a coherent character. Although British administrative supervision remained strong, villagers began to assert their own priorities, to request councils, and to question the legitimacy of electoral lists. Often, the problems raised by petitions concerned dissatisfactions with nominees or factional disagreements, but it is apparent that in some villages recourse was now had to lawyers, and complaints concerned specific issues of law. This was the case in Samakh, Galilee, when in August 1947 one party sought to void elections held in March by the district officers. The complaint stated that the officer had acted in conjunction with a small group of notables and had limited participation in the elections to ensure the outcome. Investigation by the Crown Counsel supported the contentions of the petitioners.[37]

In Tarshiha, accounts of elections held between 1943 and 1947 reflect far greater popular understanding of the mechanisms involved, but an incident in 1947 shows the power of certain traditional values to hinder rapid change. In that year, the district officer for Acre first received fourteen nominations for the council on February 22, but on February 26, thirteen of the fourteen withdrew. His description explains what had happened:

[36] A comparison of council budgets is in the *Survey of Palestine*, Vol. I, pp. 138-39. Examples of specific local council budgets are to be found in ISA 27-2631 G/418/1.

[37] The case is detailed in ISA 27-2686 T/18.

They [the thirteen] were all youngish men and seemed interested in the Labour Movement. They had put in their nominations with the idea of having a young progressive Council. The older men of the village had been caught napping but, after the nominations had been entered, they called a meeting and persuaded these young men that affairs of the village would be better entrusted to wise old heads. The young men in the face of family authority agreed.[38]

The promulgation of the Village Administration Ordinance in 1944 led to renewed activity on the part of administrators, who established councils in a few of the most "progressive" villages. One district commissioner held a meeting in Nablus in October 1944 in order to discuss application of the ordinance. It was decided that the provisions should be applied to three villages in each subdistrict.

The Councillors would be the choice of the people and acceptable to the people of the Village. . . . The bigger "hamoulehs" might be represented by more than one member. The practical method would be for the number per "hamouleh" to be fixed and then the "hamouleh" hold a meeting and select their representative by popular acclamation.[39]

The purpose of the ordinance was clearly to encourage village cohesiveness, but its application remained close to traditional customs.

A reviving British commitment to development and legal change served to concentrate official attention on particularly promising areas. Equally significant is the fact that certain villages now took the initiative in requesting that local councils be established. This initiative suggests that rural differentiation had gained momentum and was becoming evident on the political plane. The results were by no means uniform. Some villages feared that councils would lead to rapid urbanization and hence opposed them with increased vigor; others saw an advantage in the provisions for legal and political organization.[40]

By 1946, twenty-four village councils existed in areas chosen for

[38] Acting district commissioner, Acre to district commissioner, Galilee, March 12, 1947, ISA 27-2578/A282.

[39] See correspondence between district commissioner, Acre, and district commissioner, Galilee, and between district commissioner, Galilee, and chief secretary in 1942-1944, ISA 27-2578/A283.

[40] "Note on a Conference Held at the District Commissioner's Office, Nablus, on the 26th October, 1944, on the Subject of the Application of the Village Administration Ordinance," ISA 3891/4. For examples of village requests for the establishment of councils, see ISA 4 219 G/31/45 and 218 G/3/45. Opposition to a council was expressed in some cases. See ISA 27 71/4/2.

development. Only two had a predominantly Christian population, with two others having a Christian minority. None was solely Christian, and the rest, with one exception (Druze) were purely Muslim. The geographical distribution also shows marked change, particularly in the southern part of the country. Seven village councils (six of them in Gaza subdistrict) were formed in this area, and the population they served was consistently larger than that of any other area. Jerusalem District also showed rapid development, particularly in the areas around Ramallah, while the Galilee remained more static and Samaria changed gradually in this respect.[41]

It is important to interpret these factors in perspective. The growth of local institutions was predicated on village viability, and this may explain why the Haifa area had neither local nor village councils and why only one village council existed near Jaffa. These were both growing cities that drew on the peasant population in their areas for labor and thus had a greater impact on the breakdown of social cohesion than Jerusalem. In addition, the Christian population showed a far greater tendency toward urbanization than the Muslim sector, and this was probably significant in the Haifa area. Since most of the entirely Christian villages were located in Acre subdistrict, it is likely that they provided an important source of such migration.

The method followed by administrators in forming recognized councils still depended heavily upon family or religious divisions. A fairly typical procedure is described by a former district commissioner in his advice to I. L. Phillips, acting district commissioner from Gaza:

> You should first determine the total number of councillors to be chosen and the particular number to represent each hamouleh; these numbers would exclude the mukhtars (who are members ex-officio) and would be based roughly on the comparative figures of population. At Salfit we did not hold elections but required the heads of families within each hamouleh to nominate their representative or representatives. Formal elections seemed to me to be rather too advanced a procedure for such a community, and as it proved, there were no disputes over the nominations.[42]

A note on "Local or Village Council Procedure" indicates administrative interest in imbuing the new councils with parliamentary modes of procedure. The list of instructions deals with such items as the constitution of councils, arrangements for calling meetings, and the

[41] *Survey of Palestine*, Vol. I, pp. 131-32.

[42] District commissioner, Jerusalem, to acting district commissioner, Gaza, November 26, 1946, ISA 4 555 Y/133/45.

duties of council chairmen. It contains an interesting mixture of standard parliamentary rules and elementary precautions. In a paragraph dealing with "Procedure on Assembly," a sentence on quorums is followed by the instructions that a chairman "himself will *NOT* vote at first" and that voting is done by raising the right hand.[43]

This tendency to vacillate between fairly sophisticated concepts of local government and strongly paternalistic precepts supports the view that uneven development in local institutions characterized rural society at this time. While there is no doubt that family and religious segmentation remained primary in most villages, it is clear that in important respects a consensus of priorities among villagers was beginning to emerge. This change had greater impact because district officials were simultaneously altering their own perspective. These officials were now more willing to accept the views of village councillors as legitimate and were less likely to ascribe them to family divisions as had been standard in earlier years.

These generalizations can easily be countered by cases in which family disputes continued to paralyze constructive action or villagers desperately resisted taxes imposed under the expanded Roads and Works Ordinance of 1946. The conclusion to be drawn is not that village life as a whole suddenly changed radically but rather that in certain cases established uniformities in rural life were being altered. The eruption of a willingness to fight for new rights, along with an increased consciousness of what was happening in surrounding areas, were important indications of the changes that had occurred in rural areas under the Mandate.

Conclusion

The legal provisions for village government in Palestine under the Mandate concentrated almost exclusively on enabling the district administration to collect funds and maintain public security. A few larger villages had functioning local councils, but the vast majority continued to delegate communal responsibility to hamula leaders and mukhtars. The terms of the Mandate for Palestine were formulated with a view to protecting "the cultural integrity" of its Arab population. In practice, this protection was translated into a formula for the maintenance of an increasingly unviable social structure. The hamula system of control and the emphasis on collective responsibility to the state had evolved in an empire served by the grant of substantial autonomy to local communities. This pattern did not fully disintegrate

[43] "Local or Village Council Procedure," by assistant district commissioner, Tulkarm, September 8, 1946, ISA 3891/4.

during the Mandate, but a new, supplementary layer of relationships did develop.

The previous harmony between cultural and political authorities that had begun to break down in Ottoman times disappeared entirely under the Mandate. In its place, the state and nation became largely antagonistic forces. Also, throughout Palestine economic opportunity and political claims made demands upon individuals that could not be resolved through existing structures.

Conflict was not new to Palestinian villagers. Rural life had been fraught with high levels of social tension and intermittent violence for centuries. Customary norms, supported by physical interdependence, had kept such tension within socially tolerable limits. The British Mandate introduced a destabilizing factor into this tenuous system for survival. Officials of the mandatory government used unfamiliar standards of justice and sought to regulate village relationships in accordance with their own views of stability. In doing so, they inevitably weakened the pressures for conformity while not providing adequate substitutes. The result was an intensification of conflict.

Divisions within Arab society now symbolized a growing struggle to reformulate the terms of community. Access to power was no longer based on a common set of criteria. Family control could not readily be integrated into a bureaucratic structure. Notable leaders had to compete with new groups whose claims stemmed from expanded economic resources and professional expertise. An exaggerated belief in previous harmony was replaced by an equally unrealistic sense of contemporary disorientation. The anger this generated expended itself against all those who appeared responsible.

The revolt of 1936-1939 reflected the chaos that had engulfed the rural areas of Palestine. The coincidence of a growing nationalist movement with the fragmentation of village society temporarily created the illusion of a unified movement against mandatory authority. The failure of the uprising lay in the absence of a leadership able to channel village discontent into effective political action. Internal strife consumed the energies released and turned the thrust for autonomy into a cry for help.

The establishment of the Palestine government had shattered an earlier coexistence of empire with community. The mandatory political system was limited in territory and expansive in demands. A society organized in multiple collectivities could not conquer this new phenomenon. Only broader unity could transform the state into a vehicle for the satisfaction of social needs. For Palestinian Arabs, this resolution proved to be impossible. Foreign control over the state obscured the nature of the problems being faced. Transformation of communal patterns was therefore associated with defeat by strangers.

Throughout the Mandate, Palestinian Arabs thus remained divided against themselves, struggling to repudiate developments over which they felt they had little control. No expansion of opportunities would be meaningful until this internal conflict was resolved in a new form of communal existence.

CHAPTER 3

West Bank Refugees—
Between Camp and Society

by Shimon Shamir

Introduction

Becoming a refugee implies rejection by one society from which one has fled; remaining a refugee implies nonacceptance by another society in which one has sought refuge. The present article focuses on the latter conditions not with the intention of downgrading the import of the circumstances of becoming a refugee, but because it was these conditions that this author could observe directly and study subsequent to the June 1967 War.[1]

The study was undertaken in Jalazun, an average-size camp of about 4,000 persons. It is situated three miles north of Ramallah. Economically, Jalazun is closely linked to the nearby town—as is the case with most refugee camps in the West Bank. The refugees of Jalazun are of mixed urban and rural origins. Most of them come from the Bayt Naballah-Lydda region.

For the purpose of the study a random sample was constituted by picking every fifth household in Jalazun, using the forms of the 1967 Israeli census. In each household—108 altogether—all the household heads and all the men over 15 were interviewed. This gave a total of 142, consisting of 30 women and 112 men.

---

[1] This chapter is based on the author's more extensive study, "Communications and Political Attitudes in West Bank Refugee Camps" (Tel Aviv: The Shiloah Center for Middle Eastern and African Studies, 2nd edition, October, 1974), mimeographed, 72 pp. Parts of that study were sponsored by the Rand Corporation. That work, in turn, was an extension of the author's contribution to an interdisciplinary field study conducted in 1967-1968 in the Jalazun refugee camp: Yoram Ben-Porath, Emanuel Marx, and Shimon Shamir, "A Refugee Camp in the Central West Bank" (Tel Aviv: The Shiloah Center for Middle Eastern and African Studies, 2nd edition, October, 1974), mimeographed, 148 pp. (Hebrew). The work of professors Ben-Porath and Marx on the refugee problem was issued in English by the Rand Corporation under the title, "Some Sociological and Economic Aspects of Refugee Camps in the West Bank" (RAND R-835-FF, August, 1971).

The interviews were conducted by Tel Aviv University's Shiloah Center for Middle Eastern and African Studies with teams of Arabic-speaking interviewers. Each team consisted of two interviewers, one of them conducting the interview and the other taking notes. They used a list of 193 questions as a general outline for the interview—not as a structured questionnaire. The interviews usually lasted four hours, and refugees in employment were compensated for the loss of time. The women in the sample were not asked questions relating to attitudes. The 1,500 pages of the records of these interviews supply most of the data for the present study. (This vertical cross section is referred to as the "Jalazun sample.")

These data were supplemented by conversations with educated refugees, usually teachers, administrators, or other white-collar workers (many of them employees of UNRWA, United Nations Relief and Works Agency for Palestine Refugees). The conversations took place in 1968-1969 with interviewing teams from the Shiloah Center, who visited most major refugee camps in the West Bank.[2] The conversations were held, sometimes individually and sometimes in small groups, at local schools, coffee houses, camp offices and private homes. They were entirely informal and notes were written down only after the termination of the visits. The interviewers added their personal impressions and points of comparison between the various camps. In this way a horizontal cross section through the camps was achieved. (The study refers to the interviewees in this cross section by the term "white collar respondents.")

One of the first impressions gathered by the researchers was that the realities of refugees' lives in the camps were very different from the commonly held image. Refugees in the West Bank camps (the study did not apply to the more densely populated camps of the Gaza Strip) were not the impoverished, unemployed, destitute, externally supported, and apathetic people they are often taken to be. Those in the camps had belonged initially to the lowest strata of the original Palestinian society. By 1967, they were wage-earning employees, mostly in nearby towns, and the camps' rate of employment did not differ substantially from that of the West Bank in general. Through UNRWA, refugees have benefited from a level of social services, in areas such as health, education, and welfare, that is more advanced than in many Middle Eastern societies. Many of them have had the necessary aptitude and mobility to benefit from the opportunities afforded by the changing economic conditions. From social and economic perspectives, they resemble the masses of population in developing countries who have been part of a universal trend—people

[2] They included thirteen camps: 'Arub, Fawar, 'Aida, Dehayshe, Qalandia, Dair 'Amar, Am'ari, Jalazun, Balata, 'Askar, 'Ayn Bayt Alma, Tulkarm, and Jenin.

who have been uprooted from their traditional, predominantly agricultural environment and have gravitated toward urban centers to
undergo a painful process of transformation in their occupational
structure, way of life, and value system.

In the case of the refugees, however, the agonies of dislocation
seemed to be aggravated not only by the political dimension, kept
alive by the continuing Arab-Israeli conflict, but also by a more severe
problem of social inferiority and identity crisis. The camp framework
accentuated both aspects of this problem and at the same time provided an escape from them. The detachment of the camp refugees
from the political world intensified their sense of inefficacy. It was
only through the mobilization of factors affecting mostly the young
generation—such as education, vocational training, and mass communications—that the perspective on these problems began to
change. These observations serve as the central hypothesis for the
present work.

Pursuing the aim of this study confronted the researchers with
many methodological and technical problems, not all of which could
be adequately solved. The study is basically an investigation of attitudes, and "attitude" is a term so ambiguous and confused that some
social psychologists and sociologists have suggested discarding it altogether. Attitudes are not only difficult to define, they are even more
difficult to evaluate in a given person or group of people. There are
no universally accepted methods for gathering data on attitudes, and
once data have been gathered there is no acknowledged methodology
for interpreting them in any definitive way. This problem is all the
more applicable in this investigation, which was not only "cross-
cultural" but also one where interviewers and interviewees represented two societies engaged in a political conflict. Such factors as
semantic confusion, political prudence, cultural norms, and psychological motivations had to be considered in order to see the responses
in their proper light and to explain contradictions. For all these reasons, the findings given here should be regarded as broad approxima-
tions only.

It should also be noted that the present article is based on data
gathered at the end of the 1960s, a critical stage in the history of the
conflict. Following the defeat of the Arab regular armies, the Palestine
Liberation Organization (PLO) was just emerging as a significant
political factor. For the refugees it was a period of transition from
Jordanian to Israeli administration. Yet, even if the findings presented in this chapter cannot be regarded as up-to-date, many of
them still apply to the present situation.[3]

[3] For some observations on developments in the camps since the conclusion of this
study, see Emanuel Marx, "Changes in Arab Refugee Camps," *Jerusalem Quarterly*, 8
(Summer, 1978), 43-52.

Problems of Social Status

In attempts to bring out the self-image of the refugees, we sought to shed some light on some of the most crucial aspects of the refugee problem: What is the quality of being a "refugee"? What does the status of refugee mean to the refugee himself? Where is the focal point of his grievances as a refugee?

Refugees seized readily any opportunity to voice their grievances to outsiders. Indeed, they often regarded this activity as a fulfillment of a national duty and a contribution to their political struggle. Their statements, which thus bordered on the ritualistic, had to be treated by the researchers with great caution, but in many respects they undoubtedly mirrored true feelings.

In examining the records of the Jalazun interviews, the following expressions were found to be characteristic of the way in which refugees described the essence of the refugees' condition: "a cipher and a zero" (J2), "living a life of despair and humiliation" (J18/1) "only half human" (J19), "deprived of honor, homeland, and religion" (J33), "death for him is preferable to life" (J48), and "a living dead, for he who has been dispossessed of his *watan* (home country) is considered dead" (J5/1).

At first, these phrases seemed to express only the general psychological distress of a displaced people, and indeed some of the more articulate respondents spoke of their grievances in terms of mental anguish, a sense of crisis, insecurity, and unrest. Many refugees complained that what they lacked most in their present conditions was *istiqrar*—an untranslatable Arabic term that denotes a settled position and a state of stability, security, and peace of mind.

A closer examination of the refugees' responses, however, revealed that their feelings of distress were consistently centered around the problem of social status. Whenever the interviewers pursued this problem, the respondents made this point very clear, each at his own level of sophistication. Their complaints focused not on their standard of living (which in some cases equaled that of their neighbors), nor on their social services (often superior to those available to their neighbors), but on their social position.

The refugees explained that what makes them different from, and inferior to, the people among whom they now live is that these people possess land and property while the refugees have lost theirs. They claimed that their neighbors, especially the villagers on whose land a camp like Jalazun is built, call them squatters, accuse them of having sold their own land to the Jews, and tell them to go back to where they came from. Refugees believed they are regarded as "gypsies" who, having no roots in landed property, are at best "fruit thieves" and "trespassers" and, at worst, capable of committing the most heinous

acts. "The refugee is outside any binding code of traditions and customs," their neighbors often say. The refugees complained in the interviews that, because they lack landed property, the local people refuse to give them credit when they need loans, fail to assist them in
other ways, and are reluctant to allow their daughters to marry them.
Some respondents said that their most painful experience as refugees
was the humiliation inflicted on their children in their encounters
with children of the neighboring communities.

What made this situation so mortifying for the refugees was that
they themselves, in fact, shared the outlook of those who discriminated against them. Even though they had not lived on the land for
some twenty years, they still adhered to the value system of an agrarian society in which landlessness is regarded as unforgivable. They
often repeated dictums such as "the landless is despised" and "he who
has no land has no religion or homeland." The refugees claimed that
their loss of landed property had marked them indelibly; their painful inferior status, they believed, "will follow them wherever they go"
and will plague them "even after a hundred years" (J33, J116).

The realities observed throughout the West Bank did not always
substantiate this claim. The processes of modernization, especially
urbanization and occupational mobility, have rapidly reduced the importance of land ownership as a determinant of social status. The
young generation of refugees has been oriented toward white-collar
or skilled salaried occupations in the urban centers, and their status in
the communities that employ them has been determined largely, if
not entirely, by their degree of success in such careers. Indeed, the
interviews showed that educated young refugees in the camps
minimized or ignored the problems of social status and expressed
their grievances mainly in political terms.

It was only in the camps, where social and attitudinal patterns are
slow to change, that the refugees' inferior social status remained the
focus of their problems as they conceived them. Most of the humiliat-
ing experiences that the refugees recounted took place in the context
of intercommunity relations between the camp and the neighboring
village or town; only rarely did they occur on the interpersonal level
between refugees and nonrefugees as individuals. It was the framework of the camp that kept reminding the refugees that they belonged to a group marked by landlessness and were hence deprived
of their status.

The problem of social status has an additional aspect. In traditional
Arab society, and to a large extent in contemporary society as well,
status is secured by possessing a place within the complex structure of
family, clan, and community. For refugees, scattered in many camps
and towns, this social structure no longer exists. The extent of its dis-

integration varied from camp to camp. The 108 respondents of the Jalazun sample had come from as many as 18 communities and belonged to an even larger number of clans and extended families. In the camps of the Hebron area, the family structure had been somewhat better preserved. But as a group, the refugees had lost most of the benefits of belonging to an established social structure, in the traditional sense. From this came their feeling that socially they were "deficient" beings.

Problems of social status and the disintegration of stable social structures were compounded by the added problem of leadership. Refugees described themselves as a leaderless mass. The traditional leaders of their original communities had lost their credibility in the circumstances of flight. There was a remarkable consensus among refugees from many places of origin that their local notables and leaders were the first to leave. They owned vehicles, had cash or bank deposits, and found no difficulty in moving comfortably to a distant town. According to most of the refugees, it was not that these local leaders urged other people to leave but the fact that they disappeared themselves that brought about the collapse of their communities. No one remained to guide the people and thus each individual was left to his own counsel. "The leaders left first," said a 74-year-old refugee, "and when the leaders leave the people cannot remain. No one inquired about the other, everyone tried to take care of himself" (J74).

The refugees lived separately from their former leaders. Some families in the camps retained their connections with former elders and *mukhtars* of their original communities who, being economically better provided, now lived in the nearby town or even in the Jordanian capital. The refugees called on them socially or to seek their advice and intermediation with the authorities (*wasta*). Several family heads in Jalazun reported occasional meetings with their former clan or village leaders in Ramallah in which "the general situation" and "the problems of the refugees" were usually discussed (J69, J102). The authority of these traditional leaders over former communities, however, was shattered beyond repair, and what loyalty they still commanded was often merely ritual.

The problem of the loss of social standing stemming from loss of land and disintegration of social structure did not apply equally to all refugees. While these problems were perpetuated in the camp, refugees who moved into the towns joined the general flow of urbanization and traded their particular problems for those of a much larger section of society. What is more, the younger refugees, who had never experienced life as part of the old social structure, were generally free of the distress that their elders felt at their drop in social status.

For those who remained in the camp the loss of traditional ties created more psychological burdens: it meant the loss of a sense of security and protection. In consequence, as Bruhns has already noted, the refugees came to regard their camp as a substitute for the traditional social framework and tended to evade direct confrontation with the society outside.[4] This tendency to regard the camp as a refuge was also the result of the fact that, as seen above, the refugees' sense of discomfort emanated largely from what they regarded as "nonstatus" because of their lack of land and property. It is true that their belonging to the camp structure accentuated their social inferiority relative to the society in the neighboring communities, but at the same time the camp itself constituted an immediate frame of reference within which they were somewhat freed from this burden.

Refugees in Jalazun explained their reluctance to move to the nearby town, even if it were economically profitable, by the feelings of loneliness, estrangement, insecurity, and inferiority that they anticipated in that alien environment. "I want to live among refugees" (J68) was a typical statement.

This frame of mind reinforced the insistence of the majority of the refugees on 'awda, i.e., full return to their places of origin, as the only solution to their problem, and their reluctance to consider any alternative solution that focuses on personal rehabilitation in the West Bank. It is one of several reasons why many refugees rejected the possibility of accepting housing in the neighboring town and declared that they would not agree to a personal settlement that involved leaving the camp. An UNRWA sanitation worker expressed this in the following way: "I am not prepared to move to Ramallah. I have no relatives in that town and have nothing to do there. I am afraid that my children will be beaten there and afterwards I'll regret having left Jalazun" (J70). The acceptance of any alternate settlement would necessitate making personal decisions and giving up the collective security of the camp's social framework. The following reply is characteristic: "I am one of many; if all go, I'll go too" (J14). The attachment to the camp and the insistence on 'awda are, consequently, complementary.

Moreover, the retention of refugee status served as a substitute for status based on ownership, for the refugee status indicated a *potential* ownership of property and land. Thus, it became necessary to adhere to 'awda and retain all the symbols that embody the right to return. The ration card that refugees hold was thus seen as a promissory note on this right. Hence the conviction that he who sells his card, sells his honor, or that "selling the card is like selling one's land" (J18/2, J64).

[4] F. C. Bruhns, "A Study of Arab Refugee Attitudes," *Middle East Journal*, 9 (1955), 130-38.

This motive for insistence on 'awda was embedded in the traditional outlook and was characteristic of older and rural refugees, not of the young and the urbanized (who have other motives for the same demand). Among youth who grew up in the camp, and could perhaps be expected to have stronger ties with it, no attachment of the kind described above could be discerned.

Identity Crisis

Identification is the function of a two-way relationship: it is determined by the individual's attitude toward the communities around him, and the attitude of these communities toward the individual. In the case of the West Bank refugees, the complexity of their situation was intensified by the fact that the refugees felt themselves to belong to a *number* of existing or potential entities without being able to visualize any of them materializing in the foreseeable future as a political community into which they could be fully integrated. These entities may be schematically described in the form of five circles, each containing the next, like nested Chinese boxes.

The largest circle is the Islamic world community—Islam being the religion of practically all the refugees in the camps. It could be seen clearly from their statements on this subject that for most refugees Islam is inseparable from their concept of a national community and that they expected to live in a community that was predominantly Muslim. Many refugees stated, as a matter of fact, that Arab unity is only a step toward Islamic world unity, that they wished to see the *shari'a*—the Islamic law which is the basis of the Islamic state—as the law in their political community, and that it is inconceivable that a non-Muslim would be allowed to serve as head of state in a community in which the majority is Muslim. To many of them Arabism and Islam are simply identical: "A Muslim who converts to another religion loses his national identity and stops being an Arab," said one of them (J29).

When the interviewers pursued this question, however, it soon emerged that this attitude was scarcely more than a profession of faith, and on more concrete issues the refugees opted for basically secular solutions. Given the failure of the modern pan-Islamic movement and the obvious unfeasibility of its program, it is not surprising that most refugees found this concept devoid of any practical implication for their political future.

The second circle is pan-Arabism. The refugees have always been described as ardent, perhaps the most ardent, supporters of Arab unity. They received with great optimism the tide of pan-Arabism, which reached its height in the second half of the 1950s. Refugees accepted the slogan coined by Nasser, "The way to (Arab) Unity is the way to Repatriation" (*Tariq al-wahda—tariq al-'awda*), as a working formula and expected their problem to be solved within the framework of a victorious unified Arab state.

It seems that the refugees did not later repudiate their loyalty to at least some vague concept of an all-Arab political community. Observing life in the camps, we found that this loyalty was being reinforced by a process of "all-Arab social mobilization," through such channels as higher education, inter-Arab political parties, mass communication, and employment opportunities all over the Arab world.

However firm the refugees' adherence to the vision of a unified pan-Arab political community, the interviews revealed that by the end of the 1960s real expectations had dwindled considerably. Asked whether they could envisage all Arabs living under one and the same government, most respondents rejected the idea as either impractical or undesirable. The disillusionment of the refugees with the leadership of the Arab world after the 1967 War stemmed not only from the failures of this leadership in the arena of the Arab-Israeli conflict, but also from what the refugees regard as its self-interestedness in dealing with their problem. A teacher in Dehayshe repeated the cliché on this subject: "The Arab states have traded in the fate of the refugees." Alienation from the Arab regimes was also expressed in the attitude to their broadcasts. Some respondents manifested impatience with the excessive verbiage of Arab mass communications, which sharply contrasted with the actual accomplishments during the 1967 War of the Arab regimes that controlled them. "We live in a world of theories, speeches, and talk," said a teacher in Jalazun, "we are fed up with them all" (J116).

The next circle is that of the Jordanian state, the polity to which the refugees had formally belonged for almost two decades. It is remarkable that the process of the "Palestinization" of Jordan—through the influx of Palestinians into the East Bank and their large-scale recruitment for the institutions of the Jordanian state—had not reached the point where it could produce new identity symbols or modify the existing ones. In spite of all the indoctrination efforts of the Jordanian regime to present Jordan as the legitimate heir to Palestine and as the homeland of Palestinians, the refugees simply could not regard it as their own political community. None of the respondents spoke of Jordan as "our country" or of its government as "our government." On the contrary, as will be shown, refugees still spoke of the "annexation" of the West Bank by Jordan. An UNRWA employee in 'Askar complained: "The Jordanians forced us to register as Jordanian nationals—unlike Nasser who did not impose Egyptian nationality on the refugees in the Gaza Strip."

The attitude of the refugees to Jordan was in fact a reflection of the attitude of the Jordanians towards them. Refugees complained they had been accorded the lowest status in society: "In Jordan the Palestinian stood in the second place and the refugees in the third" (J11). They bitterly recalled that their refugee status had been marked in their Jordanian identity cards. They felt discriminated against in the bureaucracy, in the police, and particularly in the army. Refugees could be appointed to the administration or could enroll in the officers' school only with very heavy bribes. Even then, mobility and integration were limited: "The Jordanians," said an assistant cook in an UNRWA installation, "trusted a Jordanian corporal more than a Palestinian officer" (J61). The interviewees claimed that Jordanian bureaucrats, policemen, and soldiers treated refugees with rudeness and brutality and, whenever possible, refugees preferred not to have any business with them. They felt that the Palestinian policemen, for example, treated them much better than the Jordanian policemen. The security authorities kept a close watch over the camps and several refugees reported having been arrested without trial, beaten, and humiliated.

There were also confrontations between Jordanian authorities and the refugees that erupted into violence. At times of antigovernment agitation in the towns of the West Bank, demonstrations were held in the camps as well. In an encounter with Jordanian troops in November 1966, a 14-year-old boy was killed in Jalazun, and his father in turn grabbed a gun from one of the Jordanian soldiers and shot the man responsible for his son's death. The boy's father and uncle were sentenced to death, but later their sentence was commuted to imprisonment. The refugees were collectively compelled to pay a burdensome ransom.

For the refugees, these were the main points of contact with the Jordanian state. In the study of socialization processes in modernizing states, it has been often noted that the teacher in the state school, the officer in the national military services, and the state-employed health and welfare worker all play an essential role in "nation-building" by personifying the political community to the masses. In the ordinary life of the refugees, these figures simply did not appear. Refugees had not been called to offer national service in the army. Primary education, health, and welfare services were supplied by UNRWA, not by the state. In a camp like Jalazun, even mail was not distributed by the postal service but by the local mukhtar of the refugees, who had to be tipped for rendering this service. The state was represented in the camp solely by the police station (*makhfar*). (It is interesting to note that in the case of students and teachers who *had* been affiliated with state institutions, a more positive relationship with the state could be seen—but in these cases it was more than offset by their political animosity to the ruling Hashemite dynasty.)

It may therefore be said that, between 1949 and 1967, these limits on social mobilization among the refugees in the camps failed to encourage the assimilation of refugees into a Jordanian political community.

The fourth circle, comprising all Palestinians, is of greater, probably the greatest, import. The roots of the concept of a Palestinian identity do not go back earlier than the British Mandate period and at the beginning of that period it was even rejected by the Palestinian Arabs themselves. But gradually such an identity gained ground and was expressed in a number of collective symbols.[5] Under the Jordanian regime it was latent, but it reappeared with new vigor after the war of June 1967. For the refugees, particularly the educated, their being is an existential assertion of the Palestinian identity. A teacher in 'Ayn Bayt Alma declared in a conversation at the local school: "I am a Palestinian, a son of the Palestinian people. This is how I identify my origin and that's that."

Some refugees spoke emphatically against the Jordanian annexation of 1949. A young construction worker in Jalazun protested against the usage of the term "West Bank": "There is no such thing as the West Bank," he said, "it is a part of Palestine" (J102). Although the degree of Palestinian identification expressed in the interviews differed sharply from one individual to another, none challenged it. Most refugees showed little enthusiasm, under the political circumstances of that time, for the idea of establishing a Palestinian state in the West Bank, but many of them nevertheless expressed their hopes for the eventual emergence of some kind of Palestinian statehood.

Whatever views they supported, politically minded refugees showed that they upheld their Palestinian identity and shared a whole set of symbols that express it. Asked about their heroes they mentioned a number of Palestinian field commanders of the war of 1948—to the exclusion of Jordanian or other popular Arab figures. Above all, it was the Palestinian fedayeen organizations that, through their actions and broadcasts, nurtured this attitude after 1967. A refugee might have had doubts and reservations about the fedayeen's tactics and programs, refused to be involved in their actions, or rejected their claim to represent all Palestinians, but he nevertheless deeply identified with them. Only very rarely would refugees denounce the fedayeen organizations or their political forums. For the

[5] On this question see Yusuf Sa'igh, *Filastin wal-Qawmiyya al-'Arabiyya* (Beirut: The Palestine Liberation Organization, 1966).

refugees, the fedayeen were an authentic Palestinian expression and a source of much-needed dignity and pride.

At the same time, there were indications that for the majority of refugees in the camps in 1968, the Palestinian circle, as a community to identify with, remained an abstract and problematic notion. Palestinianism—which had never been embodied in a polity and had little to build on in the way of distinctive cultural, historical, linguistic, ethnic, or other features—was not yet a crystallized concept or the predominant focus of loyalty. It was only for the "highly politicized" group[6] that Palestinian national solidarity was already emerging as a coherent reality.

In addition to the sociopolitical atomization that prevails in Palestinian society generally, a wide gap divides the refugee camps from the Palestinian villages and towns. It seems that it was easier for the refugees in camps to identify with a distant all-Palestinian organization than with the autochthonous Palestinian society around them. The refugees recalled the cool reception they had received from the local population of this region when they fled there. They often quoted the locals as having said: "You sold your land to the Jews, and now you come to squat on our land." Reportedly, villagers sometimes denied refugees entrance to their villages, while townsmen usually showed little interest in their hardships. An old refugee said: "If they had only been able they would have denied us even a glass of water" (J43).

The refugees also questioned the loyalties of the local society and rejected its leadership as mercenary. Some educated refugees not only expressed doubts as to the viability of a state in the West Bank, but also questioned the readiness of the Palestinians to assume the responsibilities involved in establishing it. They emphasized that the Palestinians had no real leadership and that their loyalties were divided among rival families, interests, ideologies, movements, and regimes. Palestinian society, they maintained, would have to undergo further social and political development before it could become a true nation-state.

Finally, the refugees themselves constitute the innermost circle. Consisting of fragments of the former Palestinian community, they are now scattered over a wide area. The elite among the refugees have found their way into the economic and political systems and establishments of some Arab states. The Arab states have not viewed favorably any independent initiative on the part of the refugees to form

[6] For classification of refugees by level of politicization, see Shamir, "Communications," p. 29, Tables 6 and 7.

their own political institutions, and the lower classes who remained in
the camps, certainly were incapable of such initiative.

Since 1948, the refugees have not managed to produce an au-
thoritative centralized leadership that would solely represent their interests and mold the refugees into an effective political group. Nor
have the camps produced any local leadership that might undertake
this task. This lack of leadership and autonomous organization was
deplored by many refugees, who regarded it as their principal failure.
This failure, they explained, caused the continued dependence on
other Arab leaders.

The refugee thus found himself belonging and not belonging to all
these circles. At the mosque he heard that he was part of the Muslim
umma. At the camp school he learned that there was the Great Homeland (*al-watan al-kabir*), which comprises all the Arab world, and the
Small Homeland (*al-watan al-saghir*), which is Jordan. He heard in
broadcasts from other Arab countries that his one and only homeland
(*watan*) was Palestine. He himself often used the term watan in its
original sense, that which it had before it came to denote the modern
concept of *patria*. For him the watan was still his place of origin, his
village or town in present-day Israel; accordingly, the fact that he still
lived in Palestine, whatever the degree of Palestinian identification
might be, often was not enough to make him feel he was within his
watan.

Political Inefficacy

The detachment of camp refugees from any polity was closely bound
up with another main source of anxiety in their lives—their total dependence on political forces over which they had no control. In discussing this problem, just as in speaking of their social status, the refugees tended to describe the difficulties in psychological terms: they
expressed feelings of frustration, helplessness, demoralization, and
fatalism that turned out to be linked with their view of their political
position. The interviewees indicated that they had no influence in
shaping their political environment and were inevitably the primary
victims of any unfavorable development. Some said that to them
being a refugee was like being the ball in the great Middle Eastern
game of political football.

This attitude was particularly strong among the refugees who were
classified in the study as "apolitical."[7] The individuals in this group
reflected a dual concept of society by which people are divided into
those who have power and exercise it at will, and simple folk like

[7] Ibid.

themselves who have no access to power. Politics is the domain of the former while the latter are their natural prey. It is the men in power who send people to war; wars, in their turn, breed hatred—and not the other way around. Politics causes suffering to people in the same way as do natural disasters, and it is just as meaningless. A 75-year-old refugee put it this way: "Just like the plants which blossom in the spring and wither in the summer, men fight each other and in the end they all die" (J47). Another applied this concept to the experience of the Palestinians: "Since the day the world was created everybody has been trying to dominate everybody. Rulers come and go. The British replaced the Turks, the Jordanians replaced the British, and now the Israelis have taken the place of the Jordanians; in their turn they too will be gone" (J73).

Their attitude toward political vicissitudes and the suffering they inflict was one of complete resignation. God created the world this way, and the faithful must accept it. Some based their attitude on the famous Islamic dictum (Koran: *Women*, 62): "O ye believers! Obey Allah and obey the Messenger and those of you who have command" (J115). They showed hardly any tendency to evaluate various rulers or politicians or to judge their actions. They did not expect much from them and accordingly did not feel that they owed them anything besides formal obedience. They wished to avoid any involvement in the political world—feeling that such involvement would endanger their security and would produce little good in any event. A baker in Jalazun said proudly, "Neither the British government, nor the Jordanian or the Israeli governments know my name" (J14).

Although the responses along these lines are deeply rooted in the traditions of Arab Islamic society, especially as found among the lower classes, and some are simply old formulae for evading political questions, their frequency in the camp was surprisingly high. This is all the more remarkable considering the cumulative effect of the pressure of Arab politics on the individual and the high rates of exposure to mass media.

The refugees' passive stance toward politics was, of course, also the outcome of political realities. After the collapse of the Arab Palestinian community in 1948, refugees began to regard themselves as completely paralyzed by objective circumstances. They turned their attention to developments in the Arab states and placed all their hopes on the emergence and growth of "truly national" forces there. The refugees in the camps usually regarded the final triumph of these forces as inevitable, and trusted them to do all that was necessary to bring about victory—beginning with the formulation of a conceptual approach and a general strategy and concluding with a successful implementation at the right time. Their own role, they considered, was

simply to wait for the day when the triumph of Arab nationalism
would do away with their problems. The detachment of camp life
from political realities accentuated the refugees' perception that these
political forces were largely beyond their influence and control.

The combination of sociopolitical atomization, demoralization, and
loss of self-reliance, on the one hand, and great confidence in the
forces of Arabism, on the other, helps explain why the refugees in the
camps reconciled themselves to all-Arab ideological formulae instead
of searching for a pragmatic solution based on their own direct experience and concrete interests. They adopted instead the vague concepts, phrases, and slogans disseminated by the principal Arab regimes, even though these regimes never translated their words into a
clear program of action aimed at achieving results in the foreseeable
future.

In Arab society, 'awda has become an article of faith from which no
Arab patriot is exempt. The adherence of the refugees to 'awda was,
therefore, not only a measure of their sense of grievance but was actually imposed by the entire political system of the Arab world, which
reached them via the communications media and other channels. According to these concepts, it is not the refugee problem that stands in
the way of a settlement to the conflict, but rather it is the conflict that
necessitates deferring the refugee problem until victory is achieved, at
some time in the future that no Arab regime can specify. Thus, the
attitude of the refugees gradually assumed the form of what
Eisenstadt and Peres called "messianic expectation"—the long-
suffering wait for redemption through the agency of external forces,
utterly beyond the control of those who wait.[8]

The emergence of the fedayeen movement, as the interviews
showed clearly, did little to change the attitude of the refugees in the
West Bank camps in 1968, beyond arousing in them one more "messianic expectation" that was focused on the world outside and that
bore little relationship to everyday realities. "The way of the
fedayeen" (al tariq al-fida'i) was added to the stock of conceptual approaches to a resolution of the conflict that dominate the refugees'
verbal attitudes. It did not provide them, however, with a program
oriented toward concrete gains that could be implemented in the
foreseeable future. The "fida'i solution"—by the admission of the
fedayeen leaders themselves—was conceived as a protracted process
that may take generations to achieve.

The camp became the embodiment of this "messianic expectation,"
and the idea was expressed in the life of the refugees in a variety of

---

[8] S. N. Eisenstadt and Y. Peres, "Some Problems of Educating a National Minority,"
(Jerusalem: The Hebrew University, 1968), mimeographed.

symbols. In their terminology, the refugees meticulously emphasized the impermanence of the camp. They referred to their dwellings as "shelters" and not as houses. Another symbol was the UNRWA ration card, which they viewed as a sort of passport to 'awda: "The card," said an elderly laborer, "is the refugee's certificate to return to his homeland" (J66).

Accordingly, most refugees found it difficult to refer, in the interviews, to 'awda in terms of a concrete reality. When they were asked to point out the practical ramifications of 'awda and to describe how it would affect their personal lives, it often turned out that they had never contemplated the problem in these terms. Many refugees insisted that a return to their place of origin would take place only under Arab rule and with the removal of the Jewish inhabitants, but they could hardly suggest a scenario that would lead to those conditions. Others proclaimed their readiness to return and to live alongside the Jews, or even under the Israeli government, but, again, the practical implications of such a solution remained shrouded: they were unable to depict the type of political community in which they would live after 'awda, what their social and political position would be, or, in the very first instance, how they would resettle in their former localities that had undergone so drastic a change since 1948.

This attitude of camp refugees toward their general problem differed sharply from their behavior in the economic field, or any other field of their daily activities where, in contrast to their popular image, they were no less dynamic than their neighbors. Moreover, refugees could often be seen making day-to-day decisions that were incompatible with their declared political positions.

The coexistence of two different planes of reality was a salient feature of refugee attitudes. Components such as the ideological, the collective, the formal, the political, and the ritual appeared on one plane, and components such as the pragmatic, the individualistic, the material, the personal, and the concrete appeared on the other. What appeared on the first plane was usually static, rigid, and absolute, whereas what appeared on the second plane permitted maneuvering, flexibility, and compromise. These two kinds of attitudes were compartmentalized in such a way that refugees could make everyday decisions and choose courses of action independently of their formally held beliefs.

The pragmatic attitude had been applied, for example, to the question of employment. When the Arab leadership, in the mid-1950s, objected to the refugees taking employment in the "host countries," thinking that such work would prejudice their status as displaced persons, the refugees opted for employment. They rejected the pressure of the Arab leadership and of the PLO after 1967, when they began to accept employment on a large scale from the Israelis. Also in contradiction to the adherence to 'awda, refugees encouraged their sons to take vocational training, which was oriented to a large extent toward emigration (mostly to the oil-producing countries) and not toward a return to the original villages and agriculture.

On this plane, the camp was not a symbol of impermanence but rather a residence with many recognizable material advantages: housing and social services were free; the cost of living was lower than in the towns, and UNRWA guaranteed a minimum subsistence. Once again, in the mid-1950s, when Arab political leadership opposed the substitution of concrete and brick structures for tents, the refugees preferred practical considerations over ideological ones and accepted the more convenient structures that were offered to them. After 1967, refugees expected the Israeli government to introduce improvements in the camp installations. Indeed, many interviewees asked for the installation of electricity and other services and even for the "development of industry" in the camp.

Mobility and Mobilization

Among the young and the educated, the gap between these two planes of existence diminished. In their case, the practical-economic considerations often drove them away from the camp and toward a greater involvement in Arab political-ideological life. For them, the camp was not a refuge from diminished social status, competing identities, or perceived inefficacy in achieving their major goals. Thanks, in great measure, to the educational network of UNRWA, many acquired modern skills that were in demand in the local towns and the neighboring Arab countries. It can be assumed that many of them would have migrated from their villages, as part of the general process of urbanization and emigration, even without the war with Israel. But the conflict had certainly increased the political implications of this mobility.

Perhaps the most important factor in political mobilization was education. This is not merely because education usually leads to greater political awareness and involvement, but also because the schools in which refugees were educated disseminated Arab political concepts. The schools of the camps, and to an even greater extent the non-UNRWA urban high schools that served the camps, were most effective in shaping the political outlook of the next generation. By 1967, most refugees in their twenties and thirties had been imbued with a complex attitude toward political issues.

Another potent instrument of political mobilization is the mass media. At the time of the interviews, no other communication medium approached the importance of the radio in the refugee's life. "Radio plays the central role in our life," said a teacher in 'Arub, adding that most of their information on world and Arab affairs came from the radio. Of the interviewees in the Jalazun sample, about two-thirds reported daily listening. The portability of the transistor radio further increased the exposure to this medium and allowed for listening in working hours as well. Many refugees reported listening four to five hours daily and some stated simply that they listened "all day long." A refugee in Jalazun said: "The transistor radio is my constant companion, it follows me everywhere. When I have no work, I go and sit under the olive trees and listen to my transistor radio" (J57).

Although antagonism toward the Arab regimes that control broadcasting systems was found to be widespread, refugees did find in the broadcasts elements with which they could identify—each one at his own level of political awareness. Among the interviewees, there were many who found the blend of religious and nationalist concepts preached by radio congruent with their own value-system and had little difficulty in internalizing it. The "mass appeal" of the messages transmitted by radio seemed to be greater among the uprooted refugees, with their shattered social structure, than it was among many other sections of society.

The cumulative effects of these mobilization factors accounted for the growth of a politicized element in the camp. All the "white-collar respondents" in the study belonged to this category. In the Jalazun sample a "highly politicized" group was identified that included all the white-collar employees in the sample. Practically all those with high school or post-high school education in the "Jalazun sample" appeared in this group, and they were all under 42 years of age.[9]

Conversations with them revealed that they were deeply concerned over politics. They felt that what happened in the political sphere had a direct bearing upon their welfare, dignity, and hopes for the future. They were keen observers of political developments and devoted much of their time to this preoccupation. Their attitudes toward the various elements of their political world were systematically organized within enduring cognitive systems.

Most of them adhered to formally structured ideologies that are recognizable to the student of Arab ideologies by the usage of typical terms, slogans, arguments, etc. In spite of the apparent diversity of the ideas to which these refugees attached themselves—ranging from Communism to "Islamic dynamism"—they shared a broad common denominator. They all upheld their Palestinian identity and supported the Palestinian struggle. All members of the group were pri-

[9] Shamir, "Communications," p. 29, Table 7.

marily nationalists who regarded the struggle between the Arabs and their enemies as the main axis around which politics revolves. Their ultimate aspiration was to see the Arabs emerge victorious as a political, economic, and cultural power. They were also concerned with questions of social justice, and even the "Islamic dynamists" among them supported some sort of social reform. Finally, they saw all these values as compatible with Islam—a claim that was maintained even by communists.

Some elements in the politicized group acted as links between the camp and broader sociopolitical circles. A number of channels led from the town to the white-collar workers in the camps: officials, social workers, clerks, nurses, teachers—most of them UNRWA employees. The UNRWA white-collar workers were characterized by a high degree of mobility; they were in constant contact with the administrative centers in the cities and with other refugee camps, and were sometimes transferred from one camp to another.

The highest degree of mobility was reached by the teachers, who constituted an important channel of communication between the camp and the external world. In order to be trained as teachers, refugees flocked from all parts of the West Bank to the few towns, such as Ramallah and Nablus, where teachers' colleges exist. Some of them received their diplomas after having spent years at universities in certain Arab states. Studying at home by correspondence was also popular, but these students still had to travel each summer to the corresponding university to take their exams. The assignment of teachers to their various posts further facilitated interaction. In a typical camp one or two dozen teachers could be found who commuted daily to schools located in other camps and villages or in the nearby town; a similar number of teachers from the outside taught in the camp's schools.

For the camps—socially segregated from both the surrounding villages and nearby town—these teachers constituted the most important links with the autochthonous society. Teachers from camps, villages, and towns met occasionally in coffee houses, private homes, or the school's club for informal, and sometimes even formal, discussions of professional, social and, above all, political topics.

Of particularly great consequence were the channels between these politicized elements in the camp and what Stockman called the "new leadership" in the West Bank towns.[10] This leadership consisted of young (many of them in their forties) professionals—lawyers, physicians, educators, engineers, and officials—all with the inclination to an

---

[10] I. Stockman, "Changing Social Values of the Palestinians: The New Outlook of the Arab Peasant," *New Middle East* (June, 1969), 18-21.

active political outlook. They depended less on property ownership or family affiliations than on their political connections, sophistication, activism, and devotion. Their apparent knowledgeability on subjects such as Middle Eastern secret diplomacy, attitudes of national leaders, clandestine political parties, and fedayeen activities gave them status. Their influence was then channeled to receptive groups in the area, including the refugee camps within the periphery of their towns.

The interviews brought out the fact that there existed in the camps a considerable "generation gap." The lives of the young and the educated, on the one hand, and those of the older and traditional, on the other, run in two different circles. As a 16-year-old tailor's apprentice put it: "Discussions and debates are conducted by the young refugees among themselves and the old refugees among themselves. There is no rapport between the two generations" (J28/4). The young regarded the old as lacking political awareness and national consciousness. Sometimes they referred to them as "Ottomans" (J76).

On the other hand, the older generation regarded the younger with wariness and some puzzlement, and deplored the loss of control over them. "The family heads and the religious leaders have no more influence over the youth," complained the camp director in Balata. Far from being influential, parents were sometimes influenced by their sons. One father not only admitted having learned much about politics from his son, but kept citing him on political questions. "Only on questions of religion do we differ," he said (J33/1).

Nevertheless, the rate of change should not be overstated. Despite all the factors working in the West Bank toward the integration of refugees into their environment, most refugees in the camps still lived with a sense of social degradation and political void. As has been shown, the camp framework itself intensified and perpetuated this condition—which seems to suggest that only dismantling the framework may remove this barrier to more effective integration.

PART TWO

Palestinian Urban Elites

Conflictual Pressures and Cooperative Interests: Observations on West Bank-Amman Political Relations, 1949-1967

by Shaul Mishal*

Introduction: New Incongruities

The new political order that emerged in the territory of mandatory Palestine after the 1948 War afforded the Jewish community in Palestine sovereign status and the Emirate of Transjordan political authority for its independence. The war, the movement of the Palestinian population to the West Bank, the control of the region by the Jordanian Army (the Arab Legion), and its annexation to Jordan in April 1950, transformed Palestinian-Jordanian interstate relations into intrastate relations. Jordan became a dualistic society with two main political communities: Palestinian and Transjordanian.

Annexation tripled the population under Jordan's rule. In 1948 Transjordan's population was almost 400,000; the annexation added 900,000 Palestinians, half of whom were inhabitants of the West Bank, while the rest were refugees.[1]

The existence of three societies—Jewish, Palestinian Arab, and Transjordanian—in two states—Israel and Jordan—increased the incongruence between the political boundaries fixed by the armistice agreement and those boundaries demarcated by the Palestinians' collective identity. The gap between the social and political boundaries

* I would like to thank the Lady Davis Fellowship Trust for the grant which made this research possible.

[1] In 1950, the United Nations economic mission to the Middle East gave the number of Palestinian refugees as 100,905 in the East Bank and 431,500 in the West Bank. The United Nations Relief and Works Agency Report estimated the total number of refugees in both Banks on August 31, 1950, as 485,000. See United Nations, *Assistance to Palestine Refugees: Interim Report of the Director of the United Nations Relief and Works Agency for Palestine Refugees in the Near East*, General Assembly, Office Records: Fifth Session Supplement No. 19 (A/1451/Rev. 1) (New York, 1951), p. 4; Aqil Abidi, *Jordan, A Political Study 1948-1957* (New York: Asia Publishing House, 1965), p. 63.

of the Palestinian community increased Palestinian desires, inside and outside the West Bank, to regain Palestine within the mandatory boundaries. Those desires, which contradicted Jordanian interests in the West Bank, provided a focus for potential conflict between the Palestinians and the Jordanian regime.

There had always been people within the Palestinian leadership, during the 1948 War and in the first years after the annexation, who challenged Jordan's activities on the West Bank and who sought to realize Palestinians allegiance through Palestinian, pan-Arab, or pan-Islam options. In September 1949, for instance, Palestinian leaders established, under the auspices of the Arab League, the ill-fated All-Palestine Government in the Gaza Strip to regain Palestine within the mandatory boundaries.[2] From 1954 on, political groupings in the West Bank like al-Ba'th and the National Socialists tended to realize their Palestinian allegiance through the pan-Arab option that was associated with the Nasser regime, although some saw it embodied in the Damascus Ba'thist regime. Others, like the Muslim Brethren and the Liberation Party, were willing to further their political desires in Palestine through activity in pan-Islam movements.[3]

Some of the Palestinian leaders in the West Bank, especially those who belonged to the Nashashibi faction, supported King 'Abdallah's political goal of incorporating Palestinian territories into this kingdom. Nevertheless, many of them tended to make their support conditional on his willingness to include all of Palestine in his kingdom and on the termination of the political independence of the Jewish community there. This attitude was most strikingly articulated by the Jerusalem and Ramallah delegates to the Palestinian Congress, also known as the Jericho Conference, which had been arranged by King 'Abdallah and his Palestinian supporters on December 1, 1948, to endow him with legitimacy for the annexation of Palestinian territories to Jordan. Only a few, however, like Shaykh Muhammad 'Ali al-Ja'bari of Hebron and Wadi' Da'mas of Beth Jalla wanted to give 'Abdallah a free hand in solving the Palestine problem.[4] Jerusalem and Ramallah's attitudes were reflected in some of the decisions of this conference. It was resolved, for example, that "the Conference sees Palestine as a single indivisible unit. Any solution incompatible

[2] On the formation of the All-Palestine Government (Hukumat 'Umum Filastin) see 'Aref al-'Aref, *Al-Nakba* (The Disaster) (Beirut: undated), pp. 89, 703-705 (Arabic); Abidi, *Jordan*, pp. 49-52.

[3] On the activity of opposition political parties in the West Bank in the 1950s and the 1960s see Ammon Cohen, "Political Parties in the West Bank Under the Hashemite Regime" in *Palestinian Arab Politics*, ed. by Moshe Ma'oz (Jerusalem: Jerusalem Academic Press, 1975), pp. 21-49.

[4] 'Aziz Shihadah, "The Purposes of Jordanian Legislation in the West Bank," *Hamizrah Hehadash* (The New East), 20 (1970), 166 (Hebrew) (henceforth *HMH*).

with this situation will not be considered final. . . . The Conference recognizes His Majesty King 'Abdallah as King of all Palestine and greets him and his gallant army as well as the Arab armies that fought and are still fighting in defense of Palestine."[5]

One can conclude that despite internal conflict over a broad range of issues, Palestinian leaders inside as well as outside the West Bank strongly agreed about the need to preserve the Arab character of Palestine. Consequently, they were unanimous in their desire for some Arab political authority that would include the whole territory of Palestine within the British Mandate's boundaries, though the exact form and operation of this authority was a subject of controversy among the various political streams.

In this respect, for the king's Palestinian opponents and many of his supporters, the struggle between the Arab and Jewish communities over Palestine was a fundamental issue that involved a total opposition of interests. But 'Abdallah, who sought cooperation with the Jewish community in Palestine and later with Israel, preferred to see the conflict as a problem to be handled by processes of political bargaining with due regard for the balance of power in the region.[6]

These opposing interpretations were mostly a result of the contradiction between 'Abdallah's political goals and those of the Palestinians during the Mandate period—a contradiction that stemmed from 'Abdallah's desire to prevent the creation of an independent Palestinian political entity in Palestine, perceived by him as a potential rival.[7] Contrasting evaluations of the outcome of the 1948 War reflected this contradiction. From the standpoint of the Palestinian Arabs, the war had ended in utter defeat. For King 'Abdallah of Jordan, however, it enhanced the political authority of Jordan and increased his military power.

These differing evaluations of the war's outcome critically affected the way each side defined its objectives in the conflict with Israel. King 'Abdallah tended to treat the Arab-Israeli issue as a residual border

[5] 'Aref al-'Aref, Al-Nakba, pp. 877-78.

[6] On the Israeli-Jordanian discussions in late 1948 and beginning of 1949 over the possibility of political settlement, see, for example, 'Abdallah al-Tall, Zikhronot 'Abdallah al-Tall (The Memoirs of 'Abdallah al-Tall) (Tel-Aviv: Ma'arachot, 1964), pp. 301-26 (Hebrew); and also Ben Gurion's interview with the Kimche brothers. "The negotiations reached an advanced stage. Israel agreed to grant Jordan a free port—at Haifa or Jaffa—and a corridor to it. The parties were discussing the width of the corridor when King 'Abdallah was shot and killed. . . . If 'Abdallah had not been murdered a full peace would have been signed between Israel and the Kingdom of Jordan." Jon and David Kimche, Mishnei Evrei Hagiv'ah (Both Sides of the Hill) (2nd ed. Tel-Aviv: Ma'arachot, 1973), p. 263 (Hebrew).

[7] For details on 'Abdallah's attitude toward the Palestinians see Joseph Nevo, "Midiniuto Hapalestinait Shel 'Abdallah 1945-1948" ('Abdallah's Palestinian Policy), unpublished M.A. thesis, Hebrew University, 1971, pp. 1-14, 27-46 (Hebrew).

conflict. The Palestinians, on the other hand, considered it a clash of destinies, which needed a radical solution.[8] In this respect, Amman defined its political objectives in terms of the actual needs of the existing Jordanian state, while the West Bank population defined its political objectives in terms of the realization of the national ambitions of the Arab people of Palestine. Amman tended to stabilize the status quo with Israel by embarking on a process of political arrangements. The Palestinian leaders in the West Bank strove to change the status quo by military means.

Under these circumstances one might have expected that the tension between Palestinian desires and Jordanian interests would increase separatist currents within the Palestinian community and would lead to a Palestinian appeal for an autonomous existence and to an inevitable clash between the two political communities. After all, Palestinians had become the majority in Jordan. They enjoyed socio-economic superiority and a high degree of political consciousness, compared to the Transjordanians. But in reality, there was no strong separatist current on the West Bank for most of the years of Jordanian rule. Instead, Palestinian leaders in the West Bank were willing to work economically and politically with the regime in Amman. Such cooperation with Amman existed despite the fact that it had a negative effect on the West Bank political leadership by restricting it to local bases and to day-to-day political issues.

Why were the Palestinian leaders willing to cooperate with Amman? What kind of political arrangements made the coexistence between the two parties possible? How did the Jordanian regime succeed in controlling the foci of power in the West Bank without facing any durable threat from the West Bank elite? This article will focus on these questions.

Cooperation as a Mutual Need

The tendencies toward moderation of conflicts and strengthening of participation and cooperation with the Jordanian center derived from mutual needs of the populations on the West and East Banks. The gap in the level of development of the two populations led to an increase in the sense of mutual dependence after the annexation and encouraged an exchange relationship between the two parties.

Different levels of modernization and social and political development had characterized the two political communities before and during the Mandate period. Palestinians ranked higher than Transjorda-

[8] On this distinction see Nadav Safran, *From War to War* (New York: Pegasus, 1969), p. 22.

nians on a whole series of sociodemographic measures: urbanization, educational level, health standards, exposure to communications media, and growth of income per capita.[9] Despite the West Bankers' higher ranking on these measures, however, their situation after 1948—the lost war, the proximity to a hostile and threatening Israel, the annexation by a suspicious Transjordan, and the lack of a border with any third party—heightened their sense of political dependence on the East Bank population. Lower political status was aggravated by the Hashemites' monopoly of both military and economic power, elements that sealed the dependence of the West Bank on Amman.

The West Bankers' superiority in socioeconomic development, coupled with their sense of political inferiority, provided the basis for exchanges with the administrative center in Amman. Palestinians supplied skilled manpower to fill vital economic, administrative, and public service functions. In return, Amman allowed them some scope for action and freedom of maneuver in both the political and economic spheres. This interdependence of the parties increased during the years of Jordanian rule of the West Bank.

The balance struck between conflictual pressures and cooperative interests also received ideological backing, as both parties tended to define their political identity flexibly rather than adhere strictly to such concepts as nation-state or national collective. After annexation, the Palestinians of the West Bank had at least three sources for shaping and defining their political identity: pan-Arab, Jordanian, and Palestinian. Their attachments to pan-Arab and Palestinian political symbols and beliefs were based on voluntary acceptance, while their affiliation with the political entity of Jordan materialized mostly in participation in its political life and in actual dependence on resources allocated by the Jordanian government in Amman.

Even the East Bank population, however, was ambiguous about the content of Jordanian identity. Some political circles in Amman did not accept the finality of Jordan's national boundaries. 'Abdallah still saw the realization of the Hashemites' political dream in a "Greater Syria" that would encompass Syria, Lebanon, Palestine, and Transjordan.[10] By sharing with the Palestinians an ambivalence about the

[9] On these sociodemographic measures as indicators of modernization in Middle Eastern states see Daniel Lerner, *The Passing of Traditional Society* (New York: The Free Press, 1958).

[10] On the correspondence between 'Abdallah and the British government on this matter see *al-Kitab al-Urduni al-Abyad* (The Jordanian White Paper) (Amman, 1947), pp. 19-23. On 'Abdallah's repeated attempts to achieve his ends in the 1950s, including his contacts with the Syrian and Lebanese governments, see his memoirs, *al-Takmilla min Mudhakkarat Sahib al-Jalala al-Hashimiyya al-Malik 'Abdallah Ibn Husayn* (A Supplement to His Hashemite Excellency King Abdallah Ibn Husayn's Memoirs) (Amman, 1951), pp. 307-308 (Arabic), and *al-Hayat*, February 18, 1958.

definition of collective boundaries, the Jordanians made way for various possibilities of practical cooperation, even with their rivals among the Palestinians. Thus, without unequivocally committing themselves to accepting the central symbols of the Jordanian government, West Bank leadership could cooperate with Amman in terms of "temporary arrangements," which could persist for a relatively long time.

The perception of temporary arrangements had two aspects. On the one hand, it reflected the feeling of the political elite in the West Bank that they were involved in an unresolved conflict. It thus entailed nonacceptance of the status quo, at least in terms of ultimate goals. On the other hand, defining the existing situation as transitory meant that West Bank political circles could reconcile themselves to it in the short run until they acquired the means for realizing their goals. The perception of transient arrangements, then, allowed not only for the existence of a *potential* for change, but also for the possibility of maintaining the status quo.

The course of coexistence between the two sides was thus influenced by two factors: an orientation that led to tensions and created a potential for conflicts, and mutual interests that brought out the cooperative elements. These mutual interests muted the conflicts to the extent that some disagreements could be considered artificial and bound to disappear when the final goals, which would embody some sort of Arab unity, were realized.

Manipulation and Cooperation

The willingness of the major part of the West Bank elite to cooperate with Amman on the basis of temporary arrangements meshed with the government's approach, which was to develop a policy for pacifying political groupings in the West Bank as long as this did not jeopardize control over the foci of power in the kingdom. In this sense, the cooperative tendencies among the Palestinian elite enabled the Jordanian government to exercise control over this elite without the necessity of direct confrontation. Some aspects of the Jordanian approach were reflected in the political patterns that emerged in appointments and recruitment, as well as in West Bank administrative structure and electoral regulations on the national and local levels.

Extension, Appointments, and Recruitments

The military extension of Amman's authority over the West Bank in May 1948 and the formal annexation in April 1950 entailed the appointment of members of the West Bank elite to senior posts in the central political machinery. Incorporating the elite into existing political institutions meant doubling the membership of the legislature from twenty to forty, with each Bank having twenty seats. Senate membership was also doubled from ten to twenty, with parity between the Banks.[11] West Bankers were also appointed by 'Abdallah to senior executive office, and the services and scope of matters dealt with by the executive were broadened. There were three West Bankers serving as ministers in the cabinet of Tawfiq Abu al-Huda appointed in May 1949: Ruhi 'Abd al-Hadi in foreign affairs, Khlusi Kheyri in trade and agriculture, and Musa Nasir in communication.[12]

Central authorities tended to place the West Bankers in senior offices and administrative posts that were directly related to West Bank problems. Palestinians were appointed provincial governors; to positions on the Israeli-Jordanian Mixed Armistice Commission; as representatives of refugee affairs; and in the economic, educational, and judicial sectors.[13] Palestinians also held senior administrative positions in the ministries of agriculture, economics, education, development, and foreign affairs.

The policy of appointments to senior political and administrative offices and doubling the membership of the representative bodies indicates just how important Amman thought the West Bank elite was to the extension of the center's control. Amman tried to appoint loyal men from families with high social standing and to support the election of cooperative candidates. Candidates for high positions in Jordan's administration included Shaykh Ja'bari; persons from the Nashashibi camp such as Raghib al-Nashashibi; Farid Arshayyid, a notable from Jenin; and Sulayman Taji al-Faruqi, originally from Ramleh, who had cooperated with 'Abdallah during the Mandate and helped to mobilize support for annexation among the Arab Palestinians.[14] Some top bureaucrats among the Palestinians in the mandatory administration were also candidates for senior posts in the Jordan government: the former district officer Gamal Tuqan as the chief administrator of the West Bank, the judge from Haifa Ahmad Halil as

[11] Although the number of seats was doubled and parity between the Banks instituted, the first Senate after annexation was composed of twelve Transjordanians and eight Palestinians. The Senate included as part of the Palestinian delegation two members, Tawfiq Abu al-Huda and Samir al-Rifa'i, who had lived in Transjordan since the 1920s and served in the Hashemite Royal Court. See *HMH*, 1 (1950), 303. For a list of the members of the first Senate, see Zvi Ne'eman, *Mamlekhet 'Abdallah leahar Hasipuah* ('Abdallah's Kingdom After the Annexation) (Jerusalem: Israel Foreign Ministry, 1950), pp. 71-72 (Hebrew).

[12] See Abidi, *Jordan*, p. 65.

[13] *HMH*, 1 (1949), 60.

[14] On their relations with 'Abdallah in the mid-1940s see Nevo, " 'Abdallah's Palestinian Policy," p. 39.

the governor of Ramallah and the northern areas, and the former governor 'Aref al-'Aref as mayor of Jerusalem.[15]

Most of the West Bank ministers had close ties with the Nashashibi camp and were themselves members of families of high standing in the West Bank. In Sa'id al-Mufti's first cabinet after annexation, for instance, Raghib al-Nashashibi was minister of agriculture; Ruhi 'Abd al-Hadi, minister of justice; Ahmad Tuqan, minister of public works and rehabilitation; Sa'id Ala al-Din, from a notable family from Ramleh close to Nashashibi circles, was minister of trade and customs; and Anastas Hananya, a Christian from a pro-Hashemite family in Jerusalem, was minister of transport and posts.[16]

The Nashashibi faction also figured prominently in appointments to the Senate in the first years after annexation. Of the eight West Bankers appointed to the Senate at that time, five were Nashashibi supporters: Raghib al-Nashashibi; Sulayman Tuqan, the mayor of Nablus; Sulayman Taji al-Faruqi; Farid Arshayyid; and the refugee leader from Lydda, Husayn Khawajah. Other members of the first Senate were Shaykh Muhammed 'Ali al-Ja'bari, and Wadi' Da'mas, the Christian mayor of Beth Jalla. The only one not a member of the Nashashibi group was 'Abd al-Latif Salah, who became an open opponent of the Husaynis after annexation.[17]

'Abdallah also tended to use the appointments policy to placate or co-opt his enemies. Khlusi Kheyri, for example, was a member of the opposition Ba'th until 1952 when he joined the government as minister of economics and development in six of the next ten cabinets. Anwar Nusayba, a Husayni and secretary of the All-Palestine Government in Gaza, also found a place for himself in the new administration. So too did Husayn Fakhari al-Khalidi, who had formerly been a sharp critic of 'Abdallah's Palestine policy.[18]

The appointments policy did not, however, mean that the regime was allowing any real shift of power to the West Bank. Although they represented the majority of the population, West Bank representatives were never allowed to constitute the majority in such bodies as the Senate, the House of Representatives, or the cabinet.[19] Amman was also very selective in its appointments. West Bankers held most of the economic portfolios—rehabilitation, construction, economy, and

[15] Ne'eman, 'Abdallah's Kingdom After the Annexation, p. 24.

[16] HMH, 1 (1950), 303.

[17] Ibid., p. 302; Clinton Bailey, "The Participation of the Palestinians in the Politics of Jordan," unpublished Ph.D. dissertation, Columbia University, 1966, p. 102.

[18] Ibid., p. 98.

[19] Even the principle of parity in the representation of the two Banks was applied only in the House of Representatives. It was not, in fact, maintained in the Senate or in the cabinet: in only three of the twenty-nine cabinets that served from 1950 to 1965 was there equal representation of East and West Bankers. Ibid., p. 91.

trade—almost continuously. The dependence of these ministries on the Court's decisions in key economic issues generally made it possible to neutralize the political potential inherent in them and prevent their being turned into foci of political power independent of the Court. Sometimes, in order to still complaints that they were not party to important decisions, West Bankers were given the foreign and defense portfolios as well. However important these ministries may have been, they did not constitute the real loci of power in Jordan; those were the offices of the prime minister, the deputy prime minister, the minister of the interior, and, later, the minister of information.[20]

Selective recruitment into particularly critical arenas of public service was an additional means to exclude the Palestinian community of the West Bank from access to the state's most important sources of power. Such selectivity is most strikingly seen in the recruitment to the Arab Legion. Since the Arab Legion was a volunteer army, the central authorities could carefully control the selection of recruits; volunteers could be easily accepted or rejected. Selection was guided by the principle that a hard core of elite regiments composed of Bedouin troops completely loyal to the center must be maintained.[21] Thus, despite the recruitment of Palestinians into the Arab Legion, the basic policy of the army command ensuring the Bedouin character of the crucial infantry regiments and motorized units did not change. From 1953 to 1956, seven of the Legion's eighteen regiments were overwhelmingly composed of Bedouins. Most of the recruits from the West Bank served as technicians, and those who did serve with infantry regiments were not generally combat soldiers.[22] In short, while trying to give the army a national character by recruiting Palestinians, the central authorities encouraged the concentration of *loyal* (East Bank) elements in key positions and in elite combat units. Selective recruitment helped preserve the Hashemite political center's continued control of the army despite changes in the political system.

The executive's discretionary powers were also reflected in the recruitment and assignment of workers to various posts in the civil service. In 1956, for example, there were 20,550 public employees; 6,500 of them were not assigned positions in accordance with civil service standards, and some 10,000 were temporary or contract workers.[23]

[20] Uriel Dann, "Regime and Opposition in Jordan Since 1949" in *Society and Political Structure in the Arab World*, ed. by Menahem Milson (New York: Humanities Press, 1973), p. 150.

[21] P. J. Vatikiotis, *Politics and the Military in Jordan* (London: Frank Cass, 1967), pp. 17, 26-29.

[22] Ibid., pp. 82-93.

[23] U.S. Department of Labor, *Labor Law and Practice in the Hashemite Kingdom of Jordan* (Washington, D.C., 1967), p. 23.

As far as the contract workers were concerned, it was determined that promotion depended on the level of the office and responsibility it bore. In fact, though, promotion was largely a function of the candidate's seniority and family ties, of his ascriptive traits rather than his performance.[24] A similar situation prevailed in relation to the other two categories of civil servants as well. Hiring procedures and salary levels in these categories were at the discretion of the department head or the project chief. Thus, there was often a difference between the salaries of holders of similar offices in different ministries. Through a network of ascriptive ties, the Amman authorities were able to allocate positions in a manner that underscored the disadvantageous position of West Bank residents.

The absence of uniform procedures in the public service in terms of broad discretion in hiring and firing also led to weakness in the staff units of the Jordanian administrative system. Frequent changes in personnel in the top echelons of the ministries led to uncertainties. Ministers often lasted less than six months with a particular ministry, with the result that policy changes were unpredictable and the execution of policy was emphasized more than the planning.[25] It seems that the executive preferred an improvisational approach rather than a clear policy that might have highlighted the unfavorable allocation of resources to the West Bank.

In short, the recruitment policy for both the armed forces and the civil service, as well as the selectivity in appointments to political positions, indicate the mechanisms of exclusion of West Bankers from key positions and potential power posts in the governmental center in Amman. Through a combination of cooperation and restrictions, the Jordanian policy toward the West Bank elite aimed to ensure that West Bank leaders had some share in government and would not be driven to overt opposition, but that East Bank elements loyal to Amman were in control of the most important foci of power.

The Administrative Structure: The Election Process
and the Lack of an All-West Bank Leadership

Amman's success in retaining control of key positions in the West Bank while avoiding direct confrontation was also largely a function of an administrative structure and patterns of political action that limited the possibilities for action in an all-West Bank political framework. Palestinian leaders drew their limited power mainly from their

[24] See Z. R. Ghosheh, "The Process of Administrative Change in Jordan," unpublished Ph.D. dissertation, Southern Illinois University, 1970, pp. 40-41.

[25] In the ministry of education, for instance, there were five ministers in the period 1957-1959. The ministry of transport went through ten ministers in four years; Ghosheh, p. 66.

local bases. Given the narrow local foundations of their economic and social standing, these leaders lacked the broad support needed to become national figures. Formal positions on the national, Jordanian level, such as seats in the Senate, the House of Representatives, or even the cabinet, did not constitute effective and fully legitimate means of expanding these power bases, partly because of the West Bank public's ambivalence about its own political identity and its relationship to Amman. Furthermore, most of the West Bank political leaders belonged to families with commercial and economic interests, and their property was affected by government policy. Their vulnerability to adverse policy decisions in Amman discouraged them from adopting positions that might lead to an open clash with the rulers of the country.

The inability in the Jordanian period to continue to use Jerusalem as a focus for a wider power base was also due to an institutional factor that diminished Jerusalem's status. While under the Mandate, Jerusalem had been the seat of government; now Amman was the sole capital.[26] Shortly after annexation, the Jordanian regime took steps to underscore Amman's centrality. District administrative offices were made directly responsible to the ministries in Amman, and the Jerusalem offices were given absolutely no authority in the rest of the West Bank.[27] Moreover, the authorities also decided to transfer all government offices to Amman by April 1951.[28]

In sum, despite the opposition of West Bank representatives and local organizations, such as the Jerusalem City Council, the Supreme Muslim Council, and the Chamber of Commerce, the Jordanian government was determined to transfer the center of governmental gravity from Jerusalem to Amman. Besides depriving the Jerusalemite leadership of the advantage it had had under the Mandate of being close to the seat of British administrative power, the downgrading of Jerusalem also tended to increase the possibility of leadership crystallizing in other local urban centers, such as Nablus, Hebron, and Ramallah. In this respect, Amman's policy intensified "localistic" interests and the rivalry among localities over the resources to be allocated.

The system of elections to the House of Representatives and the Jordanian Municipal Elections Law permitted the Jordanian central authorities to influence election results. These were also used by the

[26] On Jerusalem's status under the Mandate as a social and political center for the Arabs of Palestine see Ya'acov Shimoni, *Arviyei Eretz Israel* (The Arabs of Palestine) (Tel-Aviv: Am-Oved, 1947), pp. 385-88, 393-95 (Hebrew).

[27] See a decree of December of 1949 in Jordan, *Al-Jaridah Al-Rasmiyiah* (The Official Gazette), December 17, 1949.

[28] See *Filastin*, November 18, 1950.

government to strengthen parochial-local interests as against all-West
Bank aspirations. For the purposes of elections to the House of Representatives, the West Bank was divided into seven constituencies that
elected half the members of the House; these were Jerusalem-Jericho,
Hebron, Nablus, Ramallah, Bethlehem, Tulkarm, and Jenin. The
elections law stated that a candidate's victory was determined by the
proportion of the total vote cast for him, in accordance with the
number of deputies allotted to each region.

This system of seven constituencies seems to have helped Amman
authorities to obtain the election of the candidates they preferred
more than a proportional representation system would have done.
The latter system would have forced the political center to campaign
along a wider front and lessened its chances of success. This view
seems to be supported by the electoral defeats of the opposition Ba'th,
al-Qawmiyun al-'Arab, and the Liberation Party, even though they
could run legally in some elections and, in others, had candidates who
fronted for them. In the elections to the third parliament of October
16, 1954, for instance, when real party lists appeared for the first
time, the Ba'thists, despite an intensive campaign and the generous
assistance they received from Syria and Egypt, were totally defeated.
The pro-Hashemite Arab Constitutional Party more than doubled its
representation from eight seats in 1951 to seventeen in 1954.

The parity system in the representation of the two Banks in Parliament limited the influence of political currents in the more populous
West Bank, while overrepresenting the more sparsely populated constituencies on the East Bank.[29] In the 1950s, for example, Ramallah
district with a population of 120,000 and Jerusalem with 150,000 had
three members; while the southern district of Transjordan, which included al-Kerak, Ma'an, and Tafilah, had five members although the
population was only about 90,000.[30]

Constituencies of whose support the regime could be certain were
also overrepresented; the more sympathetic and loyal the inhabitants
of the constituency were to the regime, the more seats were allotted to
it in parliament. Thus, Hebron District with a population of 135,000,
which tended to support the Hashemite regime, was represented by
four deputies, the same as Nablus District with a population of
175,000.[31]

Another method the Jordanians used to influence elections was to

[29] *HMH*, 1 (1950), 214-15. In 1954, according to the Jordan Ministry of Economy,
the population of Jordan was 1,400,000, 550,000 of whom were in the East Bank and
850,000 in the West Bank. See Jordan, Ministry of Economy, *Statistical Abstract* (Amman, 1955), pp. 22-24; Bailey, "The Participation of the Palestinians," p. 118.
[30] Bailey, "The Participation of the Palestinians," p. 119.
[31] See, for example, *HMH*, 1 (1950), 214.

give soldiers the right to vote wherever they were stationed on the day of the election. This regulation was particularly important in the first three elections when a force of about 10,000 men was located in the West Bank. Even General John Glubb, referring to the elections to the third parliament, admitted that the names of pro-government candidates were marked on the lists given to soldiers at the polls.[32]

Amman also tried to influence elections for the local and municipal councils in order to keep opposition groups from challenging its policies. The 1955 municipal law states that the area of jurisdiction of a municipality constitutes a single electoral district. The minister of the interior, however, reserved the right to order it split into several districts and to determine the boundaries of the districts and the number of members each would elect to the municipal council.[33] Moreover, the central authorities had the right to appoint two members to the municipal council in addition to those elected by the voters and to appoint the mayor. On October 18, 1964, for instance, the minister of the interior appointed a long-time Hashemite supporter, Shaykh Ja'bari to the Hebron City Council and to the office of mayor.[34]

The government could also influence the electorate indirectly. The Municipal Elections Law restricted the suffrage to anyone who paid a "land or any municipal tax at a rate of at least one dinar during the twelve consecutive months preceding the election, on condition that if the property is held by more than one resident each of the property-holders pays his share."[35] As a result, only men with property or capital and those in possession of some asset for which they paid taxes could vote. The more traditional property-owners thus dominated the voting list. If they paid taxes for their tenants, they assured the right of the latter to vote and thus extended support for candidates they favored with voters outside their immediate clan or religious group. In this sense, the tendency for candidates' lists to allot representation to the various clans in the municipality suited Amman's policy of strengthening parochial-local interests at the expense of West Bank-wide ones.

[32] John B. Glubb, *Soldier with the Arabs* (London: Hodder and Stoughton, 1957), p. 351. Glubb claims, however, that no attempt was made to convince them to choose any particular candidate, although ". . . [i]t is possible that a number of soldiers voted for Taufiq Pasha's men when they saw them marked as 'Government Candidates.' "

[33] For details see Ori Stendel, *Habhirot La'iriyot Bagada Hama'ravit (1951-1967)* (The Municipal Elections on the West Bank) (Israel Defence Force, Judea and Samaria Area Command, 1968), pp. 2-3 (mimeographed, Hebrew).

[34] Ibid., p. 3.

[35] Article 12 in ibid., p. 6. The other conditions were that the voter be a male Jordanian citizen, aged 21, normal, and resident in the area of jurisdiction of the municipality during the twelve months prior to the election.

Under these circumstances candidates who were not of landowning families did not stand much chance even if they had other assets, such as education or a profession. When the trend for young, educated men to run for office emerged in the 1960s, the new candidates still tended also to be members of families with high status and prestige. Thus in Ramallah, the young and educated Nadim Zaru, a candidate of the 'Awad clan, one of the oldest families in the city, became a city councilor in 1964. In short, limited change took place permitting a different type of leader to be chosen without undermining the traditional patterns of local authority centering on the prestigious clans.[36] Acquisition of power through formal position in the government continued, for the most part, to be at the "pleasure" of the political groupings in Amman.

Only in the 1956 election campaign was there a serious attempt by West Bank opposition parties to turn the parliament into a source of real political power. This was perhaps the only election campaign in which the Amman authorities did not intervene blatantly, and, consequently, the elected parliament, not the Court, constituted Prime Minister Sulayman al-Nabulsi's cabinet's main power base. The dismissal of the cabinet in April 1957 and the dissolution of the parliament indicate the Court's fear of losing its control of foci of power. This fear was reflected in its decision to draw back from its attempt at democratization by taking a hard line against the opposition.[37]

Lacking a West Bank-wide authority, local West Bank leaders tended to operate more as interest groups attempting to influence Amman's policies than as integral components of the decision-making process. Both the pro-Jordanian West Bank leaders as well as those who were inclined to opposition activity tended to act as brokers between the Palestinian population and the rulers in Amman or the Arab regimes. The West Bank came to depend largely on sources of power beyond its control. True, Palestinians played ministerial as well as parliamentary roles in Jordan, but policy was the province of a small circle in the Hashemite administration composed almost exclusively of East Bankers of Transjordanian as well as Palestinian origin.[38] Only on the local level, and even then only to the extent that resources were actually controlled by municipal authorities, local chambers of commerce, and welfare organizations, could the West

[36] For more details see Benyamin Shidlovsky, *Ramallah al-Birah, Skira Hevratit Politit* (Ramallah al-Birah, Sociopolitical Survey) (Israel Defence Force, Judea and Samaria Area Command, 1970), pp. 62-63 (mimeographed, Hebrew).

[37] On the Court's activity against Sulayman al-Nabulsi's government see King Hussein, *Uneasy Lies the Head* (London: Heinemann, 1962), p. 133.

[38] For more details see Uriel Dann, "Regime and Opposition in Jordan Since 1949," pp. 178-80.

Bank leadership truly be said to have had some control over the allocation of resources.

By concentrating on material day-to-day activity, the pro-Jordanian
leadership in the West Bank denied itself the role of solidary leadership representing the political symbols of the Palestinian community.
This leadership, however, was not really in a position to fulfill that
function; its legitimacy, such as it was, was based mostly on the social
structure of local communities and not on more integrative nationalist
values or structures. In some respects the solidary leadership's functions were fulfilled by national Arab (non-Palestinian) leaders with
pan-Arab pretensions such as Nasser or 'Abd al-Karim Qassim, particularly as the Egyptian or Iraqi mass media overcame geographical
distance to encourage Arab national solidarity outside their state's
borders. It is true, all the same, that during periods of unrest in the
West Bank, there emerged a Palestinian solidary leadership comprised of intellectuals, many of whom had been educated in other
Arab countries. This leadership was ideologically articulate and held
radical social and nationalistic views. In the main, however, it remained a medium for transmitting popular identification to the
pan-Arab leadership rather than a solidary leadership in its own
right.

The weakness of this young intellectual leadership lay in its inability
to draw power either from its institutional or its socioeconomic status.
Nor, given the lack of wide party activity, could it find effective channels for participation in the existing political system. The only route
open to the solidary leadership, then, lay underground, inside or outside Jordan, in Palestinian or other radical bodies. The existence of
this additional route for political activity and mobility, moreover, re-
lieved, to some extent, the pressure for elite rotation in the West
Bank, where the pattern of local and day-to-day political activity continued to prevail. Like the traditional elite that collaborated with
Amman, however, the opposition that relied on radical Arab regimes
remained an object of manipulation by external forces rather than an
independent element controlling resources of its own.

Within Cooperation, Without Integration: Concluding Notes

The roots of the tacit acceptance by West Bank leaders of the status
quo in Jordan as a temporary arrangement lay ideologically in their
flexible definition of the political boundaries of the Palestinian collective. Their definition emphasized the transitory aspects of the Palestinians' present existence. These leaders were cognizant of Amman's
monopoly of both military power and foreign economic aid, which
underscored the subordinate position of the West Bank. By regarding

the situation of the Palestinians as transient, the West Bank elite could put off confronting Amman over issues that had a high potential for immediate conflict, such as the question of political identity and the nature of long-term relations between the two Banks.

Amman, for the most part, contributed to the perception of arrangements as temporary by developing a strategy for pacifying the West Bank political elite and seeking compromises with it rather than direct confrontation. Despite the emphasis on accommodation by the two sides, however, the suspicious attitudes of the parties toward each other limited the possibilities for transforming the relationship of coexistence into full-fledged integration. The coexistence patterns between Amman and the West Bank remained possible as long as many of the political groups in the West Bank fostered a tendency to consider the solution of the Palestine problem as a long-term and pan-Arab matter. The operative meanings of such terms as territory, sovereignty, and national leadership, which were common in the West Bank in the first years after its incorporation into Jordan, became increasingly ambiguous and tied to the mobilization of all Arab resources. Daily politics, at the same time, were carried on by local elites lacking legitimacy or efficacy on an all-West Bank basis.

The emergence of radical Palestinian groups outside the West Bank, particularly the Palestine Liberation Organization (PLO) and Fatah Organization in the mid-1960s, constituted a serious challenge to the locally based landowning West Bank leadership that was willing to settle for coexistence through acquiescence in temporary arrangements. In order to restore the Palestinians to a central role in the political and military struggle for Palestine, the radicals sought to bypass concern with temporary arrangements and focus attention on the long-range question of a solution to the problem of Palestine.

One can also argue that the Israeli victory in the 1967 War paradoxically helped these radical Palestinian circles by shifting the emphasis of Arab concerns from daily politics to the larger question of the fate of Palestine. The removal of the West Bank from Jordanian control broke down the political arrangements that had been the basis for the coexistence of the two Banks. This breakdown was moderated somewhat by the open bridge policy between the Banks after the war and the hope held by some of the Palestinians in the West Bank that the Jordanian regime would help them extricate themselves from Israeli rule. Nevertheless, the desire to force the Israelis out of the West Bank reopened the entire Palestine question. New leaders raised alternatives that involved a radical departure from a Jordanian solution, namely, a return to the temporary arrangements of the past. Among these alternatives was the idea of Palestinian sovereignty in the West Bank, necessitating a departure from a purely localistic leadership.

CHAPTER 5

Politics and Social Change
in the West Bank Since 1967

by Mark Heller

Introduction

At the conclusion of the June War in 1967, the political elite of the
West Bank (those preeminent in its public affairs and its interactions
with outside forces) still consisted largely of notables drawn from the
historically prominent families that had long dominated Palestinian
politics. The basis of state power, however, had changed significantly
from the mandatory period. In the years 1947-1949, the elite had
been reduced substantially—in overall numbers, in the economic resources at their disposal, and in the scope of their influence beyond
their home bases. And in the two decades of Jordanian rule, the West
Bank had experienced a considerable measure of economic and social
change that further diminished the basis of elite power. At the same
time, politics had become an increasingly autonomous sphere of activity, and the elite status of the notables had become progressively more
dependent on the explicitly political roles and resources conferred on
them by the Jordanian government. Their role in mediating relationships between the local population and the central government in
Amman became a major source of their continuing authority and
prestige. For these reasons, it is appropriate to refer to the political
elite that Israel confronted in the West Bank in 1967 as the "Jordanian establishment."

In the Israeli government, those involved with the occupation regime that followed, and particularly Defense Minister Moshe Dayan,
intended to create, through a civil affairs administration, the conditions of indirect rule that would best preserve relative stability. Therefore, Dayan instructed the officer commanding the West Bank, as
early as June 7, *not* to set up an Israeli administration, but rather to
use the existing apparatus.[1]

---

[1] Shabtai Teveth, *The Cursed Blessing* (New York: Random House, 1970), p. 32. On
the structure of the military government, see Nimrod Raphaeli, "Military Government

Dayan's basic approach, however, was not unchallenged in Israel. Many leftists had long believed that the Arab *effendis*—the big land-owners and merchants—were responsible for Arab hostility to Israel, because they had incited the population in order to divert resentment away from their own privilege and wealth. These Israeli elements would have favored efforts to "democratize" the West Bank. It is interesting that they were joined by some Israeli Arabs, perhaps because they were suddenly made aware of the relative social and economic "backwardness" of their relatives and friends in the West Bank.[2]

Administrative structures and statements suggest that, at the level of official policy, it was Dayan's approach that prevailed. The irony of the occupation has been, however, that it produced many of the very changes advocated by his challengers.

For the fact of the matter is that, since 1967, the West Bank has undergone a profound economic and social transformation. This upheaval is attributable, in part, to specific government action. Despite Israel's overtly passive social policy, some officials, especially in the field of agriculture, adopted developmental goals that stimulated far-reaching changes in the economic structure of the West Bank. But by far the greatest stimulus to change was a consequence of the occupation that was initially unintended and unanticipated, namely, the West Bank's massive exposure to and interaction with the economy and society of Israel itself.

The overall effect of this transformation has been further to diminish the political resources of the "Jordanian establishment" by redistributing economic assets and undermining the economic centrality of the traditional elite, and by challenging the traditional norms, values, and social relations from which the notables' preeminence derived. Economic and social change has led to a profusion of aspirations, a confusion of roles, and a diffusion of resources, which have encouraged demands for a political transformation by local counter-elites and enlarged the political public potentially receptive to these demands.

In short, the occupation has altered the local political configuration within the West Bank and complicated the dynamics of elite forma-

---

in the Occupied Territories: An Israeli View," *Middle East Journal*, 23 (Spring, 1969), 177-90, and "The West Bank: Governing Without Administration," *Public Administration in Israel and Abroad*, 10 (1970), 27-36.

[2] In the summer of 1967, the Israeli-Arab writer Rustum Bastuni urged the immediate "unilateral Israeli modernization" of West Bank society, *Jerusalem Post*, August 8, 1967. See also Muhammad Watad, "Israeli Arabs and the Generation Gap," *New Outlook*, 14 (March, 1971), 25-30, where Israeli policy is obliquely criticized for buttressing the position of the West Bank "feudal class."

tion. It has accelerated the secular trend toward elite fragmentation and differentiation to the point where the notables are now but one element, albeit an important one, contending for the role of political elite. At the same time, the occupation has revived the saliency of the Palestine-national issue, thereby contributing to the invigoration of a vehicle—the Palestinian organizations—for other counter-elites who are external to the West Bank, but internal to an emerging Palestinian political community. But continued uncertainty about the ultimate disposition of the area allows another external actor, Jordan, to continue to make its influence felt in support of West Bank allies.

This last factor retards, to some extent, the ongoing socioeconomic displacement of the traditional elite. But it is the constraint of occupation that actually prevents this displacement from realizing itself in a political sense, that is, from expressing itself in political-institutional forms.

As a result, real signs of change in West Bank political stratification are tentative, ambiguous, and often contradictory. A kind of balance seems to have emerged. The balance, because it is delicate, permits maximum impact of external factors. Any change in the present status of the West Bank, or any widespread expectation of imminent change, would probably enhance the influence of one or another of these factors, thereby deciding the contest for elite roles and resources.

Economic Developments Since 1967

Large-scale economic transformation of the West Bank was an unintended consequence of occupation, the result of interaction between the West Bank and Israel proper. More specifically, it was a spinoff of Israeli economic expansion, and the vehicle for this was the growing employment of West Bank workers in Israel's labor-short economy. The military government first endorsed this trend, and then encouraged it. By 1972, the consequences of work in Israel had become so great that the original concept of "normalization" was recast in a much more dynamic mold, and "economic prosperity" was consciously added to the longstanding triad of Israeli objectives: nonpresence, noninterference, and open bridges.[3]

In this whole process, the "Jordanian establishment" lost its role as the main channel for external economic inputs and much of its pivotal position in the economy of the West Bank. As the economic consequences of occupation came to contradict the conscious thrust of

[3] Israel, Ministry for Foreign Affairs, Information Division, *The Administered Areas: Aspects of Israeli Policy*, Information Briefing (Jerusalem, 1972), pp. 11-13.

indirect rule, existing social and political relationships were inevitably altered. In particular, post-1967 economic prosperity in the West Bank reduced the relative scarcity of certain resources (jobs, capital) and the centrality of others (land), control of which had previously endowed the traditional notables with their instrumental importance.

Of the factors stimulating economic growth in the early years, the expansionary fiscal policy of the military government was perhaps the most important. Total public-sector expenditures (of which municipalities accounted for about 15 percent) grew continually after 1967, but revenues grew even more rapidly, so that excess demand, which was financed mainly by the Israeli government, remained fairly constant in absolute terms and dropped as a proportion of Gross National Product from 11 percent after the war to about 5 percent in 1972/73. The ratio of public expenditures to GNP exhibited a similar decline, from about 19 percent in 1968/69 to 12 percent in 1973/74. By then, the fiscal role of the government under Israeli occupation had just about reverted to the level prevailing in the last period of Jordanian rule.[4]

In the first two years of the occupation, particular attention was paid to the problem of unemployment, which was severe even before 1967 and had been greatly aggravated by the war. Budgetary deficits were planned in order to finance unemployment-relief projects, especially roadbuilding, for which over 25 million Israeli pounds were allocated in 1967/68-1968/69. But as unemployment declined, the need for make-work projects disappeared, and essential public works were increasingly mechanized and often tendered out to local contractors.[5] Once the problem of chronic unemployment had been solved, fiscal policy was made to conform to the overall policy of "noninterference."

Of greater long-term consequence was the activity of the military government in the field of agriculture. Indeed, agricultural develop-

[4] Almost half of public expenditures in the West Bank under Jordan were related to defense and security. Since 1967, defense expenditures have been defined as part of Israel's public consumption. See Eliahu Borochov, *The Economy of the Arabs of Judaea and Samaria: Background Data* (Tel Aviv: Israel Defence Forces, General Staff, Chief Education Officer—Leadership and Information Branch, n.d.), p. 43 (Hebrew), and Arie Bregman, *Economic Growth in the Administered Areas, 1968-1973* (Jerusalem: Bank of Israel Research Department, 1975), p. 72.

[5] Israel, Ministry of Defence, *The Israel Administration in Judaea, Samaria and Gaza: A Record of Progress* (Tel Aviv, n.d.), p. 34. Evidence of declining unemployment includes the number of man-days financed by the Department of Public Works: 1967—1,354,500; 1968—1,350,000; 1969—600,000; 1970—125,000. Israel, Ministry of Defence, Coordinator of Government Operations in the Administered Territories, *Four Years of Military Administration, 1967-1971: Data on Civilian Activities in Judaea and Samaria, the Gaza Strip and Northern Sinai* (n.p., n.d.), p. 59.

ment in the West Bank has been little short of revolutionary. The immediate problem of agricultural surpluses in 1967 was solved by the rapid reestablishment of trade links between the East and West Banks. But Israeli planners were troubled by the uncertainty of the East Bank market, subject as it was to political vagaries, and they feared the effects of instability or depression on a sector that was the direct or indirect source of livelihood for the overwhelming majority of the area's residents. Nor was Israel itself able to absorb these particular surpluses, at least, not without undercutting the incomes of her own farmers, who produced many of the same commodities.

Therefore, Israeli advisers and staff officers encouraged the restructuring of agricultural production and the modernization of cultivation methods in the West Bank. Their efforts included research and surveys, demonstration plots, agricultural field days, the expansion of agricultural extension services, hiring of more agronomists and veterinarians, the provision of study and training courses, and visits to Israeli farms.[6] The receptiveness of West Bank farmers to change was indicated by their adoption of new cultivation techniques (growing under plastic, sprinkling and drip irrigation) and seed strains and by the increasing capitalization and mechanization of agriculture.[7]

Partly as a result of these developments, cropping patterns changed, considerable improvements in yields were achieved, and agricultural production was greatly expanded. Between 1967/68 and 1973/74, the value of agricultural output grew from I£35 million (as compared with I£45 million before the war) to I£885 million. And the fact that agricultural employment was practically unchanged in this period indicated a marked improvement in worker productivity.[8] Some aspects of West Bank agriculture, however, remained relatively underdeveloped, particularly irrigation. In 1973/74, 95 percent of the cultivated

[6] *Four Years of Military Administration*, pp. 40-43. See, also, Eytan Israely, "The Agricultural Development of the West Bank," *Public Administration in Israel and Abroad*, 11 (1971), 97-102. Israely was Staff Officer for the West Bank in the Ministry of Agriculture from 1967 to 1970.

[7] Purchased inputs rose from I£21.4 million in 1967/68 to I£90.1 million in 1973/74. Between 1967 and 1972, the use of fertilizers rose from 2,000 tons to 60,000 tons, and that of pesticides from 5,000 tons to 40,000 tons. Tractors in use rose from 147 to 1,049 in 1974. Israel, Central Bureau of Statistics, *Administered Territories Statistics Quarterly*, 5 (1975), pp. 52, 71; Israel, Israel Information Center, *Facts About the Administered Areas*, Information Briefing, 28 (Jerusalem, n.d.), p. 50; and Vivian A. Bull, *The West Bank—Is It Viable?* (Lexington, Mass.: Lexington Books, 1975), p. 86.

[8] The number of persons employed in agriculture in the West Bank was 32,700 in 1967/68 and 36,100 in 1973/74. Therefore, output per employed person rose from I£4,128 to I£24,515. Bregman, *Economic Growth*, pp. 52-53, and Israel, Central Bureau of Statistics, *Statistical Abstract of Israel*, 1975, pp. 704, 706, 710.

area was still unirrigated. Real output, especially of olives and field crops, is therefore subject to considerable fluctuations due to yearly changes in rainfall. Nevertheless, between 1967/68 and 1972/73, real output grew at an average annual rate of about 10 percent.[9]

The Israeli administration played a less active role in other sectors of the West Bank economy, and change was therefore less dramatic. Slow but steady growth was almost entirely a function of increased agricultural output, since processing of primary goods (foods, tobacco, olives for oil) continued to account for about three-quarters of industrial sales. Overall industrial production grew, but shortages of investment capital, skilled labor, and political stability prevented any major structural changes, such as scale, composition, or size of production units, in West Bank industry.[10] Indeed, industry's share of total national product actually declined (see Table 10). Consequently, no significant entrepreneurial or urban employing class emerged during these years. The number of West Bank workers engaged in industry rose from about 12,500 in 1969 to about 22,300 in 1974. But practically the whole of this increase was accounted for by workers in Israel. In the West Bank itself, industrial employment was virtually unchanged (1968—12,500; 1974—14,400).[11]

It appears that the fiscal policy and sectoral activity of the military government, especially in agriculture, had some positive effect on West Bank economic growth. But the significance of these developments pales in comparison with the major economic byproduct of Israeli occupation: the export of labor services to Israel itself.

[9] Bregman, *Economic Growth*, p. 53.

[10] In 1974, the index of industrial sales stood at 320, in current prices (1969 = 100). When this figure is deflated for price increases (excluding housing, fruits, and vegetables), the value of sales still rose some 27 percent in real terms, i.e., about 5 percent per annum. *Statistical Abstract* (1975), pp. 714, 694. Industry, however, continued to be based largely on processing of agricultural goods, carried out in small workshops using labor-intensive production methods. The dominant form of ownership remained individual, family, or partnership. Joint-stock enterprises were rare. Before the war, there were only two factories employing more than 100 workers; by 1972, there were still only five. On industrial scale, see Bull, *The West Bank*, p. 98; "Report on Two Years of Israeli Administration," *Israel Economist*, 25 (July, 1969), 203; Israel, Prime Minister's Office, Economic Planning Authority, *The West Bank: Economic Survey*, Appendices (Jerusalem, 1967), Appendix E-1 (Hebrew); and Ya'acov Lifschitz, *Economic Development in the Occupied Territories, 1967-1969* (Tel Aviv: Ma'arachot, 1970), pp. 133-36 (Hebrew).

[11] There is no detailed information on size of industrial establishments after 1968, but the absence of any significant change in scale is indicated by the ratio of paid employees to others (owners, partners, and unpaid workers, i.e., relatives), which was constant throughout the period under review (1969—1.3:1; 1970—1.1:1; 1971—1.4:1; 1972—1.3:1; 1973—0.9:1; 1974—1.2:1). My computations from tables in *Statistical Abstract of Israel*, 1969, p. 638; 1973, pp. 713, 717; 1975, pp. 704-706.

Table 10
West Bank Industrial Output

	1966	1969	1970	1971	1972	1973
Industrial output						
(I£ current millions)	—	33.6	37.9	51.0	62.8	76.8
as % of GDP	9.0	8.4	8.8	8.8	7.2	7.7
as % of GNP	7.9	7.6	7.4	6.9	5.5	5.6

Sources: Industrial output is extrapolated from a figure for 1971 in Bull, *The West Bank*, p. 50, using an index for gross revenue from industrial sales in *Administered Territories Statistics Quarterly*, 5 (1975), p. 44. GDP and GNP figures are from *Statistical Abstract of Israel*, 1975, p. 688, except for the 1966 figure, which includes East Jerusalem and is taken from Bregman, *Economic Growth in the Administered Areas, 1968-1973*, p. 44. Apart from Bull's figures, which are reproduced from reports of the Bank of Israel's Research Department and show output for only three years (in constant 1971 prices), I have found no raw data on industrial output or income in any of the sources. The figures given above should therefore be treated with extreme caution. Although they do appear to confirm the trend of declining or, at best, static salience of the industrial sector, which has been noted by many observers, they nevertheless can be used only to indicate orders of magnitude.

Like "open bridges," the movement of West Bank workers to Israel was a spontaneous development—an unanticipated solution to the problem of West Bank unemployment, which subsequently received official endorsement and encouragement.[12] At first, West Bank workers traveled to farms or construction sites near the "Green Line" and in Jerusalem. They were recruited by intermediaries and labor contractors (called "bosses"), many of whom were Israeli Arabs familiar with market conditions. But by the end of 1968, the number of workers had reached 5,000, and the government decided to set up labor exchanges in the main towns in an attempt to regulate the process.

After that, the number of West Bankers working in Israel grew dramatically. Some of these workers continued to go "unofficially," because they could avoid taxes and other deductions at source and receive a higher take-home pay. More apparently preferred to accept employment through official channels, in order to benefit from pensions, sick-funds, transportation, insurance, etc. But regardless of how they went, the trickle soon turned into a flood, as West Bankers sought first, relief from unemployment, and then the higher wages offered by the labor-starved Israeli economy. By 1974, the number of West Bank workers in Israel reached 40,800, that is, 30 percent of the entire West Bank labor force, and over half of all West Bank employees (see Table 11). In that year, despite the war of 1973, two

[12] Oded Remba, "Israel and the Occupied Areas: Common Market in the Making?" *New Middle East*, 26 (November, 1970), 35.

Table 11
West Bank Employment and Wages

	1968	1969	1970	1971	1972	1973	1974
Total Employment (thousands)	83.5	109.9	114.6	116.8	125.2	126.4	137.0
Of which employees	40.9	49.8	56.5	63.8	71.8	72.9	78.4
Of which in Israel	5.0	7.9	14.0	25.0	33.4	36.8	40.8
% of all employees	12.2	15.9	24.8	39.2	46.5	50.5	52.0
% of all employed	6.0	7.2	12.2	21.4	26.7	29.1	29.8
Employed in West Bank	78.5	101.5	99.9	91.2	90.3	87.8	95.0
Employees in West Bank	35.9	41.9	42.5	38.8	37.4	36.1	37.6
Average daily wage (I£) of all employees	6.5	6.7	7.9	10.3	13.7	17.9	25.3
in West Bank		6.0	6.9	8.6	11.5	13.9	21.6
in Israel		10.1	11.8	13.5	17.0	21.8	28.7
West Bank wage as % of Israeli wage		59.4	58.5	63.7	67.6	69.3	75.3

Sources: Israel, Central Bureau of Statistics, Statistical Abstract of Israel, 1969, p. 638; 1971, pp. 643, 636, 638; 1973, pp. 713, 717; 1975, pp. 704, 706. Bank of Israel, Research Department, The Economy of the Administered Areas, 1972 (Jerusalem, 1974), p. 9. Bregman, Economic Growth in the Administered Areas, 1968-1973, p. 37.

West Bank families out of five, on the average, were still sending one of their members to work in Israel.

The majority of these workers were employed in construction and, to a lesser extent, in industry. As their numbers increased, the occupational profile of the West Bank was radically altered (see Table 12). But since they were almost all commuters who returned home each night, they did not undergo all the stresses usually associated with occupational change in agrarian society—stresses that were in fact experienced by many Palestinian peasants during the British Mandate. And unlike migrant workers from other labor-exporting societies, they were not uprooted from familiar social contexts and confronted with the problems of permanent marginality in alien settings. In other words, there has been no major process of urbanization despite the population increase.[13]

[13] In 1972, towns accounted for about 25.9 percent of the population, as opposed to 26.9 percent in 1967 (excluding East Jerusalem). The decrease is probably explained by differential rates of emigration. The share of refugee camps also dropped, from 9.4 percent to 7.8 percent, while that of villages rose accordingly. Israel, Central Bureau of Statistics, Census of Population 1967, No. 1 (Jerusalem, 1967), p. x, and Administered Territories Statistics Quarterly, III, No. 2 (1973), Appendix A, pp. 77, 85, from which I have computed the distribution of population. However, it should be noted that many Arab workers have taken to staying overnight in Israel, illegally, in makeshift quarters, and returning home only at weekends. Most of these are probably Gaza Strip residents who

Table 12
Occupational Distribution of West Bank Workers (percentages)

	1961 all	1967 men only June	1967 men only Sept.	1969 men	1969 all	1974 men	1974 all
Agriculture	41.2	33.4	33.7	38.5	44.8	21.0	29.6
Manufacturing	10.7	14.6	11.5	14.1	13.3	17.4	16.3
Construction	10.7	15.1	12.3	14.9	11.9	27.5	22.4
Commerce	7.3	11.9	15.3	13.7	11.7	13.4	11.2
Transportation	2.2	6.6	5.1	4.6	3.7	5.0	4.1
Services	12.6	14.2	15.7	9.8	10.3	10.7	12.2
Other	15.2	4.2	6.4	4.4	4.3	4.9	4.2

Sources: Jordan, Department of Statistics, *First Census of Population and Housing*, Vol. 3: Economic Characteristics of the Population (1961), pp. 10-13; Israel, Central Bureau of Statistics, *Census of Population 1967*, No. 4, Labour Force, Part I, p. 8; *Statistical Abstract of Israel*, 1973, p. 714; and 1975, p. 702.

Nevertheless, the massive influx of workers to Israel and the virtual elimination of unemployment had a profound impact on social and economic patterns in the West Bank. The most startling effect was simply the tremendous income earned by West Bank workers. Between 1969 and 1973, wages earned in Israel grew from I£47 million to I£361 million, at which point they constituted over one-quarter of West Bank GNP.[14] As a result, about half of the real growth in GNP (at constant 1968 prices) over these five years—which amounted to almost 60 percent—was directly attributable to net factor payments from abroad, mostly wages earned in Israel. In addition, the siphoning off of workers to Israel created an unprecedented labor shortage in the West Bank itself, which led to a considerable rise in wages there.

Two conspicuous changes resulted from these economic developments. One was a marked rise in the general standard of living in the West Bank. Between 1968 and 1973, real GNP per capita rose by 71 percent, from I£603 to I£1,031. Part of this income was absorbed by higher savings, but most was used on personal expenditure, which rose by 56 percent in this period.[15] This newfound prosperity was re-

---

live farther from their places of work. See, for example,*New York Times*, April 12, 1973, and *Yediot Aharonot*, November 15, 1974.

[14] Bull, *The West Bank*, p. 52; and *Statistical Abstract of Israel*, 1975, pp. 692, 688. By contrast, factor payments from abroad—primarily wages—to the West Bank in 1966 amounted to approximately JD7.1 million (about I£70 million), that is, 10.5 percent of GNP. Borochov, *The Economy of the Arabs*, p. 17.

[15] *Statistical Abstract*, 1975, p. 688. The rate of gross private saving out of disposable income from all sources rose from 10 percent in 1968 to 22 percent in 1972 and then fell back to 16 percent in 1973 because of the war. In that year, absolute savings were I£223 million. *Statistical Abstract*, 1975, p. 691. However, much of this saving took the form of hoarding, in gold or foreign currencies, or was sent out of the area. Only a small part of it was used for private investment.

flected in statistics on population growth,[16] food consumption, housing conditions and facilities, ownership of consumer durables, access to medical and educational services, and other things.

The second important change was a redistribution of wealth in favor of workers and peasants. The increased demand for labor brought not only a rise in real wages, but also a rise in the number of wage earners per household. Consequently, many lower-class families began, for the first time, to enjoy some measure of prosperity and financial security. Meanwhile, the whole of the white-collar class has been relatively less favored by occupation-related developments.

Many merchants and businessmen profited from a generally rising volume of sales. But clerical workers, whose services were not demanded in Israel, suffered a considerable decline in earnings relative to those of industrial, construction, and even agricultural workers.[17] The situation of civil servants was better than that of other white-collar workers, because many of them remained on the Jordanian civil list and received a second salary from Amman. Nevertheless, not a few officials, particularly teachers, were forced to take second jobs in order to cope with inflation.[18]

Those hardest hit were large landowners and free professionals. The former have had to curtail the amount of land they work with hired labor and to offer better terms to their tenants. The latter have suffered a serious loss of income, certainly relative to other occupational groups, and probably in absolute terms as well. Many lawyers have been on strike since 1967, and benefits paid by the Jordanian Bar do not compensate fully for lost earnings. Doctors have had to

[16] Between the September 1967 Census and the end of 1974, population increased by 78,600, that is, at an average annual rate of about 1.7 percent. After 1968, when the postwar outflow of refugees stopped and the Israeli labor market was opened up, the rate was closer to 2.4 percent per annum. This contrasts with a rate of 0.85 percent per annum between 1952 and 1961. For post-1967 developments, see *Statistical Abstract*, 1975, p. 684. On the effects of emigration during the Jordanian period, see Naseer H. Aruri, *Jordan* (The Hague: Martinus Nijhoff, 1972), p. 67; Hashemite Kingdom of Jordan, Department of Statistics, *First Census of Population and Housing, 18th November, 1961*, Vol. I, General Characteristics of the Population, p. 29, and, for Jordanians abroad, p. 315; and "Palestinian Emigration and Israeli Land Expropriation in the Occupied Territories," *Journal of Palestine Studies*, 3 (Autumn, 1973), 110.

[17] Before the Six-Day War, average income of service workers was 128 percent, 131 percent, and 169 percent of industrial, construction, and agricultural workers' incomes, respectively. By 1974, these figures had dropped to 104 percent, 78 percent, and 109 percent. Figures for 1967 are based on average monthly incomes in Jordanian dinars, drawn from Israel, Central Bureau of Statistics, *Census of Population 1967*, No. 4, Labour Force, Part I, Table 8, p. 12. 1974 figures are computed from average daily wage in Israeli pounds, given in *Statistical Abstract*, 1975, p. 704.

[18] Interview with Farid Baraka, director of education, Tulkarm District, May 8, 1974. See also Shimon Shamir et al., "The Professional Elite in Samaria: Preliminary Report" (Tel Aviv: unpublished mimeo, June, 1974), p. A-11 (Hebrew).

compete with Israeli medical facilities, and the reduced scarcity value of their services has resulted in declining real incomes.[19]

These developments have been felt throughout the West Bank, but nowhere more strongly than in East Jerusalem. There, white-collar workers, self-employed professionals and, especially, top civil servants were hurt by Israel's annexation of the city and the abolition of its separate administrative status, and many in the tourist industry (hoteliers, guides, travel agents, though not souvenir shopowners or restaurateurs) lost business to Jewish concerns. Finally, East Jerusalem was subjected to the full weight of Israeli taxes and compulsory loans, but only the lower-income groups really benefited from improved social services.[20]

The effect of these changes has been to challenge traditional patron-client relationships. Because of the existence of alternative sources of employment, workers and peasants are less dependent on local businessmen or landowners for jobs in the private sector; nor do they require the intervention of local notables, politicians, or well-placed relatives to secure government positions. Furthermore, the increasing ability of workers, and especially peasants, to repay debts and finance consumption out of current income means that they are less dependent on large landowners, wholesalers, and businessmen for private credit (usually for short terms, at very high interest rates).

Developments associated with the occupation have significantly undermined the economic centrality of the traditional elite, although no *Arab* counter-elite has as yet been produced. The later years of the British Mandate were marked by similar trends. But since 1967, economic developments have combined with social and cultural changes to produce a potentially formidable threat to the continued preeminence of the traditional elite.

Social and Cultural Changes During the Occupation

Since 1967, many West Bankers have been exposed to a society whose operating norms and forms are very different and, in many ways,

[19] Interview with Dr. Hamdi a-Taji al-Faruqi, el-Bira, June 17, 1974. In March 1975, the general consumer price index stood at 363.1 (1968/69 = 100), but the index of doctors' services was only 297.3. *Administered Territories Statistics Quarterly*, V, No. 2 (1975), pp. 22, 26.

[20] For more on the special problems of East Jerusalem, see Gideon Weigert, *Israel's Presence in East Jerusalem* (Jerusalem: by the author, 1973); Eliahu Kanovsky, *The Economic Impact of the Six-Day War* (New York: Praeger, 1970), pp. 163-67; Muhammad Abu Shilbaya, "Jerusalem Before and After June 1967: An Arab View," *New Middle East*, 42/43 (March/April, 1972); and Michael Bruno, "Israeli Policy in the 'Administered Territories,' " in *Israel, The Arabs and the Middle East*, ed. by Irving Howe and Carl Gershman (New York: Bantam, 1972), p. 257.

more modern than their own. If the only carriers of these values had been the relatively few civilian and military representatives of Israel working in the West Bank, then the Israeli occupation would have conformed to the pattern typical of other colonial and military occupations, that is, one in which the sociocultural impact of the occupier is mediated and, to some extent, regulated by the existing elite. But in the West Bank, the exposure of West Bankers to Israel has been massive and unmediated. It takes the form of direct contact with Israelis, direct access to Israeli media of communication, and direct involvement in Israeli social and economic institutions. As a result, many more West Bankers, whose political and national hostility to Israel is in no way abated, are nevertheless estranged from the pre-1967 social order, and from the role of the old elite in it.

Changes in patterns of economic superordination have inevitably led to some changes in patterns of status and prestige, and stories do circulate in the West Bank about the newfound arrogance of the traditionally deferential "lower" classes.[21] Nevertheless, subjective stratification appears to have changed more slowly than income redistribution, and the hierarchy of status remains generally intact, although the basis of this status allocation has shifted to explicitly occupational and secular educational criteria. Teachers, for example, who have seen their earning power decline relative to that of blue-collar workers, still prefer to find some way of supplementing their incomes, rather than abandon the profession and the prestige it brings.[22]

This apparent stability of subjective stratification is, however, misleading. Israeli occupation represents a massive intrusion of Western modernity into the West Bank, with potential consequences not only for the pattern of social relations, but also for the political culture of the area. The totality of Israel's victory in 1967 and the search for an explanation led many West Bank intellectuals to a fundamental reappraisal of their own society, very much reminiscent of the post-1948 "disaster" literature and, indeed, of the earlier reaction of traditional Muslim societies to their first catastrophic encounters with Western power in the eighteenth and nineteenth centuries. As one prominent Ramallah attorney writes:

With the June War, all previous modes of life were shattered. The whole social structure was challenged. All previous values

[21] One example involves the newly prosperous plumber, who responds to the late-night summons of a physician by exclaiming, "Do you think I am a doctor? I don't have to come running every time someone sends for me in the middle of the night." Such stories may be apocryphal, but they gain currency in the retelling, and indicate a widespread perception of "what the world is coming to."

[22] Interview with Farid Baraka. See also Shamir, "The Professional Elite," Chapter B, pp. 14-15, and Part 2.

and convictions were put to the test . . . everyone could see the progress the Jews had been able to make. Something basic was wrong. The organization of the society, the values, the ideals were all upset.[23]

Such agonizing introspection, a result of the unique emotional climate of the first postwar years, was undoubtedly moderated thereafter; the 1973 War has certainly produced a countervailing trend. Nevertheless, the occupation and interaction with Israel continued to pose a serious challenge to the organization, values, and ideals of West Bank society.

That challenge obviously does not stem from the inherent attractiveness of Israel per se. Israel does, however, embody certain Western cultural forms and values that have long inspired sectors of the West Bank population and especially the counter-elite of intellectuals and party activists that grew up during the Jordanian period. In other words, the forces undermining tradition are not specifically Israeli, but they are greatly strengthened by the Israeli presence in the West Bank.

The most visible aspects of antitraditional behavior are externalities of life style, such as dress and personal appearance. But sociocultural influence quickly transcended superficialities and affected substantive modes of behavior as well. Arab youths began to envy the independence of young Israelis and their freedom from traditional family and sex-role constraints, and this has been translated into a growing restiveness against parental control. As a result, one often hears complaints, especially in Jerusalem and other towns near the "Green Line," about lack of discipline, lack of respect for elders or authority in general, insolence toward social superiors, displays of immodesty in public, and so on.[24] Such changes are associated with the declining strength of religion and morality in general, and many traditional figures, though they concede that this is a universal phenomenon, are particularly resentful of what they perceive to be the spiritually corrosive impact of contact with Israeli modernity.[25]

The rebellion against traditional forms often implies a wholesale re-

[23] Aziz Shehadeh, "The Palestinian Demand is for Peace, Justice and an End to Bitterness—," New Middle East, 35 (August, 1971), 22.

[24] Interviews with Edward Khamis, senator, Bayt Jalla, June 19, 1974, and Shaykh Muhammad Ali al-Ja'bari, mayor of Hebron, May 25, 1974. See also Amnon Rubinstein, "The Occupation: A Sort of Social Revolution," New York Times Magazine, May 6, 1973.

[25] Shaykh Ja'bari points to the establishment of insurance companies in Hebron after 1967 as an indication of peoples' declining reliance on faith. Similar themes were raised in an interview with Shaykh Sa'ad e-Din al-Alami, mufti and qadi of Jerusalem, on June 18, 1974.

jection of the hierarchical authoritarianism of traditional Arab society. Its standard-bearers are usually young intellectuals, professionals, and journalists, enabled by the circumstances of occupation and
the peculiar constellation of political forces since 1967 to launch a vociferous assault on the values of the old political order and the status
of the Hashemite-supported traditional elite.[26] Their ideological pre-
dilections are democracy in public life and egalitarianism in personal
relations, and in the diffusion of these values, so antithetical to the
traditional political culture, the occupation itself has played a significant role.[27]

Exposure to a wide variety of Israeli institutions has produced signs
of attitudinal change in a number of important issue-areas. The first
concerns status allocation. We have already alluded to the shift in subjective status stratification away from ascriptive criteria and towards
occupational-educational determinants. Even villagers whose fathers
owed their livelihood to *effendi* notables, and whose grandfathers were
judged by them in traditional courts, no longer automatically defer to
or concede without a struggle the superiority of family notables, clan
chiefs, and big landowners. Instead, they increasingly respect the authority of those "who know more," that is, the intellectuals in Palestinian society.[28]

But beyond this, there appears to be a growing aversion to any
symbolic manifestations at all of status differentiation, even when
based on functions, roles, or achievements. This sentiment—the ob-
verse of the declining respect for authority and discipline referred to
earlier—is believed by some to have been directly stimulated by
examples of Israeli behavior—open opposition to leaders, the critical
tone of the Israeli press, the relatively relaxed relations between army
officers and enlisted men, and the general informality of Israeli public
figures.[29] Whatever the cause, it finds its expression in the rejection of
elaborate honorific titles, signs of personal servility, the sycophantic

---

[26] For example, Joseph Nasri Nasr, "Palestinians Want a New Elite," *New Outlook*, 12
(February, 1969), 39-42; and, Ahmed Barham, Muhammad Nasiriyya, and Ibrahim
D'eibis, "Palestinian Forum—Three Palestinians Speak Their Mind," *New Middle East*,
31 (April, 1971), 37-39.

[27] This is acknowledged in observations such as, "Outside influences make Husayn
seem undemocratic," or "People see the West most vividly in Israel." Interviews with
Ibrahim al-Daqqaq, Jerusalem engineer, May 12, 1974, and Aziz Shehadeh, Ramallah
attorney, May 28, 1974. See also, A. N., "Letter from Ramallah," *New Middle East*, 8
(May, 1969), 5: "The living example of a democracy on their doorstep is becoming con-
tagious."

[28] I. Stockman, "Changing Social Values of the Palestinians: The New Outlook of the
Arab Peasant," *New Middle East*, 9 (June, 1969), 18-21.

[29] Cited in interviews with Muhammad Abu Shilbaya and Nihad Jarallah, president
of the West Bank Court of Appeals, June 4, 1974.

style of Arab media, glorification of leaders, and the cult of the individual, among other things.[30]

One important aspect of this general trend concerns the traditional status of government officials. By all accounts, the prestige of civil servants has declined since 1967. Economic relations have undoubtedly played a role in this change. Perhaps a political stigma attaches to being in the employ, albeit indirectly, of Israel. But the major factor appears to be the encroachment of Israeli bureaucratic norms and procedures. It would probably surprise most Israelis to learn that some West Bankers perceive the Israeli bureaucracy, in contrast to those they know in the Arab world, to be more imbued with a service ethos and more responsive to public needs.[31] In any event, Israeli control has resulted in changes in the operation of bureaucracy, and these, in turn, have depressed the status of West Bank bureaucrats. For one thing, Israeli officers have, to some extent, discouraged the practice of *wasta* (mediation by prominent personalities on behalf of their clientele), thus broadening access to government services while simultaneously undermining the view held by most private citizens of "government" as remote and omnipotent.[32] For another, local personnel have been subjected to more government control and procedural standardization.

These changes have minimized the discretionary latitude of officials, thus narrowing both the real and the perceived gap, in both income and power, between all-powerful official and private individual. They have probably improved the overall image of the bureaucracy in the eyes of the public, but they have also diminished the relative power and authority of the official class, previously drawn from the "Jordanian establishment," thereby depriving it of much of its traditional status.

The Political Configuration Since 1967: Conflicting Sources of Identity and Authority

The Persistence of the Traditional Elites

Even before its economic and social impact began to be felt, the Israeli occupation precipitated a reexamination of the bases of political

[30] See, for example, Nissim Rajwan, "The Turning Point in Judaea and Samaria," *Keshet*, 2 (Winter, 1971), 144 (Hebrew). Also, interview with Muhammad Nasiriyya, Jericho journalist, May 13, 1974.

[31] Interview with Zafir al-Masri, chairman of the Nablus Chamber of Commerce, August 10, 1975.

[32] One example, involving the unsuccessful attempt of a Ramallah merchant to secure reunification permits for seven local families, is recounted in David Pryce-Jones, *The Face of Defeat* (London: Weidenfeld & Nicholson, 1972), pp. 119-20.

stratification in West Bank society. Initially, this reexamination was simply a visceral reaction to the rapidity and totality of defeat—Husayn's failure to defend the West Bank discredited his regime and those in the West Bank associated with it. But so long as the reversion of the West Bank to Jordan seemed imminent, overt opposition to the political order was neither practical nor prudent. The apparent helplessness of other Arabs to end the occupation, however, gave rise to a determination, reflected in the growing prominence of formally autonomous Palestinian organizations, to break away from the pattern of Palestinian dependence on Arab regimes.[33]

In the West Bank itself, there were increasing expressions of dissatisfaction with the nature of the regime in Jordan and with the pattern of relations between the two Banks. Complaints about the first issue centered on the inability of opponents of the king or his policies to propagate their views, and on the selective conferment of state favors, political and economic, on a narrow, privileged stratum. Evidence of the allegedly unequal union between the two Banks included instances of economic discrimination against the West Bank (licensing policy, state expenditures and investments, etc.) and the use of the number "3" on passports of West Bank residents, presumably to facilitate the work of the security services.

Although prominent members of the traditional elite themselves had certain reservations about existing arrangements, they were, nevertheless, collectively identified with those arrangements and, therefore, implicated in the resentment of them. Thus, evolving political-national consciousness coincided with socioeconomic change to undermine the status of the traditional elite.

The Israelis made an important contribution to this development by denying the notables, except those who happened to be mayors, their historical role of political link between occupying power and local population. Efforts by West Bank notables at the beginning of the occupation to engage Israel in some kind of direct consultation over the fate of the area were consistently rebuffed or ignored. Two weeks after the war, for example, thirty West Bank notables reportedly offered to sign a formal declaration of cooperation with Israel in return for the establishment of an Arab state in the West Bank. But their offer was rejected by the prime minister's office. And in August of 1967, West Bank activists were forced to cancel plans for a consultative assembly scheduled to be held in the *Hamra* Cinema in East Jerusalem.[34]

As a result, all those Palestinian luminaries of the Jordanian politi-

[33] See, for example, Jamil Hamad, "Palestinian Future—New Directions," *New Middle East*, 35 (August, 1971), 17.

[34] *Jerusalem Post*, August 11, 1967.

cal system—senators, deputies, former ministers, governors, ambassadors—suddenly found themselves politically unemployed. Only the mayors retained a formal political role, and that was restricted to specifically administrative matters, of instrumental importance only to their own towns and the surrounding villages. The mayors alone could not create a West Bank political center because of their inability to transcend personal and regional rivalries and because of the refusal of Israel to sanction the establishment of a representative framework for the area as a whole.

Even the powerful mayor of Hebron, Shaykh Muhammad 'Ali al-Ja'bari, who was perhaps the most quintessentially traditional leader in the West Bank, could not overcome Israeli opposition to a territory-wide political structure. Requests from Shaykh Ja'bari and others for permission to convene conferences of mayors, to establish a "Public Affairs Committee," and to implement plans for local autonomy, were all denied by Israel.[35] It was only after the 1973 War that Israel agreed in principle to the idea of "home rule." By then, of course, this was seen by West Bank activists as a transparent attempt by Israel to promote a more pliable alternative to the resurgent Palestine Liberation Organization, and local elements no longer dared to endorse the idea.[36]

As a result, the traditional notables were stripped of many of the mediation and legitimation functions that they had carried out in the past. Even as the occupation diminished the instrumental importance of access to the Jordanian government (by substituting Israeli economic control and eliminating unemployment), it also undermined the effective authority of Jordanian officeholders (by raising serious questions about the validity of Jordanian rule in the West Bank).

If the occupation altered or eliminated some of the notables' traditional roles, it also created a new role—resistance to the occupation—that some of these notables tried initially to appropriate. In the immediate aftermath of the 1967 War, it was they who led the vocal opposition to Israeli rule. Because they continued to assume that they

---

[35] On West Bank mayors' conferences, see *Jerusalem Post*, August 18, 1968, December 9, 1969, and August 17, 1971. Shaykh Ja'bari's proposal for a "Public Affairs Committee" is discussed in *Ha'aretz*, April 17, 1970, *Yediot Aharonot*, April 24, 1970, and James Feron, "Time Stands Still in an Israeli-Occupied Town: Ramallah," *New York Times Magazine*, May 17, 1970, 33. The demand for local autonomy on a supramunicipal level was raised in the aftermath of the 1972 municipal elections. *Jerusalem Post*, May 2, 1972. On local organization in general, see Abraham S. Becker, *Israel and the Palestinian Occupied Territories*, Report R-882-ISA (Santa Monica: Rand Corporation, 1971), p. 85.

[36] The "political surrender" of West Bank leaders to the PLO and their supporters after 1973 is documented in Victor Cygielman, "Voices from the West Bank," *New Outlook*, 17 (August-September, 1974), 45-48. See also *Jerusalem Post*, December 3, 1974: "West Bank Cool to Home-Rule Feelers," and "The Home-Rule Debate."

were the natural spokesmen for the West Bank population and also perhaps because they instinctively recognized that they had most to lose from a termination of the "Jordanian connection," the notables signed petitions, transmitted manifestoes, and gave interviews demanding the withdrawal of Israeli forces and the restoration of the status quo ante.

Indeed, ending the occupation was a universally shared goal, and one that, so long as it automatically implied reversion to Jordan, contained no threat to those demanding it. But the notables, because of their vulnerability to economic countermeasures, were not prepared to provoke Israel beyond a certain limit, whereas those with less at stake were willing to undertake a more activist, even violent, campaign of resistance. Furthermore, it soon became increasingly difficult to advocate the return of the West Bank to Jordan. After the Karameh battle in early 1968, sympathy for the Palestinian organizations grew enormously. The notables may have subscribed to the emotional appeals of the organizations, but if the end of Israeli occupation meant the imposition of a regime controlled by Yasir Arafat, not to speak of George Habash or Nayef Hawatmeh, then it was not at all clear that the material interests of the traditional elite would not be better served by a continuation of the occupation. In the face of this quandary, the opposition of the notables became muted and cautious, and the function of opposition, like other functions, was shared with other elements, the notables retaining a progressively smaller share.

In view of these changes in aspirations and roles and in the economic and social relations within the West Bank, the fact that the traditional elite has not been swept away itself calls for explanation. Part of the explanation lies in the continuing ability of traditional ascriptive sources of prestige to persist in the face of ideological and structural changes, or, at least, to change more slowly than economic and social networks. But more important than cultural inertia have been the external inputs into the West Bank political system. For one thing, the ranks of the potential counter-elites have been thinned by emigration of upwardly mobile entrepreneurs, professionals, and intellectuals, whose opportunities remained constricted because of the pattern of economic growth since 1967.[37] Deportations of political leaders by Israel have had a similar effect, since they have tended to disrupt the radical elements more than the established families.[38] In addition, the

[37] Aside from the refugees of 1967 and 1968, another 30,000 Arabs had emigrated from the occupied territories by 1973. Most of these were said to be high school graduates and white-collar workers. *Jerusalem Post*, September 24, 1973.

[38] Estimates of the number of deportees naturally vary. According to Aref al-Aref, the late Palestinian activist and historian, there were already 115 by the middle of 1970. Feron, "Time Stands Still," 72. Two years later, an Israeli critic put the total at "over

Israelis pursued a policy of cultivating good relations with the notables of the area. Jordanian governors, parliamentarians, and palace intimates were denied formal authority, but Israeli officials did establish informal links with leading personalities in order to gauge "relevant" public opinion and create some channel of communication with the authorities in Amman.[39]

Finally, the Israeli administrative structure left the power of municipalities intact, and even enhanced it. And the municipal bodies provided an important mechanism for the preservation of the notable families' local influence and standing. Many routine administrative duties, which affected the daily lives of citizens, devolved upon municipal councils. Mayors also had the primary responsibility for putting the population's views before the military government. Most striking was the greatly increased economic saliency of municipalities. Israeli grants and loans accounted for part of the growth in municipal expenditures.[40] But local governments also served as the main conduit for Jordanian subventions to the West Bank, and local notables who dominated the councils consequently continued to play an important role as distributors of Jordanian largesse. In fact, it was the Israeli policy of "Open Bridges" that perpetuated Jordanian penetration of the West Bank and the replenishment of the traditional elite's waning assets. Most of these assets were financial. Intermediaries disposed of monies that could be used to reward supporters of Husayn, sustain those in prison or on strike against the occupation, influence elections, and co-opt potential opponents. If the aim of these transfers was to provoke massive noncooperation with Israel, then they were clearly futile. If they were meant to buy loyalty to King Husayn, in the face of demands for support from Palestinian or other Arab factors, then their effectiveness was not provable. But very substantial sums

---

100." Mordechai Nahumi, "Israel as an Occupying Power," *New Outlook*, 15 (June, 1972), 22. However, the *New York Times* (November 27, 1974) gave a figure of "about 70" up to the October War, and an additional seventeen in the year after. The Israeli authorities openly admit that deportation of those inciting resistance is a means to minimize disorder. For example, Brig. Gen. Shlomo Gazit, former Coordinator of Activities in the Administered Areas, interview in *Jerusalem Post*, June 9, 1972. In the first few years, deportees were mainly members of the "Jordanian establishment," but as the leadership of active resistance shifted to more radical elements, deportees tended to belong more to the "counter-elite." By 1974, those deportees were no less hostile to the Hashemites than to Israel.

[39] Some Israeli officials believed that there was no one else worth consulting. Interview with David Ariel, foreign ministry liaison officer with the military government, Jerusalem, January 30, 1974. Also, interview with Shlomo Hillel, minister of police, responsible for political contacts in the West Bank, *Davar*, October 6, 1974.

[40] Total municipal expenditures in the West Bank rose from I£13.7 million in 1971/72 to I£65.7 million in 1974/75. *Statistical Abstract of Israel*, 1972, p. 673, and 1975, p. 720.

were involved, and the pattern of funding indicated that political considerations underlay that funding.[41] It is therefore reasonable to infer that the Jordanians expected that control of these disbursements would enhance the influence of those upon whom it was bestowed.

The "Jordanian connection," however, did not benefit local notables only from a current material-instrumental perspective. Despite the growth of Palestinian sentiment, the Jordanian government was, for most of this period, viewed as the logical, if not most desirable, successor regime following Israeli withdrawal. Even after 1973, there was a general willingness, based on ideological (pan-Arab) or family and economic considerations, to maintain an organic link with the East Bank and even to acquiesce in the return of Hashemite rule, if that were the only way to end the occupation. And so long as the possibility of a return to Jordanian rule was not altogether precluded, the power of those well-connected notables and dignitaries—once and potential future officials—was not something blithely to be dismissed.

The effect of these inputs on the political resources of the traditional elite is difficult to determine with any precision. Obviously, neither Jordan nor Israel was capable of authoritatively allocating political values in the West Bank. To the extent that the traditional elite is seen to contradict the emerging political formula, based on particularistic Palestinian nationalism and dissatisfaction with the traditional social order, to that extent at least must its moral standing be diminished.

On the other hand, traditional cultural norms, though in a process of atrophy, have not yet been totally supplanted. Face-to-face contacts and personalized relations, for example, are still very important. Local notables still maintain a *dawrah*, and make provisions for it.[42] Town mayors, for example, typically work, not in private offices, but

[41] According to one source, the mayor of Nablus, Hamdi Cana'an, was entrusted with JD200,000-300,000 of Jordanian funds in the first 2-3 years of the occupation. Private information (the reliability of such information is obviously problematic). In 1970, payments to some West Bank notables who criticized Husayn's relations with the Palestinian organizations were stopped. *Amman al-Masa*, July 13, 1970. After the 1973 War, when sympathy for the Jordanian regime suffered another sharp decline, it was decided to resume payments to civil servants and teachers (these had been suspended about two years before), and in 1974, Jordan granted I£34 million to West Bank municipalities. *Ma'ariv*, November 23, 1973, and *Jerusalem Post*, February 13, 1975. In early 1977, when new developments (American diplomatic initiatives, rapprochement with Syria) made it apparent that Jordan, despite the Rabat conference, was not definitely excluded from plans for the disposition of the West Bank, payments to West Bank municipalities were again resumed. *Jerusalem Post*, February 1, 1977.

[42] *Dawrah* (circle)—the typical informal grouping of Arab society, in which friends, relatives, suitors, and supplicants associate around an influential notable. On the *dawrah* and clientalism, see James A. Bill, "Class Analysis and the Dialectics of Modernization in the Middle East," *International Journal of Middle East Studies*, 3 (1972), 426.

in large rooms. The mayor's desk is usually at one end or in a corner of the room, and a larger conference table may also be in evidence. But there are always chairs or ottomans lining the walls of the room. Friends, relatives, supporters, and retainers wander in and out to present problems or petitions, exchange gossip, or simply to sit and drink coffee, to see and be seen. Furthermore, the notables, even under occupation, can still "deliver the goods." Their material-instrumental resources are not entirely self-generated and have not been for a long time. Instead, they are largely derived from Israeli and Jordanian policies. But these policies contribute much to the survival of the traditional elites.

A final consideration, one that has played a role in the past, merits attention now as well: the ability of the leading families to adjust to new circumstances. These families, which had bought up land and joined the bureaucracy during the late Ottoman period, which had created parties, women's organizations, and trade unions during the Mandate, and which had entrenched themselves in the Jordanian government after 1948, now were confronted with the challenge of Israeli occupation and the rise of the Palestinian organizations. Many again demonstrated their adaptability by balancing all aspects of an increasingly complex constellation.[43] There is, of course, no evidence that such prudential flexibility was consciously orchestrated; it is as likely that such outcomes were the result of uncoordinated, individual decisions. Nevertheless, having different family members prominent in different political environments projected the image of a political division of labor within the family, which could be relied on, *in extremis*, for mutual support and protection.

The Rise of the Counter-Elites

Israeli occupation has provided both dangers and opportunities for the traditional elite in the West Bank. The dangers arise from the acceleration of social modernization and economic development, and from the stimulation of an emotional climate in which the identity-orientation of the old elite is discredited. The opportunities stem from outside influences allowing this elite to salvage some of its instrumental resources, thereby arresting, or at least retarding, the long-run deterioration in its standing.

There is, however, one critical resource which the traditional elite

[43] In recent years, for example, the Masri family of Nablus has included a member of the Jordanian Senate, a mayor on relatively good terms with the Israeli military government, and a family elder known to be acceptable to the Palestinian organizations. Similarly, the mufti and qadi of Jerusalem, a member of the Executive Committee of the Palestine Liberation Organization, and a member of Meditran (a society to promote Jewish-Arab friendship) all belong to the Alami family of Jerusalem.

could not exploit—organization. The inability of this elite to create effective organizational structures is not a new phenomenon. As in the past, it is explained by both external and internal factors. The main external constraint is obviously the capacity of the government (Israeli, Jordanian, British, or Turkish) to proscribe or disrupt political organizations transcending the local power bases of the notable class. The internal constraint is the disunity of that class, deriving from personal and family rivalries, regional orientations, and religious or other subgroup differences. The development of supraregional loyalties was discouraged by the administrative centralization and representational divisions of the West Bank under Jordan. These minimized the need for official contact between Nablus, Jerusalem, and Hebron, and maximized the bilateral ties between each of these towns and Amman. Furthermore, there were few West Bank-wide agencies of socialization. A "national" educational system, for example, wherein close links between individuals from different regions and groups could have been forged, simply did not exist. Instead, refugees usually attended elementary and secondary institutions run by the United Nations Relief and Works Agency (UNRWA). Local Muslims used the government school system, but Christians and leading Muslim families tended to prefer private schools, especially at the secondary level. The effect of the religious issue is uncertain. Palestinian nationalists prefer to denigrate the political relevance of sectarian differences, but there is some evidence that they still impede the development of an integrated political community and a cohesive political elite.[44]

In the past, the notables could compensate for their lack of organization by resorting to traditional control mechanisms (hierarchical families, pyramidal class structures and alliances, religious and moral authority, monopoly on higher education, communications, and economic assets), and relying on support from the central authorities. Furthermore, the notables had no particular need to mobilize active support, since their potential adversaries were equally disorganized and fragmented.

Since 1967, however, there have been significant changes in the criticality and distribution of organizational resources. While the old elite has been faced with declining social and political control, elements hostile to that elite have come to constitute a serious challenge, because of the political organizations they were able to create. Some

[44] In the aftermath of "Black September," Christian clerics refused to join Muslim leaders in condemning the actions of King Husayn, claiming that this was a "political" problem in which religious dignitaries should not interfere. *Ma'ariv*, October 9, 1970. It is difficult to determine whether events in Lebanon have exacerbated interreligious tensions.

were local residents who tried, in the aftermath of the June 1967 War, to revive or build up organized groups to oppose both the occupation and the Hashemite-supported elite. Party activists, for example, attempted to maintain their fragile prewar structures, but achieved no outstanding successes. A more interesting case involved the Palestine National Front (for the Occupied Territories).

Reports of a coalition of party activists and leftist intellectuals, referred to as the "National Front" or "National Union," first circulated in connection with the wave of strikes, demonstrations, and sabotage in 1967 and 1968. At that time, the National Front was already referred to as the main influence in the "Arab street" and was cited as an indication of the diminishing control of the local notables.[45] In fact, the "National Front" was then tied to Sulayman al-Nabulsi's "National Bloc," the East Bank successor of the National-Socialist Party that had served in the 1950s as oppositionist vehicle of the notables themselves.[46] And the "Arab street" was reacting, not to the organizational efforts of the National Front, but rather to outside stimuli, particularly the growing strength and prestige of the Palestinian organizations in the Arab world at large, and to specific incidents in the West Bank, like the textbook controversy in 1967 or the Aqsa Mosque fire in 1969. After 1970, when King Husayn crushed the Palestinian organizations and the West Bank experienced a real economic boom, the political effervescence in the West Bank subsided.

For the next three or four years, little was heard about the Palestine National Front. Following the October War, however, there was a resurgence in its activity, and many of those deported in 1974 and 1975 were linked with it. By that time the National Front was explicitly identified as the arm of the PLO operating in the occupied territories, and its revival corresponded with that of the PLO itself. Its evolution therefore provides an excellent illustration of what is probably the most important phenomenon in the West Bank since 1967—the externalization of political resources. Just as the traditional elite came to depend on the material assets generated by its connections with Jordan and, to a lesser extent, with Israel, so the counter-elites came to depend on the ideological and organizational assets derived from their identification with more powerful counter-elites leading the member-groups of the PLO.

It is arguable that these groups became the institutionalized expression of the emerging Palestinian identity by default, because Israel proscribed any political organization on the West Bank itself. In 1970, King Husayn succeeded in crushing the organizations in the East

[45] Jerusalem Post, November 1, 1968, and Ma'ariv, March 14, 1969.
[46] D. Farhi, "Society and Politics in Judaea and Samaria," Ma'arachot, 215 (June, 1971), 16 (Hebrew).

Bank, but only at the cost of arousing intense animosity in the West
Bank. Even before then, but especially afterward, and until 1973,
there were individuals in the area exploring the possibilities of "seces-
sionist" political organization. They included both local notables, with
the idea of regional autonomy, and younger counter-elites (in the
Palestinian National Alignment) with proposals for a Palestinian state.
In the face of opposition to the idea of a West Bank-based "third
force" by both the Hashemites and the Palestinian organizations,
mere indifference on the part of Israel would have sufficed to frus-
trate these efforts. In fact, Israel, too, played an active role in aborting
them.[47]

Meanwhile, PLO leaders were constructing an extensive political
infrastructure, including military and paramilitary formations, information offices, communications media, research and financial
bureaus, and diplomatic legations. In addition, the organizations
carved out a territorial base in the refugee camps of Lebanon, where
they administered rudimentary welfare, educational, medical, and
police services. In many ways, the PLO came to possess the attributes
of a semisovereign government, still dependent on the support or
toleration of other Arab governments and subject to their influence,
but nevertheless representing an alternative to the Jordanian-notable
alliance in the West Bank. This Palestinian quasi-government could
dispense rewards and punishments, promises and threats. It controlled material resources and instruments of coercion. In short, PLO
leadership was able to use the organization to compound its control of
material and moral resources in order to set itself up as a counter-
elite, and elite-presumptive of the West Bank. And since it could
therefore allocate resources to others, the PLO actually became a vehicle of upward mobility for political aspirants.

The extent to which the PLO superseded Jordan in this vital regard
is indicated by the behavior of prominent deportees from the West
Bank. Before 1973, most of these went to Amman, and some, like the
mayor of Jerusalem and the president of the Shari'a Court of Appeals, were given posts in the Jordanian cabinet. But after 1973, most
deportees preferred to throw in their political lot with the PLO; three
were co-opted to the executive committee of the PLO and were later
given higher offices.[48] Indeed, many had been so critical of the
Hashemite regime that they claimed to fear for their safety on the
East Bank, and asked to be deported directly to Lebanon instead,

[47] One of the potential leaders of a "third force" described the early Israeli attitude
with the rhetorical question, "Has Israel . . . allowed them [the Palestinians] to convene
and choose their own leaders . . . ?" Ayoub Musallam, "Peace Depends on Israel," *New
Outlook*, 11 (July-August, 1968), 30.

[48] *Jerusalem Post*, June 10, 1974; *Yediot Aharonot*, November 23, 1974.

where they were welcomed by PLO officials anxious to strengthen the organization's ties with the West Bank.

As a result of widespread diplomatic recognition, the stature of the PLO grew tremendously after 1973, and most West Bankers, including those who did not sympathize with the PLO, became convinced that a return of Hashemite rule to the West Bank had become much less likely. Public opinion in the West Bank, because of the vicissitudes of Palestinian political history, is very volatile and very finely attuned to shifts in probable political outcomes. Now that the future of the area had apparently been decided by more powerful forces, there were few in the West Bank prepared publicly to contest it.[49] Those previously identified with the PLO—mainly, but not exclusively, the counter-elites—benefited most from the turn of events, because they drew on its authority to enhance their own standing.

In one sense, then, post-1967 developments conform to previous patterns, in that the formation of political elites is heavily influenced by external factors. But what is important and novel about the Israeli occupation is the role of one of those factors—the PLO. Because it coincides with an emerging Palestinian identity fostered by the occupation, and because it has succeeded in fashioning coherent organizational structures, the PLO is able to portray itself as the wave of the future. Therefore, the PLO not only influences the distribution of political resources; it also appropriates for itself many of those resources and emerges as a potential West Bank political elite.

The Fragmentation of the Political Elite Under Occupation

During the years of Hashemite rule in the West Bank, differentiation of political activity was fairly simple. On the one hand, there existed regime-support activists. These were largely local notables— landowners and businessmen—who relied on material-instrumental resources, together with some measure of traditional status; who operated through the government apparatus, local councils, and informal networks; and whose main external referent was the Hashemite Court in Amman. On the other hand, there were regime-opposition activists. They were largely professionals and intellectuals who depended on ideological appeals (the force of ideas) and outside funding (usually channeled through Arab embassies and consulates); who operated in the Chamber of Deputies, the school system, the press,

[49] But the degree of enthusiasm for this change is reflected in the phrasing of responses to questions about the PLO's legitimacy. Those who are active supporters express their endorsement without equivocation or qualification. Those who do so reluctantly imply that such questions are redundant, if not silly. "If the United Nations and the whole Arab world have recognized the PLO, what does my opinion matter?"

and the parties; and whose external referents were pan-Arab forces ruling in Damascus, Baghdad, or, especially, Cairo and, to a much lesser extent, the Palestinian organizations. There was, of course, some blurring of this dichotomy. But bifurcation was the dominant characteristic of a relatively simple political configuration.

After 1967 this configuration was immensely complicated by new social, economic, cultural, and organizational forces unleashed by the occupation and especially by new developments outside the West Bank. The major change concerns the proliferation of external referents. The Jordanian government remained a potent factor in West Bank affairs. So, too, did some foreign Arab governments, indirectly, because of their involvement with the Palestinian organizations and their leading role in the confrontation with Israel, and directly, at least until the death of Nasser, because of their emotional appeal. But Israel, through her physical occupation of the area, also became an important actor. And the Palestinian organizations assumed an increasingly prominent role in West Bank attitudes and perceptions of the future.

The multiplication of external referents increased the axes of political activity. West Bank elites and counter-elites, though still in conflict over the distribution of political resources and the proper role of Jordan in the West Bank, suddenly discovered a common enemy—the Israeli occupation. Similarly, the Israeli authorities and the local notables and mayors, at odds over the character and duration of the occupation, nevertheless had a shared interest in minimizing turmoil and instability in the area. Political participants who had previously pursued mutually exclusive courses of action now found that their conflict was complicated by a convergence of views or interests on some issues. Therefore, elements of both the elite and the counter-elite found themselves acting in unusual roles or arenas and relying on unusual resources.

Within the traditional elite in particular, many individuals responded to the erosion of their past standing by changing their political allegiances and diversifying their modes of activity. Especially in the turbulent atmosphere beginning in 1974-1975, some notables came to acknowledge openly the primacy of the PLO. Others from prominent families participated, overtly or covertly, in the marches, strikes, and demonstrations that began to rock the West Bank.[50] These kinds of behavior represented an attempt by the elite to en-

---

[50] Business strikes were, in fact, a time-honored tradition in the West Bank. But more recently, notables (usually their wives or children) began to appear in the front ranks of protest demonstrations. See *Jerusalem Post*, December 12, 1974. Furthermore, there are reports that the fines of demonstrators and curfew violators are habitually paid by wealthy merchants or local chambers of commerce. *Newsweek*, May 3, 1976.

croach on the growing resource base and activity areas of the counter-elite. They were, in effect, a counteroffensive, whose impact was to diffuse the specific resources, types of activity, attitudes, and external referents that had previously distinguished elite from counter-elite. What emerged in place of this distinction and what seems now to describe the West Bank political configuration is a fluid mixture—one in which traditional "types" adopt modern political forms and radical postures, while counter-elites recognize the potency of traditional norms and the necessity of survivalist behavior.

Conclusion

In the broadest sense, the social and economic development of the West Bank since 1967 has continued to debilitate the political resource base of the traditional elite. Because of the peculiar pattern of socioeconomic change fostered by the Israeli occupation, however, an unequivocal and uniform modernization of political-cultural values has not come about. Political structures failed accurately to reflect changes in social and economic structures. The traditional elite, because of the persistence of traditional values and because of its own adaptability, managed to preserve a sphere of political power and status that was diminished, but still larger than its own resources would appear to warrant.

This was not due simply to a time lag, although that may be a contributing factor in the usually incomplete covariance between "substructure" and "superstructure." In the West Bank, chronology seems to play a secondary role in the attenuated nexus between the two, because external factors, by engendering a particular climate of political expectations, bypass that nexus and penetrate directly into the process of resource distribution. The sensitivity of the West Bank to external shifts in power relationships, because of its historical experiences and the impermanence of its present situation, has rendered the socioeconomic substructure increasingly irrelevant to its political superstructure. Recent changes in West Bank politics are therefore due more to changing identity symbols and expectations of the political public than to changes in its composition. And the present unstable balance is more a reflection of the relationships between Arab and other forces outside the West Bank than of the relationships of social forces within.

CHAPTER 6

The Dialectics of Palestinian Politics

by Donna Robinson Divine*

Few people seriously question the value of political independence. What is debated is the nature of the problems engendered by its absence. Various authors have argued that political subordination cultivates violence, social and economic dependency, or ethnic and tribal fragmentation.[1]

Given the historical record, it makes sense to begin an analysis of Palestinian society by examining the effects of conquest and political dependence. We want to establish the connection between these critical elements of the society and the particular texture of its politics. In spite of the semantic problems surrounding the term "society," there are ways for us to learn more about the social apparatus. It is not simply a matter of uncovering new data, but rather of looking more closely at the old. This paper is an attempt to transcend the bare facts of Palestinian existence by focusing on the factors animating Palestinian social life, and particularly by examining its social structure. Whatever the ultimate structures supporting the society may be, it is evident that it has been sustained, in some way, by external political powers, if only because Palestinians have been embedded in larger Islamic or Arab or European societies. Social and political arrangements have developed or been adopted in response to the presence of

* I want to express my gratitude to Gerald F. Hyman and Thomas M. Divine for their helpful comments.

[1] Frantz Fanon, *A Dying Colonialism* (New York: Grove Press, 1967); Frantz Fanon, *The Wretched of the Earth* (New York: Grove Press, 1968); Shlomo Avineri (ed.), *Karl Marx on Colonialism and Modernization* (Garden City, New York: Doubleday, 1968); one survey of the literature is contained in Chong-do Hah and Jeffrey Martin, "Toward a Synthesis of Conflict and Integration Theories of Nationalism," *World Politics*, 27 (April, 1974), 361-87; a critical view is taken by Anthony B. Smith, *Theories of Nationalism* (New York: Harper and Row, 1976); Elie Kedourie (ed.), *Nationalism in Asia and Africa* (New York: World Publishing, 1970); Stanley French and Andres Gutman, "The Principle of National Self-Determination," in *Philosophy, Morality, and International Affairs*, ed. by Virginia Held, Sidney Morgenbesser, and Thomas Nagel (New York: Oxford University Press, 1974), pp. 138-54.

non-Palestinian political forces in charge of Palestine or of the Palestinians.[2]

Political subordination entails, to one extent or another, the coexistence of different cultures, different institutions, and/or different values.[3] Far from failing to affect one another, two coexisting societies, though often antagonistic, interact, continuously and intensely. It is my thesis that this interaction provides the major dynamic of social change for the subordinate society. It is almost inevitable that the two societies would lay down different political goals, and thus varying standards of acceptable public and private behavior evolve.[4] Such variations cause tensions for the subjugated population, unsure of which standards to apply, which institutions to employ, which set of values to hold sacred. Such ambiguity tends to reinforce patron-client relationships, strengthening political hierarchy while often attenuating concern for the essentials of tradition.[5] Thus change can occur and does occur in these kinds of sociopolitical circumstances.[6]

[2] Some common surveys of Palestinian political development can be found in: William Quandt, Ann Mosely Lesch, and Fuad Jabber, *The Politics of Palestinian Nationalism* (Berkeley: University of California Press, 1973); Gerard Chaliand, *The Palestinian Resistance* (Baltimore: Penguin, 1972); David Pryce-Jones, *The Face of Defeat* (New York: Holt, Rinehart and Winston, 1972); Yehoshafat Harkabi, *Palestinians and Israel* (New York: John Wiley and Sons, 1974); Shlomo Avineri (ed.), *Israel and the Palestinians* (New York: St. Martin's Press, 1971); Hisham Sharabi, *Palestine Guerrillas* (Beirut: Institute for Palestine Studies, 1970); David P. Forsythe and J. L. Tauble, "The Palestinians and the Arab States" in *Ethnicity and Nation-Building*, ed. by Wendell Bell and Walter R. Freeman (Beverly Hills: Sage Publications, 1974), pp. 187-202.

[3] This notion stems from my reading on "pluralist" societies; a good summary of the literature appears in Leo Kuper and M. G. Smith (eds.), *Pluralism in Africa* (Berkeley: University of California Press, 1969).

[4] Clifford Geertz, "Primordial Sentiments and Civil Politics in the New States" in *Old Societies and New States*, ed. by Clifford Geertz (New York: The Free Press, 1963), pp. 105-57; Robert I. Rotberg, "African Nationalism: Concept or Confusion?" *Journal of Modern African Studies*, 4 (May, 1966), 33-46; Aidan Southall (ed.), *Social Change in Modern Africa* (London: Oxford University Press, 1963), pp. 3 and 5; Ronald Cohen, "Conflict and Change in a Northern Nigerian Emirate" in *Social Change*, ed. by George K. Zollschan and Walter Kirsch (New York: John Wiley and Sons, 1976), pp. 743-69.

[5] Cohen, "Conflict and Change"; and A. G. Frank, "Goal Ambiguity and Conflicting Standards: An Approach to the Study of Organization," *Human Organization*, 17 (1959), 8-13; Richard Rose, "The Dynamics of a Divided Regime," *Government and Opposition*, 5 (Spring, 1970), 166-92. Referring to Northern Ireland, Rose writes (p. 189): "The multiplicity of affiliations enhances the chances of cross-pressures in primary political loyalties. A Catholic will be cross-pressured by trying to combine prudential, common-sense judgments with religious and national affiliations. The character and intensity of those identifications implies a substantial amount of individual instability in crisis situations. The aggregate effect is to make it difficult for leaders (or opponents) of a political regime to predict the actions and reactions of those whom they seek to govern."

[6] From the perspective of social structure, they are "changes within type" not "changes of type." Bernard Barber, "Change and Stratification Systems" in *Social Change*, ed. by Amitai Etzioni and Eva Etzioni (New York: Basic Books, 1964), p. 203.

Palestinians have always had to adjust their ways to the demands and political needs of outside powers; they are no more free today from such dependence than they were during the days of the Ottoman Empire or the British Mandate. Such dependence on what have been perceived as alien regimes induced Palestinians to continue to rely on long-established social organizations and on traditional social structure. The result has been the endurance of several critical cleavages in society that one might have expected to disappear under the impact of rapid social mobilization and modernization.[7] Present-day Palestinian politics, though in some ways radically different from the politics of a generation ago, continues to reflect some of these longstanding cleavages. And the cleavages, in turn, have continued to pose an obstacle to political solidarity among Palestinian political organizations.

In this view, subjugated societies contain no single center, no paramount political power around which the whole system pivots. Rather society is composed of a number of power centers, organized in terms of a finely calibrated status hierarchy, whose power and influence change with time, with issue, and with their own mutual relationship. The political subordination of the Palestinians has at any one time forged two societies—the conqueror and the conquered—into a dialectical relationship whose stages can be made clear by looking at Palestinian Arab social structure. We will first turn to the Ottoman and Mandate periods in which five major social and political cleavages can be discerned: (1) shaykh-notable; (2) interfamily; (3) Jerusalem-other towns; (4) Christian-Muslim; and (5) intertribal. We will explain the nature of these cleavages and the impact of the ruling Ottomans and British on their development.

The Historical Cleavages

The formative period of contemporary Palestinian society occurred in the nineteenth century, when Palestine was part of the Ottoman Empire. Ottoman political structure consisted of a monarchy supported by military and civil bureaucracies.[8] But this governmental

[7] While it is true that independence does not eliminate longstanding social and cultural differences in a society and may, in fact, exacerbate these differences, Palestinian political leadership has not been affected by the experience of a struggle for national independence characteristic of many of the societies of Asia and Africa. Indonesia may serve as a model. R. William Liddle, *Ethnicity, Party, and National Integration* (New Haven: Yale University Press, 1970), p. 3.

[8] Stanford J. Shaw and Ezel Kural Shaw, *History of the Ottoman Empire and Modern Turkey*, Vols. I and II (Cambridge: Cambridge University Press, 1976 and 1977).

structure, applied and operationalized most fully in Constantinople, did not completely order the political system of Palestine.[9] The political powers Palestinians confronted in actual experience rested less on the often fragile arms of Ottoman military might and civil administration than on political and economic powers locally based and indigenously organized. Palestinians had their own great families—urban and rural; their own religious dignitaries—Muslim and Christian; their own military levies and tribal forces.[10] The Ottomans, in fact, usually sought control only of cities, and then only in times of turmoil or local challenges to their rule. Ottoman power almost completely stopped in the hinterland—the smaller towns, villages, and rural areas.[11] Day-to-day local administration, therefore, was shared by Turks and indigenous notables in major cities or socially prominent rural families elsewhere. Paralleling this bifurcation of political power was a split in control over religious life, part remaining in the Ottoman court hierarchy and part with local nobility, both Muslim and non-Muslim.[12] Thus, no uniform process of legitimizing a single source of political power existed for any Palestinian. It was a society in which the sources of power, the instruments of rule, and the bases of legitimacy were separately located, forming a sort of social and political balance of power.[13] Not only did Palestinians oppose Ottomans, Palestinians opposed one another, their rivalry rooted in the different social networks to a large extent sustained by the presence of Ottoman power.

In eighteenth-century Palestine, political and social power were concentrated in the hands of village and rural shaykhs whose families,

[9] Amnon Cohen, *Palestine in the Eighteenth Century* (Jerusalem: Magnes Press, 1973); A. N. Poliak, *Feudalism in Egypt, Syria, Palestine and the Lebanon, 1250-1900* (London: The Royal Asiatic Society, 1939).

[10] Jacob M. Landau, *The Hejaz Railway and the Muslim Pilgrimage* (Detroit: Wayne State University Press, 1971), Introduction. Albert Hourani, "Ottoman Reform and the Politics of Notables" in *Beginnings of Modernization in the Middle East*, ed. by William R. Polk and Richard L. Chambers (Chicago: University of Chicago Press, 1968), pp. 333-51. Abdul Karim Rafeq, "The Local Forces in Syria in the Seventeenth and Eighteenth Centuries" in *War, Technology and Society in the Middle East*, ed. by U. J. Parry (London: Oxford University Press, 1975), pp. 277-308.

[11] H.A.R. Gibb and H. Bowen, *Islamic Society and the West*, Vol. I, Part 1 (London: Oxford University Press, 1957), pp. 173-99.

[12] Bernard Lewis, *The Emergence of Modern Turkey* (London: Oxford University Press, 1968), pp. 95-96. Moshe Ma'oz, "The 'Ulama and the Process of Modernization in Syria During the Mid-Nineteenth Century," *Asian and African Studies*, 7 (1971), 77-88.

[13] Uriel Heyd, *Ottoman Documents on Palestine 1552-1615* (Oxford: Clarendon Press, 1960); Myron Weiner, "Political Integration and Political Development" in *Political Modernization*, ed. by Claude E. Welch, Jr. (Belmont, Mass.: Wadsworth, 1967), pp. 150-60.

owning large tracts of land, had been able to defeat the Bedouin or at least minimize the ravages of their raids.[14] Through this local social and political power, the shaykhs in turn managed the economy by dealing directly with agents of foreign trading and merchant houses. Family structure underpinned their power as generations of the same family maintained their position, serving as intermediaries between local inhabitants and all external forces. It is worthwhile to point out the longevity of these traditional arrangements for often disputes between powerful families reflected no more than the difference between the tribal confederations of Qays and Yaman, which trace their roots back to the birth of the Arab nation in the seventh century in the Arabian Peninsula.[15]

But social structure does change over time, and the family networks headed by rural shaykhs were not the only significant structural components of the Palestinian community. The administration of Palestine by shaykhs clearly did not provide the Ottoman Empire with enough financial and military benefits for the Empire to acquiesce forever in such an arrangement. In response to what were perceived by the Ottoman rulers as the sources of imperial weakness, Ottoman administrators undertook a series of reforms, collectively known as the *Tanzimat*, in order to govern the Empire more effectively, thereby insuring greater centralization and increasing tax revenues.[16] Through this series of reforms, local councils were established in regions of Palestine, empowered to levy taxes and bestow upon certain individuals the responsibility for collecting tax revenue in particular regions.[17]

Interested principally in greater income the Ottomans permitted the councils to award the position of tax collector to the highest bidders, thus assuring the central treasury of larger revenues. In the nineteenth century, because of the increased opportunities for becoming rich through foreign trade or through holding government offices, the tax-farmers were often urban notables rather than village and rural shaykhs. In an effort to weaken the military and financial power of the rural shaykhs, the Ottoman Empire encouraged this trend, hoping to reestablish its own imperial authority by dividing

[14] Some of these families were themselves of Bedouin origin, though they cooperated with the central powers.

[15] A. L. Tibawi, *A Modern History of Syria* (London: Macmillan, 1969), p. 28. Miriam Hoexter, "The Role of the Qays and Yaman Factions in Local Political Divisions: Jabal Nablus Compared with The Judean Hills in the First Half of the Nineteenth Century," *Asian and African Studies*, 9 (1973), 249-312.

[16] Lewis, *The Emergence of Modern Turkey*, pp. 106-28.

[17] Edward B.B. Barker, *Syria and Egypt Under the Last Five Sultans of Turkey: Experiences, During Fifty Years, of Mr. Consul-General Barker*, Vol. I (London: Samuel Tinsley, 1876), pp. 144-45.

local political and administrative power between rural and urban notable families.[18] The urban notable, the *a'yan*, became a powerful political and social figure in the Palestinian community, partly because the
Tanzimat program provided increasing opportunity for him to hold
important administrative positions in newly created provincial political structures. This in turn enabled the a'yan to increase his economic
power through administrative decisions that he helped fashion. For
example, after the Ottoman Land Law was promulgated in 1858, the
urban notables secured possession of vast tracts of rural land, becoming patrons of large numbers of *fellahin*, or peasants, who worked
small plots as tenant farmers.[19]

The interconnection between administrative, social, and economic
power in Palestine was cemented with the rise of the a'yan. The urban
notable constantly attempted to expand his power and to take advantage of every opportunity to do so. For that reason, notable families
were among the first in the Palestinian community to seek a "modern"
education in order to assure continued appointments to official
posts.[20] They proved to be the only people in Palestine who could staff
the councils of the Tanzimat, modeled as they were on Western
European administrative councils. The urban notables monopolized
the nominating procedure for members of parliament after the
promulgation of an Ottoman Constitution in 1876.[21] They directed
the major administrative units of Palestine—police, judicial, financial—as well as the central economic institutions, such as banking.[22]
They began to control the religious offices in Palestine, so crucial for
resolving disputes and collecting revenues.[23] Finally, they helped to
strengthen the military capacity of the Empire by insisting on training
in advanced military techniques and the use of sophisticated
weapons.[24] In short, Tanzimat changed the contours of social struc-

[18] Herbert L. Bodman, Jr., *Political Factions in Aleppo, 1760-1826* (Chapel Hill: University of North Carolina Press, 1963), pp. x, xi.

[19] Yehoshua Porath, *The Emergence of the Palestinian-Arab National Movement 1918-
1929* (London: Frank Cass, 1974), p. 12.

[20] Niyazi Berkes, *The Development of Secularism in Turkey* (Montreal: McGill University
Press, 1964), pp. 157ff.

[21] Robert Devereux, *The First Ottoman Constitutional Period* (Baltimore: Johns Hopkins
Press, 1964), Ch. V and VI.

[22] Moshe Ma'oz, *Ottoman Reform in Syria and Palestine 1840-1861* (Oxford: Clarendon
Press, 1968), pp. 88-89ff.

[23] Richard L. Chambers, "The Ottoman Ulema and the Tanzimat" in *Scholars, Saints
and Sufis*, ed. by Nikki R. Keddie (Berkeley: University of California Press, 1972),
pp. 33-47. I. M. Lapidus, "Muslim Cities and Islamic Societies" in *Middle Eastern Cities*,
ed. by Lapidus (Berkeley: University of California Press, 1969), pp. 47-80.

[24] M. E. Yapp, "The Modernization of Middle Eastern Armies in the Nineteenth
Century: A Comparative View" in *War, Technology and Society in the Middle East*, pp.
348-49.

ture in the Palestinian community by advancing the interests and
power of urban notables at the expense of the formerly dominant
rural shaykhs.

No longer was Palestine constantly prey to the raids of nomads,
with occasional relief provided only by local shaykhs. It had become a
more orderly, if not ordered community, with power shared by rural
and urban leaders. Both derived their power from external supports.
The urban notables could take advantage of the political arrangements established during the Tanzimat, demanding education and
the means to acquire technical competence in both administration
and military affairs. The rural shaykhs, who managed to retain control of large tracts of land and hence of extensive agricultural production, still provided important sources of taxes for the imperial treasury. Because of their economic positions and the associated status,
they could not be overlooked totally as local authorities by Ottoman
rulers.[25]

The rise to power of the urban notables itself created additional
communal divisions among the Palestinians. First, rivalry existed between the notables of different cities. Jerusalem notable families engaged in competition with their counterparts from Nablus, Jaffa, and
Acre for the most prestigious Ottoman posts. Jerusalem itself played a
special role in that competition. This city had been the focus of Palestinian attention from early times. Because of its religious status, the
Palestinians devoted much of their religious attention to its mosques
and to festivals involving its shrines. While this would seem to constitute a centralizing influence on the Palestinian community, in fact
Jerusalem did not foster political solidarity; rather it aroused the
jealousies of notables in other cities not favored by special status in
Islamic theology.[26] While prominent families from Jerusalem argued
that because of the city's importance theologically, it should fulfill an
equivalent *political* role, notables from other cities argued just as vo-
ciferously for curbing its administrative and consequent political
dominance.

Second, intense competition took place among prominent residents
of the same city. Different families of notables sought to obtain and
preserve certain influential and profitable administrative positions for
their own members and, as new families rose to participate in this
competition, the positions sometimes had to be divided among
greater numbers of people. This pattern, for example, is the origin of

[25] Of course, the patron-client ties between rural shaykhs and peasants, on the one
hand, and urban notables and peasants, on the other, differed. E. P. Thompson de-
scribes such differences in English society in his "Patrician Society, Plebian Culture,"
Journal of Social History, 7 (Summer, 1974), 382-405.

[26] Porath, *The Emergence of the Palestinian-Arab National Movement*, pp. 14-15.

the competition between the Husaynis and the Nashashibis, both
Jerusalem families and absentee landowners with aspirations toward
high political and religious positions.[27] Local family rivalries existed in
almost every other important Palestinian city, but the prestige of
Jerusalem, as a religious center of the Ottoman province, made the
competition among families there more intense and more significant
for the population as a whole.

Cleavages also existed between the Muslim and Christian populations. Christians, in the minority, sought some influence by securing
political or administrative positions in the Empire. But since under
Ottoman rule they had little chance of competing with their Muslim
counterparts, they often turned to outside powers, British, French, or
Russians, for security of life and livelihood in what they considered to
be an alien political environment.[28] Moreover, Christians were profoundly concerned with the rules governing religious worship for
non-Muslims in the Ottoman Empire. For long periods of time, they
were forbidden to display crucifixes, restricted from founding and
repairing churches, and, in general, encouraged to practice their religion in as modest and quiet a fashion as possible, in order to avoid
even the appearance of equality in status with Muslims.[29] This situation disturbed Christian Arabs, and especially their clergy, for when
the Ottoman rulers finally did relax their restrictions on non-Muslim
religious devotion, several Christian populations immediately sought
to emphasize their religious devotion through public religious
parades and new church construction. This activity upset many Muslims, who, in turn, rioted against Christians.[30] Such outbreaks then
reinforced the tendency of the Christian communities to seek support
from the European powers active in the area, and sometimes even to
adopt Western political techniques—such as political parties—for
their own ends. Muslims and Christians developed a different set of
primary political loyalties and different kinds of political organizations to express those loyalties.[31]

Finally, it is impossible to ignore, in outlining the types of fundamental divisions within the Palestinian community, the confrontation
between different tribal groups. In at least one major city, Nablus, the
family rivalries between the 'Abd al-Hadis and Nimrs, on the one
hand, and the Tuqans, on the other, reflect ancient loyalties to
Yamani and Qaysi tribal confederations.[32]

[27] Ibid.   [28] Ma'oz, *Ottoman Reform in Syria and Palestine*, pp. 189ff.
[29] Ibid., pp. 230-40.   [30] Ibid.
[31] Robert Haddad, *Syrian Christians in Muslim Society, An Interpretation* (Princeton,
N.J.: Princeton University Press, 1970).
[32] Ya'acov Shimoni, *Aravei Eretz Israel* (The Arabs of Israel) (Tel Aviv: Am-Oved,
1947), p. 17 (Hebrew).

It can be said, then, that the Palestinians lived in no single political order, and that political, social, and economic behavior were determined by the structures of local authority in particular regions. Political rivalries did not merely constitute competition for scarce resources or for political rewards, but represented a dispute over the basis of legitimate political power. The various families and religious groups did not simply challenge one another's economic or political position; they sometimes contested each other's right to hold any religious or political position at all. While the Ottoman Empire would appear to have provided a framework for their political competition, in fact it created no single or clear political environment. Tanzimat-created elites competed with pre-Tanzimat elites (educated vs. uneducated, urban vs. rural), all of whom, in turn, opposed pre-Ottoman Empire political leaders.[33] What was the appropriate political context, what were the acceptable rules and procedures, were issues dividing both the Palestinian elites and the Palestinian masses. Was the area to be totally Muslim-dominated or more religiously pluralistic? Was it to be an entity largely controlled by Jerusalem or by several different cities? Which prominent families were to exercise power? These were the unresolved questions. The Tanzimat, as the major Ottoman attempt to integrate the society, did nothing to dissolve these cleavages. The outcome of the imposition of Ottoman hegemony on Palestinian society was not an increasing unification in opposition to external control, but a deepening differentiation of its components.[34]

The disintegration of the Ottoman Empire brought new political and social changes to the Palestinian Arabs. These developments were a function of British hegemony and the Zionists' rival claim to Palestine. In spite of new institutional, cultural, and economic contexts, however, the traditional Palestinian political and social configurations continued to operate, though with different force. The differences were partly the result of differences between regimes.

On the surface, at least, Palestinians still had to contend with an imperial power that resembled the Ottomans insofar as the British hoped to rule Palestine efficiently and inexpensively.[35] Above all the British needed, as did the Ottomans, local compliance. This com-

[33] Moshe Ma'oz, "The Balance of Power in the Syrian Town During the Tanzimat Period, 1840-61,"*Bulletin of the School of Oriental and African Studies*, 29 (1966), 277-301.

[34] This is not an unexpected outcome given the pluralist nature of the society. See M. G. Smith, "Institutional and Political Conditions of Pluralism" in *Pluralism in Africa*, pp. 27-65.

[35] On this see Briton Cooper Busch, *Britain, India, and the Arabs, 1914-1921* (Berkeley: University of California Press, 1971); Elie Kedourie, *Arabic Political Memoirs and Other Studies* (London: Frank Cass, 1974); and Elie Kedourie, *The Chatham House Version* (New York: Praeger, 1970).

pliance was not easy to achieve, as many Palestinian political leaders
read acceptance of a British constitution for Palestine, with attendant
participation in governmental institutions, as capitulation to Zionist
ambitions for a Jewish state. Because of the persistent Arab rejection
of proposals for a common framework of government for Jews and
Arabs in Palestine, the British resorted to religious institutions as the
mechanism for securing at least tacit Arab support for their rule.
Elevating the position of mufti of Jerusalem to grand mufti, the first
British High Commissioner of Palestine, Sir Herbert Samuel, later
ensured the accession of the socially and politically prominent al-Haj
Amin al-Husayni to that post.[36]

England was a much stronger power than the Ottoman Empire had
been during its last centuries. Consequently, British rule of Palestine
endowed the imperial structures of government with much more
power and dignity, and one result was the exacerbation of the struggle for political power between segments of the Palestinian community. The election of al-Haj Amin al-Husayni as mufti, for example,
enhanced the Husayni family position significantly and qualitatively.
When the mufti succeeded in using his religious post as a lever to capture the presidency of the Supreme Muslim Council, the action appeared to confirm the worst fears of other notable families, who believed that political spoils were being distributed more unequally and
unfairly under the British than they had been under the Ottomans.
The balance between the Husaynis and the Nashashibis was upset in
favor of the Husaynis.[37]

The reinforcement of urban elite rivalry came to be the first and
most prominent political consequence of the British Mandate. Hence,
the imposition of British rule on Palestinian Arab society did not
undermine traditional elites or create totally new cleavages in the
community; it reinforced old divisions partly because it entailed so
much distinct and palpable political power and administrative authority.

Even the young Palestinian activists who began to agitate against
the British Mandate reflected the prominent family structure. These
people consisted, for the most part, of younger members of elite
families who would have acquired political or administrative positions
in the normal course of Palestinian politics. The British commitment
to create a Jewish national home impelled these young men to press

[36] Christopher Sykes, *Crossroads to Israel 1917-1948* (Bloomington: Indiana Univer-
sity Press, 1973), p. 43; Yehoshua Porath, "Al-Hajj Amin al-Husayni, Mufti of
Jerusalem—His Rise to Power and the Consolidation of His Position," *Asian and African
Studies*, 7 (1971), 121-56.

[37] *Palestine, A Study of Jewish, Arab and British Policies*, Vol. I, published for the Esco
Foundation for Palestine (New Haven: Yale University Press, 1947), p. 468.

for political power at relatively young ages. Forming organizations to strengthen their positions, the young activists created two famous groups, *al-Nadi al-Arabi* and *al-Muntada al-Adabi*. But in terms of the membership and leadership structure of Palestinian politics, these groups did not represent a new development in the community's politics. The first organization was led by members of the Husayni family, and the second, by members of the Nashashibis. Immediately after the end of World War I, both groups urged that Palestine be incorporated into a Syrian state ruled by the Hashemite king, Faysal.[38]

Moreover, political organizations continued to be closely identified with particular families throughout the days of the British Mandate.[39] The degree to which urban notable rivalry came to be institutionalized in Palestinian society during the Mandate can perhaps best be expressed by some of the major events of the Arab Revolt of 1936-1939. During that period, the urban Nashashibi family went so far as to begin to organize an army called the "Peace-band Movement," designed to quell the rebellion by attacking Palestinian Arab rebels.[40] And the organization formally responsible for conducting the revolt, the Arab Higher Committee, was often beset by internecine family quarrels, unable to secure distribution of supplies or to coordinate activities.[41]

The struggle for preeminence between Jerusalem and other major cities of Palestine often fueled urban notable competition. Not only did jealousy of Jerusalem persist, it intensified under the British as cities of the north were for the first time in recent history incorporated into a Palestinian political structure. These northern areas experienced particular difficulty with the new political arrangement, due to their recent administrative history.

> In the Ottoman period, Nablus and Jerusalem were connected by a number of interlocking institutions, particularly in the legal and military spheres. The Galilee, on the other hand, was never tied to Jerusalem. Palestine north of the Valley of Jezreel, was variously part of the Acre, Sidon or Damacus districts, never Jerusalem. There was certainly no tradition of relations, assuming that social and administrative links aid in the formation of political identity.[42]

[38] Yehoshua Porath, "The Political Organization of the Palestinian Arabs Under the British Mandate" in *Palestinian Arab Politics*, ed. by Moshe Ma'oz (Jerusalem: Academic Press, 1975), pp. 8-9.

[39] J. C. Hurewitz, *The Struggle for Palestine* (New York: W. W. Norton, 1950), Ch. 4.

[40] T. Bowden, "Politics of the Arab Rebellion in Palestine 1936-1939," *Middle Eastern Studies*, 2 (May, 1975), 147-74.

[41] Hurewitz, *The Struggle for Palestine*, Ch. 8.

[42] Porath, "The Political Organization of the Palestinian Arabs Under the British Mandate," p. 13.

The persistence of these cleavages in Palestinian society is not meant to suggest that British mandated Palestine was the same as Palestine under the Ottoman Empire. But no matter how different in political, cultural, and social style Britain was from the Ottomans the fact that both powers wanted to fashion a political system in Palestine that, above all, would include mechanisms for the peaceful resolution of conflicts, meant that both imperial powers had to adopt agents who could form the backbone of such a system and help implement imperial aims.

Although urban notables achieved a kind of hegemony over local Palestinian political life, they by no means controlled all of its dynamics—they were not the only local political actors. The British Mandate and its partial creation of a modern state bureaucracy laid down greater demands for officials than had the Ottomans; officials now had to be more educated and skilled than ever before. Since public offices were considered economically valuable and socially important positions in Palestine, fierce competition developed for appointments to the Mandate administration. To claim that working for the Mandate amounted to becoming an agent of a foreign power is to distort the view Palestinians held of public employment. They associated these positions with relative wealth, social status, and, most importantly, political power. Nothing was more attractive. Western intrusion increased employment opportunities for the literate, the multilingual, and the university graduate. But as would be expected, the rich (that is, the urban notables), who were already sophisticated, were able to take advantage of educational and training opportunities for their children more readily than the population as a whole.

An unexpected consequence of the improving standards in administrative employment derived from the social differences between the Christian and Muslim sectors of the Palestine population. More Christian Arabs, attending English and French language missionary schools and universities, met British entrance requirements than did Muslims. The visibility of Christian officials aroused the suspicions of Palestinian Muslims, who accused the British of favoring the Christian community and of trying to elevate its economic and social position at the expense of that of the Muslims. Thus Palestinian society became more divided along religious lines under the British.[43]

This bifurcation does not mean that examples of Muslim-Christian cooperation cannot be found. In the early days of the Mandate, Muslim-Christian societies emerged in several cities to protest against British sponsorship of a Jewish national home in Palestine.[44] In addi-

[43] Adnan Abu-Ghazaleh, *Arab Cultural Nationalism in Palestine* (Beirut: Institute for Palestine Studies, 1973).
[44] Porath, *The Emergence of the Palestinian-Arab National Movement*, pp. 90-93.

tion, several all-Palestinian congresses were held with leaders from both religious communities,[45] and women's organizations apparently included Christians and Muslims.[46] But such joint efforts were short-lived and diminished over time. Palestinian Christians and Muslims essentially lived in separate societies. Christians tended to live in cities rather than in villages, to engage in trade rather than to live on the land, and to stress cultural affinities with Christian Europe by attending church-sponsored schools or by earning university degrees in England or France. Family life was different, as Christians began to structure their family units on a nuclear, Western model, weakening their extended kinship ties, while the power of the extended family did not decrease for Muslims. Palestinian Muslims tended to marry within clans, or if that proved impossible, among their fellow villagers. Christians more typically married outside of clan and village. Needless to say, Palestinian Christians and Muslims rarely married each other.[47]

All religious groups were formally opposed to Zionism, but no single political position existed with respect to the issues of Jewish immigration, Jewish land purchases, and Jewish political autonomy. The 1936-1939 Arab Revolt again dramatized this major cleavage in Palestinian society, for the Revolt was more concentrated in rural (Muslim) areas than in urban locations, particularly in its later stages. Christians tended to oppose the Revolt, sometimes refusing to provide food and shelter for rebels and sometimes cooperating with the British government's efforts to capture rebel leaders.[48]

In contrast to the situation in colonies and territories elsewhere, the primary impact of British rule in Palestine was not economic, though there were some social and political consequences of economic changes in this period. The British considered Palestine to be primarily of strategic significance, so the economic measures they undertook served first to enhance their imperial defense network.[49] For this

[45] *Palestine, A Study of Jewish, Arab, and British Policies*, Vol. I, pp. 474-75.

[46] M.E.T. Mogannam, *The Arab Woman and The Palestine Problem* (Westport, Conn.: Hyperion Press, 1976).

[47] These observations are based on the following anthropological studies of Palestine Arabs: Hilma Granquist, *Birth and Childhood Among the Arabs* (Helsingfors: Soderstrom, 1947); Hilma Granquist, *Muslim Death and Burial* (Helsinki: Societas Scientiarium Fennica, 1965); Henry Rosenfeld, "An Analysis of Marriage and Marriage Statistics for a Moslem and Christian Arab Village," *Internationales Archiv Für Ethnographie*, 48 (1958), 32-66; Henry Rosenfeld, "Change, Barriers to Change, and Contradictions in the Arab Village Family," *American Anthropologist*, 70 (August, 1968), 732-52.

[48] Yehoshua Porath, "Social and Communal Aspects of the 1936-1939 Arab Revolt in Palestine," unpublished.

[49] William R. Polk, David M. Stamler, and Edmund Asfour, *Backdrop to Tragedy* (Boston: Beacon Press, 1957).

reason they built roads, constructed railways, and developed good port facilities. These measures affected the Palestine Arab community differentially. Merchants could take advantage of the new transportation system to expand their commercial activities, particularly since the roads tended to link urban centers between the coast and the interior. The new network permitted Palestine Arab entrepreneurs to establish ties not only with Europe, but also with Arabs in other states now with increased access to Palestine. Again, Christians were occupationally better placed to take advantage of this situation than Palestinian Muslims.

Great Britain did not attempt to lay the foundations of a modern economy in Palestine. The grand monuments of the British Mandate are not factories, but roads. But the British did try to improve Palestine's economy by introducing credit facilities to aid the growth of a small independent landed gentry and to decrease the financial dependence of tenant farmers on absentee landlords.[50] These measures affected the smaller rural and urban notables, reducing the number of such *effendis* (notables). But considering all of the other British political overtures to the notables, the political and social power of the effendi class, as a whole, was not weakened. Zionist economic activities also seemed to have the overall effect of reinforcing the position of the landowners while enlarging the gap between Arab rich and poor. In short, the major new forces of the post-World War I era—British rule and large-scale Jewish settlement—did not totally transform Palestinian society. Rather they greatly strengthened tendencies already evident during the first intrusions of the West in the eighteenth and nineteenth centuries and helped sustain the major landowning elite.[51]

Continuing Cleavages in a Dispersed Society

In the wake of the 1948 War, the Palestine diaspora, for all its personal traumas, came not as a new departure disrupting a delicate social or political balance, but rather as a continuation of a centuries-long Palestinian experience of living without a state of their own. The rise of the state of Israel and the creation of a larger Palestinian refugee community did not lead to a totally new politics as it did not lead to a totally new Palestinian society.

As enfeebled as the Palestinian community had been by subjugation and military defeat, it retained a political structure of sorts. In 1948, a

[50] *Palestine, A Study of Jewish, Arab, and British Policies*, Vol. II, pp. 722, 760, 1049.

[51] Henry Rosenfeld, "From Peasantry to Wage Labor and Residual Peasantry: The Transformation of an Arab Village" in *Process and Pattern in Culture*, ed. by Robert A. Manners (Chicago: Aldine, 1964), pp. 211-36.

"Government of All Palestine" was established, with its headquarters
in Gaza, then under the dominion of Egypt. To be sure, the Egyptians
exercised control over the statements and actions of this "govern-
ment-in-exile," but it was, perhaps, typical of the Palestinian situation
that the forces behind this political structure were urban notables,
specifically the Husaynis and their followers. Palestinian refugee politics came to be shaped in the context of an unequal distribution of
power between Palestinians, on the one hand, and their Arab host
governments, on the other. Yet the right to rule Palestinians was still
partly an organic ingredient in Palestinian social structure. The degree to which power was determined by the social structure can
perhaps be appreciated by the extent to which Palestinian notables
changed foreign partners and patrons between 1948 and 1967,
searching for the Arab government that seemed most willing to provide them with support and the promise of greater political power.[52]
Palestinian politics can be described as both a contest among notables
and a rivalry between Arab states. Palestinian notables were never
simply attendant politicians.

But what of the present moment? In the 1960s, several Palestinian
political movements arose that devised a set of tactical and strategic
goals to serve as the unifying political program for all Palestinians. An
overall political framework, the Palestine Liberation Organization
(PLO), eventually incorporated most of these movements. In many
ways, they have provided a radical departure from previous Palestinian political organizations. Referring to El-Fatah, the largest of these
fedayeen groups and the one that has captured the major offices of the
PLO, Michael Hudson wrote:

> ... to a large extent the guerilla groups did not simply penetrate
> a national elite, but actually reconstituted it. El-Fatah had a net-
> work of political and military branches that appeared to engage
> all sectors of the Palestine community: refugees, villagers and
> peasants, urban proletariat outside the camps, middle-class pro-
> fessionals and business people and very well-to-do commercial
> elite.[53]

[52] These changes are described by a number of surveys of Arab politics. One good
study is Paul Y. Hammond and Sidney S. Alexander (eds.), *Political Dynamics in the Middle East* (New York: American Elsevier, 1972). The connections between certain local
political leaders and families and particular Arab states precede the establishment of
the state of Israel. On this political linkage see Gabriel Sheffer, "The Involvement of
Arab States in the Palestine Conflict and British-Arab Relationship Before World War
II," *Asian and African Studies*, 10 (1974), 59-78, especially p. 63.

[53] Michael Hudson, "The Palestinian Resistance Movement Since 1967" in *The Middle
East*, ed. by Willard A. Beling (Albany: State University of New York Press, 1973),
p. 108.

But despite these social changes, some of the traditional social structural elements continue to be evident because Palestinian society and Palestinian political movements still remain in a state of political dependence. Much of the kind of political activity that took place in the refugee camps, for example, can be explained by the traditional social structure of the Palestinian community and the fact that political subordination has left much of that structure intact. Powerful features of the older Palestinian society persist even in the face of the refugee camp experience. The camps are organized along village and clan lines. Kinship groups that lived together in Palestine continue to live together, somewhat isolated from others in the camps. Hence, with but a little encouragement from their more powerful Arab rulers, many Palestinian political organizations continue to be rooted in kinship networks, which are perceived as enhancing the coherence and integrity of the entire community.[54]

Anthropological studies of the refugee camps confirm that the traditional Arab *hamula* (clan) organization is still viable. It is interesting to note that in Israel, as well, the hamula is a strong force among Arab citizens; its strength is attributed to the alien and hostile environment in which Israeli Arabs must live.[55] The camp experience may provide no less an alien environment for Palestinian refugees, despised, ridiculed, and severely controlled by the Arab state governments.[56] But however hostile the political climate, the most important reason for the hamula's continued viability may be the absence of Palestinian political sovereignty.[57]

Dependence has contributed to reliance on longstanding social structures and traditional patterns of political recruitment. While it is impossible to gather data on all of the people belonging to El-Fatah, it is possible to describe typical El-Fatah adherents. Such an account can be constructed by examining the obituaries of Palestinians who were killed in raids against Israel as part of missions conducted for the mili-

[54] Yoram Ben-Porath and Emanuel Marx, *Some Sociological and Economic Aspects of Refugee Camps on the West Bank* (Santa Monica: Rand, 1971), pp. 13-20. Peter Dodd and Halim Barakat, *River Without Bridges* (Beirut: Institute for Palestine Studies, 1968).

[55] Abner Cohen, *Arab Border-Villages in Israel* (Manchester: University of Manchester Press, 1965).

[56] This conclusion appears consistent with the descriptions of Palestinian refugees in such works as: Halim Barakat, *Days of Dust* (Wilmette, Ill.: Medina University Press International, 1974); Ghassen Kanafani, *Al-Adab al-Filastin al-Muqqadimmah Taht al-Ihtilal* (The Literature of Resistance Under the Occupation) (Beirut: Institute for Palestine Studies, 1968); Leila Khaled, *My People Shall Live* (London: Hodder and Stoughton, 1973); Fawaz Turki, *The Disinherited* (New York: Monthly Review Press, 1972).

[57] This notion is comparable with the argument of A. L. Tibawi, "Visions of the Return: The Palestine Refugees in Arabic Poetry and Art," *Middle East Journal*, 17 (1963), 507-26.

tary arm of El-Fatah. What is striking about the results of this research is the number of Palestinians among these activists who were
members of families that had been associated with the Husaynis in
Palestine before 1948.[58] That is, the overwhelming number of El-
Fatah activists consisted of sons of people who had worked land
owned by the Husaynis or who had entered into some sort of relationship with the Husayni clan.[59] One reason for the cohesion of El-Fatah,
it can be postulated, stems from family ties. When it is remembered
that Yasir Arafat, its leader, is himself a Husayni, and had been personal secretary to Abd-al-Qadir al-Husayni (one of the members of
the Husayni family who was killed fighting the Israelis in April 1948),
the ties between leaders and followers of El-Fatah become more ex-
plicable. Moreover, the organization responsible for setting policy in
El-Fatah is staffed by Husaynis or men married to Husaynis. The
Gehaza, as this organization is called, also now helps to initiate policy
for the PLO as a whole.[60] Amid great changes, political traditions
persist.

Another traditional cleavage in Palestinian society that continues to
have a great impact on Palestinian politics is religious in nature. The
membership of the Popular Front for the Liberation of Palestine
helps illustrate some of the enduring religious divisions. P. J. Vatikiotis has remarked that Arab Christians and heretical Muslims are
normally attracted to "radical," "extreme," "secular" ideologies as a
way of trying to transcend "the real, live question of sectarianism in
the Islamic Arab Middle East."[61] The intensely sectarian character of
Palestinian nationalist politics has often been noted, but not, I think,
as often understood. The point is that religious differences continue
to influence political organization and affiliation and preside over
political aims. The PFLP, headed by Christians, with a largely Christian following, carries on a Christian political tradition in Palestinian
politics by borrowing heavily from political movements outside of the
Middle East.[62]

Most simply put, then, in the contemporary Palestinian idiom, the
welfare of the nation proceeds first from the excellence of certain

---

[58] This has been ascertained from an examination of obituaries of fedayeen, *Al-
Muharrar*, Beirut. Out of 50 obituaries surveyed, 30 activists had had family ties with
the Husaynis.

[59] Ibid., and Shimoni, *Aravei Eretz Israel*.

[60] Ibrahim Sallah Hajjar, "The Mafia of the Husayni Family," *Ma'ariv*, September 9,
1972 (Hebrew).

[61] P. J. Vatikiotis, *Conflict in the Middle East* (London: George Allen and Unwin, 1971),
p. 162.

[62] Tareq Y. Ismael, *The Arab Left* (Syracuse: Syracuse University Press, 1976). Walid
W. Kazziha, *Revolutionary Transformation in the Arab World* (London: Charles Knight,
1975).

families, and their excellence stems from the legitimacy of their religious ties. These traditional Palestinian political and social patterns have been reinforced by foreign rule. This outcome of the presence of external powers occurred whoever the ruler might be, or whatever the circumstances of his rule.

There are specific limits within which the public life of the Palestinians has taken place, and a conqueror can affect Palestinian society only within those limits.[63] But while Palestinian society has retained its own distinctive features, it is a society that has long been submerged in a political world not entirely its own, divested of sovereignty and of areas of experience that might have made possible different political developments and social changes. Political subordination is, then, the best register of the kinds of political and social experiences actually encountered by Palestinian society—the reason why traditional social networks, amidst radical historical and political changes, have still not lost their thrust.

[63] This is true of all societies. Explained, theoretically, by Arthur L. Stinchcombe, "Merton's Theory of Social Structure" in *The Idea of Social Structure*, ed. by Lewis A. Coser (New York: Harcourt Brace Jovanovich, 1975), pp. 11-34. One empirical demonstration is Ian Whitaker, "Tribal Structure and National Politics in Albania, 1910-1950" in *History and Social Anthropology*, ed. by I. M. Lewis (London: Tavistock Publications, 1968), pp. 253-93.

PART THREE

Modes of Interaction
between Elites and Masses

Legal Protection and Circumvention of Rights for Cultivators in Mandatory Palestine*

by Kenneth W. Stein

In the immediate wake of communal violence that plagued Palestine in August 1929, High Commissioner Sir John Chancellor, himself favorably disposed to Arab claims to Palestine, succinctly defined the intermediary role His Majesty's Government was playing between Arab and Jew. He said that "there is a tendency here to regard the Government as sort of umpire and scorer, trying to hold the balance between the two races, noting when one scores off the other, and regarding it as only fair that the next point in the game should be scored by the race that lost the preceding one."[1]

The general ebb and flow of policy in Palestine was determined by the confines of the Mandate's articles and the Balfour Declaration, which appeared as its preamble. When the High Commissioner, Colonial Office, or Palestine administration officials strayed from those bounds, protests were heard in threatening decibels from segments of both the Arab and Jewish communities. In November 1921, for example, after the riots of the preceding May, High Commissioner Sir Herbert Samuel somewhat allayed Arab apprehensions about all of Palestine being turned over to the Zionists, by conferring upon some 2,500 Arab cultivators the exclusive right to farm some of the most fertile land in Palestine. The signing of the Beisan Agreement, in turn, angered those Zionists who had prematurely contemplated easy access to these 300,000 metric *dunams*[2] of state domain.

After the 1929 disturbances, the Passfield White Paper of October

---

* This article is expanded from a paper of similar title delivered at the Ninth Annual Meeting of the Middle East Studies Association in Louisville, Kentucky, November 1975. A slightly altered version will appear in Hebrew in the Israel Oriental Society Journal, *Hamizrah Hehadash.*

[1] Chancellor to his son Christopher, September 1, 1929, Chancellor Papers (hereafter CP), Box 16/3, Rhodes House, Oxford.

[2] One dunam equaled approximately one-quarter of an acre.

© 1979 by Princeton University Press, *Palestinian Society and Politics*
0-691-07615-4/79/0233-28$01.40/1 (cloth)
0-691-02193-7/79/0233-28$01.40/1 (paperback)
For copying information, see copyright page

1930 temporarily put the Zionists on notice that implementation of
the national home concept would be postponed. But the MacDonald
Letter of February 1931 neutralized Chancellor's intent of protecting
the civil rights of Palestine's Arab majority. The limitations placed
upon Jewish immigration and land purchase by the White Paper of
1939 evolved directly as a response to Palestine Arab grievances, as
they meshed with larger British geopolitical requirements both in the
Middle East and elsewhere.

The pendulum of most policy-making for Palestine swung between
the jaws of Arab or Jewish protest and the instrumentation of the
Mandate's articles. Yet, there were some axioms of policy that were
basically unalterable. England wished to retain her additional strategic presence in the eastern Mediterranean with the least possible expense to the British exchequer and taxpayer. Throughout the Mandate, an overwhelming predominance of administration expenditure
was allocated toward bolstering Britain's strategic presence, while
only small amounts of governmental revenue were made available to
ameliorate the economic and social conditions of either the Arab or
Jewish communities. Lastly, the British chose to encourage the official
and then unofficial participation of Palestinian Arab notables in consultations regarding the Mandate's daily operation and direction.

The Zionists who wanted to fulfill the maximum perceived goal for
the creation of a Jewish national home required two essential ingre-
dients: immigration and land purchase. Periodically denied the
privilege of owning land in countries of previous residence, land acquisition in Palestine filled both personal and larger nationalistic
needs for immigrating Zionists. For the Arab of Palestine, agricultural
and pastoral occupations were central to his very existence. Political
conflict unavoidably ensued as both the Zionists and Arabs engaged in
a tug of war over land.

Though land use and its control had an emerging centrality in the
Arab-Zionist dispute in Palestine, as a political issue Jewish land acquisition and Arab land sales were often muted, for various reasons,
during the Mandate. My argument is that the convenient and mutually beneficial symbiosis that developed between the Arab land owner
and the Jewish purchaser was a prominent factor. The purpose of this
paper is twofold: to discuss why and how the protection of the agricultural tenant became the least objectionable alternative to complete
prohibition of land transfer for British, Arab, and Jew, and how it
also became an object of dissension and rancor within the Arab community; and to document where possible those instances when Arab
tenants' protection was summarily and dispassionately circumvented
despite increased efforts by the British to eliminate legal loopholes in
existing legislation.

During the first decade of the Mandate the political leadership of the Palestine Arab community all came from the landed classes,[3] or from segments of the political community that had a direct financial interest in land, including lawyers, merchants, moneylenders, and religious leaders. The British eagerly encouraged the introduction of Jewish capital into Palestine through land purchase and Jewish immigration. Not wishing to endanger continued monetary inflow and out of a desire to maintain reasonable working contacts with the Arab political community, no concerted effort was made to change or tamper with Palestine's land regime. Each time the topic of land transfer prohibitions was seriously broached, in 1929, 1930, and 1931, Arab vendors and Jewish purchasers prevailed by maintaining free transfers. After the imposition of the Land Transfer Regulations in February 1940, land continued to be sold to Jews in areas prohibited to them.[4] A convenient alternative to land transfer prohibitions evolved in Britain's choice to protect legally the rights of cultivators.

Both the Arab vendor and the Jewish purchaser found the legal protection of tenants a nuisance, but more bearable than land transfer prohibitions. Though there were repeated efforts by the Palestine administration to maintain tenants on their holdings, no government legislation ever totally favored the tenant against his landlord. As a consequence, the Arab vendor continued to satisfy his desire for capital, and the Jewish purchaser, an insatiable desire to own land. The British believed that if efforts were not made to prevent the wholesale removal of tenants from their land, a class of brigands, highwaymen, and landless peasants would ultimately become a financial burden on the Palestine administration. That had to be avoided at all costs. Tenants' protection put the onus of financial or compensatory responsibility upon the vendor and the purchaser and not the British government in London or Palestine. The British were repeatedly myopic in the belief that legislation could protect the rights of cultivators in situations where the Arab vendor and Jewish purchaser sought each other out with abounding vigor and discretion. Yet, the ordinances encompassing tenants' protection gave the administration demonstrable paper evidence that the civil rights of tenants were being protected. The fact that these ordinances had to be revised periodically because of prodigious circumvention by vendor, purchaser, and tenant merely adds credence to the supposition that legislative palliatives did not suffice in Palestine. In this instance, the British government was an umpire trying in vain to implant new regulations into the land

[3] Yehoshua Porath, *The Emergence of the Palestine Arab National Movement, 1918-1929* (London: Frank Cass, 1974), p. 56.

[4] For an example of the mechanisms employed after 1940, see methods outlined for 1943 alone in Colonial Office (hereafter CO) 733/453/75042/9, folios 1-43.

transfer game that, as time wore on, became increasingly complex, devious, and uncontrollable.

The population of Palestine in November 1931 numbered 1,035,821 of whom 759,712 were Muslims, 174,610 were Jews, 91,398 were Christians, and 10,101 were classified as others.[5] Over 440,000 persons were supported by ordinary cultivation. Of these 108,765 were earners and 331,319 were dependents. The earner category was divided: 5,311 (5 percent) derived their livelihood from agricultural rents, 70,526 (65 percent) were cultivating earners, and 32,539 (30 percent) were agricultural laborers.[6] Among the cultivating earners there were thought to be approximately 56,000 (80 percent) *fellahin* who owned the land they worked and 14,000 (20 percent) agricultural tenants.[7] A legal distinction was made by the Palestine administration between the agricultural tenant who had an express or implied agreement with a landlord and cultivated a holding, and the agricultural laborer who did not cultivate a holding, even though he was hired to do agricultural work. The definition of an agricultural tenant was broadened as the Mandate progressed to encompass a larger number of agricultural laborers, but at no time was any legislation enacted to protect the owner-occupier. Protection of the owner-occupier was contemplated by the Palestine administration in early 1936, but that legislation was postponed owing to the outbreak of the Arab general strike in April of the same year. In simple numerical terms, therefore, the legal protection offered to agricultural tenants applied to only a very small proportion of the total number of fellahin engaged in agricultural pursuits. Owner-occupiers and agricultural laborers were never entitled to legal protection offered by the mandatory government.

In passing it should be noted that one-quarter of those engaged in some form of ordinary cultivation, approximately 26,000 earners, returned a subsidiary income. Rent receivers, owner-occupiers, agricultural laborers, and grazers of flocks engaged in fruit growing and picking, became tenants on another's property, bred grazing animals, hired themselves out as day laborers, or worked as tailors, weavers, or cobblers. In the early 1930s when an increasing number of owner-occupiers were selling uneconomically tenable small parcels of land,

[5] Government of Palestine, *Census for Palestine, 1931*, Vol. 1, p. 96. The demographic statistics available for the socioeconomic composition of Palestine's population are only partially reliable. But in the absence of more precise information, the Census of Palestine of 1931 is our most detailed source.

[6] Ibid., Vol. 2, Table XVI, p. 282.

[7] High Commissioner Arthur Wauchope to Phillip Cunliffe-Lister, secretary of state for the colonies, December 22, 1932, CO 733/217/97072.

there was a corresponding change in the number of tenants and agricultural laborers. Tenants already engaged with a landlord were displaced by a landlord's sale, effecting in turn a reduction in the number of agricultural laborers who could be employed in seasonal work such as plowing and harvesting. Many owner-occupiers who sold remaining parcels of land, instead of engaging in per diem labor in the urban building trades in Palestine, swelled the tenant ranks, preferring to remain in agricultural pursuits despite a perennial succession of poor crop yields.

The land transfer process had a profoundly debilitating effect upon relationships between landlord and tenant. The landlord, sometimes exclusively interested in his own financial betterment, saw the land he possessed as merely a potential remunerative object. Some eagerly entered into collusive arrangements with Jewish purchasers in efforts to rid their lands of "tenant encumbrances" prior to notification of the administration of an impending land transfer. When the administration was finally informed that a land area was to be transferred and registered, there was most often no physical evidence of previous tenant occupation.

Agricultural tenants and laborers who were prevented from practicing their traditional forms of livelihood not only expressed their hostility toward some of their landlords, brokers, and intermediaries who acted in consort with Jewish purchasers, but directed their antagonism against the British Mandatory and Zionism. But, due in large measure to their exceedingly poor economic state and inability to find sustained support from social classes above them, the expression of their enmity did not emerge until the 1936 general strike. Further accentuating hostility toward the Mandate, besides its tacit support of the establishment of a Jewish national home, was the notion that the mandatory government did not care about them or intentionally harmed them.[8]

Arab cultivator feeling toward the British was exacerbated by the understanding that they would receive land from the government through the efforts of the Development Department in the process of resettling "landless" Arabs. From the claims brought before the government under the Protection of Cultivator's Ordinance of 1933, many believed that their rights to land, lost in the transfer process, would be rightfully restored to them. Both beliefs proved illusory and only further contributed to Arab cultivator animosity toward the British and Zionists.

[8] Commissioner of lands to chief secretary, May 12, 1931, Israel State Archives (hereafter ISA), Box 3280/file 2; see fn. 11.

Cultivators and Protection, 1918-1929

The first real effort made by the mandatory government to keep all classes of agricultural workers tied to land came in 1918 with the closure of Palestine's land registry offices. Under the Ottoman regime no special legal protection was offered to cultivators, though some debtor protection existed under an 1871 law and in Egypt through the Five Feddan Law of 1912. The latter, though trying to tackle the problem of indebtedness, was successfully evaded by both fellahin and moneylenders.[9] In Palestine, Arab landowners before World War I could and did evict tenants without offering them compensation.[10] Moreover, when land was transferred, all tenants could have been dismissed by the owner, and, indeed, the purchasers made it a condition of purchase that the land be transferred free of cultivators.[11]

Since many Palestinian fellahin had informally mortgaged the lands that they possessed prior to and during World War I in order to "purchase" a military exemption from the conscription officers, foreclosure upon those lands by creditors would have necessitated the Mandate's provision of poor relief for those subsequently turned off their lands.[12] For this reason and because of the administrative turmoil left by the retreating Turkish armies in Palestine, the British military administration declared all dispositions in land null and void in November 1918 and closed subdistrict land registry offices.

By its Public Notice of April 1919, the military administration acknowledged that circumvention of its prohibition was occurring. Apparently, promissory notes or other written instruments legally acknowledging a debt were executed, providing for the debtor either to pay back the face value of the promissory note or sell his land or

[9] Gabriel Baer, *Studies in the Social History of Modern Egypt* (Chicago: University of Chicago Press, 1969), p. 75. No tenant protection existed in Transjordan, Syria, or Iraq. As in Palestine, the landlord in Transjordan terminated his contractual obligations with his tenants at the end of each year. In Syria, the first legal protection offered to tenants came in 1958, with stipulation that regulated relations between the landowner and tenant. In Iraq, a 1933 law enumerated the rights and duties of cultivators, but gave the landowner the right to retain his tenant unless the latter could pay his debt. For further information on the condition of tenants in these countries see Central Zionist Archives (hereafter CZA), Record Group S25/file 3490; Eva Garzouzi, "Land Reform in Syria," *Middle East Journal*, 17 (Winter-Spring, 1963), 83-90; Saleh M. Dabbagh, "Agrarian Reform in Iraq," *American Journal of Economic and Social History*, 28 (1969), 61-76. See also Andre Latron, *La Vie rurale en Syrie et au Liban* (Beirut: Impr. Catholique, 1936).

[10] Note by Mr. Bennett of the Palestine Lands Department, June 1930, ISA, Box 3768/file 4.

[11] League of Nations, *Permanent Mandates Commission—Minutes*, October 28, 1924, p. 58.

[12] Great Britain, *Report on Palestine Administration July 1920-December 1921*, 1922, p. 110.

share of land as satisfaction of the debt at some future date, presumably when land transfers would again be officially sanctioned. Because of a severely depressed economic condition, one fellah sought to have his advance paid in terms of a given amount of olive oil. A second mechanism used to circumvent the prohibition on land transfers involved the potential seller signing irrevocable powers of attorney that could be exercised in the future.[13] Though there was considerable success at frustrating the prohibition's intent, the ultimate goal of maintaining fellahin on their land from 1918 to 1920 was accomplished. Credit for that success was more due to general capital scarcity in Palestine than assiduous British guardianship of fellahin rights—not that British administrators wished to harm the Palestinian peasant, though they were unjustly accused of this.[14] There was a familiarity gap with local customs, procedures, and conventions among foreign military men immediately entrusted with maintaining the political and economic status quo.

When the Land Transfer Ordinance (LTO) of October 1, 1920 sanctioned a reopening of the land registry offices, no provision was made to clarify the confused state of land ownership and land tenure in Palestine. No cadastral survey was suggested or otherwise implemented. The LTO had a threefold objective: to reduce speculation in land, to assure the intent of a person or company to cultivate a holding, and to maintain the small owner and tenant on the land he worked. To oversee the implementation of these objectives, it was legally required for the district commissioner to give his consent to all land transfers.

The LTO was the first piece of legislation under the British civilian administration aimed at binding the owner-occupier and tenant to their land. Since the 1880s, tenants had been periodically rotated from plot to plot because landowners feared that their tenants might acquire prescriptive rights to the lands tilled. This custom had caused some tenants to leave lands in the Jezreel Valley in favor of tenancy on the Sultan's land in Beisan where such a practice was not employed.[15] By article 6 of the LTO the district governor was charged "to withhold

[13] *Proclamation, Ordinances, and Notices Issued by OETA-South to August 1919* (Cairo, 1920), pp. 31-32; ISA, Box 3744/file R525.
[14] Statement of the Arab Executive refuting the English White Paper of October 1930, in 'Abd al-Wahhab al-Kayyali, *Watha'iq al-Muqawama al-Filastiniyyah al-'Arabiyyah didd al-Ihtilal al-Baratani wa al-Sahyuniyyah, 1918-1939* (Documents of Palestinian Arab Resistance against British and Zionist Occupation, 1918-1939) (Beirut, 1968), p. 192 (Arabic).
[15] George Post, "Essays on Sects and Nationalities of Syria and Palestine-Land Tenure," *Palestine Exploration Fund Quarterly Statement* (April, 1891), p. 106; Alfred Sursock, *Memorandum on Sursock Lands*, September 30, 1921, ISA, Box 3544/file 21; Arthur Ruppin, *Syrien als Wirtschaftsgebiet* (Berlin: Kolonial-wirtschaftsliches Kommittee, 1917), pp. 64-65.

his consent of a transfer, unless he was satisfied that in the case of agricultural land either the person transferring the property, if he is in possession, or the tenant in occupation, if the property is leased, will retain sufficient land in the district or elsewhere for the maintenance of himself and his family." The precise amount of land to be left to the owner-occupier was to vary according to region of the country, based upon the land quality as determined by the district governor.

In its effort to reduce speculation in land, the LTO clearly forbade the district governor to give assent to transfers where property was valued in excess of 3,000 Egyptian pounds or in area of 300 dunams in the case of agricultural land. The High Commissioner had the prerogative to overrule a decision of a district governor in granting permission for a transfer. Such government interference in the land transfer process greatly angered Arab landowners, who were themselves severely in debt by World War I's conclusion. Landowners and scions of Arab landowning classes fervently desired the repeal of all these restrictions. They never betrayed any enthusiasm for them.[16] Many wanted the option to engage in land speculation for remunerative and personal purposes, while others were keen to sell portions of their land to immigrating Zionists.

The Zionists, too, showed no deep affection for the land transfer restrictions imposed by the government. Official purchasing organizations such as the Palestine Land Development Company were on the verge of consummating the transfer of some 65,000 dunams of land in the Jezreel Valley owned by the Sursocks of Beirut. The Colonial Office took careful note of the likely removal of these tenants and suggested that due safeguards be maintained for their protection. That vast sums of money were not available to the Zionists at this time for large-scale land purchases contributed to the Colonial Office's belief that the removal of the land transfer restrictions would not greatly endanger the Arab population's future.[17] Without any objection by Arab representatives at the Advisory Council meeting of December 6, 1921 and in concurrence with the Colonial Office's directives to protect tenants, the LTO of 1920 was amended, limiting government interference in land transfers.[18]

In its amended form, which remained legally in force until superseded in June 1929, all area and value restrictions on land to be transferred were removed. The Transfer of Land Amendment Ordinance (LTAO) of December 1921 no longer provided any legal protection to

---

[16] High Commissioner Herbert Samuel to secretary of state for the colonies, November 22, 1921, CO 733/7/58411; H. F. Downie of the Colonial Office, *Note on the Palestine Land Problem*, March 8, 1935, CO 733/272/75072.

[17] Minutes by Mr. Mills of the Colonial Office, no date, CO 733/7/58411.

[18] Minutes of the 13th meeting of the Advisory Council, CO 733/8/63972.

a person transferring his own land, be that person a large landowner with marketable surpluses or the small owner-occupier. No protection was offered the agricultural laborer. Only the occupying tenant, of which there was no working legal definition, was to be protected. By our estimates, more than 80 percent of the population dependent primarily upon an agricultural income was *not* entitled to legal protection either then or later in the 1930s when cultivators' protection was ostensibly enlarged.

The legal protection offered to tenants between 1921 and 1929 was systematically circumvented by Arab landlords and Jewish purchasers. British officials, charged with tenants' protection, were unable to enforce provision of a maintenance area because they lacked data about land in Palestine—its ownership, its tenants, and its use. In the period of time between the initial purchase negotiations, which sometimes lasted for months and even years, and the official notification of the administration of a pending transfer, tenants' rights were easily compromised. Testifying before the Shaw Commission in 1929, the director of lands noted that

A vendor would come along and make a contract for sale and purchase with the Jews. We would know nothing of this until 4, 5 or 6 months later when the transaction would come to the office. We then instructed the District Officer to report on the tenants. He would go out to the village and in some cases he would find that the whole population had already evacuated the village. They [the tenants] had taken certain sums of money and had gone, and we could not afford them any protection whatever. In other cases it was found that a large percentage of the population had already gone before the transaction came to us, and we could not find out who the tenants were, they had no written contracts, and we did not know what compensation they were getting.[19]

An overwhelming preponderance of the tenants for whom we have records preferred monetary compensation to a maintenance area. Moreover, contrary to the director of lands' testimony, the Palestine administration did know in some cases what compensation tenants were receiving, since agreements between Jewish purchasing agents and Arab tenants were usually registered by the notary public at local subdistrict offices of the government.[20] It is difficult to prove conni-

[19] Great Britain, *Report of the Commission on the Palestine Disturbances of August 1929* (Shaw Report), Cmd. 3530, March 1930, p. 115; Cf. League of Nations, *Permanent Mandates Commission—Minutes*, June 6, 1930, p. 61. In the villages of Kneifis, Solam, Tel-Tora, and Jabatta purchased from the Sursocks in the Jezreel Valley in 1925, the villagers vacated their lands prior to administration notification of the transfer.
[20] See Appendix I.

vance on the part of administration officials regarding intentional frustration of tenants' protection, but susceptibility to traditional business practices cannot be ruled out entirely.

The amount of money given to Arab tenants to vacate a land area prior to official transfer was often equal to or greater than the net amount of a tenant's yearly income, after rent, tax, and debt payment. A tenant's annual income was variously estimated to range anywhere from 9 to 30 Palestine pounds.[21] Average compensation paid to the 688 tenants formerly employed by the Sursocks approximated 40 Palestine pounds per tenant and his family.[22] The amount of compensation was usually based upon the amount of land actually worked by a tenant reckoned in terms of *feddans* plowed. In instances where there were agricultural workers in occupation, but not legally entitled to any form of compensation, Jewish purchasers in some cases paid amounts ranging from 5 to 15 Palestine pounds in order to give them funds to live on while not working and to find work elsewhere. It was not uncommon for the Palestine Land Development Company to make liberal payments to local village *mukhtars*, to better persuade their villagers to vacate their lands.[23]

The absolute cost of compensating tenants increased as legal protection was steadily strengthened and tenants became increasingly aware of their rights under the law, as the problem of land availability grew more acute, and as the price of land sharply increased.[24] In order to ease further their evacuation from recently bought land, agents for Jewish purchasing organizations made additional payments on behalf of tenants for tax and debt arrears and for crops in the ground but not harvested.

An unknown number of tenants did receive alternative land as prescribed by LTAO. They eventually arranged to convert it into monetary compensation, left the area for agricultural pursuits elsewhere, moved to neighboring Arab villages and subsisted on per diem in-

[21] Government of Palestine, *Report of a Commission on the Economic Condition of Agriculturists in Palestine and Fiscal Measures of Government in Relations Thereto*, 1930, p. 44; Arthur Ruppin, "Jewish Land Purchase and Reaction upon the Condition of the former Arab Cultivators," CZA, S25/4207.

[22] See Appendix II. Further research is necessary to determine the total number of Arab tenants who received monetary compensation to vacate the land they worked.

[23] Yehoshua Hankin, a Jewish land purchasing agent to the central office of the Palestine Land Development Company, March 11, 1932, CZA, S25/7620.

[24] Palestine Land Development Company to Palestine Zionist Executive, May 5, 1925, S25/685; S. Kaplansky, "The Land Problem in Palestine," 1929, CZA, Z4/3444/III; Protocol of the JNF directorate meeting, December 28, 1928, CZA, KKL 5/Box 1048. In 1925, the compensatory amount paid to tenants raised the total purchase price of rural land 15 percent, in 1930 it approximated an additional 20 percent, and by 1938 land that cost five Palestine pounds per dunam required an additional sum of two pounds.

come, or migrated to the urban areas and often there to the building trades. Many Arab tenants who received monetary compensation moved alternatively eastward, and distinctly away from Jewish settlements.[25]

Thus, during the 1920s, precedents were established for tenants' protection for the remainder of the Mandate. Legislative protection only applied to a very small percentage of the agricultural population; buyer-seller collusion was a common method of circumventing tenants' rights; tenants readily accepted monetary compensation to vacate the lands they worked; and Jewish purchasers developed the belief that any piece of land could be purchased if the price were right.

The Protection of Cultivators Ordinance, 1929, and Amendments

By the end of 1926, members of the Palestine Lands Department recognized the inefficacy of existing tenants' protection and the need to reduce circumvention of the 1921 legislation. Before drafting any additional legislation, High Commissioner Field Marshal Lord Plumer consulted with the head of the Palestine Zionist Executive. Not only was the Palestine Arab Executive not consulted about the proposed intention to plug existing loopholes in tenants' protection, its opinions were not solicited for the drafting of the legislation as were the Palestine Zionist Executive's. The Palestine Zionist Executive was keenly interested in the shape and structure of any contemplated tenant legislation: it wished to avoid the creation of legitimate Arab grievances obviously engendered by Jewish land purchase; and it wished to assure itself that any such legislation would not impede land acquisition and Jewish settlement in Palestine.

At least from August 1928, when the Protection of Cultivators Ordinance (POCO) first appeared in draft form, until its promulgation in June 1929, the Palestine Zionist Executive actively contributed to the revision of the bill. The Palestine administration lacked information about the details involved in the land sale process. That, in conjunction with their avowed policy, as stated in the Mandate's articles, to consult with the Zionists about matters affecting the establishment of the Jewish national home, provided for unfettered Jewish land purchase and monetary compensation procedures to continue.

Not surprisingly, therefore, compensation in land was not made compulsory under the POCO of 1929. Legal sanction was given to the

---

[25] Mr. Bennett, secretary to Sir John Hope-Simpson to John Stubbs, director of lands, July 4, 1930, ISA, Box 3768/file 4; League of Nations, *Permanent Mandates Commission—Minutes*, June 22, 1926, p. 116.

existing practice of monetary compensation. In response to the practice of producing a land sale agreement at the land registry documenting that land was free of tenant encumbrances, the new ordinance stipulated that a landlord had to provide written notice at least one year prior to the termination of a valid tenancy. In instances where the tenant had failed to pay his rent within a reasonable period of time, failed to cultivate the land in accordance with good husbandry, or where an order of bankruptcy was in force against the tenant, such written notice was not required. From June 1929 until the end of 1932, no case was referred to the High Commissioner whereby the tenant was declared bankrupt or deemed to have failed to cultivate a holding properly resulting in an order for eviction made by a landlord.[26]

Though the POCO demanded that a landlord pay fair compensation to his tenants for improvements on the land made by them, no tenant could receive such compensation, in the event of eventual eviction, unless either the landlord had given written prior consent to such an improvement or the tenant had informed the landlord in writing of his desire to effect a particular improvement. In those few cases where improvements were made by tenants of long standing and agreements were made between the landlord or his local agent and the tenant, agreements were predominantly oral and not written. POCO further protected the *landlord* by enabling him to give his tenant(s) one year's written notice of a rent increase, forcing the tenant unwilling or unable to pay the increment to quit the land on the date when the increased rent would become due. Where a tenant received notice to quit, the landlord could either pay compensation to the outgoing tenant for the preparation of the land for the next crop, or the landlord could anticipate selling his land free of tenant encumbrances by giving required written notice to the obliging tenant, or announcing a rent increase to the recalcitrant tenant. He could then prepare his land for a future crop, and receive from the purchaser compensation for either the prepared land or for the crop already in the ground.

In April 1929, the Jewish National Fund (JNF) purchased 30,000 dunams at Wadi Hawarith south of Hedera. The future whereabouts of the 1,200 Bedouin who had at various times inhabited portions of this land greatly worried the Palestine administration, especially High Commissioner Chancellor, members of the Shaw Committee, and Sir John Hope Simpson.[27] The concept of a landless Arab population

[26] High Commissioner Wauchope to Phillip Cunliffe-Lister, secretary of state for the colonies, December 22, 1932, CO 733/217/97072.

[27] *Shaw Report*, p. 123; minutes of the Executive Council of the Palestine government, January 17, 1930 and February 7, 1930, CO 814/26.

created by Arab land sales and Jewish purchasers greatly distressed Chancellor. From both moral and practical points of view, he wished to stop the collusively arrived-at land sale agreements made between Arab and Jew. He could not understand how the claims by Jews resident in Poland and Russia to land in Palestine should have preference over the claims of indigenous Arab cultivators. Furthermore, he could not as High Commissioner permit these Arabs to become a landless class, draining administration revenue and posing a potential threat to the stability of the country.[28]

Chancellor's preoccupation with the condition of the Arab agriculturist translated itself into an unsuccessful attempt to award the Arabs of Palestine privileges commensurate with those enjoyed by the Jewish community under the articles of the Mandate.[29] By March 1930, Chancellor recognized that the POCO was inadequate in protecting Arab agriculturists. He took particular note that the JNF had purchased lands through the legal mechanism of a public auction ordered by the Nablus District Court in satisfaction of a collusively arrived-at mortgage debt.[30] Tenants on such lands had no tenancy privileges and were therefore liable to eviction.[31] Chancellor also recognized that landlords were terminating tenants' occupancy by increasing the rent beyond their means to pay. He also wished to stop land sales in excess of 1,000 dunams and thereby return to the principle embodied in the LTO of 1920. In his proposed draft ordinance to amend the 1929 legislation, Chancellor sought to increase tenants' protection.[32]

Unlike his predecessor and successors in Government House in Jerusalem, he was willing to abet the wrath of the Arab landowner who wanted freedom to dispose of his land. But Chancellor was stymied in his effort. The British first had to consider the repercussions of the publication of the Shaw Report in March 1930, with its anti-Jewish settlement overtones, upon the domestic political situation and on the minority government of Ramsey MacDonald.[33] In Chan-

---

[28] Chancellor to secretary of state for the colonies, March 5, 1931, CO 733/40/87402 (I); Chaim Arlosoroff, *Yoman Yerushalaim* (Jerusalem Diary), n.d., p. 20 (Hebrew). Chancellor to Christopher, January 15, 1930, CP, Box 16/3; Hope-Simpson to Chancellor, June 26, 1930, CP, Box 15/2.

[29] For Chancellor's attitude toward the Mandate see his dispatch of January 17, 1930, CO 733/182/77050, part II.

[30] A. Ashbel, ed., *Shishim Shnot Haksharat HaYishuv* (Sixty Years of the PLDC) (Jerusalem: Hamcoar, 1969), pp. 81-88 (Hebrew).

[31] Judgment of the Court, June 11, 1930, CO 733/190/77182; Michael F.J. McDonnell, *Law Reports of Palestine 1920-1933* (London, 1934), pp. 471-73.

[32] See the draft POCO Amendment Ordinance in Chancellor to Lord Passfield, secretary of state for the colonies, March 29, 1930, CO 733/182/77050, part II.

[33] Gabriel Sheffer, "Intentions and Results of British Policy in Palestine: Passfield's White Paper," *Middle Eastern Studies*, 9 (January, 1973), 43-60.

cellor's second of six proposed pieces of legislation dealing with land,
he advocated the prohibition of land sales from Arab to Jew, thus raising a larger, politically sensitive issue of discrimination on the basis of
race and religion, otherwise prohibited by article 15 of the Mandate.[34]
Since the Shaw Report requested an expert to investigate aspects of
immigration and land settlement (resulting in Sir John Hope
Simpson's Report of October 1930), all land legislation was held in
abeyance until the British government issued a policy statement,
which appeared in the form of the Passfield White Paper.

Chancellor's proposals had to wait. While the Passfield White Paper
of October 1930 faulted Zionist settlement for creating a landless
Arab class and hinted at the institution of land transfer prohibitions,
the MacDonald Letter of February 1931 recanted such implications.
All that was contemplated was temporary control of land dispositions
and transfers.[35] Through their contacts at the Colonial Office, the
Zionists were able to translate contemplated "temporary control," into
the reformulation of tenants' protection, a far cry from containment
of Jewish settlement as envisaged by Chancellor.

Having been consulted about the interpretation of the Passfield
White Paper between November 1930 and February 1931, the expanded Jewish Agency (JA) insisted that such consultations continue
in order to abort Chancellor's proposed land transfer restrictions.
Fearful of Jewish invective prior to the submission of its annual report
to the League of Nations, the Colonial Office allowed Dr. Selig
Brodetsky, Lewis Namier, and other Zionists frequent input into all
amending legislation pertinent to land.[36]

The juxtaposition of the proposed land transfer prohibitions with
the passage of the POCO not only increased the actual monthly sales
of land to Jewish purchasers, but it caused Arab landowners to refuse
to lease land to hitherto permanent tenants.[37] Some landowners, fearful of the prohibitions, did not want to bind themselves and impede
free disposition. A steady decline in the availability of large unoc-
cupied or partially occupied lands concurrent with the passage of the
POCO forced many Jewish purchasing agents to concentrate on the
acquisition of land from small Palestinian landowners, after such

[34] See Proposed Transfer of Agricultural Land Bill in CO 733/182/77050, part II.

[35] League of Nations, *Permanent Mandates Commission—Minutes*, June 15, 1931,
pp. 78-80.

[36] Minutes by John Shuckburgh of the Colonial Office, May 22, 1931 and Passfield to
Chancellor, April 22, 1931, CO 733/199/87072, part II. Lewis Namier of the London
Zionist Executive to Chaim Weizmann, January 20, 1931, CZA, 525/7455; secretary of
state for the colonies to High Commissioner, January 29, 1931, and High Commissioner to secretary of state for the colonies, January 31, 1931, CP, Box 13/5.

[37] Zvi Botkovsky, a Jewish land purchasing agent, to the Palestine Zionist Executive,
March 3, 1931, CZA, S25/9836.

holdings had been accumulated into large areas by Arab intermediaries and land brokers.

At all costs, those sellers and purchasers interested in unfettered
land transfers vigorously opposed any centralized government control. Legislation that Chancellor had drafted promised to constrain
severely the methods of Jewish land purchase and Arab land sales.
The JA and its affiliated land purchasing institutions did not want an
amended version of the POCO or land transfer controls that would
guarantee tenants' protection in the interim period between the signature of an option to purchase and the actual transfer of the land.
Past willingness of Arab tenants to accept monetary compensation
prior to legal transfer reinforced the belief among Jewish purchasers
that such payments would be no less effective in the future.

But Chancellor was adamant about the need to provide wider protection for cultivators of all varieties. In early 1931, he was upset by
the plight of cultivators at Shatta village near Beisan, who were being
evicted because they possessed no legal protection. There, the landowners had moved tenants from one plot to another and had the land
rented to tenants by another tenant acting as an agent for the landlord. Under the existing POCO, tenants of tenants were not protected
legally against eviction.

The politic manner in which the Palestine Land Development
Company handled the Shatta tenants' future considerably moderated
Chancellor's immediate fears about their becoming landless and
"highwaymen." Not only was monetary compensation paid to the sub-
tenants who did not qualify legally as tenants, but efforts were made
to resettle them elsewhere. Chancellor did not insist upon the inclusion of a subtenant in any new definition of "tenant" nor did he insist
upon a more comprehensive definition of a holding. He succumbed
to the pressure placed upon him by the secretary of state for the colonies to enact additional legislation for cultivators early in 1931, so
that His Majesty's Government could go to the League of Nations
meeting in June stating that action had been taken to protect the Arab
cultivator.[38]

In May 1931, the Protection of Cultivators Amendment Ordinance
(POCAO) was enacted. It was drafted after being submitted to the JA
no less than four times for comment and emendation.[39] Not all of the
various objections raised by the JA were removed from the drafts of
the amendment. Legislation for the first time protected grazers who
had been in continuous occupation of a particular area for five years,
even though lawyers for the JA feared that any fellah who merely

[38] Secretary of state for the colonies to Chancellor, April 22, 1931, CP, Box 13/5.
[39] S. Horowitz, lawyer for the JA, to the JA, June 8, 1931, CZA, KKL5/536.

exercised the practice of grazing could move onto the land and take possession of it and defy the landlord to have him removed, except in payment of some compensation. The JA's trepidation was justified. Grazers did request compensation from landlords on whose land their flocks once moved about readily. In April 1932,[40] the administration refused to sanction such retroactive compensation. It is noteworthy that some grazers who were otherwise predominantly illiterate and shunned direct contacts with landowners were sufficiently wily and forward in seeking compensatory sums.

The 1931 amending legislation, contrary to Jewish purchasing interests, protected tenants who were evicted by the order of a court or judge. A 1932 amendment included the execution officer as well, suggesting that circumventions took place between May 1931 and April 1932 in which the execution officer of the court, and not the court or judge, had orders for eviction comprehensively applied.

The protection of grazers and the protection of those evicted by the order of a court or judge were direct administrative responses to the protracted problem of Bedouin grazers at Wadi Hawarith, where a purchase had been effected through collusive mortgage and debt forfeiture. An additional blow to Jewish purchasing interests was the directive in the 1931 legislation that the High Commissioner or his deputy could refuse monetary compensation as equivalent provision secured toward the livelihood of the tenant. According to all interpretations made by the legal advisers of the JA, this gave Chancellor de facto if not actual control over land transfers. But since this provision worried members of the Palestine Land Development Company and others, a letter of explanation was procured by Chaim Weizmann, the former president of the World Zionist Organization, from the Colonial Office almost refuting the intent of the new amendment. In that letter of May 20, 1931, monetary compensation was not to be excluded.[41] Once more, Robert Drayton, the acting attorney general, pointed out that the High Commissioner (nor anyone else) could not control agreements reached among the tenant, landlord, and purchaser.[42]

The definition of a tenant continued to exclude agricultural laborers receiving a monetary wage and owner-occupiers. The legal protection offered in 1932 still only applied to perhaps no more than

---

[40] Protection of Cultivators Amendment Ordinance (No. 1) 1932, *Official Gazette*, April 22, 1932.

[41] Dr. Thon of the Palestine Land Development Company to the JA, June 8, 1931, CZA, KKL 5/Box 536.

[42] For Drayton's comments on the POCAO see CO 733/199/87072. For the POCAO of May 1931 see *Official Gazette*, May 29, 1931, pp. 414-16.

20,000 of the more than 100,000 fellahin engaged primarily in culti-vation.

The Protection of Cultivators Ordinance, 1933, and Amendments

In an effort to streamline, redefine, and broaden tenants' protection, a new ordinance was enacted in August 1933 superseding all previous POCO legislation. Unlike earlier POCO legislation, drafts of the or-dinance were not communicated to the JA for comment. Consider-able input into its drafting came from Lewis French, the director of development, who had recommended both a Homestead Protection Ordinance for the owner-occupier and a new POCO. As the High Commissioner, Sir Arthur Wauchope believed that tenants formerly displaced would be resettled through the efforts of the Development Department's Landless Arab Inquiry and future displacement would be prevented by the new POCO. Wauchope and the Palestine admin-istration were naive in believing that legislation and the bureaucracy could effectively provide tenants' protection, but his consummate commitment to tenants' protection was evidenced by the immediate promulgation of the ordinance by publication in the *Official Gazette*, a procedure reserved generally for changes in tariff and custom dues.

The principal element in the Protection of Cultivators Ordinance of 1933 provided that no "statutory tenant" (person, family, or tribe) of one year could be disturbed by the owner, unless he was provided with a subsistence area whose adequacy was determined by a govern-mental board. Additionally, the tenant was given security against dis-turbance, was protected against unrestrained rent increase, and was entitled to compensation for improvements if evicted. In making it-self the final arbiter between two segments of Palestinian Arab society, the Palestine administration generated societal conflicts, splintering further an Arab population already divided by regional, religious, so-cial, and political affiliations.

While there was a concerted effort made to enhance the rights of the tenant, squatter, and landless Arab, the British government did not commit itself to the protection of the owner-occupier or to the ag-ricultural laborer, nor did it forsake totally its informal alliance with landowning and land-benefiting classes. High Commissioner Wauchope acknowledged that the Palestine administration could not undertake to resettle agricultural laborers, if for no other reason than the financial expenditures involved.[43] The POCO of 1933 permitted

[43] Wauchope to Cunliffe-Lister, December 22, 1932, CO 733/217/97072.

landowners the prerogative to petition government to resume a
tenanted holding for purpose of upgrading its cultivable capacity, its
development, or for closer settlement, colonization, or disposal for
building purposes. Many landlords did seek governmental assistance
in ridding their land of tenants under these provisions in section 15 of
the POCO.[44]

This POCO prevented the tenant from selling or mortgaging his
tenancy right, but did not prevent him from giving up his land to the
landlord before the granting of "statutory tenancy." Where tenants
did make prior agreements with their landlords to vacate land, and
then claimed "statutory tenancy," the government board established
to protect the tenants' rights ruled in favor of the landlord. Informal
agreements were sometimes made between the landlord and his tenants, in which the landlord, interested in freeing his land of tenants,
did not collect a portion of the crop as annual rent and paid the tenant's tithe, for which the tenant left his land.[45]

The immediate result of the ordinance's enactment was an increase
in the number of disputes over the right to use and dispose of land.
There were surprisingly few claims to tenancy rights from Arabs with
respect to Jewish-owned land. This lack of claims was evidence that
Jewish landowners were finding little difficulty, by means of payment
of liberal compensation, in persuading Arabs who claimed rights to
abandon their claims. There was the case of eleven cultivators in the
Ramleh subdistrict who had their claims for "statutory tenancy" upheld against the Hanotiah Company, a Jewish colonization company.
Three days after the judgment in their favor they chose to leave their
lands after receiving 600 Palestine pounds.[46] Most disputes that arose
under the ordinance's jurisdiction were between Arab landlords and
their tenants.[47]

Most of the claims submitted in early 1934 concerned land in the
coastal plains and not the hill regions of Palestine, reflecting Jewish
land purchase concentration and Arab land sales in general. Between
early 1934 and January 1937, 271 claims were heard with 167 upheld
and 104 dismissed in the Tulkarm subdistrict.[48] Once claims were ac-

[44] See below on landlords' actions under section 15 of the POCO.
[45] Case of Faris Ali Salameh vs. Mohammad al-Sheikh Nasir and partners, ISA, Box
3922/TR 34/33/a. There were numerous instances where this procedure was practiced.
[46] J. Hawthorn Hall for the High Commissioner to Cunliffe-Lister, April 27, 1934,
CO 733/252/37272/1 folios 17 to 30.
[47] Ibid. This point is corroborated by the more than 250 claims from the Tulkarm
subdistrict that we read.
[48] H. M. Foot, assistant district commissioner, Samaria to northern district commissioner, January 28, 1937, CO 733/345/75550/33F. Claims should not be confused with
individuals. There were single claims in which there were as many as seventy tenants
seeking "statutory tenancy."

cepted by the boards set up to investigate them, they were handled with dispatch, which had a positive effect upon the minds of the people.[49]

From the records of the claims in the Tulkarm subdistrict, testimony of village mukhtars carried great weight in the decisions made by investigating boards. Records of tithe payments were in most cases insufficient evidence of a tenant's cultivating tenure. Though the ordinance did not precisely require written documentation of previous cultivation or grazing, in cases where it was the landlord's word against the claimant, the commission most often held against the claimant. Many times no written tenancy agreement existed, because the tenant feared any possible knowledge by the government of his whereabouts. Furthermore, if a claimant were working land that had never been registered in the land record books, the establishment of rightful ownership first had to be determined by the land courts, a lengthy process in its own right. If it could then be shown that the claimant owned land in addition to the land in which he was a tenant, and that area was deemed adequate for his subsistence, then his "statutory tenancy" claim was not upheld.

The new ordinance, like its predecessors, was open to abuse, misuse, and circumvention. Some cultivators saw in the new POCO an opportunity to enhance themselves financially, either by seeking to extract monetary compensation from a landlord interested in selling his land free of tenant encumbrances or by squatting on land and expecting to use it until a decision was made about the claim. Some bona fide tenants plowed areas larger than their normal capacity would allow in order to deny the area to other agricultural workers who might otherwise have squatted on a landlord's property for the purpose of gaining compensation or working the land legitimately. The bona fide tenants believed that they might be entitled to larger compensatory amounts with fewer claims against the same landlord.[50] The impact of anticipated monetary demands caused some landlords to reduce the actual amount of land under cultivation, reducing in turn the crop yield and their rents, calculated on a fixed percentage of the yield. There were instances where the Arab landlord concurred with a claimant's request for "statutory tenancy" after the land had been purchased and legally registered. Such a practice resulted in the signing of contracts between Arab sellers and Jewish purchasers, stipulating that the seller was responsible to hand the land over free of tenants.[51] Provision of the money for the compensation came either from the seller or the purchaser depending upon the land sales

---

[49] Wauchope to Cunliffe-Lister, March 10, 1934, ISA, Box 2464/file G 195.
[50] ISA, Box 3922/TR 94/33.   [51] ISA, Box 3922/TR 79/33.

agreement. Another simple means of evading tenants' rights was the production at the board hearings of a receipt and agreement signed by the claimant acknowledging that he worked the land without the consent of the landlord, thus negating "statutory tenant" classification.[52]

Before the passage of the POCO of 1933, some landlords drew up lease agreements with tenants for a certain rental amount to be paid in cash rather than in kind. The tithe on such lands was often paid by the tenants directly to the tax collectors or to agents working for the landlord who also collected the rents. But the existing Commutation of Tithes Ordinance obliged the landlord to pay the tax directly. After the passage of the POCO of 1933 some tenants believed that the tax collection procedure would not permit the landlord to evict them from their land. Hence, many of them ceased paying the amount of the tax due the landlord and in turn due to the government and ceased paying the rent as well. Landlords, responding to their tenants' refusal to pay rent, appointed guards to watch the threshing floor, or, if the landlord was resident far distant from his lands, requested the administration to collect the rent and the tax on his behalf.[53] On at least one occasion the tenants killed the guard employed by the landlord to collect the rent and tithe.[54]

Tenants in some cases were appropriately coached about their rights. In one instance claimants repeated, parrot-like, the block and parcel numbers of the lands in which tenancy rights were claimed, yet were unable to state the block and parcel numbers owned and occupied by themselves in the same village.[55] The extent to which Palestinian Arabs, involved in the nationalist cause, incited recalcitrance on the part of some fellahin against their landlords and against the Zionists is in need of further study. There is evidence that "intriguers and blackmailers redoubled their efforts to obtain money from landlords by inciting others to enter land in which they had no rights."[56]

The recourse left to landlords was in section 15 of the POCO, which permitted resumption of a holding. In some cases, the Arab landlord was able to gain eviction of his tenants because he wished to upgrade his holding to cash crop cultivation of oranges.[57] In other cases, the landlord sought resumption of a holding and eviction of his tenants

[52] ISA, Box 3922/TR 61/33.

[53] ISA, Box 3890/TR 94/33, especially Ahmed Qabbani to assistant district commissioner, February 26, 1936, folio 61.

[54] Ibid.

[55] *Memorandum submitted to the Palestine Royal Commission on behalf of the Jewish Agency for Palestine*, November 1936, p. 143.

[56] Note by H. M. Foot, December 11, 1933, CO 733/252/37271/1.

[57] ISA, Box 3384/TR 114/33, and TR 41/33.

because he considered himself helpless and poor.[58] Another Arab landlord, who served in the Palestine administration, asked and received the resumption of his holding and the eviction of his tenants because their tenancy threatened his future with serious material loss. The landlord argued that he should not be forced to suffer, merely to provide a tenant with means for his living.[59]

An immediate effect of the new POCO was a particular reluctance on the part of Arab landowners to lease or release their lands to tenants. In the southern district of Palestine, Arab landlords evaded the spirit of the ordinance by not permitting resident cultivators to begin plowing for the coming agricultural season, thus not evicting them, but making their already precarious economic situation more tenuous. Landlords in the coastal plain sometimes left all their lands fallow rather than run the risk of tenancy claims.[60] As a result of this practice, many tenants spent hours appealing to sympathetic magistrates, police officers, and other administration officials who were, however, in no position to help them legally. By shutting tenants out of land they previously occupied and denying them the opportunity to cultivate the winter crop immediately after the summer crop, optimum seeding and land preparation time was lost.

The most unanticipated result of the POCO was its stimulating effect upon land transfers. Many landowners who still possessed reasonably large estates of 1,000 dunams or more sold their lands to Jewish purchasers rather than run the risk of tenancy claims. In some instances, landlords approached the JNF, requesting and receiving money to compensate their tenants of prior years in preparation for eventual sale to Jewish purchasing agents.[61] As far as it concerned the process of Jewish land purchase, this procedure enabled the Arab landlord to deal directly with his tenants, while the Jewish purchasing organization only supplied the compensatory amounts. This had the dual effect of cutting down on the number of bogus claims that might otherwise have been lodged against a Jewish company, and reducing the frequency of Jewish-Arab tenant contact, always susceptible to overtones of antagonism, resentment, and disquietude.

Not unexpectedly, the JA, its affiliated land purchasing organizations, and the Palestine Arab community reacted strongly and negatively to the implementation of the newly written POCO. As was evident from the Palestine Arab press, most Arab response to the new POCO was negative. Many articles pointed to the inadequacy of the

---

[58] ISA, Box 3922/TR 204/33.   [59] ISA, Box 3922/TR 114/33.

[60] Cf. fn. 46; League of Nations, *Permanent Mandates Commission—Minutes*, June 5, 1935, p. 51.

[61] Interview with A. Ben Shemesh, then legal adviser to the Jewish National Fund, May 3, 1973.

POCO, for it did not totally prohibit land sales. *Al-Jami'ah al-Islamiyyah* of August 3, 1933 remarked in one article that the POCO came too late, since the coastal plains had already been transferred into Jewish hands. Moreover, noted the paper, in the future the Arab landowner will shun the fellah and will not allow him to cultivate his property lest he remain on it permanently, and so the poor fellah will be chased by the Zionists. *Filastin* of August 5, 1933 said that "if the government seriously cared for the interest of the masses it would prohibit land transactions which prejudice the fellahin and cause them more harm than any number of successive bad (agricultural) seasons."

'Awni 'Abd al-Hadi, a lawyer and active member of the Istiqlal Party, noted that he did not believe the ordinance would be enforced, just as other ordinances (protecting tenants) since 1920 had not been enforced. He suggested that the government take effective measures to stop Jews from appropriating lands before compensating Arab cultivators with other lands. Interestingly enough, he did not advocate prohibitions on land sales, but rather urged the government to force a purchaser or seller to provide land in compensation for an eviction, with failure to comply to result in a seven- to ten-year prison term.[62] 'Awni took similar note of the inefficacy of the previous POCOs in his reply to the reports submitted by Lewis French. There he noted that no individual member of a nation had the right to dispose of his land in a manner that might prejudice the rights and position of the nation to which he belonged.[63]

Only immediately after the enactment of the POCO was there serious discussion of its merits. Most attention paid to the land question by Arab politicians in the period from 1933 until the promulgation of the Land Transfer Regulations of 1940 centered around the total prohibition of land sales interspersed with virulent attacks against land brokers. There is ample evidence to suggest that the fellahin took welcome advantage of the ordinance but were considerably disillusioned when the government failed to return many of them to their lands of previous occupation.

The new POCO created serious problems for Jewish land purchase. Because it gave a tenant rights against the landlord and did not prejudice those rights when land was transferred, the new owner was as liable to tenancy claims as the seller. Even if the seller contracted to sell his land free of tenancy encumbrances, the purchaser could not be sure that he would not face numerous tenancy claims. As a result of tenants' rights to occupy land as protected under the Land Dis-

[62] *Al-Jami'ah al-Islamiyyah*, September 8, 1933.
[63] 'Awni 'Abd al-Hadi to the High Commissioner, March 17, 1933, CO 733/230/17249.

putes Possession Ordinance, the Jewish owner of newly acquired land often found himself involved in very costly and lengthy judicial proceedings. Settlement with claimants to tenancy often necessitated out-of-court payments, sometimes forcing the purchaser to pay compensation to the tenants twice, once before the transfer and once after the transfer was effected.

The second major criticism of the POCO lodged by Jewish purchasers concerned the limitations placed upon the landlord. By virtue of the ordinance, as soon as a tenant received administrative recognition of "statutory tenancy," he became the charge of the landlord for life. If the tenant decided that he preferred another parcel of land, for whatever reason, the landlord was obliged to reserve both the land from which he moved and the land to which he moved as maintenance areas. Since no area limit was placed upon a tenant's holding, some claimed that more land was necessary for their livelihood than they actually needed or could work, farming portions of it out to others who in turn paid the "statutory tenant" rent for its use.

While many landlords, as noted, resorted to the resumption of their holdings, the ordinance deprived the landlord of absolute freedom to dispose of his land in whatever manner he wished. Land became, as a result, an illusory security forcing financial institutions to be cautious in granting credit or allowing collateral for what might well be encumbered land. The JNF argued that the ordinance perpetuated the practice of grazing at the expense of favoring more intensive use of otherwise cultivable lands.[64]

In an effort to broaden further the definition of a "statutory tenant" and increase cultivators' protection, the Protection of Cultivators Amendment Ordinance of 1936 was enacted in June 1936. The definition of a "statutory tenant" was finally apparently widened to include a person who was hired by the landlord to do agricultural work and who received a monetary wage. At least that was the definition as it appeared in the draft ordinance of May 7, 1936. When the amendment was promulgated on June 25, 1936, agricultural laborers were specifically excluded from the "statutory tenant" definition. It is not clear whether their inclusion in the draft ordinance was merely a typographical error, or whether there was actual intent to provide protection for agricultural laborers. It is highly unlikely that Wauchope, who was already in the midst of fending off the Arab general strike in May, would have been willing to allocate vast funds sorely needed for security purposes to pay for the administrators and bureaucracy necessary to hear the claims of this large class of cultivators.

[64] *Note on the Cultivators (Protection) Ordinance*, July 1934, CZA, S25/6932.

Conclusion

Had there not been an outbreak of Arab disturbances in April and May of 1936, the mandatory government would have enacted protection for owner-occupiers through retention of a maintenance area known as a "lot viable." This would have protected the largest and most economically vulnerable agricultural class in Palestine. But as a result of the riots and general strike, such legislation awaited the findings of the investigatory (Peel) commission. No owner-occupier legislation was ever enacted.

Wauchope had understood that for practical, financial, and economic reasons he had to stop or minimize the displacement of Arab cultivators. At the same time he did not wish to restrict land transfers or have restrictive land transfer regulations instituted as had been suggested earlier by Chancellor.[65] Obliged legally through the articles of the Mandate to facilitate the growth of the Jewish national home and unofficially to court Arab (landowning) notable participation, or at least tacit acquiescence to British presence in Palestine, support of tenant's and cultivator's protection was considered the most advantageous and least antagonistic solution in the land sphere. No radical rearrangement of land ownership patterns and no overt legal restrictions upon Jewish land purchase (until 1940) were enacted.

Blind faith in British-imposed law was the most appalling aspect of British policy in the land sphere. The British did not comprehend the depth of Zionist commitment to own land nor did they understand why Palestinian Arabs were positively eager to sell portions of their patrimony. As a result they did not conceive of the artful deceptions conjured up by purchasers and sellers to satisfy their respective needs.

In 1940, the British changed their role from umpire to advocate. The land transfer restrictions were as much an effort to stop Jewish land purchase as to protect the Palestinian Arab against his own willful indiscretion. British paternalism was aimed not only at shielding the Palestinian Arab population, but designed to retain Britain's political dominance in Palestine.

The dispute over land was not just an Arab-Zionist controversy. It tore at existing societal differences within the Palestinian Arab community. Accession to positions of political authority had been acquired via land acquisition. Later, such authority was preserved by exchanging money for land. Once a protected birthright, land increasingly became relegated to commodity status for some Palestinian Arab notables. Social cleavages widened as tenants were forced to leave traditional areas of residence and adjust their life styles to exist-

[65] Wauchope to Cunliffe-Lister, April ? 1932, CO 733/230/17249.

ences that were increasingly less dependent upon direct agricultural and pastoral occupations. Continued economic disorientation and physical dislocation contributed to the inability of many former Arab tenants, and other agriculturists for that matter, to develop some common political voice. Once displaced and compensated, the Arab tenant could not depend upon a former landlord as his political spokesman. Land sales to Jews hastened the divisions within Palestinian Arab society.

Two factors played significant roles in British misperceptions: lack of well-trained administrative personnel who could understand the complexities of the land regime; and a gross underestimation of the effects of a plummeting rural economy upon a cultivator's ability to maintain, in what were good years, adequate subsistence. As a consequence of these deficiencies, the Palestine administration was compelled to rely upon information judicially supplied to it by the JA.

Nevertheless, Arab tenants gladly took compensation to vacate their holdings. Some relished the opportunity while others were reluctant to accept anything but land. Ultimately the peasants were defenseless against the process of dispossession and the legalized but relentless pressure that went with it.[66] Such pressure emanated simultaneously from Arab sellers, Jewish purchasers, and an agricultural economy that was precarious at best. Many who received monetary compensation saw these lump sums as means toward debt extrication. Most squandered the money given them. Very few invested the proceeds in other, more profitable commercial or agricultural pursuits.

Colonel C. F. Cox, the Nazareth district governor in 1920-1921, zealously defended the rights of tenants to receive land as compensation. Yet, even he came to the unalterable conclusion that the mandatory government was interfering in a matter where it had not been asked and where tenants preferred to receive money.[67] Nonetheless, the Palestine administration, particularly after 1929, appointed itself as judge between Arab landowning and Arab tenant classes. It is not surprising, therefore, that on looking back upon the effectiveness of the various POCO's promulgated, the administration found in 1941 that they comprised "one of the most contentious pieces of legislation on the statute books for Palestine."[68]

Inter- and intra-communal ill-feeling was catalyzed by the various

[66] For a similar conclusion see George Antonius, The Arab Awakening (New York: Capricorn Books, 1965), p. 398.

[67] Abraham Pevsner of the Palestine Land Development Company to the head of the Palestine Zionist Executive, September 12, 1928, CZA, S25/7456.

[68] Report of the Committee on State Domain on the Proposal to Exempt State Domain from the Provisions of the Cultivators (Protection) Ordinance, enclosure in a letter from Sir Harold MacMichael, High Commissioner for Palestine, to Lord Moyne, secretary of state for the colonies, June 28, 1941, CO 733/447/76117.

versions of the POCO. Certainly, in the absence of such legislation, the cultural, religious, political, and economic animosities that plagued Palestine for almost three decades under the Mandate would still have been evident, though without it the hostilities might also at times have been somewhat less vitriolic.

UNDERTAKING[69]

Mr. Yehoshua Hankin
   through the District Officer, Nazareth

We, the undersigned, cultivators of the lands of the village of Afuleh, as shown by the Register of Commuted Tithe for 1924, hereby admit and acknowledge that the lands and houses situated in the village of Afuleh are the property of Nicola and Michel, sons of the late Ibrahim Sursock, of the City of Beirut, and that after the death of the said Michel his share devolved by way of succession according to Miri Law to his heirs, viz., his widow Lisa Sursock and to his sons from his said wife, who, being still infants are under the lawful guardianship of their mother, and that the said lands and houses are still their property to this present day, without any objection or adverse claims by another person, and no other person has any rights to the said properties:

And whereas, you have purchased the said lands and houses with all the rights and benefits appurtenant thereto on behalf of the Palestine Land Development Company, and the American Zion Commonwealth, and you caused the said properties to be surveyed and to be registered in the names of the said two companies.

And whereas, we are not in a position to purchase the said properties or any part of the same, owing to our inability to pay the price, and you have offered us sufficient land for cultivation,

We therefore, of our own free will do hereby inform you that we decline your said offer, as we have obtained lands for cultivation elsewhere, and we are not in need of land, and we undertake that by the 5th of January, 1925, we shall evict and deliver for your use our houses, and remove from the said houses our families and our cattle, and we shall deliver the said houses to you free from any impediment

---

[69] Central Zionist Archives, S25/3368.

and we shall leave the lands of Afuleh, its houses and other buildings and deliver the same to you.

And we further undertake to deliver to you four camel-loads of fodder per feddan,

And we acknowledge with thanks the receipt from you of £25 twenty-five pounds per feddan, viz., I, Selim al-Saadi, received from you £50 for two feddans, and I, Salem (al)-Saadi, received £25 for one feddan; and I, Mustapha al-Shari, received from you £25 for one feddan; and I, Ali al-Khalaf, received from you £25 for one feddan; and I, 'Abdullah Muhammad Jawish, received from you £50 for two feddans, and we Arifeh and Atfeh, heirs of Kamel Assad, for ourselves and in our capacity as guardians of our infant brother, Farla(?) and the other heirs, received from you £50 for two feddans, and this by way of compensation for the crop and any other work done by us on this land, and as consideration for our refusal of your said offer of land for cultivation, and we hereby waive by way of full and irrevocable waiver any rights which we may have had to the said lands and houses, and we declare that we have no further right to demand the purchase of the said land or any part of the same, nor do we demand land for cultivation nor any rights to the crop, nor any other rights whatsoever.

If we fail to comply with the above terms or if we fail to deliver the said lands and properties (viz., the said houses) and to leave the said village within the aforementioned period, we shall be liable to pay you by way of rental for the said houses and lands at the rate of half-a-pound per day for each feddan, and in addition to this if we fail to leave and deliver, or we fail to comply with any of the terms herein mentioned, we shall be further liable to pay you the sum of £50. per feddan by way of damages for the damage caused to you and of any Court or other fees which you may incur without the necessity of any Notarial or other notice, and our failure to deliver, or our default shall be deemed to be sufficient notice within the meaning of Article 107 of the Ottoman Code of Civil Procedure.

Yours, etc.

28th December 1924. (Signed) *'Abdullah Muhammad Jawish*

Finger print of

Ali al-Khalaf al-Adad
Salem Mahmud al-Saadi
Salim Mahmud al-Saadi
Mustafa Omar Shaari
Arifeh bint? Kamel Assad
Atfeh bint? Kamel Assad

We personally know the above five men and two women and they signed the above document in our presence after it was read over to them.

Witness (Signed)   Hassan Mubari
                     Mahmud 'Abd al-Hassani

Certified by the Notary Public of Nazareth under number 388 of 26/12/24.

APPENDIX II*

Table 13

Number of Arab Tenant Farmers on Tracts Acquired by Jews in the Plains of Esdraelon (Jezreel Valley) and Acre and Compensatory Amounts Paid

Land	Sellers	Area in Metric Dunams Purchased	Previous Tenanted Area	Number of Tenants	Compensation Paid (£)
Nuris Block	Sursock	27,018	5,514	38	615
Nahalal Block	Sursock	20,034	6,433	64	333
Ginegar	Sursock	10,568	5,927	20	256
Tel Adas	Sursock	19,758	8,271	34	492
Hartieh Shayk Abreik Harbaj	Sursock	23,894	14,244	59	3,314
Jabatta Kneifes	Sursock	22,056	11,028	57	2,032
Jedda	Sursock	9,465	9,190	54	3,338
Tel-Shemmen	Sursock	6,341	5,973	22	1,103
Kuskus-Tabun	Farah	9,281	6,984	40	1,628
Afule	Sursock	14,244	12,406	47	2,603
Shunam	Sursock, Ra'is, Atala	9,373	5,514	14	1,051
Abu-Shusha	Karkabi	4,870	1,929	17	432
Warakani	Karkabi	3,308	2,757	9	513
Jidro	Sursock	40,976	14,704	117	3,568
Majdal and Kafratta	Sursock	19,023	18,380	96	6,156
Totals		240,209	129,254	688	27,434

*Central Zionist Archives, S25/7620.

CHAPTER 8

Peasants into Workmen:
Internal Labor Migration and the Arab Village Community under the Mandate

by Rachelle Taqqu

Elites and Masses: Toward a History from Below

The study of the Arabs in mandatory Palestine has long suffered from a preoccupation with elites that has produced a static, one-dimensional image of the Palestinian community. This emphasis has grown out of a primary interest in Palestinian nationalism and has sought justification in the structure of Arab politics and society under the Mandate. Nevertheless, an exclusive concern with the role of elites overlooks the social and economic transformation that was overtaking Palestine. If the popular identification with the hegemonic classes and culture remained strong, profound imbalances within Arab society were also emerging. Traditional social relations were shaken as landholding patterns shifted, as agriculture and markets expanded, and as the burgeoning capitalist economy centered in the coastal plain drew increasing numbers of Arab peasants into urban wage labor.

Among the pressures for socioeconomic change, the recruitment of an Arab wage force was perhaps the most dramatically obvious development: by the 1940s, when labor mobilization reached a wartime peak, the total Arab wage force had expanded to include nearly one-third of the entire male Arab population of working age. The transition to wage labor had far-reaching consequences. It led to a loosening of customary bonds that was particularly fateful for Palestinian nationalist politics, since the nationalist movement lacked central institutions and rested heavily on informal traditional ties. In addition, changes in class and group loyalties helped shape popular attitudes to a series of critical issues, from Zionism and Jewish immigration to the widening notion of the Palestinian community. Despite the centrality of this transformation, however, we still know very little about it. Recent research has begun to pay increasing attention to the questions of class formation and proletarianization in these years;[1] but the human dimensions of this process—the evolving relationships, solidarities, and identity among peasant-workers—have seldom been explored.

This paper is an effort to help fill that gap. In order to clarify the changing class situation of the Palestinian peasantry, it singles out the transition to wage labor for special study, tracing the impact of labor migration on both the structural position of peasants and the identity of *fellah* workers. It also emphasizes the sharp discontinuities within the mandatory period itself. For, rather than representing a continuum, the Mandate was marked by important shifts in official policy and in patterns of economic development. In particular, the wartime years of the 1940s can be seen as a radical departure from previous times.

Following a brief survey of the size of the Arab wage force over time, developments of the 1920s and 1930s are considered apart from and in contrast to those which followed them. The transition to wage labor did not evolve from a more generalized process of agrarian differentiation and growth, but was hastened instead by opportunities outside the Arab economy. Labor migration did not necessarily lead to proletarianization, and proletarianization did not always imply solidarity. In the 1930s, the simultaneous economic backwardness and sociocultural strength of the village, and the prevailing patterns of labor recruitment and organization of work, together reinforced the mutual attachments among peasant workers. A shared sense of deprivation with clear class overtones emerged.

These village bonds, however, were greatly weakened by the prolonged Arab Revolt of 1936-1939; and the soaring demand for Arab labor in the 1940s strained peasant relationships beyond their limits. Ironically, wartime labor recruitment also intensified a process that traced its origins to earlier decades, but had not previously achieved significant proportions. This was the growth of self-consciousness and solidarity among a sizable number of workers. At the village level, however, the effect of the wartime mobilization of labor was social dislocation and confusion.

The Arab Labor Force: Size and Distribution

In Ottoman Palestine, the payment of money wages to Arab cultivators and workers in traditional industries had not been common.

---

[1] Talal Asad, "Anthropological Texts and Ideological Problems: An Analysis of Cohen on Arab Villages in Israel," *Economy and Society*, 4 (May, 1975), 251-82. Elia Zureik, "Toward a Sociology of the Palestinians," *Journal of Palestine Studies* VI, 4 (Summer, 1977), 3-16. Shulamit Carmi and Henry Rosenfeld, "The Origins of the Process of Proletarianization and Urbanization of Arab Peasants in Palestine," *Annals of the New York Academy of Sciences*, 220 (March, 1974), 470-85.

It was only with the establishment of the Mandate and the implanta-
tion in Palestine of a capitalist sector that an Arab wage force began to
grow. The number of wage workers, whether casual or permanent,
was at first extremely small, for the Palestine economy was expanding
in fits and starts and was plagued by a serious depression from late
1926 through 1928. In the 1930s, however, the Arab wage force
began to increase steadily, largely as a result of redoubled Jewish immigration. Despite the determination of Labor Zionists to build a
self-sufficient economy that did not rely on the exploitation of cheap
Arab labor, their autarchic aspirations were not even approximately
realized until the Arab boycott and strike of 1936 brought about a
sudden segregation of the two economic sectors. Before then, substantial numbers of Arab workers were directly employed by Jews on
citrus plantations and in other agricultural jobs, and in a wide range
of other enterprises from construction and quarrying to industrial
concerns. The mandatory government also helped transform the
economy, despite its preference for very gradual development. It
provided vast opportunities for Arab employment by reorganizing
the railways, improving communications, building a new harbor at
Haifa, and making way for a number of foreign concessions. The
Arab economy, too, was stimulated by the influx of capital and by the
growing demand for housing; but expansion within the Arab sector
was by itself unequal to the task of closing the widening gap between
population and productivity.

Most Arab laborers were temporary migrants from their villages or
casual workers on nearby public works. Arab urbanization never
reached major proportions. Still, the Arab populations of Jaffa and
Haifa did grow remarkably. In the intercensal period between 1922
and 1931, Jaffa's Arab population increased by 63 percent, and Haifa's by 87 percent, although the overall growth rate of the Arab population in the same years was 28 percent and the general urban growth
rate among Arabs was 24 percent. Other towns where the Arab population grew at a rapid rate were Jerusalem, at 37 percent, Ramleh, at
43 percent, and Lydda, at 39 percent.[2] In these towns, the private
building trade and allied work in quarries and in cement manufacture
absorbed the largest portion of the migrants.

The size of the overall wage force can be only imprecisely gauged,
since the statistical data are largely rough and unreliable. Much Arab
labor eluded enumeration because it was casual or strictly rural. The
figures in Table 14 should therefore not be interpreted too closely.
They exclude the thousands of peasants who worked seasonally in
various forms of agricultural employment, or in public works in the
countryside.

[2] Palestine Government, *A Survey of Palestine* (Jerusalem, 1946) (afterwards, *Survey*),
I, pp. 147-49.

Table 14
Estimated Arab Wage Force, 1930-1935

			Other indices of growth†		
	Workers per annum		Avg. no. of permits/yr.	Avg. value 1933-35	Avg. munic. expend. on public wks.
Branch of production	1931*	1931-35	1933-35	(1930=100)	1933-35
Agriculture					
Total wage force[3]	na	30,000			
Citrus culture[4]		(1939)			
Arab groves					
(peak of season)	na	15,000			
		(1938)			
Jewish groves					
(peak of season)	na	8,000			
		(1935)			
Permanent workers					
(Arab and Jewish groves)	na	5,000-7,000			
		(1938)			
Railways[5]	1,750-2,000	3,000			
Harbors[6]					
Jaffa	1,500**	2,000			
Haifa	—	800-1,600			
Industry[7]					
Non-Jewish	na	4,000			
Jewish	na	1,500			
Oil Companies	na	1,000			
Construction and quarrying[8]					
Total	8,900	na			
Haifa harbor construction	—	2,000			
Urban building activity					
Jaffa			241	641	598
Haifa			306	912	154
Acre			103	369	130
Ramleh			114	323	243
Lydda			118	406	117

* Census data for 1931 on occupational distribution are included only in instances where the census distinguishes wage labor from other earners.
** Includes boat owners.
† This category is included to help gauge labor force growth in construction and quarrying, in the absence of reliable estimates of wage force size.

[3] For the government's estimate of 30,000 agricultural workers, see PRO CO 733/469/76284, Employment Committee, First Interim Report, 27.X.44.
[4] Survey, I, p. 340; Central Zionist Archives (afterwards, CZA) S25/4569, "Memorandum on the Influence of Jewish Employment on the Non-Jewish Population." See also CZA S25/10342, "Arab-Jewish Economic Interrelations in Palestine" (1936), by Dr. A. Bonne.
[5] Palestine Government (afterwards, PG), Report of the General Manager on the Adminis-

The seasonal flow of underemployed village labor was halted during the economic depression that began in 1935 and reached serious proportions by 1939 and 1940. Although it had roots in the international economy and in declining Jewish immigration, the depression was also directly related to the Arab Revolt, which threw large numbers of semiurbanized fellahin back into total dependence on indigenous agriculture. Unemployment was seriously aggravated by the shipping crisis that virtually closed the Mediterranean in 1940. Masses of agricultural workers from the citrus plantations together with many hundreds of port workers found themselves without work.

In mid-1941 economic depression among the Arabs shifted suddenly and radically into a wartime boom, as demands on local agriculture, industry, and manpower escalated. By 1942, a severe labor shortage developed. Some 30,000 Palestinian citizens, most of them Jewish, had in the meantime joined the armed forces, thus adding to the strain on the labor market.[9] Recruitment of Arab wage workers consequently reached unprecedented proportions.

To prevent a mass rural exodus—and also as a bulwark against soaring wage rates—government and military authorities imported thousands of unskilled workers from neighboring Arab countries.[10] Imported labor, however, met only a fraction of Palestine's manpower needs in the 1940s. An officially constituted Employment Committee in 1944 cited a reduction of the agricultural work force by some 57,000 males since 1939: this figure included 10,000 Jews, with the remainder Arabs who had previously derived most of their income from agriculture. The depletion was greater if one considered the entire pool of underemployed agricultural labor when calculating the prewar base figure.[11]

tration of the Railways, 1932, p. 51, and ibid., 1936, p. 133. PG, Census of Palestine, 1931, Vol. I, pp. 288-89, gives the lower estimate of 1,750 for 1931.

[6] Israel State Archives (afterwards, ISA) I/Lab/39/44, Report by Margaret Nixon, 24.I.36. On Haifa harbor, see CZA S9/1135, Haifa Workers' Council to Labor Department, Jewish Agency, 23.IX.36.

[7] PG, Office of Statistics, Statistical Abstract of Palestine, 1939 (Jerusalem, 1939), p. 52; CZA S25/10342, "Arab-Jewish Economic Interrelations in Palestine" (1936).

[8] Census, 1931, I, pp. 288-89, listed 7,000 workers in construction and 1,900 in mining and quarrying. Figures on harbor construction come from ISA PWD 7/5 (2) and 7/5 (3), Reports of Resident Engineer, Haifa Harbor Works, from 17.XI.31 to 16.V.34. See CZA S25/10495, 12.VI.32, for the report that the total number of workers then at the harbor was 1,700. Indices on building are derived from PG, Statistical Abstract, 1939, pp. 52-53.

[9] PG, Department of Labor, Annual Report, 1942.

[10] On foreign Arab labor in Palestine, see Survey, I, pp. 213-14; ISA Galilee District files 943:25/3, Major, PLCO to assistant district commissioner, Haifa, 19.III.47. See also the statistical estimate by the Histadrut (June, 1947), in CZA S25/3107.

[11] PRO CO 733/469/76284, Employment Committee, First Interim Report, 27.X.44, para. 8.

Although it is impossible to take an exact measure of the Arab wage force because of its seasonal fluctuations, certain figures do reflect a degree of stability. It is helpful at this point to set out a schematic estimate of the number of Arab wartime workers near the peak period of employment in 1943. Two important reference points are the contemporary analyses of the Arab work force by the government's statistician, P. J. Loftus (Table 15), and by the Histadrut (Table 16). Loftus admittedly understated the size of the Arab labor force, since he excluded part-time family labor. The chief drawback of his assessment, however, is its lack of distinction between wage laborers and other earners. The 1947 Jewish study, on the other hand, specifically enumerated the number of Arab wage workers. It probably errs on the side of overestimation.

If fishing, business, services, professions, and agriculture are eliminated from the estimates in Table 16, the total number of wage earners outside agriculture is 100,000. This assessment approximates the rough estimate made by the Labor Department in 1942, which included fellahin in temporary and seasonal employment. It should be noted, however, that the Histadrut's calculations represent an upper limit, since they are exceptionally liberal.[12]

The Impact of Labor Migration: The 1930s

The steady recruitment of labor before 1940 was closely related to conditions in the Arab countryside. As a combined result of population growth, land pressure, and agricultural stagnation, a large labor surplus was emerging. Between the two censuses of 1922 and 1931, the Arab population increased from 660,641 to 848,607, representing an increment of 28 percent. From 1931 to 1940, the Arab growth rate

[12] The number of railway workers thus appears to include not only Palestinian Arabs (some 5,000 by the account of the management), but also 1,500 Egyptians and 500 Transjordanians. The computations of workers in handicrafts and industries take account of various occupations omitted from the 1943 industrial census. They include, for example, 2,000 tailors' employees and 2,000 cobblers' workers above and beyond the 6,163 industrial wage earners enumerated in 1943. Again, the large number of workers in the "miscellaneous" category reveals the very broad scope of the survey, for this classification includes wage earners in religious institutions, school teachers, barbers' employees, engineers—and even 200 salaried artists ("photographers, actors, musicians, etc."). In addition, the survey assumes that certain occupational categories assessed in the population census of 1931 grew at the same rate as the general population, and there appears to be a degree of overlap between its classifications. See Department of Labor, *Annual Report, 1942*; PG, *Report of the General Manager on the Administration of the Railways, 1946*, p. 147; industrial censuses of 1940 and 1943 in PG, *General Monthly Bulletin of Current Statistics* (afterwards, *GMBCS*) (April, 1945); *Census of Palestine, 1931*. For monthly statistics on fluctuations in employment, see *GMBCS*, 1945-1947.

Table 15
Estimated Number Engaged in Each Branch of Production and Average Output per
Head in the Arab Community, 1944*

Branch of production	Number engaged (thousands)	Total income (£P mil.)	Average income per person (£P)
Total	300	49.6	165
Agriculture, livestock, fisheries, and forests	152	20.4	134
Industry and handicrafts	13	3.3	254
Housing	—	2.9	—
Building and construction	20	2.9	145
War Department, civilian employment	26	2.7	104
Palestine troops	2	0.2	121
Transport and communications	15	3.5	233
Commerce and finance, hotels, restaurants, and cafes	29	6.9	238
Government and local authorities	32	4.8	150
Other	11	2.0	182

* From P. J. Loftus, *National Income of Palestine* (Jerusalem, 1946), p. 27. £P stands for
Palestinian pounds.

Table 16
Histadrut Estimates of the Arab Wage Force, 1946*

Occupation	Number
Government workers	24,000
Army	27,000
Railways	7,000
Municipalities	3,250
Arab industries and handicrafts	11,000
Arab workers in non-Arab industry	2,500
Miscellaneous small enterprises	500
Mining	1,300
Harbors	1,700
Fishing	3,000
Oil companies	4,000
Construction	7,000
Transport	4,000
Business, services, professions	14,000
Agriculture	30,000
Miscellaneous	6,750
	147,000

* CZA S25/3107, "Arab Workers in Palestine in 1946" (June, 1947).

was nearly 26 percent according to government estimates. Growth was almost entirely due to natural increase, deriving in part from improved standards of hygiene and preventive medicine under the Mandate: death rates fell off sharply and infant mortality showed a significant decline, in urban areas in particular.[13] Together, population increase and land transfers to the Jews combined to throw growing numbers of Arabs onto the labor market.

The central propelling motive for labor migration, however, was the slow pace of agrarian modernization. As the Israeli anthropologist Henry Rosenfeld has pointed out, the existence of a large labor surplus was endemic to nonintensive agricultural cultivation, since farming rarely occupied the fellah fully.[14] Although Arab citriculture expanded during the period before 1940, capturing an enlarged local and foreign market, the capital accumulated in the export sector of Arab agriculture found its way only slowly to the traditional sector.[15] To a considerable extent, Arab citrus plantations formed an enclave in the Arab economy. Expansion and innovation did take place in other plantation farming, such as banana cultivation, although it still remains to determine the extent of such modernization. Before 1940, however, this trend did not offset the general stagnation in the larger nonintensive sector.

The reasons for agrarian backwardness have yet to be investigated in full. They include the attitudes and priorities of the landowners as well as the perennial indebtedness of the bulk of the peasantry. Official government policies and the creation of a local Jewish market for Arab produce both tended to sustain the extreme dependence of fellahin on landowners and urban moneylenders. Significantly, the proliferation of external, seasonal, and erratic labor opportunities also contributed considerably to the persistent underdevelopment of the countryside. Before 1940, most undertakings that employed Arab labor took advantage of the seasonality of this labor pool and its relative exclusion from the capitalist economy to serve their own fluctuating manpower needs and to keep wages low. This was as true of mining, quarrying, and roadwork as it was of citriculture or even of various industrial workshops in town. Outside employment thus provided fellahin with supplementary income rather than alternative oc-

[13] PG, Department of Statistics, *Vital Statistics Tables, 1922-1945* (Jerusalem, 1947), p. 1. See also, *Survey*, I, pp. 140-60.

[14] Henry Rosenfeld, "From Peasantry to Wage Labor and Residual Peasantry: The Transformation of an Arab Village" in *Process and Pattern in Culture*, ed. by Robert A. Manners (Chicago: Aldine Publishing Company, 1964), pp. 211-34.

[15] But see, however, Ya'akov Firestone, "Production and Trade in an Islamic Context: Sharika Contracts in the Transitional Economy of Northern Samaria, 1853-1943," *International Journal of Middle East Studies*, 6 (April, 1975), 185-209, 6 (July, 1975), 308-24.

cupations. Moreover, unskilled wages remained relatively low both in
and out of agriculture as a result of the loose demand for labor, the
existence of a large reserve of underemployed villagers, and the seasonal influx of impoverished Hawranis who lived in squalor and
worked for a pittance in the coastal region. The spread of wage labor
in the interwar years was thus a partial phenomenon that contributed
little toward peasant solvency or agrarian innovation.[16]

Patterns of labor recruitment in the countryside frequently reinforced the existing social structure as well. Thus, the government
Public Works Department, a major employer of Arab labor, relied on
the traditional structure of village society, recruiting workers on a
personal basis, through communal agents such as village *mukhtars*.
The organization of work was informal, following the lines of social
organization among the villagers. Mixing workers from different villages was not favored, and bringing laborers from afar was discouraged since this would require either transportation arrangements or
the erection of labor camps. Officials of the department strongly opposed the centralization of recruitment or the delegation of hiring authority to impersonal agencies except when absolutely necessary.
They did not relish the development of an uprooted labor army, dependent on public works for a livelihood.[17]

The Public Works Department respected traditional patterns of organization and stratification both because it was economical to do so
and also because of the social role that the government had given to
roadwork: short-term public works became the predominant form of
relief for seasonal rural unemployment.[18] Numerous customs and incidents attested to the successful fusion of seasonal wage labor and
traditional village organization. The practice of giving preference in
roadbuilding work to nearby villages encouraged peasants to claim
the right to work on all projects on or near their village lands; and
plentiful petitions for work presented by village mukhtars and *hamula*
leaders on behalf of their followers indicated that recognition by the

[16] Ya'akov Firestone, "Crop-Sharing Economics in Mandatory Palestine," *Middle Eastern Studies*, 11 (January, 1975), 3-23, and 11 (May, 1975), 175-94; David Horowitz and Rita Hinden, *Economic Survey of Palestine with Special Reference to the Years 1936 and 1937* (Tel Aviv: Jewish Agency, 1938), pp. 40-45; Talal Asad, "Anthropological Texts and Ideological Problems"; Rosenfeld and Carmi, "The Origins of Proletarianization." On wages scale, see PRO CO 733/152/57204, Report of the Wages Commission, 1928, u/c Plumer despatch, 17.VII.28.

[17] ISA, Galilee District files, 2629: G311, district engineer, Nazareth to district officer, Nazareth, 27.VII.41. See also PRO CO 733/152/57204, Wages Commission Report, 1928, p. 9; ISA PWD 7/5(2), f. 166, director of public works to chief immigration officer, 25.I.31.

[18] PRO CO 733/266/37543, Hathorn Hall to Cunliffe-Lister, 27.X.34; CO 733/339/75343, High Commissioner to Ormsby-Gore, 7.IX.37. See also CO 733/469/76284, Employment Committee, First Interim Report, 27.X.44, pp. 4ff.

Public Works Department had effectively enhanced the social position of these traditional leaders.[19]

Still, by the 1930s, the determination for cultural continuity in the countryside collided with economic realities, for poverty was forcing growing numbers of peasants to seek their livelihood in town. A period of severe agricultural depression coincided with a time of urban prosperity and expanding opportunities in the coastal plain. While agricultural yields were extremely poor from 1930 to 1933 and not much better in 1934, money wages paid to Arab workers in the coastal towns generally followed an upward trend until mid-1935. Among the thousands of urban migrants, many remained in town for extended periods, despite the temporary and seasonal nature of most Arab employment.[20]

Incoming workers found themselves in an alien and confusing milieu. The Jewish presence constituted the most formidable symbol of urban hostility. But veteran Arab urbanites also held themselves aloof from the rough newcomers and extended them a cold welcome. Independent artisans and skilled workers in town earned perhaps four, five, or six times as much as casual day laborers could hope for. Many of them were Christians, and this too set them apart from the largely Muslim migrants. The shantytowns that sprang up in Haifa and Jaffa were further evidence of an inhospitable environment where poverty, insecurity, and marginality were the lot of the fellah worker.[21]

Migrant workers often sought a psychic haven by maintaining village social ties in new circumstances and surroundings. Recruitment patterns and the continuing vitality of the village community facilitated their efforts. Since the quarries, the oil companies, and the construction industry all found it convenient to engage unskilled labor through traditional village leaders, rural workers from a single village were frequently employed together away from home. In the Jewish-owned Nesher quarries, Arab workers struggled to bring their wives and families to settle with them near a worksite outside the village of Balad al-Shaykh. Their efforts to reconstruct a village environment on the outskirts of the limestone quarries led them to strike against the management in 1936.[22]

[19] See, for example, petitions filed in ISA PWD 7/5(2), passim.

[20] PG, *Wage Rates Statistics Bulletin*, no. 1/1937; *Statistical Abstract, 1936*, p. 32. Eliahu Agassi, "The Palestine Arab Worker and his Organization under the Mandate" (unpublished paper, in Hebrew, Tel Aviv, 1959). Migrants did winter work in the orchards and the ports; in the summer they worked in construction, or did painting, whitewashing, or quarrying, for example.

[21] On urban wages, see *Wage Rates Statistics Bulletin*, no. 1/1937. George Mansur estimated the number of Arabs living in shantytowns around Jaffa at some 11,000. See *The Arab Worker Under the Palestine Mandate* (Jerusalem, 1937), p. 14.

[22] Eliahu Agassi, "The Palestine Arab Worker," p. 11; see also Tel Aviv Labor Ar-

Sometimes, the migrants joined together in urban associations. In Haifa, for example, workers established a small number of benevolent societies, each providing social and financial services and composed of workers from a single village. Hamula divisions were apparently overlooked. Where such links with a specific village could not be preserved, laborers forged ties with broader groups of migrants like themselves. They proved particularly receptive to the efforts of urban leaders to organize them into semipolitical voluntary associations. Many flocked around the various youth groups, religious associations, and nationalist clubs that sprang up in the 1930s. Among these, some half-dozen so-called labor associations attracted many migrant workers. The powerful Husayni family in Jerusalem, their arch-rival Fakhri al-Nashashibi, and a leading Haifa businessman and notable, Rashid al-Hajj Ibrahim, all made brief attempts to lead loosely knit workmen's societies.[23]

Yet most of these new associations provided only an illusory refuge. They were fragile partly because the laborers were so mobile. More important, however, was their inability to provide the leadership that the migrants missed. Notable-led associations held out the lure of patronage, a familiar relationship to Arab villagers that now proved of little substance: since the bulk of Arab labor was employed outside the Arab economic sector, urban politicians were neither accustomed nor able to secure special favors for their supporters on a large scale. The organizations they dominated were often sporadic and hollow. They subjected peasant workers to the dissonant claims of factional rivalries without granting them the advantages of either material gain or social accommodation.

To a great extent, it was the continuing vitality of the village community that enabled the migrants to resist the splintering impact of the coastal towns; and the new urban associations helped in turn to preserve the village foundations of the migrants' identity. Their nationalist rhetoric buttressed rural loyalties by idealizing the agrarian past and calling for cultural resistance to change. Even in the few cases, such as factory strikes, where peasants banded momentarily with skilled urban workers, the urbanites generally asserted their separateness and social superiority.[24] Paradoxically, moreover, the organizational and functional weaknesses of nationalist voluntary societies underlined the migrant workers' marginality *as a group*.

During much of the Arab Revolt, the disaffection of displaced peas-

---

chive, 237.IV. 26, minutes of Histadrut Arab Committee, 28.II.36, on Nesher strike of 1936.

[23] Tel Aviv Labor Archive, 250.IV.435, report by Eliahu Agassi on Jewish work among the Arabs in Haifa, 1934-1935 (in Hebrew).

[24] Ibid.

ants provided a strong motive for insurrection.[25] Despite the internal disorganization of the Revolt and the spread of anomic violence, however, the involvement of fellah workers in the rebellion did not just derive from the disruptive impact of the coastal cities on individuals. It stemmed more fundamentally from a real sense of collective oppression. This, as we have seen, was rooted in an active identification with village culture and with the lower peasantry in particular. Rather than erasing or dislocating this awareness, patterns of labor recruitment had reinforced it. In the summer and fall of 1938, the Revolt turned for some months into an assault of the countryside on the towns. Semiurbanized fellahin, who had returned in great numbers to their villages after 1936, joined with other villagers to terrorize the Arab inhabitants of several towns in a mounting campaign of anger.[26] If there was a class dimension to the Arab Revolt, it was not related to proletarianization as much as to a militant identification of interests among an impoverished peasantry.

War and Workers

This sense of solidarity did not last. In 1939, following the intensification of British efforts to quell the Revolt, villagers were subjected to conflicting pressures from many directions. By the end of the uprising, the village population found itself internally divided and poorly prepared for the swift economic upheaval that came with the outbreak of the Second World War.

The immediate effect of wartime labor.mobilization in Palestine was to fragment the rural community still further. Mounting requirements of the large British military garrisons in Palestine spawned a vast, unskilled Arab labor force. New employment opportunities were concentrated to a considerable extent in the countryside: approximately half of the Arab workers engaged by the War Department and almost all public works labor were employed outside urban areas. Rural-to-urban migration resumed and quickened in the 1940s, but in no way corresponded to the inflation of the Arab wage force.[27]

As a result, rural patterns of social organization frequently prevailed over the depersonalizing or rationalizing effects of labor

[25] Yehoshua Porath, "Social Aspects of the Emergence of the Palestine Arab National Movement" in *Society and Political Structure in the Arab World*, ed. by Menahem Milson (New York: Humanities Press, 1973), p. 132, notes that the men around 'Izz al-Din al-Qassam were displaced villagers.

[26] Ibid., and Yuval Arnon, "Fellahim Bamered Ha'aravi B'Eretz Yisrael," unpublished M.A. thesis, Hebrew University, 1970, pp. 91ff.

[27] CZA S25/7170, General Federation of Jewish Labor, Survey of the Situation in War Department Work (September, 1942) (in Hebrew).

mobilization. Jewish sources recorded that fellah workers in army installations often invited their military overseers home, and that they commonly presented gifts of produce or livestock as inducements to gain employment.[28] The fact that many laborers could return with relative ease and regularity to seasonal work in their villages also placed limits on the differentiation of the rural wage force. For many fellahin who worked near their own villages, particularly in the Galilee and in the south of Palestine, military employment simply took the place of previous projects in the Public Works Department.

Nevertheless, in contrast to the experience of the previous decade, social dislocation did emerge at the village level. Not all peasant workers stayed near home, and the attractions of more distant opportunities exerted growing force. The mobility of nonurban wage laborers challenged village elites simply by separating villagers from their leaders for prolonged periods. Throughout Palestine, day laborers traveled significant distances to work in military installations. These migrant workers frequently lived in temporary encampments near their worksites or were billeted in nearby villages. As early as 1941, an official memorandum on the labor situation remarked that "thousands of daily labourers have been brought from Gaza, Lydda, Nablus and other areas to work in the [northern] sub-district[s] as well as a few hundred of Hurani [sic] labourers who are engaged on road construction."[29] This situation was not confined to the north.

The rate of labor turnover was relatively high. Thus, the Public Works Department, which accounted for well over half the government's employees, possessed no large, regularly employed group of workers, but engaged a vast labor force on a temporary basis. The department usually dispensed with the services of workers upon completion of the particular work in the area.[30] Continuing mobility among workers was encouraged by the great variability of market rates for labor in different regions.[31] The sheer size of such an itinerant labor force taxed the capacity of the village to maintain the affiliation of the migrants on unchanged terms.

Increased opportunities for supplemental labor helped improve the economic situation of the peasantry, particularly since wages in

[28] Ibid. See also ISA I/Lab/106/44, Vol. I, petition from villagers of 'Amqa village, Acre subdistrict, to the chief secretary, complaining that the Jewish manager of the aerodome required gifts of eggs, chickens, etc., for employment, or else that the Arabs join the Histadrut.

[29] ISA 65:2211, f. 32a, "Extracts from a Memorandum on the Labour Situation in May, 1941," quoting agricultural inspectors of the Department of Agriculture and Fisheries.

[30] ISA I/Lab/82/43, director of public works to chief secretary, 2.VI.45.

[31] On the variability of rural wage rates for day labor, see ISA U/602/47, minute dated 14.VII.47.

rural employment rose to market demands. Thus, together with labor mobilization, rising rural prosperity also undermined many traditional relationships. War Department wages kept pace with the rising cost of living, estimated at over 250 percent for the Arab community between 1939 and 1945. Before the war, the average daily pay for unskilled Arab labor in public works had been 120 mils. In 1945, according to the assessment of an officer in command, War Department projects paid unskilled Arab labor from 230 to 370 mils per day. Earnings of unskilled rural labor in other government departments were on a higher scale: in 1947 they ranged from 200 mils a day to 600 mils, with top-ranking wages increasingly cited.[32]

Rural prosperity also grew out of the inflated price of agricultural produce during the war. Yet another index of rising village income was the continuous climb in agricultural wage rates: the upswing was universal and dramatic. Manpower shortages and competition from nearby construction works pushed real wages in agriculture up. The average wages paid to Arab labor in Arab employment outside of citriculture in the winter season of 1946-1947 represented an increase of 355 percent over those paid in 1939, when general agricultural workers had earned an estimated 80 to 120 mils daily.[33] Although landlords had similarly profited from good farm prices, previous patterns of stratification in the countryside were nevertheless shaken.

Greater inequalities in the wealth and social position of fellahin also emerged as money wages became more prevalent and cultivators freed themselves from debt. Some, for example, were able to invest their earnings in land and agrarian development in their home villages. At the same time, the inflated prices of the 1940s pressed heavily on many of the poorest, who had difficulty even finding access to work that was more highly paid.[34]

The decline of traditional authority in the countryside impelled the government to shore up village elites by reviving the administrative functions of local notables and hamula leaders. The debate on priorities and goals for the rural population was a complex one and

[32] CZA S25/7201, Dr. E. Koenig to M. A. Novomeyski, 28.V.47; ISA I/Lab/82/43, major-general cmdg. Br. trps. in Palestine and Transjordan to chief secretary, 8.VII.45. See also PRO CO 733/439/75156/143 (1942-1943), High Commissioner telegram to colonial secretary, 26.I.43, which gives the figure of 151 percent as representing the Arab cost-of-living in 1943 as compared with 1939. For the monthly index during the war, see ISA DLab 1440 K/1, f. 65, Wages Committee Index, Quarterly Announcement no. 19 (October, 1947).

[33] *Survey*, II, p. 737; *GMBCS* (April, 1947), p. 223; PRO CO 733/469/76284, Employment Committee, First Interim Report, 27.X.44, p. 5.

[34] Y. Firestone, "Production and Trade," part 2, p. 311; and Z. Abramowitz, "Wartime Development of Arab Economy," *Palestine Yearbook*, 1 (1944-1945), 137-38.

falls beyond the range of this study.[35] It is significant, however, that economic upheaval in the countryside coincided with the government's decision to reinstate traditional village councils of elders, to retain mukhtars as its direct representatives, and to recognize the role of notables in arbitrating local disputes.

The government realized that the customary councils had lost their effectiveness in many cases or had fallen into disuse, and that village mukhtars had increasingly lost the respect of their countrymen as their administrative functions grew while their representative role shrank. Against the recommendations of the Royal Commission Report, and despite the advice of the district commissioners, the government chose to base any further rural development and reform upon a solidly traditional foundation.[36]

Instead of reversing the dissolution of traditional rural structures, this program served as a partial remedy which added to the confusion. Not only was the administrative reform itself incomplete and partially applied, but it stood alongside a welter of contrary influences. Among these were official efforts to intensify and modernize agricultural production. The government occasionally tried to resolve this incompatibility by sponsoring small agricultural development projects under the supervision of village mukhtars. Frequently, however, attempts to expand productivity entailed broader forms of agricultural modernization, extending to the introduction of additional machinery and the establishment of several experimental farm stations. The question of how far agricultural modernization proceeded during this period and to what extent it altered social relationships still remains to be answered: it is an important key to a deeper understanding of the transformation of the countryside.[37]

Wartime Recruitment Patterns

Wartime recruiting practices and patterns of work organization weakened the mediating role that village leaders had formerly assumed in supplying unskilled labor. When labor grew scarce, the customary engagement of villagers from the area of the works lapsed; and, as respect for local and regional integrity receded, reliance upon traditional rural authorities to marshal and control workers also waned. Moreover, the urgency of many war works frequently

[35] Ylana Miller, "From Village to Nation: Government and Society in Rural Palestine, 1920-1948" (unpublished Ph.D. dissertation, Berkeley, 1975), Part II.
[36] ISA Chief Secretariat files G/140/37, f. 57a, memorandum, 25.XI.38; PRO CO 733/448/76164, Report of the Bailey Commission, 2.X.41, pp. 18-19.
[37] On agricultural modernization, see *Survey*, II, pp. 724ff.

brought about a new emphasis on efficiency that left but little scope
for the small services of village notables.

Instead, the country's Arab and Jewish contractors took a large
share of responsibility for the recruitment of labor; and they showed
a marked disregard for the village connections of their workmen. To
the contractor, consideration of regional boundaries was rarely ob-
ligatory or economical. Transport of unskilled workers from one part
of Palestine to another was freely and frequently undertaken.[38] Military employers also showed impatience with the allocation of work
along local and communal lines. One military officer in the Royal Engineers expressed typical sentiments when responding to such a
claim: "Whether Nazareth enlisted men are rich or poor, agricultural
or town bred, Christian or Moslem, does not really concern me. I
merely want a good working gang which I have got."[39]

The rising demand for scarce labor led to the multiplication of private Arab employment agencies. Like the contractors, they were interested in immediate profit, and they too contributed to the displacement of local rural elites from recruitment processes. The social
composition of the work force was to them a matter of indifference;
together with many of the contractors, they encouraged the importation of labor across the country when profitable. In the absence of
other alternatives, the government modified its former opposition to
private, fees-charging agencies into an unofficial acquiescence.[40]

The dispersal of rural labor throughout the country thus eroded
the traditional relationship of the workers with village administrative
elites and altered the fabric of rural life. Just as recruitment procedures became increasingly impersonal, organization of work was no
longer patterned deliberately to accommodate the village attachments
of the workers. Although bands of villagers continued in many instances to work in closely knit groups of kinsmen and neighbors,
employers considered this only rarely as a criterion for engaging unskilled labor. The contrast with earlier works programs, which had
frequently been designed to relieve rural underemployment, was
marked.

There were occasions when government or the military pressed
mukhtars and other village notables to provide scarce labor; some
were confronted with ultimatums and deadlines. The services of local
leaders, and of mukhtars in particular, were sought when disciplinary

[38] ISA PWD 7/5/2 (3), f. 170, C. Wilson Brown to district commissioner, Haifa,
7.VII.39; see also f. 255.
[39] ISA Galilee District files 2629:G 311, f. 34, Lt. Col. in RE #73 CRE Works to assistant district commissioner, Nazareth, 28.X.41; see also Tulkarm District files 3885:T/
20/1, officer commanding to assistant district commissioner, 12.II.46.
[40] ISA PWD 7/5(3), f. 228, R. M. Graves, minute, 5.IV.41, and following replies.

difficulties arose as well.[41] Such resorts to the authority of local elites clearly undermined their social position still further. By their nature, these pressures dramatized their role as agents of external authority at a time when their representative function as regular suppliers of seasonal labor was sharply curtailed.

The reaction from the countryside indicated the extent to which village sensibilities were hurt. When local notables did receive appeals to supply labor or to restore discipline, their responses often disclosed a sense that their authority was in jeopardy. Thus, one mukhtar's son in Qalqilya offered to provide laborers to the Public Works Department but only under stringent conditions. His men must be paid at a relatively high rate, they could work at a maximum distance of five kilometers from the village, and each work gang must be composed of men from one family or party of the village.[42]

A further indication of rural dissatisfaction was the flood of aggrieved petitions from villagers to employers, protesting the violation of their rights when outsiders were hired in works on their own lands.[43] The response of the Public Works Department to such claims showed how radically its labor recruitment procedures had been transformed. More often than not, departmental officials replied brusquely to the village mukhtars who importuned them. As the district engineer of Nablus District explained to the mukhtar of the Arab Kafr Saba, the department now believed that "[n]o village [had] any monopoly of Public Works carried out in their village land."[44] The impulse toward regularization of hiring procedures found further expression in a departmental decision to post a locked box outside the offices of district engineers, for applications to work. Although this system, initiated in 1946, was barely used, its installation represented a great change in the department's attitudes to labor mobilization.[45]

Recruitment of civilian Arab labor for army and RAF works became more formalized as well. Laborers were engaged through the nine district offices of the Pioneer and Labor Department. At the Pioneer Labor Office in Haifa, an army employment exchange was developed under the administration of an army lieutenant; as indi-

[41] ISA PWD 7/5(3), acting director public works to district commissioner, Lydda, 19.IX.42; ISA PWD 7/5(3), foreman, Tulkarm to district engineer, Nablus, 7.IX.42. ISA PWD 7/48/1 (1), N. Y. Bulos, district engineer, Nablus to director, public works, 8.XI.46; ISA I/Lab/106/44, Vol. I, Nimr Abu Ghosh to High Commissioner, 19.II.42.

[42] ISA PWD 7/5/(3), H. Khatib to executive engineer, 4.IX.42.

[43] I/Lab/106/44, Vol. I, passim; ISA Tulkarm files 3885:T/20/1, passim; ISA 65:00496, petition of 44 laborers to High Commissioner through district officer, Tulkarm, 22.V.40.

[44] ISA PWD 7/5(3), f. 171, district engineer, 5.IX.39; see also petition from Yahudiya village to director of public works in the same file, 20.IX.39.

[45] PWD 7/5/12, minute, 31.VIII.46.

cated by the following official report, it operated in a highly formalized manner:

> There is a large reception office with three clerks, who deal
> with the registration of workers. Each applicant must produce an
> identity card, or a passport with three photographs and must
> submit the names of two persons as referees. If a man is engaged,
> the identity card is stamped and he is given a registered number.
> A "blacklist" is kept of persons who are not to be employed for
> security reasons. . . . Brief details are taken of the persons en-
> gaged, qualifications or experience, and the person is classified as
> unskilled or skilled. The man is then referred with a letter to the
> employing officer. In the case of military workshops, the employ-
> ing officer will immediately apply a trade test if a man presents
> himself as a tradesman.[46]

Through this exchange, from twenty to thirty tradesmen and about
fifty unskilled workers were engaged daily during the height of wartime employment.[47] A large proportion of these were Arabs, since the
Histadrut provided a major share of Jewish labor to the military authorities.

These impersonal methods of labor recruitment were not, however, institutionalized into a permanent, formal machinery for the allocation of employment. Recruitment patterns continued to be as erratic as the unpredictable fluctuations in the wartime labor market.
The change in hiring policies, bypassing village authorities, only fleet-
ingly signaled the beginning of an orderly, contractual system of labor
recruitment. The recruitment offices of the Pioneer and Labor Corps
(PLCO) were not intended to be permanent, and were certainly never
expected to serve as a general labor exchange. Pioneer and Labor
Corps staff was sharply reduced just as the discharge of many War
Department workers increased the pressure on its offices.[48] Nor had
other employers of labor developed new methods of labor recruitment; they relied instead on their customary practice of hiring labor
at the gates of the works. In the period of labor shortage, both the oil
companies and some municipalities acknowledged the inadequacy of
this system. Together with the PLCO, they indicated the need for a
government employment exchange, which they pledged to patron-

---

[46] ISA 65:2123, C. E. Cousins, inspector of labor for the northern region to chief
inspector of labor, 24.III.43.

[47] Ibid.

[48] ISA 65:2123, J. Young, Major, SPLCO to DDPL Hqtrs., 6.IX.45; H. E. Chudleigh
to chief inspector, 7.IX.45.

ize.[49] Despite much discussion, no officially administered employment exchange was ever established.

Perhaps the most damaging consequence of the confusion in recruitment methods was the widespread corruption that it encouraged. Since few effective channels were available for the mobilization of manpower, various purveyors of labor were able to charge disproportionately high sums for their services. Corruption among clerks, timekeepers, foremen, and overseers was also common: as many sources attest, laborers were normally obliged to purchase the favor of such people in order to obtain work.[50] War Department workers in particular were victimized. Thus, in matters of labor supply, traditional authority was often replaced by a stratum whose association with labor was anonymous, unscrupulous, and transient.

The dependence of workers on the favors of their superiors helps to explain why the elimination of the traditional middleman's role did not lead more frequently to the spread of independent behavior and assertiveness among bands of rural workers. Now and again spontaneous protest erupted; but, except for a major strike effort by public works employees in 1947, such demonstrations were sporadic and confined to very small groups.[51] Haphazard recruitment practices, together with the generally unstable circumstances of nonurban Arab labor, retarded the development of such embryonic associations.

In addition, the overwhelmingly unskilled character of the rural labor force obstructed the evolution of new networks of affiliation based on occupational differentiation. Not only were most rural unskilled laborers engaged on a casual basis; they also continued to be isolated from the potential leadership of skilled cadres. In 1943, the War Department and the RAF employed some 27,000 civilian Arab workers on a full-time basis. Of these, approximately 10 percent were classed as skilled. Skilled labor, moreover, was heavily concentrated in urban locations and in the three large military camps situated within close reach of urban centers—Serafand, Bayt Naballah, and Rafah. Outside the largest installations there were seldom more than twenty-five skilled Arab workers at any single worksite, and fre-

[49] ISA DLab 1452 CL/83-Me/1, C. E. Cousins to chief inspector, 14.X.43; ISA 65:2123, C. E. Cousins to chief inspector, 31.III.43; H. E. Chudleigh to chief inspector, 7.IX.45.

[50] ISA 65:2212, A. H. Couzens to chief secretary, 10.VIII.47. CZA S25/7170, General Federation of Jewish Labor, Survey of the Situation in War Department Work (September, 1942).

[51] For instances of such protests, see PWD 7/5(3), H. Khatib to executive engineer, Report on Labor, 4.IX.42; acting director, public works to district commissioner, Lydda, 19.IX.42. ISA Tulkarm files 3885:T/20/1, Captain J. S. Collinge to acting district commissioner, August 15, 1942.

quently there were none at all. In rural locations, skilled Arab labor was employed chiefly through the central plain and in Samaria. As before, public works labor in the countryside was largely unskilled.[52] Technical training for the Arab population, both urban and rural, remained undeveloped throughout the Mandate.

The segregation of unskilled Arab labor from skilled cadres was reinforced by occupational stratification along ethnic lines. Although skilled Jewish labor was spread throughout the country, unskilled Jewish workers were concentrated at a small number of sites, and in the Haifa area in particular. At mixed sites outside the major camps, unskilled labor was rarely Jewish. Thus, in many of the smaller sites, and particularly in the south, skilled work was performed by a small stratum of Jewish labor whose contacts with the numerous unskilled Arabs were minimal. Ethnic and occupational barriers thus coincided: Arabs and Jews were engaged in dissimilar work, earned widely disparate wages, and generally identified with different status groups. It is important to recognize these distinctions, particularly because of a tendency in some of the literature of the time to see wartime labor mobilization as an equalizing force.[53]

Some Arab workers did adopt the standards and aspirations of their organized Jewish counterparts; and some of the social dislocation of the 1940s was in fact translated into a sense of commitment and identity among Arab workers. But such developments were confined for the most part to the towns, where working conditions, together with several extraeconomic circumstances, helped foster the reemergence of an Arab labor 'movement. With the support and guidance of the government's newly established Labor Department—and under the influence of leftist leaders—the revitalized Arab unions of the 1940s diverged distinctly from their predecessors in their rhetoric, methods, and goals.[54]

Although Arab labor organizations created many village branches and counted many fellah workers among their followers, rural conditions obstructed their efforts to penetrate the countryside. The extensive recruitment of Arab villagers into wage labor had been the hasty byproduct of war, accomplished over a brief span. It was necessarily

[52] CZA S25/7170, General Federation of Jewish Labor, Survey of the Situation in War Department Work (September, 1942). On PWD, see Survey, II, p. 775. The decline in real wages resulted from inflation and from the fluctuating demand for labor.

[53] See, for example, Council of Jewish-Arab Co-operation, Bulletin (August, 1944-December, 1949).

[54] The establishment of a Labor Department sympathetic to Arab labor, the promulgation of wartime defense regulations to control manpower, and the Histadrut's organizational efforts among the Arabs all promoted Arab trade unionism. See Rachelle Taqqu, "Arab Labor in Mandatory Palestine, 1920-1948" (unpublished Ph.D. dissertation, Columbia, 1977), Chapter 8.

an incomplete and inconsistent process with a divisive impact on Arab village society. Although the disruptions of the peasant economy undermined traditional patterns of social organization and increased the individual freedom and mobility of many fellahin, the emergence of a distinct identity among laborers was impeded by the incompleteness of the transition to wage labor. The rural concentration of the work force, the random techniques of recruitment, the instability of most wartime employment, the undisguised official intention to prevent permanent proletarianization—all these militated against any widespread assumption of a working-class identification. Furthermore, the new distribution of Arab labor was uneven to the point of lopsidedness. While the ranks of unskilled village labor swelled, the emergence of skilled and semiskilled cadres continued to be retarded, both through circumstance and through governmental design.

To the extent that the labor movement did reach out to the migrant workers of the villages, it generated insecurity and confusion rather than a consolidation of interests. For the class and the ideology that' the nascent unions were coming to represent were based on a new principle of social cohesion. At many levels they challenged and competed with existing notions of peasant community; and in several instances they aroused the enmity of the elites. The implicit tensions between traditional patterns of social organization and the new labor movement undermined village—and nationalist—consensus on one hand, and helped thwart the clear emergence of a working-class identity on the other. As a result, peasants in wage labor had few signposts to guide them through their rapidly changing social environment.

The Postwar Economy

Occupational mobility and the continuous existence of a large wage-earning labor force were phenomena that outlasted the war itself, despite the reduction in war-related employment. Although it is difficult to assess the economy of 1948, it is quite clear that, through 1947, Arab workers were frequently reluctant to return to their villages, and that many of them remained in nonagricultural employment. Neither the large-scale unemployment fearfully anticipated by the government nor the reassuring resettlement of fellah workers in their villages anxiously advocated in official circles accompanied the end of World War II. Despite the progressive discharge of thousands of civilian laborers from the War Department and from other "war service occupations," the labor market remained extremely fluid from 1944 through 1947.

It appears from descriptions of the rural economy that many Arab workers continued to move frequently from one temporary job to another, without reestablishing roots in the countryside. In 1946, the Arabs actually showed "a tendency to migrate from the country into the towns, despite the discouraging nature of the circumstances for such a movement."[55] The employment index in government and the services—which engaged a preponderance of Arab workers and therefore provide a useful gauge of Arab employment—showed continuous variation both upward and downward from April 1945 to May 1947. It was only in the second half of 1947 that employment figures began to deteriorate steadily.[56] This continuing mobility was accompanied by a decline in real wages from 1945 and took place within an atmosphere of general economic instability.[57] Not surprisingly, the postwar years saw the outbreak of a rash of Arab strikes and mounting assertiveness on the part of organized Arab labor.

In part, the reabsorption of fellah labor into the villages was delayed by the sheer mass of the uprooted work force. But there were other factors. Abundant short-term work was still available outside agriculture. The employment of Arabs at the refineries of the international petroleum companies continued at high levels,[58] while the volume of government employment dropped only slowly. Throughout 1946, the monthly survey of "Expected Fluctuations in Employment" included this sanguine observation:

> It must be observed that, so far, the contraction in employment has not been as great as was expected. On one hand, employment by the Services has not declined seriously, and on the other hand, private employers (more particularly building contractors) and Government Departments have tended to increase the number of their employees in recent months.[59]

Work at Jaffa port and Haifa harbor was resumed gradually. The general economy continued to be buoyed by the presence of numerous troops who were not immediately evacuated.

Military discharge of civilian personnel was deliberately staggered, as a matter of official policy at the highest levels.[60] These tactics

[55] Department of Labor, *Annual Report, 1946*, pp. 4-5.

[56] *GMBCS* (December, 1947), p. 775. See ISA DLab 1445 O/4, minutes of meeting at regional office, 3.I.47. DLab 1426 A/9, Annual Report of the Southern District, 1946, by J. R. Hughes. On the scarcity of agricultural labor, see *GMBCS* (December, 1946), p. 711.

[57] Z. Abramowitz, "Wartime Development of Arab Economy in Palestine," *Palestine Yearbook*, 2 (1945-1946), 223.

[58] *GMBCS* (December, 1946), p. 709, gives the actual number of Arab and Jewish employees in mineral fuels, refining, and distribution as 4,116. Arabs still comprised the majority of these.

[59] *GMBCS* (September, 1946), p. 507.

[60] PRO CO 733/469/76284/1944, minute by Eastwood, 8.VIII.44.

achieved their immediate purpose of averting a crisis of unemployment, but they also perpetuated the mobility of the thousands of
Arabs still employed by the War Department in 1946 under unmis-
takably insecure conditions. The release of about 10,000 Arab civilian
workers in 1944 was followed by a slight expansion of the War
Department labor force in 1945 and by subsequent piecemeal dis-
charges.[61] In addition, many laid-off workers were reemployed in
new military construction operations, undertaken in the Gaza region
and also around Lydda starting in 1945. A large part of the work
force near Gaza reportedly came from the hill districts. The protrac-
tion of military works thus continued to propel an internal migration
of labor.[62]

Eric Mills, as controller of manpower in Palestine, raised a lone dis-
senting voice against the artificial prolongation of military works not
necessary for the direct purposes of war. As an immediate remedy for
the "lack of rhythm" between the labor market and the prospects of
continued employment he proposed a large program of public works
and construction, financed from public loans.[63] The unemployed
would thus be absorbed through the expansion of a permanent economic infrastructure. Although official opinion was unanimous on
the need for some supplementary works programs to uphold the viability of an Arab agrarian nucleus, most administrators favored an ad
hoc approach to such programs, which were, they argued, supplementary by design.[64] This bias, together with the scarcity of supplies
and the political tension that beset Palestine in these years, meant that
the continuation of military works comprised the single major official
attempt at cushioning the country's transition from a war economy.
These military works differed from earlier supplemental works programs in their impersonal recruitment methods, in the generally
greater distances of work sites from the workers' homes, and in the
higher scale of wages offered. They hardly bolstered rural reintegra-
tion.

The Arab economic sector also offered employment opportunities
at the end of the war. While certain industrial enterprises closed
down, such as the Eastern Match Factory at Nablus, others were embarking on a new future as Arab capital accumulated during the war
found its way to industrial investment. A glass factory opened at Jaffa,
a large spinning mill was established nearby, and a furniture factory

[61] ISA I/Lab/58/45, conference of Labor Department and War Department personnel, 2.XI.45.
[62] ISA I/Lab/22/46/x, Report on Unemployment, 21.XI.46.
[63] ISA DLab 1452 O/16, E. Mills, minute, 9.IV.44.
[64] See PRO 733/469/76284, Employment Committee, First Interim Report, 27.X.44;
response of the Palestine Government may be found in ISA DLab 1452 O/16.

began operating at Haifa, to name a few.[65] Private construction in the Arab sector was also expanding; but the Arab economy was not stable. J. R. Hughes, inspector of labor for the southern region, reported on labor conditions there in 1946: "Military contracts were not replaced by an expansion in production designed for peace time needs and local manufacturers were unable to compete with overseas producers on the assumption of imports from the soft currency areas."[66] Employment levels in Arab industry fluctuated rapidly. The textile industry in particular was disrupted in 1946 by successive setbacks and recoveries.[67]

The slow reabsorption of labor into the countryside also derived from the nature of agriculture itself. Despite official confidence in the capacity of Arab agriculture to accommodate the bulk of the wartime workers, Palestine's agrarian base proved less immediately "resilient" than many administrators had hoped, for it depended on a complex web of variables. Thus, the full-scale revival of citrus cultivation was delayed by continued shipping difficulties, while grain prices in 1945 declined.[68] In 1945-1946, abnormally heavy rains interfered with cultivation; in 1947, drought reduced agricultural employment substantially in the Jerusalem, Gaza, and Hebron districts and in parts of Galilee.[69] The possibility remains that the increased wartime land transactions among Arabs led to a consolidation of middle-sized Arab estates; this, together with wartime agricultural development, may have affected the social basis of reassimilation in ways that must still be investigated.

It was in this social setting that the events surrounding partition and independence unfolded at the end of the war. The failure of the Palestine Arabs to meet the various challenges which followed World War II was, of course, the result of a host of different circumstances, many of which were external to the Arab community itself. But labor migration and the social dislocations it created played a major though forgotten role in the paralysis and panic that overtook the Arab masses in 1948.

By the end of the Mandate, then, the transition from peasantry to

[65] Z. Abramowitz, "Wartime Development of Arab Economy in Palestine" (1945-1946), 216ff.

[66] ISA DLab 1426 A/9, Annual Report of the Southern District, 1946, by J. R. Hughes.

[67] Ibid., and Z. Abramowitz, "Wartime Development of Arab Economy in Palestine" (1945-1946), 224.

[68] Z. Abramowitz, ibid., p. 22.

[69] ISA I/Lab/22/46/x, Department of Labor Unemployment Report, March, 1947, 18.V.47; ISA Galilee District files 2614:G/67, acting assistant district commissioner, Beisan to DCr, Galilee District, 30.VIII.47. PG, Department of Agriculture and Fisheries, *Annual Report, 1945-46*, p. 5.

wage labor did lead to an increasing differentiation of the Arab work force at some levels and to the formation of an incipient working class. But proletarianization should not be viewed mechanistically as leading directly to class solidarity and the decline of an older order. In Palestine, this was an incomplete, contradictory, and hardly unilinear process whose consequences were frequently most disruptive for the Arab community.

Index

'Abdallah, King, 36ff., 46, 170ff.
Acre, population in 1895, 16n
Alami family, 205n
'Ali, Muhammad, 9, 12n
All-Palestine Government in Gaza, 170, 176, 226
Antoun, Richard, 112, 122
Arab Constitutional Party, 180
Arab Executive Committee, 20, 21, 243
Arab Higher Committee, 25, 30, 222
Arab League, 30, 170
Arab Legion, 169, 177
Arab Revolt: British suppression of, 29; clash of values in, 86; delay of British legislation, 256; internal cleavages, 222, 224; outbreak of, 24-25, 236; village relationships in, 134ff., 144, 237, 262ff.
Arafat, Yasir, 3, 202, 228
Arshayyid, Farid, 175, 176
'Awad family, 182
'awda, 152ff., 160ff.

Bailey Report on Village Administration of 1941, 138, 139
Balfour Declaration, 20, 124, 233
Barakat, Halim, 78
al-Ba'th, 170, 176, 180
Beisan Agreement, 233
Black September, 206n
Brodetsky, Selig, 246

Cana'an, Hamdi, 49, 204n
capitalism, world spread of, 5-6, 78-79, 88, 99
Chancellor, Sir John, 233, 244ff., 256
Christians: cleavages with Muslims, 219; in agriculture during Mandate, 22; in schools, 206, 223; local councils, 133, 142; migration, 59, 70; moneylenders, 14; percentage of West Bank population, 45; population in 1946 and 1947, 23; radical, 228; sample selection, 89; urban, 25
clan, see hamula
Collective Fines Ordinance of 1936, 136
Collective Punishment Ordinance of 1925, 132, 136

communism, 163, 164
Commutation of Tithes Ordinance, 252
Cox, Colonel C. F., 257

Da'mas, Wadi, 170, 176
dawrah, 204
Dayan, Moshe, 185
al-Din, Sa'id Ala, 176
Disturbances, 1929, 233
Dodd, Peter, 78
Dowbiggin, H. L., 110
Drayton, Robert, 248

Education Ordinance, 133
Egypt: agreements with Israel, 83; conquest of Palestine, 1832-1840, 9; haven for the Mufti, 30; land law, 238; pan-Arabism, 183; role in Jordanian elections, 180; rule of Gaza Strip, 38, 99, 154; village chief in nineteenth century, 109, 115, 118, 121; workers in mandatory Palestine, 266n
Eisenstadt, S. N., 160

al-Faruqi, Sulayman Taji, 175, 176
El-Fatah, 184, 226, 228
Faysal, 19, 222
fedayeen, see Palestine Liberation Organization
French, Lewis, 249, 254

Gaza, population in 1875 and 1895, 16n
Gaza Strip, 38, 61, 99, 154, 192n
Glazer, Myron, 90-91
Glubb, John, 181
Government of All Palestine, see All-Palestine Government in Gaza
Granott, A., 13
Granquist, Hilma, 120
Gur-El, Arye, 47

Habash, George, 3, 202
al-Hadi, 'Awni 'Abd, 254
al-Hadi family, 22, 219
al-Hadi, Ruhi 'Abd, 175, 176
Halil, Ahmad, 175
hamula: and local councils, 133, 141, 142;

Related Books Written under the Auspices of the Center for International Affairs, Harvard University

Entrepreneurs of Lebanon, by Yusif A. Sayigh (sponsored jointly with the Center for Middle Eastern Studies), 1962. Harvard University Press.

Somali Nationalism, by Saadia Touval, 1963. Harvard University Press.

The Dilemma of Mexico's Development, by Raymond Vernon, 1963. Harvard University Press.

People and Policy in the Middle East, by Max Weston Thornburg, 1964. W. W. Norton & Co.

The Rise of Nationalism in Central Africa, by Robert I. Rotberg, 1965. Harvard Univesity Press.

Political Change in a West African State, by Martin Kilson, 1966. Harvard University Press.

Political Order in Changing Societies, by Samuel P. Huntington, 1968. Yale University Press.

Political Development in Latin America, by Martin Needler, 1968. Random House.

Protest and Power in Black Africa, edited by Robert I. Rotberg, 1969. Oxford University Press.

The Process of Modernization: An Annotated Bibliography on the Socio-cultural Aspects of Development, by John Brode, 1969. Harvard University Press.

Authoritarian Politics in Modern Society: The Dynamics of Established One-Party Systems, edited by Samuel P. Huntington and Clement H. Moore, 1970. Basic Books.

Lord and Peasant in Peru: A Paradigm of Political and Social Change, by F. LaMond Tullis, 1970. Harvard University Press.

Political Mobilization of the Venezuelan Peasant, by John D. Powell, 1971. Harvard University Press.

Peasants Against Politics: Rural Organization in Brittany, 1911-1967, by Suzanne Berger, 1972. Harvard University Press.

New States in the Modern World, edited by Martin Kilson, 1975. Harvard University Press.

Politics and the Migrant Poor in Mexico City, by Wayne A. Cornelius, 1975. Stanford University Press.

No Easy Choice: Political Participation in Developing Countries, by Samuel P. Huntington and Joan M. Nelson, 1976. Harvard University Press.

The Arabs, Israelis, and Kissinger: A Secret History of American Diplomacy in the Middle East, by Edward R. F. Sheehan, 1976. Reader's Digest Press.

Cuba: Order and Revolution in the Twentieth Century, by Jorge I. Domínguez, 1978. Harvard University Press.

Israel: The Embattled Ally, by Nadav Safran, 1978. Harvard University Press.

Library of Congress Cataloging in Publication Data

Main entry under title:

Palestinian society and politics.

  Includes index.
  1. Palestinian Arabs—Addresses, essays, lectures.
2. Elite (Social sciences)—Palestine—Addresses,
essays, lectures.   I. Migdal, Joel S.
DS113.7.P35   301.5′92′091749275694   79-84002
ISBN 0-691-07615-4
ISBN 0-691-02193-7 pbk.